THE GUERILLA DYNASTY

THE GUERILLA DYNASTY

Politics and leadership in North Korea

ADRIAN BUZO

I.B. Tauris *Publishers*
LONDON • NEW YORK

Published in 1999 by I.B.Tauris & Co Ltd
Victoria House, Bloomsbury Square, London WC1B 4DZ
175 Fifth Avenue, New York NY 10010

ISBN 1 86064 414 7 (hardback)
ISBN 1 86064 415 5 (paperback)

A full CIP record for this book is available from the British Library
A full CIP record for this book is available from the Library of Congress

Library of Congress catalog card: available

Typeset in Goudy by DOCUPRO, Sydney
Printed and bound by KHL Printing Co. Pte Ltd, Singapore

CONTENTS

TABLES

ABBREVIATIONS

AA	Australian Archives
CC	Central Committee
CCP	Chinese Communist Party
CPC	Central People's Committee
CPRF	Committee for the Peaceful Reunification of the Fatherland
CPSU	Communist Party of the Soviet Union
CRS	Commonwealth Record Series
DCRK	Democratic Confederal Republic of Koryo
DFAT	(Australian) Department of Foreign Affairs and Trade
DJP	Democratic Justice Party
DMZ	Demilitarized Zone
DPRK	Democratic People's Republic of Korea
EIU	The Economist Intelligence Unit
FBIS	Foreign Broadcast Information Service
FEER	The Far Eastern Economic Review
FETZ	Free Economic and Trade Zone
IAEA	International Atomic Energy Agency
ICC	International Chamber of Commerce
KCNA	Korean Central News Agency
KCP	Korean Communist Party
KH	The Korea Herald
KPA	Korean People's Army
KWA	Korea and World Affairs
KWP	Korean Workers' Party

LDP	Liberal Democratic Party
LSWY	League of Socialist Working Youth
NAM	Non-Aligned Movement
NEAJUA	Northeast Anti-Japanese United Army
NKVD	(Soviet) People's Commissariat for Internal Affairs
NPT	Nuclear Non-Proliferation Treaty
PT	*The Pyongyang Times*
RDP	Reunification Democratic Party
ROK	Republic of Korea
SNCC	South–North Coordinating Committee
SPA	Supreme People's Assembly
UNDP	United Nations Development Program
VP	*Vantage Point*

PREFACE

North Korea or, as I will refer to it throughout this work, the Democratic People's Republic of Korea (DPRK) has developed its identity in four distinct phases: revolutionary struggle (up to 1945), communist oligarchy in power (1945–58), dominant leadership by Kim Il Sung (1958–67), and personal autocracy under Kim Il Sung and his son Kim Jong Il (1967 to the present). The leading role of Kim Il Sung and the pursuit of the goals of economic development and Korean reunification under the leadership of the Korean Workers' Party (KWP) has been common to all four periods as has been the pursuit of these objectives under the ideological guidance of a Leninist party. Otherwise, each period is distinct in terms of leadership characteristics, policies, and personnel.

The purpose of this book is to describe the evolution of the DPRK state. This is not a comprehensive history of the DPRK, for such a work cannot in truth be written on the basis of information currently available. Instead, I have concentrated attention on events and developments which seem to me to best explain the history and current prospects of the DPRK. I have therefore sought to link a detailed interpretive framework, covering such factors as Leninist party culture, Korean political tradition, the history of the Korean nationalist and communist movements, the military community, and Stalinist principles of organisation and state-building to actual events over an extended period of time. To date, the most thorough example of this type of approach to the DPRK remains Scalapino and Lee (1972), and their interpretation of Korean communism through the 'overarching variables of communism, development and tradition', (Scalapino and Lee 1972:xx). Time has tended to validate many of their key assessments, but equally has delivered the opportunity to view aspects of their variables more clearly.

In retrospect, the genesis of this work was the six months I spent as an Australian diplomat in Pyongyang during 1975. Through a long gestation period I meditated on this extraordinary society and in the process incurred a number of debts to individuals and institutions. Many may have forgotten the debt and even forgotten me, but it is a pleasant task to recall my colleagues and benefactors here. Foremost thanks must go to my immediate colleagues at Monash University and Swinburne University of Technology for providing the time and the facilities to enable this work to proceed. This work grew out of a dissertation for which I must thank Bruce Jacobs as a very support-ive supervisor, and Professors Robert A. Scalapino and Byung-joon Ahn as examiners. In addition, Mike Godley, Murray Frazer, and Kelvin Rowley have provided advice, encouragement and support in a number of ways.

I first began to write about the DPRK at the behest of the Royal Asiatic Society Korea Branch, whom I also addressed on the subject in 1981. I also owe a considerable debt to Derek Davies and others at the *Far Eastern Economic Review* who offered advice and then a long-standing arrangement as occasional contributor and writer of the North Korea section in their *Asia Yearbook*. These *Asia Yearbook* pieces forced me to constantly re-examine my assessments of the DPRK and also provided a valuable starting point for this present work. Over the years I have also enjoyed and benefited from a continuing informal relationship with the Australian Department of Foreign Affairs and Trade (DFAT) and have always found discussions with officers in Canberra and Seoul stimulating. This was particularly so when I was Project Manager and a contributor to a Departmental study *Korea to the Year 2000: Implications for Australia* in 1991–92. DFAT officers also went to particular trouble to arrange access to Australian Archives (AA) material on the DPRK, and for this I owe particular thanks to Jeff Robinson and Moyra Smythe. In addition, like so many other foreign scholars, I also remain struck by the generosity of many scholars and government officials in the Republic of Korea (ROK). My particular thanks over the years go to Professors Byung-joon Ahn, Wan-kyoo Cho, In-young Chun, Eui-gak Hwang, Ki-jun Jeong, Jun-yop Kim, Kyoungsu Lho, and also to the Under-wood family. More formally, the time I spent at Dankook University, Seoul, in 1979–81 was a valuable experience and enabled me to re-evaluate much of what I had observed in the North in the light of extensive reading in Korean history. I am especially grateful to former President Chung-Shik Chang, Professor Sok-Ha Kim, and especially to my then supervisor, Professor Pung-Hyun Nam for two productive and enjoyable years.

Finally, I thank my wife Erica and children Elizabeth, Michael and Eva for so many supreme blessings over the years. It was not easy for a wife and sub-teen children to accept a professional academic lifestyle, for it seemed so unlike anything to which they themselves could relate. Their husband/father was often at home but closeted away; there was no nine-to-five rhythm and weekends were rarely free. He seemed to play with the same toys—paper, stationery, books, word processors and printers with which they played but positively howled if anything was upset or rearranged. I cannot express with words the appreciation and gratitude I feel for the part they have played in bringing this work to fruition. I dedicate this work to them.

In referring to publications written in English, I have placed the author's family name last. In all cases, to avoid misunderstanding or ambiguity I have adopted a standard practice of inserting a hyphen between the two elements of the authors' personal names. Thus 'Han Shik Park' becomes 'Han-Shik Park'.

For other names, places, titles, and terminology, I have followed the McCune-Reischauer (M-R) system of romanisation with the following modifications:

- For technical reasons I have omitted the diacritic marks.
- For Kim Il Sung and Kim Jong Il I have used the official DPRK romanisations as carried in English-language DPRK publications such as *The Pyongyang Times*, since this is how they are known internationally.
- I have romanised DPRK place names and ideological terminology (e.g. 'Juche') according to DPRK practice.
- In the case of ROK public figures I have used the spellings carried in Yonhap News Agency's *Korea Annual* since this is how these people are most widely known.

1

THE ORIGINS OF THE GUERILLA TRADITION

In a state governed by personal autocracy the significance of the character, personality and life experiences of the leader is self-evident. His imprint on society is heavy, his shadow is long, he himself is an agent of transformation. His achievements and failures are also usually measured on a grand scale, and this encourages considerable speculation on his personality and formative influences. This is especially true when we consider the case of Kim Il Sung, for few individuals have shaped the character and destiny of a modern state as thoroughly as he has, to the extent that the past history and present dilemmas of the Democratic People's Republic of Korea (DPRK) cannot be understood apart from his life and career. Other shaping factors such as Korean nationalism, social forces, class conflict, Japanese colonisation, Soviet hegemony and Cold War rivalry all have their place in the story of the DPRK, but the DPRK has been shaped and driven primarily by a vision of the nature of politics, economics and international affairs which had profound meaning for Kim.

This vision emerged from an infusing of elements drawn from Kim's early experiences, the times in which he lived, and above all from his experience as an anti-Japanese guerilla fighter in Manchuria in the 1930s, with the Stalinist model of state-building. For Kim the guerilla years were a profound and protracted experience, covering many years as a young adult under arms in an isolated and forbidding environment. They shaped his perspective of the world and especially shaped his view of the purpose of political power and state-building.

When Kim emerged from this environment in 1941 he entered upon a sustained period of exposure to the Stalinist state, first as an officer in the Red Army (1941–45) and then as a key cadre—soon *the* key cadre—in Soviet-occupied North Korea. In Stalinism, Kim saw a model for the rapid construction of a modern industrial nation-state under the aegis of a revolutionary party, capable of expelling all vestiges of imperialism from the Korean peninsula, and he applied its prescriptions and formulae accordingly. The anti-Japanese guerilla movement and Stalinism shared many common points of ideology and this allowed Kim to meld the two together into the state ideology of Juche ('self-reliance'). Our search for an understanding of Juche and the state policies it continues to underwrite in the DPRK begins with an account of Kim Il Sung's background and his rise to power.

Kim Il Sung was born Kim Song-ju in the village of Mangyongdae near Pyongyang on 15 April 1912.[1] The eldest of three sons, Kim is usually described as coming from a peasant background, although his father, Kim Hyong-jik (1894–1926), married the daughter of a prominent local Presbyterian family, and no members of the family ever seem to have directly engaged in farming. Kim's parents were Christians and engaged in anti-Japanese activities. A maternal uncle died in prison while serving a long sentence for armed insurrection, and Kim's father, himself, took an active stance against the Japanese, participating in Christian-led nationalist groups. In 1917 Kim Hyong-jik played a prominent role in the establishment of the anti-Japanese Korean National Association. He was imprisoned for this in 1917 and only released in late 1918 or early 1919. In the wake of the March First Movement of 1919, Kim Hyong-jik and his family left Korea for Manchuria where the Japanese authorities had less reach and where nationalists could conduct their activities with greater freedom. At age 7, therefore, Kim Il Sung went with his parents to Manchuria, and returned only for two years of schooling in 1923–24. From 1925, when he turned 13, to 1941 when he turned 29, Kim lived in Manchuria. There the privations of immigrant life seem to have contributed to the deaths of his father in 1926 at the age of 32, his mother in 1932 at the age of 40, and a younger brother during the early 1930s.

In Manchuria Kim entered the Chinese school system, even though Korean alternatives were available. He left school in 1927, aged 14, while still a few months short of completing three years of Chinese middle school and soon became actively involved in Communist activities. A contemporary Japanese police document records him present at a meeting called to form a Communist youth group

2

in 1929 (Dae-Sook Suh 1967:266), and he was arrested and imprisoned for eight months soon after for various anti-Japanese activities (Dae-Sook Suh 1988:7). Upon his release in 1930, Kim spent two years in Kut'un, a small Manchurian village with a predominantly Korean population. Some time after the death of his mother in 1932 he joined the Chinese Communist Party-led guerilla movement which had become operational after the Japanese takeover of Manchuria as Manchukuo in September 1931. The earliest date of surviving comrades' recollection of Kim under arms is early 1933 (Sung-Chul Yang 1981:81), while the earliest contemporary record of Kim's military activities dates to early 1935 (Dae-Sook Suh 1967:268).

Kim's entry into anti-Japanese activism was part of a much broader movement which first arose with the steady Japanese penetration into Korea, beginning with the Treaty of Kanghwa in 1876 and ending with the annexation of Korea as a Japanese colony in 1910. This penetration opened Korea to a wide range of modernising influences, and in the process many members of the Korean intelligentsia became aware of their country as an independent nation-state for the first time. Modern Korean nationalism dates from the first sustained perceptions of the threat posed by imperialism in the 1880s and the need to adopt state-strengthening countermeasures. It developed at a time when government efforts at self-strengthening were largely ineffective, and grew to maturity under a harsh colonial regime. It was conditioned both by subsisting features of the traditional political culture and by the context of a failing dynasty and colonial rule. Although Kim Il Sung had little contact with other sections of the nationalist movement, he shared a number of common features with them.

Korean nationalism differed from the nationalism of most other colonies in that Korean nationalists did not have to manufacture a new nation out of heterogeneous parts. Korea had well-established geographical and cultural boundaries, a powerful sense of cultural distinctiveness and a long, discrete history as a unitary state. The major task of the nationalists was not to convince people that 'Korea' existed, but to mobilise countrymen to transform the homogeneous ethnic community and its existing, traditional politico-social order, into a modern, independent nation-state. But despite this strong cultural identity, Korean nationalism under the Japanese was marked by lack of cohesion—and even outright hostility—between the nationalist groups themselves. Many factors contributed to disunity, including Japanese repression, but even when this repression was not present it emerged that while Korean nationalists had a strong sense of belonging to a single ethnic community, this did not mean that they perceived this community in the same fashion. To individual Korean nationalists, 'Korea' was an abstract concept which they extrapolated from concrete experiences within particular groups, usually ordered around a dominant personality, a common education background, a common regional identity or a common clan affiliation.[2] While the nationalists dedicated themselves to reclaiming Korea, in another sense they were really reclaiming a multitude of Koreas.

Religious institutions, ideology or eminent individuals might have transcended these barriers of class and region but in the Korean nationalist movement, as in China, the lack of effective nationalist leadership and cohesive ideology was especially significant. While many Koreans were well aware of the dilemmas facing their country, nationalist activists had few avenues for effective mobilisation. They tended to be aroused, mobilised, then frustrated and disillusioned by lengthy periods of ineffective activities. Increasingly, those who remained active within the movement resorted to terrorism and other extreme options. Moreover, with few exceptions, members of the former Choson dynasty (1392–1910) elite did not play a prominent role in the nationalist movement. Their traditions and allegiances belonged to an old order and when that order fell, few of them redirected these allegiances toward nationalist movements. The result was a lack of cohesion in joint activities with other groups and little capacity to mobilise people in the name of new, effective symbols of Korean identity. No section of the nationalist movement established a broad base of support that cut across social status boundaries, and consequently Korean nationalism was never able to mount a sustained threat to Japanese rule.

An efficient Japanese repressive apparatus restricted the scope for nationalist activity within Korea and meant that Korean exile groups played a prominent role in nationalist activities. However, while the Soviets provided some assistance to the Korean Communist cause, and while the Chinese Nationalists were in the main sympathetic, the other major powers in the region tacitly accepted Japan's argument that Korea had lost the capacity to rule itself and that its people would benefit from Japanese colonisation. No foreign power offered significant material aid or an effective base of operations to Korean nationalists, and so activities abroad remained sporadic, small-scale and uncoordinated. While the Koreans managed to establish a Korean Provisional Government in Shanghai in 1919, this entity failed to rally a sizeable portion of the movement, and by the 1930s was virtually defunct (Dae-Sook Suh 1967:11, Henderson 1968:314–15, Dae-Sook Suh 1973:190).

The protracted nature of the anti-Japanese struggle had other consequences. Many would-be national leaders were absent from Korea for long periods of time and did not experience first-hand the modernisation process which the country underwent, especially after 1930. Moreover, in various ways they had set down cultural and intellectual roots in the various countries which had been their homes, in many cases, for more than twenty years. When they returned, they were out of touch with their homeland, out of sympathy with the experiences and models of development to which Korea had been exposed, and prone to contrast and justify their record of resistance in exile by attacks on the 'collaborationism' of those who stayed in Korea. Their return to Korea in 1945 marked the gathering of often mutually hostile groups, and the inception of a cycle of political violence and recrimination.

Ideologically, the net effect of these factors was a brand of resentful nationalism which characteristically evinced a profound sense of injustice, impotence and inequality and which had little faith that the world could ever be anything but a threatening place. The result was also a nationalist movement which had little impact on the Japanese regime prior to Korea's liberation in 1945. The nationalist movement was disadvantaged by many factors beyond its control but, whatever the contribution of individuals and groups, it was always a movement which added up to considerably less than the sum of its parts. Its level of actual achievement is symbolised, somewhat sadly, by the fact that in 1945 neither the US nor the USSR included even a token Korean contingent in the first wave of their occupying forces, nor did they extend political recognition to any of the exiled movements.

The characteristics of the nationalist movement as a whole also applied to the prewar Korean Communist movement. The strong sense of cultural identity and the task of reclaiming the homeland from the Japanese meant that Korean Communists operated in an environment charged with nationalist sentiment. In practice, therefore, there was little distinction between Communist and nationalist as nationalists became Communists, Communists became nationalists with all manner of shadings in between.[3] However, this did not lead to effective united front activities between the two movements, for while they could often appear similar in outlook, Communist strategy assessed the struggle against bourgeois nationalism as equal in

importance to the struggle against the Japanese. Accordingly, relations between Communist and nationalist groups were marked by
bitter animosity in the prewar period.

This lack of distinction between Communism and nationalism
also reflected the Korean Communists' lack of ideological sophistication. Although their movement attracted relatively educated, urban
dwellers, and although some Communists such as Pak Hon-yong
received training in the Soviet Union,[4] conditions for the development of serious interest in ideology and theory such as a stable,
cosmopolitan learning environment were absent. As a result, theoretical issues played very little role in either attracting Koreans to
Communist activism or to sustaining their interest in it. Not only
did the movement lack any notable theoreticians or indeed any body
of theoretical writing, there was little internal party debate on theoretical issues, nor were such issues significant in factional disputes.
As far as the Soviet-led Communist International (Comintern) was
concerned, the Korean Communist movement quickly acquired a
reputation for poor defences against bourgeois-nationalist deviation-
ism and for the practice of revolutionary violence of an adventurist
or putschist variety (Dae-Sook Suh 1967:51–2).

The Korean Communist movement was also marked by diversity
and disunity. Like the nationalists it was hampered by a strong
tradition of localism and regionalism. Moreover, the movement operated in a number of countries, and each section of the movement
developed individual characteristics. These ranged from the underground agitation and propaganda activities characteristic of Korean
Communists in Japan and in Korea itself, to the armed guerilla
struggle in Manchuria, to more regular political and military activities
in other areas of China. In matrix fashion, all of these theatres of
operation had their own subsets of regional and small-group affiliations which militated against unified command and activity.

In particular, the movement's diaspora-based character after 1928
meant that each element in the overall movement acquired its own
history, traditions, networks of association, tactical imperatives and
ideological colouring. Poor communications and the distances
involved meant that they rarely had contact with each other and
could refer to no shared event or incident such as a Long March or
an October Revolution. Even within Korea, the uneven impact of
the Japanese colonial government's economic policies, contributed to
new forms of regional identity among domestic Communists and in
the broader politicised community.[5] As members of a minority ethnic
community who were subject to the discipline of foreign parties

during 1928–45, the status of Korean Communists abroad remained insecure. This environment of poorly defined ideological and strategic priorities, poor communication, and a steady diet of failure often caused them to turn their attention inward toward issues of leadership and tactics, and internecine conflict was a constant problem.

The only source of significant foreign assistance to the Communist movement was the Soviet Union through Comintern. However, here too the relationship was difficult. The Korean Communist Party (KCP) was established on Korean soil in 1925, but because of the KCP's minuscule size, its reputation for undisciplined or difficult behaviour, and its lack of ideologues capable of putting effective arguments at the right level, it attracted little attention from Comintern. Comintern correspondence with the Koreans and Korean participation in Comintern councils and conferences was infrequent (Dae-Sook Suh 1970:227), and although contacts between the Korean Communist movement and Comintern had begun in the early 1920s, the KCP's admission to Comintern was not ratified until September 1928. This came too late to encourage the Koreans because two months earlier, in July 1928, the KCP had officially dissolved itself after a fourth and final attempt to establish a KCP on Korean soil ended in failure. Formal relations with Comintern therefore began with bitter analyses of the reasons for failure and wide-ranging Comintern criticisms of the Korean Communist movement. These included factionalism, failure to address agrarian issues, failure to broaden a membership base that was overwhelmingly petty bourgeois in background, failure to preserve security in agitation and propaganda activities, and the repeated tendency to jeopardise clandestine activities by premature, public demonstrations (Dae-Sook Suh 1967:178, Scalapino and Lee 1972:90–3, 106–11). The Korean Communist movement, therefore, derived little benefit from its Comintern relationship and, as we shall see, the memory of this earlier, acrimonious relationship lingered to influence Soviet judgments as it set about the establishment of the DPRK in 1945.

The Korean Communist movement, therefore, functioned as a collection of different movements, each possessing distinct organisations, hierarchies, histories and personal networks. By 1945 it had not attempted to hold a Party Congress, nor had it held any broadly representative meetings.[6] It had no recognised headquarters, it published no theoretical journals, and its platform and policies were poorly developed and articulated. It had no widely recognised leader or leadership group, nor any individuals with reputations for providing ideological, theoretical or practical guidance to the movement as a whole. As a diaspora-based movement working in an environment of efficient Japanese repression, it had suffered high rates of attrition in armed struggle. It possessed no means of building a grass-roots organisation within the country. Few, if any, of its members had ever set foot in the settled areas of Korea and were, therefore, unknown to most Koreans.

The Korean Communist movement in Manchuria, of which Kim Il Sung was a part, struggled with the same set of disabilities that afflicted the movement generally. After the dissolution of the Korean Communist Party, Korean Communists in Manchuria faced the choice of either accepting a Comintern-directed merger with the Chinese Communist Party (CCP), which took effect in 1930, or else leaving the movement. Many refused to join, but Kim Il Sung was one of those who accepted the new arrangement. For roughly ten years Kim was a member of the CCP and fought in the Northeast Anti-Japanese United Army (NEAJUA), a Chinese Communist guerilla army which brought a number of scattered Chinese and Korean guerilla bands under unified command after the Japanese declared the establishment of Manchukuo. From 1933 on, the NEAJUA came under extreme pressure from a sustained Japanese offensive, and by the end of 1935 it had been driven out of settled areas. According to official Japanese estimates at this time, it consisted of six armies with a total of about 15 000 men, mostly under arms, conducting anti-Japanese guerilla activities deep in the countryside (Dae-Sook Suh 1988:17).

During 1936–38 the NEAJUA armies were reorganised into three route armies. The Korean guerillas were concentrated into the First Route army whose area of operation was closest to the East Manchuria–Northeast Korea border, and it was in this army that Kim attained prominence, rising to be one of the dozen or so top-ranking Koreans in the command structure. By this time, organised operations of any description had either ceased or else were being conducted by isolated guerilla units whose only link to the Party was the presence of a political commissar in their ranks (Scalapino and Lee 1972:162, Dae-Sook Suh 1967:277–8). Kim's command varied from 50 to 300 men engaged in hit-and-run operations with the enemy and in extracting supplies from the local population, mostly by means of kidnapping, robbery and extortion (Dae-Sook Suh 1988:39).[7] His largest and most famous operation was the June 1937 attack on the Japanese garrison at the border village of Bochonbo, in which he led a company of about 200 men. Kim continued to conduct operations under extremely adverse conditions before retreating from Manchuria to the Soviet Far East in the second half of 1940, whereupon a new phase in his career began.

When we examine Kim Il Sung's prewar career, the strength of his basic convictions is immediately apparent. We do not know exactly why he joined the Communist guerilla movement, but his moment of decision was early—he was barely seventeen years old when first arrested for Communist youth group activities—and apparently unassisted, for no record survives of early role-modelling or mentoring. This was clearly his vocation and he never seems to have wavered in pursuing it. In this he was probably aided by his youth but also because the traditional Korean political culture into which he was born had little to offer a person of his background and temperament. The lack of a military tradition and the concept of a political centre which abhorred autocracy and sought to balance monarchical and bureaucratic interests were especially useless to a revolutionary who had chosen a life of guerilla warfare. Strong social status barriers and localism were likewise barriers to a man who would still be a 'commoner' in the eyes of many, and who did not complete a middle school education. In Kim's later career we can detect the influence of such traditionalist traits as personalism and localism, but within traditional Korean political culture we find no sanction for the later major DPRK regime traits of despotism, militarism, the suppression of particularistic and small-group ties, and pervasive state interference in the lives of families and individuals.

It is also clear that Kim demonstrated leadership qualities and was given command over significant numbers of men. Many of these men became bound by personal ties of loyalty to him and later formed the nucleus of his leadership circle after 1945. In assessing Kim's record we may speculate that this was not a highly competitive environment, and that Kim's education record of having nearly completed middle school compared well with his Korean guerilla comrades, many of whom were barely literate.[8] In addition, his status as the eldest son in a family with respectable anti-Japanese credentials may have given him a certain bearing and innate self-confidence. His Chinese language education may have helped him to function as a go-between in the often difficult relationship between the CCP command and the Korean guerillas and, according to the accounts of Soviet officers with whom Kim came into contact during 1941–45, he was personable and self-disciplined (Goncharov et al 1993:131–6). From his post-1945 record, we can surmise that he was affable, ruthless, and a strict disciplinarian.

But perhaps the most striking feature at this stage of his career is the extent of his isolation—physical, political, social and cultural. He went into virtual exile at the age of seven and spent his formative years as a mobile guerilla operating in a harsh climate in remote areas. As a member of the CCP and of the NEAJUA, Kim operated outside the mainstream of the Korean Communist movement and was therefore unknown within it (Dae-Sook Suh 1970:429–30). He may have occasionally read newspapers and heard radio broadcasts, but he would rarely, if ever, have spent any significant time in a Korean or Chinese settlement of more than a few hundred people, let alone lived in a town or city. Until 1941 his exposure to the modern world was very limited, for during these years there were no trappings of government-in-exile, no liberated areas to administer, no intellectuals at his elbow, and no foreign advisers.[9]

This isolation shaped his intellect by limiting his exposure to outside ideas and moulding the ways in which he conceptualised and dealt with practical problems. Guerilla life instilled in him the habits of self-reliance, perseverance and unremitting struggle, but we may also see in this period the roots of his later attitude of deep suspicion and mistrust toward 'outsiders' and more broadly the diversity and pluralism of the external world. He lived in a predatory, political subculture of force which encouraged in him an outlook that accepted callousness and criminality as a daily reality. Judging by his post-1945 actions, he also came to possess the deep conviction that his experience of people and politics in the guerilla movement held true for people and politics everywhere.

This contrasts with other branches of the Korean Communist movement. Even though most Communist activists were driven out of Korea proper, many of their activities in exile were still carried out in cosmopolitan centres and in contact with the broader cultural and political horizons which urban China and Japan provided. Moreover, from the mid-1920s, the broader world of Korean nationalism took on specific cultural orientations involving language, literature, and the promotion of national identity by reclaiming what was felt to be a specifically Korean historical and cultural tradition (Robinson 1988). Kim had little or no exposure to such movements, and when he returned to Pyongyang in 1945 he was almost entirely ignorant of the cultural and social world in which his compatriots had lived under the Japanese.

These formative influences were not, of course, unique to Kim. Within the wider context of the anti-Japanese nationalist struggle, by 1945 the Korean Communist movement as a whole had acquired a set of characteristics born of a protracted, ideological struggle within an intricate, long-established political culture, and a distorting colonial context. Its experience of conspiratorial struggle and the efficacy of violent means would be a continuing theme as it launched the process of class struggle in North Korea in 1945. Crucially, its members had never engaged in large-scale organisation and mobilisation themselves, and by 1945 had been exposed to only one practical model of governance: the Stalinist mobilisation state.

When Kim left Eastern Manchuria and crossed into the Soviet Union in 1941, he was transported into the midst of an immense socialist state where the air rang with appeals not to socialist internationalism but to Russian nationalism, and he was given a role to play, albeit a small one, in a massive mobilisation effort for a great and desperate military struggle which ended in a glorious victory. For Kim the Soviet Union must have been a startling and exhilarating revelation, especially as a model for military mobilisation and rapid post-revolutionary modernisation. After routine internment by border security guards Kim was assigned to the Khabarovsk Infantry Officers School,[10] and in August 1942 was assigned to the 88th Brigade, a brigade which absorbed the remnants of the Manchurian guerillas then in the Soviet Far East. The brigade, which functioned within the Soviet Army command structure, consisted of four battalions, each with a strength of about 150 men. Its training regimen centred on reconnaissance and infiltration, not combat activities. Kim took command of one battalion with the rank of captain. This brigade brought together many cadres who rose to high office in the DPRK in the era of Kim Il Sung's personal autocracy (1968–94), including Chon Mun-sop, Ch'oe Hyon, Ch'oe Yong-gon, Han Ik-su, Kim Il, O Chin-u, Pak Song-ch'ol, So Ch'ol, Yi Ul-sol, Yi Tu-ik, and Yim Ch'un-ch'u (Seiler 1994:85–88).

The extent to which Kim was able to travel within the Soviet Union and observe its society and economy is not clear. He appears to have made at least two extended trips to Moscow (Seiler 1994:35–6), but given his military duties it is doubtful that he moved very far beyond military circles. He seems to have been well-liked by his Soviet superiors, and he quickly gained a reputation for strict discipline. In particular, Soviet officers recall his strict rules against heavy drinking (Goncharev et al 1993:131ff).

The Soviets entered the Pacific War on 8 August 1945 but the Japanese surrender seven days later meant that the Korean elements in the 88th Brigade saw no active service. Surplus to requirements, they were excluded from even symbolic participation in the actual Soviet entry and occupation of Korea north of the 38th parallel, reportedly because Stalin saw them as a potential complication to Soviet occupation plans (Seiler 1994:46), and the Brigade itself was disbanded soon after the Japanese surrender. However, another door soon opened as Kim and 66 other former Korean officers of the 88th brigade were reassigned to assist the Soviet occupation authorities in liaison with the local population. This placed them in strategically important positions throughout the occupation forces apparatus, and it was in this capacity that they returned to Korea on 19 September 1945. In this manner began what North Koreans at the time termed 'the Age of the Rule of the Interpreters' (Weathersby 1990:196).

In re-establishing government in North Korea after the Japanese surrender, the Soviet Union assembled and gave power to a Communist oligarchy comprising elements of the pre-1945 Korean Communist movement and a cadre of Soviet citizens of Korean heritage. This oligarchy contained a number of mutually antagonistic elements, but in the period 1945–50 its members displayed considerable unity of purpose as they set about a wide-ranging social and political transformation of the North and prepared for a war of national reunification against the South. On 25 June 1950 these preparations culminated with the outbreak of the Korean War.

Post-liberation political activity in the Korean peninsula proceeded amid intense popular expectations of wide-ranging change, but also amid a political vacuum created by the departure of the Japanese colonial administration after thirty-five years. There were exile movements, but there was no broad-based government-in-exile waiting to assume power. There were politicians, but no mass political movements or parties waiting to re-emerge. Instead, political influence was largely wielded by prominent individuals who derived their authority from their social standing in Korean society and from their record of nationalist resistance to the Japanese. There were intense political expectations in both the Soviet zone of occupation north of the 38th parallel and the US zone in the south, but no coherent political centre capable of effectively addressing those expectations. In both occupation zones, military governments adjusted to their new and unaccustomed role as de facto governments. There were many points of contrast between the US and Soviet approaches but, in confronting an unfamiliar local political culture, both needed Korean political allies who shared their respective political philosophies and who could become reliable instruments of rule.

There is general agreement that the Soviets had only the most general plans for their occupation prior to August 1945 (Scalapino and Lee 1972:317, Weathersby 1990:184, Hak-Soon Paik 1995, van

Ree 1989:50–1). Until the end of 1945 they saw the nationalist leader Cho Man-sik and his Democratic Party as the major political force in the North, and viewed Kim Il Sung primarily as a military leader. However, growing Soviet disenchantment with Cho led them to opt for Kim as a more compatible figure. By January 1946 the Soviets had given members of the prewar Korean Communist movement collective status as a ruling oligarchy with Kim at their head.

The Korean Communist oligarchy contained four distinct elements: domestic Communists, former Manchurian guerillas, Korean soldier-guerillas of the Yan'an group, and Soviet–Koreans. The most significant group, the domestic Communist group, comprised Communists who had conducted operations within Korea for much of the Japanese colonial period. Their major strengths were their established record as anti-Japanese agitators and their local networks which they revived and extended in the South after liberation. Their major weaknesses were the advocacy of a doctrinaire, urban, proletariat-based political ideology in an overwhelmingly rural and agricultural society, and their adherence to a radical political tradition that associated political activity with small-group political agitation and violence. Although they were present in the North where, throughout the 1930s, they had attempted to build support through the tiny industrial proletariat that existed in the Hamhung–Hungnam area in the northeast, they had concentrated their activities in the area around Seoul where there was a greater concentration of industrial workers. Accordingly, as many Communists emerged from prison or hiding, they re-established the KCP in Seoul immediately after liberation, and pursued tactics of confrontation and often violence against the US military occupation authorities.

The second major group in the oligarchy, the former Manchurian guerillas, was led by Kim Il Sung. Like Kim, most members of this group were in their twenties and early thirties, of limited education, and of low social status. They had fought under CCP command and were virtually unknown to the rest of the Korean Communist movement as well as to the population at large. Numerically small, this group was, for the most part, highly disciplined and tightly knit after long years of guerilla warfare. The Manchurian guerillas entered Korea in October 1945 after some four years of training in the Soviet Union and, although its members lacked political stature, they possessed the decisive advantage of close ties and clear compatibility with the Soviets. By early 1946 Kim Il Sung had emerged as the clear Soviet choice as the future political leader of the country, and the fortunes of his group rose accordingly.

The third major group in the oligarchy, the Yan'an group, also based itself in the North after August 1945. Its members comprised a group of Korean Communists who left Manchuria and made their way to Yan'an in the late 1930s, where they fought against the Japanese and the Chinese Nationalists under the leadership of the CCP. Dae-Sook Suh (1970:379) notes that the term 'Yan'an' is misleading, because they were based not in Yan'an but in Southeastern Shaanxi province, where they fought on the front line, and sometimes behind enemy lines, against the Japanese. With few exceptions, the Chinese Communists appear to have remained largely indifferent to this group of Koreans. They evidently made little effort to either integrate them into the CCP during the war, or else to support them in the postwar period (Dae-Sook Suh 1967:230). As a group, Yan'an veterans were generally older, better educated and more sophisticated than most other Korean Communists by reason of their exposure to large-scale military and political activities in China. In post-liberation North Korea, initially they maintained their distinct identity by establishing the New People's Party (*Sinmin-dang*) in February 1946 and by appealing primarily to the intelligentsia, but their strategic position was weak. Like the Manchurian guerillas, long years in exile had left them with tenuous roots in Korea. They had no big power patron, their service in China was grounds for deep Soviet suspicion, and they had no independent power base. In order to compensate for these weaknesses, they soon entered into a strategic alliance with the Manchurian guerilla group, with whom they merged to form the North Korean Workers' Party in August 1946. Their survival hinged upon recognition of their military and ideological proficiency, and upon the emergence of a broad-based Communist party, capable of accepting distinct groupings within its ranks.

The fourth major group in the oligarchy, the Soviet–Koreans, had no affiliation with the prewar Korean Communist movement. It consisted of a cadre of Soviet bureaucrats and Party officials of Korean background who were dispatched to the North to fill the administrative and bureaucratic vacuum left by the departure of the Japanese. Much as they did in Eastern Europe, the Soviets drew on the valuable resource of cadres in the Communist Party of the Soviet Union (CPSU) who possessed what were described as special 'national characteristics' for organisation and guidance activities at appropriate levels of government.[11] During this period an estimated two hundred CPSU cadres of Korean background occupied senior positions in the bureaucracy up to Vice Minister level and were also in overall charge of Korean Workers' Party (KWP) organisation and propaganda.[12] To occupy such positions in a government established under Leninist party auspices was, of course, to play an active role in support of Soviet objectives. In fact, so seamless was the relationship between the KWP and the CPSU that the Soviet–Koreans who were CPSU members automatically became KWP members in Korea while retaining their Soviet citizenship and CPSU party membership. By contrast, Korean members of the Chinese Communist Party had to relinquish their membership and reapply to the Korean party (Chong-sik Lee and Ki-wan Oh 1968:287). Soviet–Koreans played senior and influential policy roles within the KWP until their leaders were dismissed in the wake of the Second Plenum of the Second KWP Congress in August 1956, whereupon most of them returned to the Soviet Union (Ginsbergs 1976).

As a ruling oligarchy, the Communists were divided by the legacy of the movement's prewar antagonisms, but were united by the common problem of popular indifference. Their esoteric ideology had little obvious relevance to the problems of an overwhelmingly backward, rural society, and their prewar record was not impressive. With liberation came vigorous grass-roots political activity in the form of local People's Committees which reflected the turbulence of the times in their advocacy of wide-ranging transformations in Korean society, but this advocacy was made with little or no specific reference to the Korean Communist movement or to Marxism–Leninism. Assessments of the Communists' popular support vary, as does the nature of the evidence on which these assessments are based, but the overall picture emerges of limited popular support. Communists, though of course campaigning under adverse conditions, still comprised only 4 per cent of the elected members of the first legislature in the South in December 1946, with left-wing members comprising a further 7 per cent (Sung-Chul Yang 1990). As Kim Il Sung himself observed in 1955, 'If we had yelled about building socialism in the period of construction directly after liberation, who would have accepted it?' (Paige 1964:230).[13]

Another problem shared by all Communist groups was that between them they had few individuals recognised as political leaders by the general population. Social upheaval and dislocation on the peninsula in the period leading up to 1945 had been considerable, and upon liberation in the North the disciplines of traditional society and Japanese authority were replaced by the disciplines of state terrorism and class warfare, but there is no compelling evidence that core features of the Korean political tradition were significantly set aside. The four key attributes of age, social status, educational background and place of origin were still important determinants of Korean attitudes toward political leadership, and the Communists had to contend with better credentialled rivals in all these categories. This was especially the case with Kim Il Sung and his Manchurian guerilla colleagues who typically were at least a generation younger than veteran nationalist leaders such as Cho Man-sik, were of peasant background, had received little education past the middle school level and who mostly came from remote areas such as Manchuria and the Hamgyong Provinces in the northeast of the peninsula. The guerillas compensated for these drawbacks to a degree through their record of anti-Japanese resistance, but while anti-Japanese nationalism translated into public respect and even formed the basis for a prominent political role in many parts of East and Southeast Asia after the Japanese surrender, Korean Communist activities had been mainly sporadic, low-level, unheroic in nature or else carried out in remote regions on foreign soil in obscure circumstances. Moreover, Japanese censorship was such that there was little public awareness of their deeds. The Communist campaigns lacked the power on the public imagination that might have come through eminent leadership, large-scale, sustained campaigns or notable accomplishments.

A further serious problem for the Communists after August 1945 was that they did not gain access to power as a result of any mass-based political or military campaign, but were handed power by foreign occupation authorities. This, of course, had its benefits. Soviet backing meant control of the political centre, and hence a means of building and consolidating a power base that bypassed the intense localism of Korean political culture and the rough, village-level democracy of the times. Moreover, Soviet backing provided essential resources such as practical bureaucratic expertise and a cadre of Soviet–Koreans who were experienced at political mobilisation. This was invaluable for a movement which had specialised in underground political agitation, protracted military and small-scale guerilla operations, and crude transactions such as banditry and terrorism. However, the Soviets also had exacting standards of loyalty, and these required the Communists to offer regular and elaborate public praise for a liberator that by late 1945 was rapidly becoming a coercive foreign power. Over time, constant public praise for the Soviets in the lavish style dictated by Stalinist political culture served to underscore their status as a marginal political movement with strong external linkages. Unquestioning support for unpopular policies in the Soviet interest, such as the December 1945 Moscow Agreement on trusteeship for Korea, also placed a heavy political burden on the oligarchy.[14]

Nevertheless, many Communists were prepared to accept close and public identification with the Soviet Union despite undoubted feelings of resentment at the overbearing nature of Soviet control, because most North Korean Communists in 1945 considered themselves to be members of an international brotherhood of socialist parties which freely acknowledged the pre-eminence of the Soviet Union and the CPSU, and which deeply admired the achievements of Stalin as an individual leader. To be a Communist meant identification with a friendly major world power which had a long history of support for anti-colonialist movements and which had just helped to defeat Japan. Korean Communists owed much to the Soviet Union, and were they to compare their prospects in 1945 to their situation only five or ten years previously, those who did not experience or else were prepared to overlook the appalling behaviour of the Soviet occupation troops in the period immediately after liberation would have had much reason to give thanks to their big brother.[15]

Although fulsome public expressions of praise for the Soviet Union, the CPSU and Stalin were mandatory for the oligarchy during this period, there seems little doubt that in many cases they reflected genuine sentiment. Amid widespread expectations of radical, even utopian change and great hope for the future, the Soviet military government speedily addressed expectations that collaborators should be called to account, that there should be an end to social status discrimination, a new distribution of wealth, and that there should be a better life for workers and peasants, marked by access to education, health care and other social services.

While many may not have consciously identified such a program with socialism per se, in the ideology of the CPSU under Stalin, the new recruits who now swelled the ranks of the Party in the North would have found much with which to identify. Like so many of the cadres who rose in the CPSU under Stalin, they too were relatively unsophisticated, recently educated young idealists who were not interested in cosmopolitan ideological debate, but instead were attracted by calls to conduct class warfare against the established political and social orders, and by the discipline, intensity and violence of mobilised political life. With time and experience, a nationalistic brand of communism would come to the fore, but in the atmosphere of 1945, to be a good Communist in North Korea was to be heir to the way in which Soviet-style communism had evolved ideologically and organisationally since 1917. In short, to be a good Korean Communist in 1945 was to praise the Soviet Union and to be a good Stalinist.

Moreover, the continuing division of the country gave a vital measure of unity to the movement on policy grounds for, whatever else on which they might disagree, the movement was united on the proposition that the revolution would not be finished until the South was liberated. In this task each group of the oligarchy needed the others, for together they contributed a highly complementary set of strengths to the task of reunification. Kim Il Sung and the Manchurian guerillas had formidable state resources at their disposal, but had little formal education or administrative experience, and had no network in the South, where well over half the population lived. Japanese census statistics in 1944 estimated the population south of the 38th parallel as 15.9 million, with 9.2 million in the North, but by September 1946 the figure for the South had risen to 19.4 million, much of which came from the northern exodus and from the repatriation of Koreans, who were mainly former Kyongsang Province residents, from Japan. The Yan'an group contained cadres with higher levels of education and broader experience than the Manchurian guerillas. They could also offer considerable military expertise but likewise had no network in the South. The domestic Communists led by Pak Hon-yong operated at the grass-roots level in the South, and claimed to have built a substantial Party structure. In any drive for reunification this network would be indispensable.

The search for a local Party leadership which was compatible with the Stalinist system posed a number of dilemmas for the Soviets. The domestic Korean Communist movement, now based in Seoul, had ties with the Soviet Union in the prewar period through the Comintern but, in Soviet thinking, ties from this era were now irrelevant, if not dangerous. They dated from a period when the Comintern was still under the control of the old Bolshevik stratum of the CPSU, and this stratum had been a key target of Stalin's Terror of the 1930s, as had foreign Communists living in the Soviet Union. Under Stalin there were wide-ranging changes to CPSU organisation and it was now a very different entity to the CPSU of the 1920s. In the 1930s Stalin had abandoned the Bolshevik-style organisational pattern of the Party as an elite, revolutionary vanguard in favour of a mass party headed by an autocratic genius-leader, and in the process made far more stringent demands on foreign parties for loyalty to the Soviet Union than the Bolsheviks with their commitment to proletarian internationalism had ever done.[16]

One notable feature of Stalin's personal autocracy was an attitude of deep suspicion toward national Communist movements in Soviet-occupied countries. Wherever possible, he sought to replace them with cadres who were more directly dependent upon Moscow, and this worked against not only the domestic Communists but also the Yan'an group with its Chinese connections. This effectively narrowed the field of Koreans felt to be politically reliable down to the former Manchurian guerillas. The guerillas had come of age politically in the post-Bolshevik 1930s, and had been in training in the Soviet Union since 1941. They had become familiar with the Stalinist system and the Soviets had had the opportunity to make a thorough political appraisal of them. Within North Korea, Kim Il Sung's credentials for political leadership were almost nonexistent, but the fact that he had virtually no links with any branch of the prewar Korean Communist movement became a perverse strength in the eyes of the Soviets since it meant that he had no vestige of an independent power base. At the time the Soviets would certainly have noted his youth and inexperience, but they seem to have been attracted by more positive qualities—rigorous self-discipline, ability to command men, an exceptional work ethic and little intellectual interest in ideological matters. In short, he possessed all the desirable attributes of the subordinate client—and of the typical Stalinist cadre. This quality of outward conformity to type helps us to understand how the Soviets could have come to promote to leadership a man who, from the mid-1950s onward, spent more time working against their interests than for them.

Would Kim have attracted significant support as a potential leader without Soviet patronage? The immediate and obvious answer is that if he had, the Soviets would never have promoted him. Kim's first hurdle was the Soviet authorities, not public opinion. But beyond the issue of Soviet approbation, the later promotion of Kim's image as a hero of the anti-Japanese resistance should not cause us to lose sight of the fact that despite his record of guerilla leadership, in 1945 Kim was still only 33 years of age, with no structured education beyond middle school, no obvious personal magnetism,[17] and no significant family or institutional networks in Korea itself. In Korean terms, these were serious drawbacks for a would-be leader seeking to attract a mass following in 1945. In Manchurian guerilla circles, Kim evinced qualities of leadership such as physical and mental toughness, self-discipline, attention to detail and ability to keep men in line. In the broader public arena, age, education, social background, charisma and affiliations with particularist groups were important ingredients of a political base, and here Kim had major limitations. One of Kim's few assets was his choice of nom de guerre, for in Korea in 1945 the name 'Kim Il Sung' was widely associated not with Kim himself but with an older guerilla who had performed legendary feats in the anti-Japanese struggle, but who has never been identified as an historical person. Initially Kim may have benefited from having his nom de guerre identified in the popular mind with this other 'Kim Il Sung', though of course this benefit would not have continued past his first public appearances.

Kim and his group proceeded to consolidate power by a combination of continuing Soviet support, ability and good fortune. In his relations with the Soviets he evinced self-discipline and sound strategic sense in avoiding all semblance of conflict. He astutely applied united front tactics to contain, absorb and eliminate the weaker groups within the oligarchy in the North, and exploited the military expertise of the Yan'an group while keeping its leaders under careful political control. He was ruthless and forthright in purging such domestic Communist leaders in the North as O Ki-sop and, as the southern Communists began to retreat north under pressure from the US military government from late 1946 on, he effectively screened them off from power.

Kim's good fortune was that the Party operated under a dualistic structure at this stage, whereby the northern and southern branches remained distinct in personnel, organisation and tactics. In Seoul, Pak Hon-yong and the KCP were conducting a revolutionary struggle in the face of a hostile political centre, while in the North, Kim was leading a process of political and social mobilisation under the protective wing of the Soviets.[18] The northerners acknowledged nominal KCP authority, but in practice operated with an independent power base and in a vastly more favourable political environment. As time passed, the southerners' lack of success reduced their standing within the Party, while the strong material base created in the North, especially in the military sector, increased the power of the northern branch. When the showdown came in the early months of the Korean War, this strength proved decisive.

The Korean War destroyed the basis for unity among Korean Communist oligarchy members and precipitated a struggle for supremacy among its groups. The great task of planning a war of reunification had submerged the various latent antagonisms, but these quickly re-emerged under the stress of military reverses in the period from August to October 1950. On the one hand, Kim Il Sung felt misled when the local uprisings in support of the Democratic People's

Republic of Korea (DPRK) invasion failed to materialise on the scale promised by Pak Hon-yong. On the other hand, decisive intervention by US-led United Nations forces via the Inchon landing in August 1950 removed the prospect of early reunification. Kim therefore had little further need of Pak, open recriminations followed and Pak began the slide that culminated in his execution in December 1955.

Meanwhile, an immediate victim of the early reversals of the Korean War was the senior Yan'an group military leader and commander of the KPA Second Corps, Mu Chong. At the Third Plenum of the Second KWP Congress, held at Kanggye in the far north during 21–23 December 1950, Mu was dismissed from office and died soon afterwards. Mu was charged with a series of crimes, ranging from failure to defend Pyongyang to the unlawful execution of subordinates, but ostensibly he was called upon to shoulder chief blame for the reverses suffered after the Inchon landing. Kim Il Sung may also have assessed that Mu's Chinese military connections from the pre-1945 period were a potential threat now that the Chinese People's Volunteers were in Korea in large numbers and doing most of the fighting.[19]

However, Kim's elimination of potential rivals for power was only part of the solution to the problem of political survival in the face of military disaster. During the war the KWP had witnessed the fragility of its control of the population, with the widespread collapse of local-level Party structures and organisations and evidence of open collaboration with UN forces (Scalapino and Lee 1972:411). As the battle front stabilised in the first half of 1951, the Party faced the need for massive reorganisation. In a considerable feat of organisation, achieved with great energy under wartime conditions of widespread destruction, despair and recrimination, Kim Il Sung directed the task of re-establishing the KWP at the grass-roots level and emerged as the dominant leadership figure within the Party. The first move, taken under the authority of the Soviet–Korean Ho Ka-i, was a campaign of wholesale dismissals, but this was soon countermanded by Kim Il Sung. Kim dismissed Ho, reinstated the dismissed Party members and, during the course of 1952, enrolled a further 450 000 members to bring the total membership to just over one million by December 1952. Radically altered criteria for membership resulted in the recruitment of over 600 000 members between 1951 and 1956, and by 1956 the Party had more than made good its wartime losses, with membership rising from 800 000 in 1949 to 1 164 000 in 1956 (Scalapino and Lee 1972:712).

The restored Party mainly comprised people of poor peasant

background who were enrolled for their class background rather than their grasp of ideology. Its experience of—even its memory of—the prewar anti-Japanese Communist struggle was limited, since by 1956, 50 per cent of its members had joined since 1950, and 90 per cent had had no experience of political participation prior to 1945 (Scalapino and Lee 1972:469ff). Moreover, they were drawn from a population which had not joined the large-scale exodus south after 1945, and which had remained loyal despite enormous wartime privation and suffering. Like participants in many other wars, the North Korean population had lived through experiences of great intensity and this bonded the people to the state and the state ideology. In turn, Kimist ideology, with its constant warnings of external threats and high level of military-style mobilisation, helped to reinforce this dependency. Neither education nor experience qualified people to assess critically either the Kimist ideological training they now received or the later massive rewriting of the history of the pre-1945 struggle. Having led his country into a disastrous war, Kim himself was politically vulnerable but, with a combination of assiduous attention to organisation at the lower levels of the Party and decisive, ruthless and timely action against his opponents, Kim and his supporters progressively isolated and purged leaders of rival groups within the oligarchy.[20]

Some idea of the changes wrought on the KWP oligarchy by the Korean War can be gained from a consideration of the fate of the leaders of its major elements. By the time of the signing of the Military Armistice Agreement on 27 July 1953, Pak Hon-yong, the most prominent member of the domestic Communist group, was under arrest and would be executed within eighteen months. Mu Chong, the most prominent military member of the Yan'an group, had been purged and was now dead, and Ho Ka-i, the most prominent of the Soviet–Koreans, had committed suicide while under political attack from within the KWP. Kim Il Sung's authority had grown substantially, and his enhanced status was symbolised by the first signs of a strong cult of personality as the Party sought a new focus for loyalty.[21]

The attitude of the DPRK toward its major foreign allies also underwent transformation as a result of the Korean War. Chinese assistance strengthened the DPRK–China bond, but the DPRK viewed the Soviet Union in a changed light. The DPRK had secured Soviet support for the June 1950 invasion because Kim and Pak Hon-yong, backed by the judgment of Soviet military advisers in Korea, had persuaded Stalin that they could achieve a swift victory

(Goncharov et al 1993:149). When this did not happen, the Soviets were prepared to settle for a stalemate and a negotiated settlement which would leave the country divided. They were also prepared to force acceptance of this fundamentally unpalatable outcome on Pyongyang. While the DPRK had not engaged in open criticism of the Soviet role in the Korean War, Kim Il Sung's intense drive to control his own destiny arose as Soviet strategic interests came to determine the outcome of the Korean War.

The KWP approached the immediate post-1953 period in an atmosphere of deep uncertainty. In the Korean War the DPRK experienced human and material losses on a scale hitherto suffered only by the major protagonists of World War II. It suffered around 300 000 military casualties, 400 000 civilian casualties, and approximately three million of its citizens had fled to the South. Intensive bombing by the UN forces effectively destroyed every major centre of population and production in the North. The basis of agricultural production was severely damaged and the threat of widespread famine was averted only by substantial food aid from the Soviet Union and China. Defeat and recrimination had exacerbated bitter internal Party fighting, and the Party harboured serious doubts about the loyalty of the population.

In these circumstances the defining ideological struggle within the KWP took place in the period 1953 to 1955. This struggle pitted the 'leftism' of Kim Il Sung, who sought immediate and strong levels of investment in heavy industry in a rapid, forced pace of postwar reconstruction, against the 'rightism' of Pak Ch'ang-ok of the Soviet–Korean camp, Ch'oe Ch'ang-ik of the Yan'an camp, and others who argued for a rehabilitation phase marked by a greater concentration of investment in light industry and agriculture.[22] In turn, the economic debate was symbolic of a wider political and ideological struggle which in many ways paralleled the Stalin–Bukharin struggle in the Soviet Union of the late 1920s. In pushing his case, Kim attacked his opponents as 'dogmatists' and 'formalists' for uncritically imitating current trends in Soviet economic policy, especially a renewed emphasis on consumer goods production in the Soviet Union that emerged under Malenkov's influence in the immediate post-Stalin period.[23] Against this, he contrasted his own determination to apply the principles of Marxism–Leninism to Korean realities and so, in a landmark speech on 28 December 1955, the ideological framework that was gradually to be systematised and exalted as Juche ('self-reliance') began to emerge. Paradoxically, in its early stages Juche coexisted with continuing strong, effusive acknowledgments of the central role played by the Soviet Union and Stalin personally in the international Communist movement, and the two themes may well have continued to exist side by side were it not for the death of Stalin in 1953 and Khrushchev's subsequent denunciation of Stalinism in 1956.[24]

Also like the Stalin–Bukharin clash, the conflict ended in the complete triumph of the 'leftist' option of early and rapid socialist transformation and in the entrenchment of a high degree of commandism and autarky within the system. As victor, Kim drew more and more on the core features of the Stalinist command political and economic system.[25] These features included central planning of all production in accordance with politically determined targets, the intensive mobilisation of the labour force, the widespread employment of ideological incentives in the absence of material ones, a drive for rapid, extensive industrialisation with particular stress laid on developing the means of production, the rapid collectivisation of agriculture, and the harnessing of the DPRK economy to the collective needs of the Socialist Bloc under the direction of the Soviet Union. These features in turn were a reflection of Kim Il Sung's own talents and his predilection for military-style economic organisation and mobilisation. The DPRK in 1953 was a fearful, bitter, intensely mobilised state. Under Kim's postwar leadership it would remain so.

Wider events also played a role in the emergence of a distinctive Kimist ideology during this period. Khrushchev's denunciation of Stalin posed an important challenge to Kim, whose ideological and organisational debt to Stalin was considerable. Not only did he advocate a policy of rapid, forced heavy industrialisation for which the Stalinist policies of the 1930s were the chief blueprint, but he himself was a convinced Stalinist who had based a good deal of his legitimacy on conscious identification with Stalin's Soviet Union as a model state and with Stalin as a model genius-leader, ruling through cult of personality. He did not share the Soviet need for revision of Stalinism. Accordingly, as Kim blended the essential features of Stalinism into his new, emerging ideology of Juche, the divergence in the ideologies of the two parties gathered pace.

The promotion of Juche was also a valuable tool for Kim in the ongoing intra-party struggle, and in his hands the accusation that opponents of his rapid postwar reconstruction policies had important Soviet linkages—the Soviet–Korean technocrats amongst these opponents were, of course, still Soviet citizens and members of the CPSU—further established the nationalistic colouring of Juche. In clear, simple terms he accused Soviet–Korean opponents such as Pak

Ch'ang-ok of ignorance and neglect of Korean history and traditions, and of mechanical borrowing from other socialist countries' experiences.

As a result of these developments the KWP that assembled for the Third Congress in Pyongyang during 23–29 April 1956 was very different from the KWP of the Second Congress in 1948. Most of the key members of the pre-1950 oligarchy and most of the Party's intellectual elements had disappeared, and those who survived did so either at the sufferance of the Kimist group or because their profuse public expressions of loyalty to Kim served a useful purpose. A mass Party had grown up under the influence of Kim's organisational skills, and increasingly it reflected the personality of its chief architect— rural, patchily educated, ideologically unsophisticated, suspicious of outside linkages, rigidly disciplined, and inured to hardship. This achievement was durable, for the Party preserved this essential character in the decades that followed. The Congress achieved the consolidation, but not the total domination, of Kimist control over the Party, and this was expressed in the composition of the Political Committee, where seven of the eleven Political Committee members elected at the Congress came from the Kimist group.[26]

The April 1956 Congress also took place against a background of unrest in the Soviet Bloc. On 25 February 1956 at the Twentieth Congress of the CPSU, Nikita Khrushchev delivered his denunciation of Stalin. This forced many Eastern European states, whose leaders had been installed by Stalin, to follow suit, and also led to wider social unrest in Poland in June and most notably in Hungary in October 1956. In the DPRK the effects of Khrushchev's denunciation were not evident at the Third KWP Congress, but soon after the Congress concluded, Kim Il Sung's opponents also openly challenged Kim's policies and leadership style. At the First Plenum of the Third KWP Central Committee, held during 30–31 August 1956, Kim's opponents, comprising Politburo members affiliated with the Soviet–Korean group such as Pak Ch'ang-ok, and members affiliated with the Yan'an group such as Ch'oe Ch'ang-ik, accused him of over-concentration on developing the means of production at the expense of light and medium industry and provision of adequate food, clothing and housing. Kim's opponents attacked his growing cult of personality and accused him of failing to denounce the extremes of the Stalinist cult.

However, by now the anti-Kim forces were operating from a much-reduced base of support within the Party and their leaders were dismissed from all positions. Joint Soviet and Chinese intervention secured their formal reinstatement in September 1956, but a Party campaign against them began almost immediately, leading to their final ouster at the First KWP Conference in March 1958. The successful countering of this threat by Kim and his followers removed the remaining non-Kimists from the Party. The Soviet–Koreans who had installed and who ran much of the Party and government infrastructure were expelled with profound effect in terms of loss of expertise. The final downfall of Kim's Politburo opponents in the months following the Third KWP Congress in April 1956 thus heralded the consolidation of Kim's personal power and the apotheosis of Juche as the ideological touchstone of the Party.[27] It also laid the groundwork for the consolidation and intensification of radical policies of mobilisation and militarisation that had so far only been adumbrated. Kim Il Sung had not yet established his personal autocracy, nor had his cult of personality achieved its later level of intensity but by 1958 he was clearly the dominant leader in the Korean Workers' Party.

The destruction of the Communist oligarchy during the Korean War was a decisive moment in the history of the DPRK, for Kim's successive purges of non-Kimist oligarchy leaders directly laid the foundations for his subsequent personal autocracy. These purges eliminated not just all the leading figures in the Party outside the Kimist group, but also radically narrowed the intellectual base of the Party. The many and varied strains of the prewar Korean Communist tradition disappeared as Kim established a leadership group dominated by former Manchurian guerillas. As a result, the generic influences of Stalinism melded with a post-Korean War ideological and policy framework in the DPRK that strongly reflected the tastes, prejudices and experiences of the Manchurian guerilla mind-set—militarist, Spartan, ruthless, conspiratorial, anti-intellectual, anti-bureaucratic, and insular.

A second major consequence of the oligarchy's destruction was that the Party did not participate in the de-Stalinisation process initiated in the Soviet Union after Stalin's death in 1953. While non-Kimist members of the oligarchy joined in criticism of the excesses of Stalinism following Stalin's death, for the Kimists, Stalinism remained the nonpareil recipe for the economic transformation of the DPRK, and especially for the rapid creation of a military-industrial base. They viewed Stalinist policies as necessary for the nation to atone for the humiliation of the Korean War and to reverse the outcome of that war in the not-too-distant future.

The hallmarks of Kim's personal leadership style also emerged during the 1950s. One pointer to the future was that in his campaigns against fellow Communist oligarchs, Kim unhesitatingly adopted radical policies that involved high elements of risk. He engaged in sustained political combat against many other elements in the Party's leadership while the country was still engaged in a disastrous war, and in the immediate post-Korean War period he tested the allegiance of the population by forcing them into the immediate and rapid pursuit of heavy industrialisation at a time when virtually no one outside the Party elite could claim access to anything like adequate food, clothing or housing. Moreover, Kim pursued these policies against the advice of the Soviet Union and China, and at a time when significant voices within the Party leadership were advocating more moderate policies.

In the course of this struggle against factional opponents, for the first time Kim began to emphasise nationalism as a means of rallying the population to the enormous sacrifices needed for postwar recovery. This was a nationalism that first took shape in the environment of the anti-Japanese guerilla movement and developed into a creed through the destruction of both the non-Communist nationalist forces and much of the leftist intellectual tradition of the domestic Communists. Kim's nationalism did not draw inspiration from Korean history, nor did it dwell on past cultural achievements, for the serious study of history and traditional Korean culture soon effectively ceased in the DPRK. Rather, DPRK nationalism drew inspiration from the Spartan outlook of the former Manchurian guerillas. It was a harsh nationalism that dwelt on past wrongs and promises of retribution for 'national traitors' and their foreign backers. DPRK nationalism stressed the 'purity' of all things Korean against the 'contamination' of foreign ideas, and inculcated in the population a sense of fear and animosity toward the outside world. Above all, DPRK nationalism stressed that the guerilla ethos was not only the supreme, but also the only legitimate basis on which to reconstitute a reunified Korea.

2

THE POLITICAL INSTITUTIONS OF THE DEMOCRATIC PEOPLE'S REPUBLIC OF KOREA

In the previous chapter we have seen the emergence of a distinctive political culture in the Democratic People's Republic of Korea (DPRK), culminating in the triumph of the Kimists at the March 1958 Korean Workers' Party (KWP) Party Conference. The chapters that follow examine the Kimist state in its post-1958 phase and deal primarily with the policy outcomes that flowed from Kim's establishment of a personal autocracy during the 1960s. Since an appreciation of the institutional setting in which Kim and his colleagues operated is also important for an understanding of the nature of this personal autocracy, we first consider the characteristics of the Party and government institutions of the DPRK.

Under close Soviet supervision, Leninist principles of party organisational work provided a blueprint for the fledgling Korean Communist oligarchy to consolidate power in 1945. The result was the establishment of a network of Party and state institutions directly inspired by Soviet models and precedents, and this in turn led to a polity in which the process of political, social, and economic change was conceived and directed by a numerically small political elite. The KWP stands at the apex of this network and functions in accordance with its mission as a self-proclaimed vanguard party. It is elitist by the nature of its ideology and by virtue of the monopoly it claims on the resources of the state. It is at the core of a political culture marked by exclusion, centralisation, strict accountability, hierarchy and discipline, while its style also reflects its ex-guerilla leadership—ruthless, Spartan, secretive, suspicious of intellectual activity, resourceful, predatory, and improvisatory.

At the grass-roots level, the KWP is active through the operation of an elaborate net of specialist and mass organisations encompassing the government, the military, and subgroups such as the technocracy, the intelligentsia, trade unions, youth, and women's organisations.[1] These organisations constitute what Stalin once referred to as the 'drive reins' of the populace (Volkogonov 1995:86). They do not exist to present views in a political process of competition and mutual accommodation, but rather they exist to be coordinated and subsumed into the chain of command of the Party itself. Powell's (1992:195) description of the CPSU as '. . . an elaborate network of institutions, demands and expectations designed to promote the proper political socialization of the entire population [and inculcate] predictable, habituated responses from the citizenry . . .', and Rigby's (1977:53) likening of Communist Party of the Soviet Union (CPSU) control over these organisations to a wartime 'Supreme Command [which] directs and orchestrates the numerous formations, branches, and services operating in a particular theater of war' have obvious relevance for the role of the KWP. The KWP selects and closely supervises the key personnel in these organisations, and in the process exercises a monopoly on all significant forms of political activity. It also exercises more general control over DPRK society by means of the deployment of a formidable reward–punishment system and a ruthless coercive apparatus which, as we saw in Chapter 1, was originally developed and for many years run by Soviet–Korean People's Commissariat for Internal Affairs (NKVD) officers.

As in the Soviet and Chinese parties, the KWP leadership attains formal legitimacy through election at periodic Party Congresses. The Congress is described in the KWP bylaws as 'the highest organ of the party',[2] to be convened every four years. However, as was also the practice in the Soviet Union and China, during Kim Il Sung's lifetime congresses were convened at far less frequent intervals. The first three congresses were convened in 1946, 1948 and 1956 respectively, and the last three were convened in 1961, 1970 and 1980. At the time of his death in July 1994, Kim had given no sign of any intention to convene what would have been the Seventh Congress. KWP Party congresses bring together about 2000 carefully chosen delegates from the lower levels of Party organisation. They assemble primarily to endorse the policies of the leadership and to provide an authoritative platform from which to announce or reconfirm Party aims and objectives. After the comprehensive purge of Kim Il Sung's opponents between the Third Congress (1956) and the Fourth Congress (1961), these congresses ceased to act as forums for policy debate and assumed the character of Party rallies. Should serious Party problems require some form of debate and public resolution, the Party has the option of convening a Party conference, and has held two of these, in March 1958 and October 1966. In both cases they confirmed a major purging of leading cadres who had disagreed with Kim Il Sung on policy matters.[3]

Congress delegates elect members to two major committees which deal with Party matters between congresses, namely, the Central Committee (CC) and the Political Committee/Politburo. These two committees define inner precincts of power and enforce both the hieratical symbolism of Party leadership and the reality of its rigid elitism, remoteness and privilege. The Central Committee, a body consisting of several hundred cadres divided into the categories of full and alternate members,[4] meets regularly in plenary sessions to deliberate on matters relating to ideology, state policy and organisational matters.[5] From 1980 until Kim Il Sung's death it tended to hold semi-annual plenums. Kim Jong Il's attitude to them is not yet clear. Plenum communiques record the gist of discussion on major economic and political mobilisation campaigns, and ratify major organisational and personnel decisions reached elsewhere. While it is always hard to reach definitive judgment on the basis of scant information, in the years before the final establishment of Kim Il Sung's personal autocracy in 1967, the plenums seem to have had a more substantive agenda.[6] As occurred in the Soviet Union—but seems less the case with China—few decisions of either real or symbolic significance can be associated with plenum meetings.

This subservience is further reinforced by the high turnover of KWP Central Committee members between congresses (see Table 2.1 below). From 1956 to 1980, typically 65–70 per cent of the membership of each Central Committee did not gain reappointment at the following Congress, and this suggests that for most cadres Central Committee membership was a one-term only reward, rather than a

Table 2.1   Turnover rates in the KWP Central Committee 1946–80

Party congress	Full CC members	New members	% new
First (August 1946)	43	–	–
Second (March 1948)	59	29	49.2
Third (April 1956)	71	42	63.0
Fourth (September 1961)	85	56	66.0
Fifth (November 1970)	117	85	72.2
Sixth (October 1980)	145	60	41.4

Source: Chun In-yong (1990:221).

stepping stone to higher levels.[7] This may also be the reason why the alternate members do not typically proceed to full membership,[8] since in practice this makes alternate membership another, lesser category of reward.

Between plenums, day-to-day control of Party affairs rests with the Politburo, or the Political Committee as it was called in the DPRK until 1980.[9] Historically, the institution of the Politburo came briefly into existence in Russia in October 1917 to provide political leadership during the Revolution. It became institutionalised at the Eighth Congress (1919) with an initial membership of five as a small inner circle handling day-to-day policy-making tasks on behalf of the unwieldy larger Central Committee.[10] Its particular task was to ensure that matters of state, whether great or small, did not proceed before thorough examination from an ideological viewpoint. While no documents relating to KWP Politburo deliberations have ever become public, the content of the CPSU Politburo work plans for 1926 and 1928 are known, and they reveal discussion and action on a broad array of issues affecting Soviet life.

The KWP Politburo comprises full and alternate members who are elected at Party congresses. Between congresses the Central Committee ratifies further promotions and dismissals at its plenums. The size of the KWP Politburo has fluctuated over the years. The Fourth KWP Congress in 1961 elected eighteen members (twelve full and six alternates), and increased membership to twenty-three (seventeen full and six alternates) at the Second Party Conference in October 1966. The Fifth KWP Congress elected fifteen members (eleven full and four alternates) in 1970 and the Sixth Congress elected thirty-four members (nineteen full and fifteen alternates) in 1980. Dismissal and natural attrition reduced the Politburo to about twenty members at the time of Kim Il Sung's death. KWP Politburo members may also perform roles as members of Party Committees and Commissions, as members of the Government, and also as members of the Party Secretariat. Party bylaws state that the Politburo should meet at least once every month (Dae-Sook Suh 1981:535), but there is no evidence that the KWP follows this procedure since the media does not refer to Politburo meetings. Anecdotal evidence and Stalinist precedent both suggest that the Politburo functions as a support staff for Kim Il Sung and that he meets with them in select groups, rather than en bloc (Scalapino and Lee 1972:727–30).

The complexion of the Politburo has changed over the years. During the period of the Communist oligarchy it contained a diversity of outlook and experience which accommodated, among others, the poorly educated Manchurian guerillas such as Kim Il Sung and his followers, domestic Korean Marxist intellectuals such as Pak Hon-yong, second generation Soviet–Koreans who were veterans of provincial Party work in the Soviet Union such as Ho Ka-i and Pak Ch'ang-ok, and Korean veterans of the Chinese revolution such as Mu Chong, many of whom had also received regular Party and military training. During the 1950s, this diversity and its associated expertise disappeared from the KWP as Kim Il Sung and his group purged rival groups and established monopolistic control over the Party. Thereafter, the KWP Politburo evinced a striking uniformity in the characteristics of its members, who were usually male, aging, of Manchurian or North Hamgyong origin, poor or middle peasant in social origin, and of limited formal education. They had little or no foreign contact of any substantive nature in their backgrounds and were military or Party-bureaucratic in career orientation. It is no coincidence that, with the exception of his Chinese middle school education, these characteristics described Kim Il Sung himself.

With the possible exception of professional military men, who are in any case more Party-military men rather than military special-ists as such, no KWP Politburo members qualify as 'experts' in the sense of having obvious expert or specialist knowledge. They have been bound by the perception of a world in which socialist states were perpetually under threat from surrounding capitalist states, and are products not just of physical insularity, but of an intellectual insularity in which policy formulation has demanded the application of set ideological formulae and dogma to a broad array of practical problems. The use of the term 'technocrat', as applied to senior Party cadres after the demise of the Soviet–Korean group in the 1950s, refers more to specialisation in Party work, rather than specialisation by dint of education or professional experience, and should be seen against the background of the controlling influence on ideology, education and technology exercised by the older guerilla generation. A legitimate question to ask of an isolated (and isolationist) society is how its leaders can impart pragmatic skills and perspectives which they themselves do not possess, and to which they in many cases are hostile, to their successors.

In the KWP under Kim Il Sung, as in the CPSU under Stalin, Politburo members had little or no independent standing and, like the KWP Central Committee as a whole, there was a high attrition rate among members. Eighteen of the top thirty cadres appointed at the Fourth KWP Congress in 1961 were missing from the Politburo and the Fifth Central Committee elected in 1970, and leading

Politburo members such as Han Ik-su, Yu Chang-sik and Kim Tong-gyu disappeared during the 1970s. After the purge of Kim Tong-gyu in 1977, no more senior Politburo members were purged outright, though several suffered significant demotions in the offices they held and in Central Committee ranking.

When assessed against policy outcomes, the absence of observable independent political behaviour, and the blandly loyalist public pronouncements of KWP Politburo members, the stability after 1970 and the lack of purges after 1977 confirms the broad impression of a compliant Politburo which functioned much as the CPSU Politburo did—as a collection of people with little or no independent standing or power base who existed to carry out the directives of the leadership, who accepted and maintained a rigid discipline, and who kept any misgivings private. The defection of KWP Secretariat member Hwang Chang-yop in Beijing in February 1997 and the wide-ranging criticism that Hwang subsequently directed at KWP policies revealed that members of the elite do, in fact, harbour significant misgivings about basic Kimist policies. However, throughout the period of Kimist rule it is not possible to reliably associate particular Politburo members with any particular line of policy, such as economic pragmatism or dogmatism, nor have any senior cadres been reliably reported as harbouring, let alone expressing, views that differed in any important respect from those of their leader.

Nor was the Party Secretariat permitted any vestige of independence. The institution of the Leninist party Secretariat developed in the Soviet Union where it was created at the Eighth CPSU Congress (1919) along with the Politburo.[11] The objective was to regularise the CPSU's chaotic system of organisation and decision-making, which relied strongly on personal contact and secretive channels of communication. The Secretariat was the instrument by which the CPSU exercised central control over local party organisations in matters such as appointments, registrations, dismissals, the training of cadres, and CPSU election supervision and validation. The subsequent importance of the Secretariat owed a great deal to Stalin, who built it into a powerful instrument of personalised political control after becoming the CPSU's first General Secretary in 1922.

The CPSU Secretariat typically consisted of a leading cadre (often *the* leading cadre) acting as General Secretary with support staff. It never functioned as a committee of cadres of more or less equal standing, nor as a grooming stable for potential leaders. In times of collective leadership, such as after Lenin was incapacitated in 1922 or after the death of Stalin, it provided a key power base for their successors—Stalin after Lenin, Khrushchev after Stalin. During the Andropov-Chernenko interregnum period (1982–85) the CPSU leadership recognised the significance of this key post and went to considerable lengths to ensure that no individual dominated the Secretariat (Roeder 1993:113). However, when a dominant personality was actually in power, such as Stalin or Khrushchev (in his later years) the CPSU Secretariat members were very much cast in the role of servants of the leader, not wielders of power in their own right.

Their Korean counterparts have played the same subservient role. In the KWP the Secretariat did not emerge as an institution until the Second Korean Workers' Party Conference in October 1966. Called at a time of significant internal Party unrest, this conference abolished the posts of Party Chairman and Vice Chairman and replaced them with the post of General Secretary who, with a support staff of ten secretaries, comprised the Secretariat. The announced functions of the Secretariat were similar to those of its Soviet counterpart, namely, overseeing the implementation of Party policy and supervising Party organisational work. Kim Il Sung assumed the post of General Secretary and held it until his death, and it was the first significant post assumed by Kim Jong Il after the 1994–97 period of mourning which followed his father's death.

As with other KWP organisations, it is not possible to determine precisely how the Secretariat has functioned in practice. It is noteworthy that the KWP functioned until 1967 without the benefit of an institution that was so important in other Leninist parties. It is also significant that the Secretariat was established at a time of acute confrontation in leadership circles between Kim loyalists and a number of senior cadres who challenged his policies and leadership style. The creation of the Secretariat seems to have been a means of extending Kim's reach more directly into the Party's grass-roots activities, and the earliest members of the Secretariat were, therefore, loyalist full or alternate Politburo members.

However, after Kim restablished his personal autocracy during 1967–68, he faced no further challenges within the KWP, and with the ensuing consolidation of this personal autocracy, the activities of the Secretariat declined in importance. This has been reflected in the lower status of cadres appointed to the Secretariat in recent years. The careers of the ten secretaries appointed at the Sixth KWP Congress in October 1980 illustrate this trend (see Table 2.2 below).

By 1980, the average Politburo ranking of Secretariat members had fallen in comparison with the original Secretariat members appointed in 1967. If we exclude Kim Il Sung and Kim Jong Il from consideration, we note that only three of the remaining eight were full Politburo members, two were alternate members, and three were not Politburo members at all. The decline in the standing of Secretariat members continued during the 1980s, so that by 1990, apart from Kim Il Sung and Kim Jong Il, none of the Party Secretaries held Politburo rank.[12]

In addition to the decline in the status of Secretariat members, there is no evidence to show that service in the Secretariat has helped cadres in their subsequent careers. Consider, for example, the cases of the eight cadres appointed to the Secretariat in 1980:

1. Kim Chung-nin: demoted from full to alternate Politburo membership in December 1984, left the Secretariat soon after,[13] dropped altogether from the Politburo in 1986. Reappointed as a Party Secretary in 1990 but did not regain his former Politburo status.
2. Kim Yong-nam: left the Secretariat some time after his appointment as Foreign Minister in December 1983. His Politburo ranking has remained essentially unchanged since 1980.
3. Kim Hwan: left the Secretariat in 1986, ranking remained intact until dropped from the Politburo in 1987.
4. Yon Hyong-muk: left the Secretariat around 1984. Ranking apparently unaffected by tenure in Secretariat. Appointed Prime Minister in 1988, removed and demoted from full to alternate Politburo membership in 1993.
5. Yun Ki-bok: left the Secretariat in December 1983, subsequently

Table 2.2 **Members of the KWP Secretariat 1967 and 1980 (Politburo ranking at time of appointment in parentheses)**

1967		1980	
1)	Kim Il Sung (1)	1)	Kim Il Sung (1)
2)	Ch'oe Yong-gon (2)	2)	Kim Jong Il (4)
3)	Kim Il (3)	3)	Kim Chung-nin (11)
4)	Pak Kum-ch'ol (4)	4)	Kim Yong-nam (12)
5)	Yi Hyo-sun (5)	5)	Kim Hwan (14)
6)	Kim Kwang-hyop (6)	6)	Yon Hyong-muk (15)
7)	Sok San (12)	7)	Yun Ki-bok (21)
8)	Ho Pong-hak (13)	8)	Hong Si-hak (-)
9)	Kim Yong-ju (18)	9)	Hwang Chang-yop (-)
10)	Pak Yong-guk (19)	10)	Pak Su-dong (-)
11)	Kim To-man (-)		

Sources: For 1967 members Dae-Sook Suh (1981:328); for 1980 members *PT* 15 October 1980.

lost Politburo ranking and disappeared from public view until reappointment as a Party Secretary in 1990. Had not regained Politburo status by 1994.

6. Hong Si-hak: also left the Secretariat in December 1983, gained alternate Politburo status in 1986 and has held a steady ranking since then.

7. Hwang Chang-yop: retained Secretariat membership throughout the 1980s with no significant change to his CC ranking.

8. Pak Su-dong: left the Secretariat in 1982, has not been reported as holding any significant public office since then.

Time spent in the Secretariat has not been of particular benefit to these cadres in their subsequent careers. Some, like Yon Hyong-muk and Hong Si-hak, later received promotions but this was some time later and cannot readily be connected to their time in the Secretariat. Others like Kim Chung-nin, Kim Hwan, Yun Ki-bok and Pak Su-dong suffered demotion, while Kim Yong-nam and Hwang Chang-yop held a consistent Party ranking throughout this period. These career paths suggest that the Secretariat comprises a mix of high-ranking Politburo members and more junior-ranking Party people who do not derive power from their positions, but who are routinely rotated in and out of the Secretariat without effect on their substantive Politburo or Central Committee ranking. Despite the importance of the Secretariat as a Party institution in the Soviet Union and China, in the DPRK under Kim Il Sung the evidence argues against viewing this institution as important either in itself or as a career stepping stone for its incumbents. The pattern of appointments to the Secretariat suggests that Kim Il Sung viewed a high-powered Party Secretariat as important during the period of acute intra-Party tension during 1967–68, but that in times of unchallenged personal autocracy the Secretariat had a far less significant role to play.

The current constitutional order was promulgated through the Supreme People's Assembly (SPA) on 27 December 1972, and provides the framework for the machinery of government.[14] The 1972 constitution superseded the 1948 constitution, and reflected many of the changes in the balance of state and Party power that had occurred in the interim. In broad outline and overall institutional structure, the 1948 constitution of the DPRK was very similar to the 1936 Soviet constitution. The Supreme People's Assembly closely resembled the Supreme Soviet, and the electoral and governmental structures closely followed the Soviet pattern (Chin-Wee Chung

1983:21). This is hardly surprising for, as we have already noted, the basic laws and the 1948 constitution of the DPRK were written in Russian, either by Soviet–Koreans or Soviet advisors, and then translated into Korean (Hak-Soon Paik 1993:791).

The 1972 constitution, which comprises 149 articles, contains a more elaborate description of the basic political, economic and cultural principles of the state than its 1948 predecessor, and also effects major changes to the administrative organs of state. Article 4 downplays the formal commitment to Marxist–Leninist principles in its statement that 'The Democratic People's Republic of Korea is guided in its activity by the Juche idea of the Korean Workers' Party, a creative application of Marxism–Leninism to the conditions of our country'. The basic principles section elaborates on Juche and Three Revolutions ideology, and includes extensive references to the economy (the 1948 constitution contained only vague references to these), explicit reference to the KWP's politico-economic philosophy (the 1948 constitution had no direct references to Party ideology), the designation of private enterprises as unconstitutional, except where conducted for personal consumption (private businesses were allowed under the 1948 constitution), the granting of formal constitutional status for the KWP's dictatorship, and the changing of the designated capital of the DPRK from Seoul to Pyongyang. These changes all reflected the evolution of the DPRK state under Kim's personal autocracy.[15]

The administrative changes, which in formal institutional terms seem patterned after the Chinese system (Dae-Sook Suh 1981:502), included the creation of the post of President and the creation of a deliberative body, the Central People's Committee (CPC), composed of high Party cadres and government functionaries. The creation of these two institutions in effect downgraded the roles of the SPA as the supreme legislative and deliberative body and the Administrative Council as the main administrative organ. The changes created a series of parallels between Party and governmental institutions; the SPA resembles the KWP Central Committee as a mass ratifying body; the CPC resembles the Politburo as an elite deliberative body;[16] the Administration Council and the various commissions of the CPC, including the National Defence Commission, resemble the Party Committee structure; and the role of the DPRK President in the governmental sphere is similar in scope to the role of the KWP General Secretary in the Party sphere.

From the point of view of understanding subsequent events in the DPRK, the changes to the administrative structure in 1972 reflected the explicit supremacy of the KWP and its general penetration of the governmental process. Party principles were given formal status as state principles; leading Party cadres sat in the CPC, designated as 'the highest leadership organ of State in the DPRK' (Article 100), where their duties placed them over the Administration Council and the SPA, both of which lost substantial power.[17] Kim Il Sung was formally designated as both Supreme Commander of the armed forces and Head of State, a position previously held by the Chairman of the SPA Presidium. The 1972 constitution was promulgated after Kim Il Sung had established his personal autocracy, and it achieves meaning only in the context of personalised rule. Thus it contains many loose ends and ambiguities that could only be resolved by the exercise of personal power. Instead of seeking firmer functional differentiation, as one might expect in a modernising, industrialising state of growing complexity, the key characteristic of the 1972 constitution is functional fusion (Chong-Wook Chung 1988:108).

The creation of a powerful presidency in the 1972 constitution provided a symbolic endorsement on the governmental level for the type of power that Kim Il Sung exercised in reality. Under the constitution, the president is elected by the SPA to a four-year term. He is designated head of state and also exercises wide powers such as the promulgation of laws and ordinances of the SPA, the ratification or abrogation of foreign treaties, guidance and control of the CPC and the Administration Council, control of the judicial system and command of the armed forces. The sweeping, ill-defined extent of presidential power is also reflected in the absence of any provisions making him formally accountable to any governmental bodies in the exercise of these powers. There is no precedent for such a concentration of power in the Chinese or Soviet state constitutions, obviously because the 1972 constitution celebrates personal autocracy, rather than seeks to prevent its recurrence.[18]

The major change in the governmental structure of the 1972 constitution was the creation of the Central People's Committee, elected by the SPA to function as the 'highest leadership organ of sovereignty of the DPRK' (Article 100). Articles 103–4 detail wide-ranging powers which place the CPC in a position of superiority over the SPA, despite the fact that in theory the CPC exercises these powers on the SPA's behalf. However, trends in personnel appointments to the CPC over the years suggest that the CPC's authority is largely symbolic. Initially there was an average 70 per cent or so overlap between membership of the CPC and the Politburo, but this has fallen away over the years. The majority of CPC members elected at the first session of the Ninth SPA in May 1990 were not members of the Politburo,[19] and for past non-Politburo members of the CPC, the CPC has not been a stepping stone to higher office. For example, by the time of Kim Il Sung's death in July 1994 not one of the six non-Politburo members listed alongside nine Politburo members in the CPC in 1987 had risen to Politburo membership.

There are other indications that the CPC's governmental role is largely symbolic. The DPRK media does not report the deliberations and personnel movements of the CPC on a regular basis. Judging by published references, the CPC's role in state affairs is to endorse major decisions taken elsewhere by the Party, usually where these decisions involve major national issues. For example, an unprecedented joint meeting with the KWP Politburo on 19 February 1981 discussed the outcome of the Foreign Ministers' Conference of Non-Aligned Countries, held in New Delhi from 9–13 February. The presence of the CPC as a body at a meeting called to discuss a seemingly trivial topic carried the symbolism that it was not simply the Party involved in Non-Aligned Movement affairs but the State itself. For the same reason, the 10 January 1984 tripartite talks proposal was made jointly in the name of the CPC and the Standing Committee of the SPA (*PT* 14 January 1984), and implementation measures on Kim Il Sung's 1 January 1988 proposal on a 'north–south joint conference attended by persons in authority of both sides and the representatives of all the political parties and social organisations and people of all social standings' were discussed by the CPC, Administration Council, political parties and public organisations at a 13 January 1988 joint meeting (*PT* 23 January 1988). In 1993 the DPRK projected a similar sense of national *gravitas* when the CPC endorsed the decision to pull out of the Nuclear Non-Proliferation Treaty (NPT) (*PT* 20 March 1993).

The chief legislative body in the DPRK is the SPA. As in other Leninist party states, the deliberations and decisions of the SPA are designed to convey a symbolic seal of approval on behalf of the entire population for decisions of the Party leadership. This function of the SPA did not change under the 1972 constitution, but the changes removed many of its formal powers and redistributed them to the Presidency and the CPC (Chin-Wee Chung 1983:24). From 1973 to 1994 this 615-member body continued to meet for single annual sessions, typically held in April and lasting less than a week. The size, the high turnover of members,[20] and the short duration of sessions mark out the SPA as a rubber-stamp institution. There is no evidence of debate. All publicly reported votes have been unanimous.

The agenda usually consists of three or four items, comprising reports on major issues presented by senior members of the government. The passing of the annual budget is perhaps the most significant action.[21]

In addition to appointing the Central People's Committee, the SPA also appoints the Administration Council of the DPRK, which is often referred to as the DPRK Cabinet. It consists of about thirty or so Government ministries presided over by a number of Deputy Premiers and a Premier (or Prime Minister). During the 1980s the number of ministries fluctuated constantly as they were established, reconstituted, split and amalgamated, reflecting their status as operational units in specialist areas with no genuine political role as such. According to one defector's report, the economic ministries of the Administrative Council do not have final authority in many areas of the economy. Both the Party and the military operate separate economic systems, and the National Defence Committee, in particular, exercises substantial power through control of production and exports of weapons and other military supplies (VP vol. XVIII, no. 8, p. 31). The importance of the Administrative Council was markedly reduced in 1972 when it was made subordinate to the President and the CPC (Chin-Wee Chung 1983:37, Chong-sik Lee 1976:212), and the average Party rankings of its members during the 1980s fell accordingly. The Prime Minister is drawn from the ranks of the Politburo, and after 1980 the appointment was accompanied by an automatic promotion to No. 5 in the Party hierarchy, immediately after Kim Il Sung, Kim Jong Il, Kim Il and the top military cadre, O Chin-u. After Kim Il's death in 1984 the incumbent Prime Minister occupied the No. 4 position. In addition, a handful of other Ministers, typically about five or six out of thirty, also enjoyed Politburo status at any given time during 1980–94, often concurrently with a Vice-Premiership. For the rest, however, service on the Administration Council, once again, did not signal a career on the rise.

Even from this brief description of DPRK party and government institutions, it is clear that for sustained institutionalisation of personal rule, only Stalin's system at its height can remotely compare with the authority exercised by Kim Il Sung from 1967 to his death in 1994. After 1967, and for much of the period 1958–67 as well, he exercised enormous political authority in all major areas of government, and his judgment prevailed on all matters of state policy, whether great or small. His son has begun his rule in a similar fashion. Attempts to describe the extent of this autocracy usually transcend descriptions of political authority and emphasise the extent to which the personal authority of the leader subsumed Party ideology and organisation.[22] Kim was not only the source of all actual power, but he defined the very ideology which legitimated political power in the DPRK.

Passing reference to the various ways in which Kim Il Sung was influenced by the life and works of Joseph Stalin has already been made. As the role of Kim Il Sung changed from that of dominant leader within the KWP to personal autocrat, supreme architect of the DPRK as a would-be modern industrial state, and originator of a belief system that claimed universal validity, this influence became more and more pronounced.[23] Various commentators place different emphases on aspects of Stalinism, but they all agree on the interrelated political phenomena of extreme centralisation, high levels of social mobilisation, and personal autocracy reinforced by cult of personality. In its mature stage from the mid-1930s on, Stalinism combined a personal autocracy with the use of terror as an instrument of rule in order to seek the economic transformation of the Soviet Union. It sought this transformation by means of rapid, heavy industrialisation, featuring the mass mobilisation of labour, high levels of reinvestment, and the almost complete suppression of social forces. The result was, in Conquest's (1973:180) words, 'a command economy and a command society'.[24] Its most distinctive political trait was the cult of personality, whereby the leader assumed the mantle of benevolent genius, his every utterance providing definitive guidance in the political realm, and becoming a source of self-evident truth in all economic, social and cultural matters as well.

The term 'Stalinist' is often applied to Kim Il Sung and the DPRK system, but the nature of the Stalinist influence on Kim and hence on the DPRK polity is rarely analysed. Even detailed accounts of the life and career of Kim by Scalapino and Lee (1972), Sung-Chul Yang (1981), and Dae-Sook Suh (1988) devote relatively little attention to the phenomenon of Stalinism and its influence on Kim. More recently, Cumings (1993) has attempted to downplay, if not discount, the influence of the Stalinist model, but offers little systematic comparison of the Kimist DPRK and the Stalinist Soviet Union.[25] Yet even after setting aside the formal party, bureaucratic and social mobilisation structure also common to the pre-Stalin and post-Stalin eras, and indeed to avowedly Marxist–Leninist constitutions everywhere, we find that influences of a specifically Stalinist nature on Kim Il Sung are considerable. They include the following:

In Party organisation and political style:

- The transformation of the KWP into a mass party and the practice of maintaining a high turnover of Central Committee members between Party Congresses.
- The irregular Party congresses and general violation of socialist legality.
- The permeating of the political language with military imagery (a Trotsky innovation).
- The wholesale incorporation of grossly abusive language into public political debate.[26]
- The exaltation of violence as a legitimate revolutionary means to an end.

In ideology:

- The pursuit of early socialist transformation through 'acute class struggle' rather than through a more gradual pursuit of the dictatorship of the proletariat.
- The emphasis placed on remoulding human nature and creating 'a new type of man'; the hallmarks of the 'Juche-type man' in the DPRK are virtually indistinguishable from those of the 'New Soviet Man'.
- The strongly voluntaristic 'man is the master' ideological position.[27]
- The heavy use of kinship metaphors (e.g. 'the Fatherly Leader') to reinforce political hierarchical relationships.[28]
- The expropriating of the revolutionary past to diminish or delete altogether the contribution of people and groups other than the Leader.[29]
- The practice of attributing the basis for all policies and actions of the Party and government to the works of the Great Leader, introducing and supporting them with relevant quotations.[30]

In economic policy:

- A highly centralised, planned economy in which the Party exercises a monopoly over resource allocation.[31]
- The basic theme of Socialism in One Country (Juche in its Korean context) and its associated statism.
- The sustained emphasis given to the development of heavy industry and the associated suppression of consumer demand.
- Collectivisation in agriculture.[32]
- Heavy, sustained reliance on ideological motivation and Stakhanovite 'speed' campaigns.

- Grandiose projects of transformation—canals, dams, remaking nature in general, 'transforming the face of the capital' via skyscrapers etc.[33]

In personal style:

- The title Leader, and the formulation of the 'Under the wise direction of our great genius teacher and leader . . .' which became standard in the Soviet Union from 1929 on.
- The ceremonial typesetting of the leader's name in the print media, and its accompanying string of laudatory descriptive phrases.
- Suspicion and outright rejection of mathematical, scientific and technical planning aids.[34]
- Canonical pronouncements over a broad range of subjects, including economics, history, philosophy and linguistics.
- The characteristic way of communicating with the outside world through interviews, sometimes in person, but mainly in the form of extended responses to questions submitted by the representative of a friendly foreign news agency.[35]
- A highly interventionist working style,[36]
- Construction of a museum of gifts from foreign personages, with Kim Il Sung's Myohyang-san edifice paralleling Stalin's in his birthplace of Gori, Georgia.

This list covers both the form and substance of DPRK political practice and ranges over virtually every significant area of state activity—politics, leadership, ideology, economics, and social mobilisation, such that it is hard to imagine the DPRK as we know it without a Stalinist blueprint.

Moreover, these common features are not a matter of some esoteric or eccentric affinity, for we are looking at two systems which had close and important historical linkages. Kim Il Sung's sojourn in the Soviet Union during 1941–45 and his exposure to nation-building in the Stalinist fashion occurred at a pivotal time of his life. Although Kim's training in the Soviet Union seems to have been largely confined to military affairs, the practical appeal of Stalinism must have asserted itself strongly not just to Kim but to other Korean Communists as well because it provided a model for modernisation at a time when the only pre-existing model of economic development and modernisation—the Japanese colonial model—had been emphatically rejected. Moreover, in contrast to Marxist–Leninist theory, which provided few practical guidelines to the problems of development, Stalinism offered an organised, systematic and thorough blueprint for economic development that had been employed, seemingly successfully, in the Soviet Union for the best part of fifteen years. It is therefore not surprising that Kim Il Sung should have been attracted to Stalinism, nor that this attachment should have extended past the level of broad principles to detailed practice.

The establishment of a Soviet military occupation government, the Soviet promotion of Korean Communists as political leaders, and the presence of significant numbers of Soviet–Koreans possessing joint KWP–CPSU membership ensured that the North had early experience of the Stalinist state-building model and in particular of the Stalin personality cult. Stalin's portrait hung in people's homes, classrooms and at every railway station. Thoroughfares and other landmarks began to be named after him, and both the First [North] Korean Workers' Party Congress in August 1946 and the Second NKWP Congress in August 1948 elected Stalin as Honorary Chairman (Hak-Soon Paik 1993:47). The basic laws and the constitution of the DPRK were written in Russian and then translated into Korean, and the agendas for significant conferences involving North Korean representatives were vetted by the Soviets. Both contemporary accounts and later studies have demonstrated in considerable detail how Soviet political and economic practices became the norm.[37]

The Stalinism implanted by the Soviet occupation authorities did not become indigenised until the immediate post-Korean War period. As we have noted, the DPRK's political struggles in the period 1953–56 bear a strong resemblance to the Stalin–Bukharin struggle of the late 1920s and, as in the Soviet Union, the DPRK conflict ended with the intensification of trademark Stalinist economic policies, social mobilisation techniques, and leadership practices. Extremely high rates of investment in heavy industry became the norm, the state essentially abandoned responsibility for consumer goods production by devolving responsibility to local units, and personal autocracy buttressed by cult of personality became the fundamental organising principle of politics.

Another indication of Kim Il Sung's debt to Stalinism is the extent to which it displaced many core features of traditional Korean political culture. A number of analysts have commented on shared characteristics between the Yi Dynasty and DPRK political and social orders (Scalapino and Lee 1972:753, Henderson 1987:102, Brandt 1983:627–8, Cumings 1993:209–12), and the difficulty is not so much in detecting these affinities but in evaluating them. While some attribute these affinities to Kim's nationalism, it is more persuasive to view Kim's traditionalism as deriving more from the neo-traditionalism that is inherent in Stalinism than from a specifically Korean source.

Stalinism was first and foremost a blueprint for rapid economic transformation, but various commentators have drawn attention to its inherent neo-traditionalism. Perhaps foremost among these has been Tucker (1963, 1977), who lists the causal factors explaining why the Stalinist phase occurred, or why it took the form it did in the Soviet Union, as 'the heritage of Bolshevik revolutionism, *the heritage of old Russia*, and the mind and personality of Stalin' [*italics added*].[38] Tucker further argues that traditionalist elements became embedded in an avowedly revolutionary ideology as the Bolshevik revolution-from-above strategy matured under Stalin. This strategy drew obvious inspiration from the practices of earlier rulers, most notably Ivan the Terrible and Peter the Great, who both became overt political antecedents and legitimisers. By means of this strategy, the Soviet Union progressed economically, especially in the military-industrial sphere, but regressed socially and politically for, intentionally or unintentionally, conditions of extreme centralisation, mono-organisationalism and personal autocracy proceeded to recreate one of the central pillars of traditional society—a strong political centre capable of decisively shaping social and cultural life and severely limiting the modernisation process from moving beyond the parameters set by, or inherent in, the political ideology of the centre.

Before turning to the specific case of traditionalism in the DPRK, we should further note that while political and social practices under the Choson Dynasty contained features that were unique to Korean tradition, they also contained many features such as behavioural patterns, symbols of social and cultural identity and patterns of social and political legitimation that are part of the broader definition of traditional society. We take Eisenstadt (1973:4–5) as representative of the literature on the subject when he notes such common characteristics of traditional societies as:

- comparative lack of differentiation and specialisation in organisational structures;
- the major focus of collective identity deriving from a past event, order or figure;
- legitimation of change, delineation of the limits of innovation, and access to positions of power determined with reference to this past given;
- legitimation of the ruler in religious terms, with the incumbents

assuming the mantle of the only legitimate interpreters of religious revelation;

- the political role of the population embedded in their societal
roles; and
- limitation on the access of members of peripheral groups to the
political centre.

With these points in mind, we find that the traditionalist features
in the DPRK commonly cited by commentators fall broadly into three
categories: political leadership, ideology, and social structure. In political leadership we find on-the-spot guidance, the image of father of
the people, the role of military hero (Scalapino and Lee 1972); a
high degree of centralisation and weak grass roots (Henderson 1987);
heredity, charismatic practice and ascriptive recruitment (Brandt
1983); and the role of philosopher-king (Cumings 1993). In ideology
we find intensity in commitment and' all-embracing premises (Brandt
1983); in society we find exclusion from political participation (Henderson 1987) and caste-like status ascription linked directly to
sumptuary control (Brandt 1983). To what extent, then, do the
traditionalist traits cited for the DPRK reflect the operation of a
specifically Korean tradition and to what extent are they alien to
traditional Korean practices?

ON-THE-SPOT GUIDANCE, THE PHILOSOPHER-KING

This trait implies activism and interventionism, for which there is little
Korean precedent. Choson monarchs performed the role of passive moral
exemplars under the intense scrutiny of the bureaucracy and were
neither mobile nor interventionist.[39] In the realm of philosophy,
although the intensity of the personal bond between teacher and disciple
has strong sanction within the Confucian tradition, the traditional
political system did not assume that the political leader was a philosopher. On the contrary, the bureaucracy was deeply suspicious of any
tendency to combine the roles of political leader and active philosopher
and devoted considerable energy to restraining the monarch. Choson
monarchs did not leave behind reputations as philosophers, nor were
they expected to. The political leader's relationship to the dynastic
ideology of Neo-Confucianism was institutionalised as a passive and
derivative one, lest he challenge the scholar-official class's prerogatives.
In this point Kimist political leadership differs strongly from Choson
Dynasty political leadership.

THE MILITARY HERO

While literate Koreans were familiar with classical Chinese military tales, there was little in the way of an indigenous military tradition and little expectation that the political leader should be involved in military affairs. Haboush (1985:197–8) notes that in the early part of the dynasty the king was expected to be proficient in such martial arts as horse riding and archery, but that this had died out by the sixteenth century to be replaced by 'a more sedentary and bookish life'. Accordingly, the king is absent from the battlefields of the Imjin War (1592–98) and the Manchurian raids (1627, 1636). During the Choson Dynasty the role of military hero was seen as antithetical to the moral exemplar role, and while the DPRK has evolved a highly militarised culture, it does not seek historical precedents for this, since the early exploits of Kim Il Sung are evidently deemed sufficient in themselves. Modern DPRK militarism developed under Japanese and Soviet models, with little input from Korean tradition.

THE FATHERLY LEADER, CHARISMATIC PRACTICE

While some of the more cathartic expressions of loyalty to the fatherly leader invite participants to indulge in practices that would appear to have antecedents in Korean popular religions such as shamanism, Kim Il Sung departed significantly from the ideal of Confucian kingship in his reliance on charismatic leadership. First, with reference to Weber's three ideal types of leadership (Weber 1964:328), the Choson kings conformed to the bureaucratic-legal ideal, as opposed to the charismatic ideal. Second, although the monarch was a revered figure whose relationship with subjects could be described as a father–children relationship, this was a normative, passive relationship. By contrast, DPRK cult of personality politics is proactive in constantly seeking overt, emotional displays of loyalty and affection. Third, the image of the kindly, caring father-figure (*oboi-suryongnim*) conforms to the Stalinist model but contrasts with the role of the father within the traditional Korean household, who was a stern, remote figure who did not encourage displays of emotion.[40]

INTENSITY, ALL-EMBRACING IDEOLOGICAL PREMISES

Under the Kimist personal autocracy Kim Il Sung and Kim Jong Il have been the only sanctioned philosophers. The bowdlerised intellectual life that resulted is a gross parody of the creativity and passion of the Choson Dynasty Neo-Confucian debates. Intensity is present in the language of official pronouncements, but this intensity was very different from the traditional intensity of Neo-Confucian debate. Kimist ideology is handed down for unconditional acceptance and is not debated at all, let alone with passion or intensity. More-over, while the Confucian perception of a rational and moral universe and its faith in the capability of the human intellect to comprehend and act in accordance with the universal way is certainly all-embrac-ing, unlike Kimism it did not place the ruler above accountability.[41]

EXCLUSION FROM POLITICAL PARTICIPATION, STATUS ASCRIPTION, SUMPTUARY CONTROL

These are undoubtedly tendencies that the Choson Dynasty and the DPRK share but, in the terms that we have presented above, they are general enough to present as universal features of traditional societies, not to mention modern authoritarian regimes. They are not features that are specific to Korean tradition.

While the above traits resemble the universal orientations of traditional societies, few are specifically Korean. On the contrary, the cult of the fatherly leader, reliance on charismatic leadership and cult of personality in politics, militarism, executive activism and pervasive government intrusion into what was previously the highly self-regu-latory realm of clan and family life find no antecedents in Korean political tradition. They are, however, features of Stalinism.

The most striking Stalinist borrowing was the charismatic form of political leadership, or cult of personality, as a fundamental organising principle of politics. By definition, this entailed the vesting of supreme political and ideological authority in an individual at the expense of the institutions of the Leninist party. The adoption in the DPRK of the cult model developed by Stalin in the Soviet Union beginning in 1929,[42] was a conscious foreign borrowing that owed little to native tradition. Central to both cults were efforts to substitute family and kinship loyalties for transcendent political and state loyalties. Both cults rein-forced this concept by the pervasive use of kinship images of Stalin/Kim as the all-wise, benevolent parent caring for the extended family of Russia/Korea.[43] We also find strikingly similar themes and language employed in both cults to suggest nonpareil genius, the initiator and creator of a new way of life, and indeed the source of life through identification with the sun. Thus before Kim, Stalin was also hailed as 'the greatest man, the leader and teacher, our genius', 'the greatest man on our planet', 'the greatest thinker and leader of the socialist era of the development of mankind', and 'the greatest genius of mankind' (Gill 1990:291). We also find the same projection of intense, extrovert feelings of love and loyalty through public events and media reports. Moreover, Kim's personal appearances were ritually accompanied with prolonged stormy applause, calls of praise and manifestations of emotional frenzy. These displays are often assumed to be peculiarly Korean, but in fact find close parallels in the public receptions accorded Stalin.[44]

We conclude, therefore, that Kim Il Sung conscientiously and in often stunning detail saw the Stalinist model of political leadership and mobilisation as appropriate for the post-Korean War development of the DPRK state, and, in particular, for the rapid acquisition of a heavy industry sector and an armaments production base. Key factors in his life experience that predisposed him to Stalinism included extreme alienation from established Korean cultural and social norms, the revelation of Stalinism during his time in the USSR (1941–45), the innate appeal of the Stalinist notion of applying wartime methods of mobilisation to economic problems, and lack of exposure to, or even awareness of, alternative models, including alternative Marxist models. It was the essence of cult of personality politics that virtually every deed of the leader—good, bad, indifferent, self-contradictory, consistent, great, or small—should have been vested with special significance and be transmitted as an integral part of the leader's vision. This characteristic in turn mitigated against selective adoption of Stalinist traits, and helps to account why Stalinism became such a comprehensive blueprint, not just for the DPRK but for other Leninist party leaders such as Mao, Hoxha and Ceausescu. In Kim Il Sung's case he did not know what to leave out, nor did he know how to leave it out.

One unique feature of Kim's personal autocracy was his ability to share power with his son, Kim Jong Il. Despite the enormous difficulties inherent in grooming proteges to inherit personal political power, from the mid-1960s onward, Kim Il Sung gradually developed the role of his son as designated successor. In the 1970s the younger Kim began to play a substantial behind-the-scenes role in ideological mobilisation activities, and in 1980 emerged publicly as a high-ranking Politburo member. By the early 1990s the younger Kim was in substantial charge of the affairs of state, though at all times he exercised authority within the ideological parameters that his father had established.

The potential for confusion and acrimony between a dominant leader and a designated successor called upon to serve a lengthy period in waiting is considerable, but from the time Kim Jong Il first began to exercise broad, substantial authority within the KWP in the 1970s until his father's death, there is no credible evidence of this. We shall deal with Kim Jong Il's career in greater detail in later chapters, but meanwhile it is sufficient to observe that there is no record of conflicting public statements or policy guidelines between father and son. In fact, a distinguishing feature of Kim Jong Il's career is that he has left no mark or trace of influence on major state policies independent of his father after many years in senior positions. The literature on DPRK affairs is rich in speculation and hypothesis, but no one has ever seriously raised the issue of possible friction between the two Kims. Father and son seemed to share an almost seamlessly complementary relationship bound by the filial tie, the strong influence of Kim Il Sung's personality on his son, common ideological commitment and clear functional differentiation. The father set the major ideological, economic and diplomatic parameters while the son attended to the mobilisation work that flowed from the ideological parameters, and concentrated mainly on what might best be termed social policy. He aimed at improving the citizens' quality of life—aesthetically through direction of the 'arts' and prestige public architecture, and materially through association with construction of major leisure facilities and distribution of bounty to individuals that is somehow reminiscent of charismatic First Lady-type activities. The release of extra rations of consumer goods, such as meat, to coincide with Kim Jong Il's birthday; regular media reports of the younger Kim awarding special privileges to aging, loyal workers and former guerilla revolutionaries; and a 43.4 per cent general wage increase timed to coincide with his fiftieth birthday on 16 February 1992 (*PT* 22 February 1992) are examples of these activities.

A long-standing, harmonious arrangement for the political succession was a special DPRK characteristic, but it did not detract from the essential identity of the leadership as a personal autocracy supported by an extravagant personality cult on the Stalinist model. A veil of secrecy remains tightly drawn around the leadership decision-making process, but there is little doubt that Politburo members undertook no task, exercised no power, and tended no constituency that was not directly sanctioned by the Kims. Kim Il Sung enforced his authority by occupying the leading positions in the Party, government and military hierarchies, and it is also clear from anecdotal evidence that he also enforced it by means of multiple and overlapping domestic security and surveillance organs, by a strong work ethic, and by the force of an overbearing personality. Beginning in the mid-1960s Kim Jong Il exercised power through the support of his father, and from 1980 until his father's death the younger Kim also exercised power as a member of the Presidium, as No. 2 in the KWP hierarchy after 1984, and as supreme commander of the Korean People's Armed Forces after December 1991. When he was delegated authority by his father, Kim Jong Il also relied on a network of cadres who would not necessarily have held high Politburo rank, but who were widely known to have close ties with Kim Jong Il. They constituted more than just a personal staff, which Kim Jong Il obviously had as well, but not enough is known to characterise them other than as an irregular but sanctioned network paralleling formal Party and governmental structures and intervening in a manner determined by prior arrangement between father and son.[45]

There were, of course, institutional limits to Kim Il Sung's personal autocracy. Although the elder Kim could intervene at will in Party and state affairs, his judgments on when and how to intervene would have been affected by sometimes severely selective information flows. The canonic status of Kim's every utterance, the rigidity of his ideology, and the fate of those who challenged his judgment in the 1960s encouraged sycophantic responses, rather than objective analysis from advisors, and in time the tendency toward self-censorship and distortion must have become extreme. This affects not so much information gathering as interpretation. In foreign relations, for example, the DPRK bureaucracy gathers and disseminates among Party cadres a considerable body of information on international and Republic of Korea (ROK) affairs on a daily basis.[46] Of itself, this provides a factual background for policy formulation, and DPRK cadres are much better informed about the world than is generally thought. However, at the senior policy-making level, the Kimist ideological framework has clearly and stringently affected their capacity to absorb and use broadly based, objective analysis of international political and economic trends.

Reliance on the bureaucracy for sustained oversight of policy implementation imposes a further limitation, for by its very nature the bureaucracy is dedicated to routine and stability, rather than to responding to the high level of political and economic mobilisation demanded by Kimist ideology. Moreover, high-level defectors with experience in the DPRK bureaucracy have described in detail the demoralising experience of grappling daily with the problem of applying an often irrelevant or dysfunctional ideology to practical economic and diplomatic problems. The Kims themselves seemed to sense potential opposition from this quarter, for in their speeches and writings they clearly identified the bureaucracy as an adversary and as a major impediment to socialist construction. Moreover, since the mid-1970s, they have launched repeated anti-bureaucratic campaigns under the Three Revolution Team Movement.

Most importantly, the very triumph of Kim's personal autocracy imposed its own limitation. It introduced a zero-sum equation into policy-making, whereby the police-state necessary for ensuring compliance with his will undermined policy objectives in other areas. For example, Kim sought economic development, but effectively prevented the establishment of many of the key conditions essential for economic and social modernisation, such as freedom of information, reasonable autonomy in the economic decision-making process, and reasonable access to international capital and technology. These were, of course, incompatible with his demand for unlimited personal autocracy. Similarly, Kim sought modern, efficient armed forces, but the needs of regime security produced an inefficient, highly centralised command and communications structure.

While DPRK institutions are constrained by the presence of personal autocracy, they are not static in their operation. In the years between the Sixth KWP Congress in 1980 and the death of Kim Il Sung in July 1994, Party and government institutions in the DPRK began to demonstrate a number of characteristics that are significant for the analysis of state affairs during this period. The most significant of these features are as follows.

THE DISCONTINUATION OF PARTY CONGRESSES

Party congresses were held in 1946, 1948, 1956, 1961, 1970, and 1980. The intervals grew progressively longer and, prior to his death, Kim Il Sung gave no sign of any intention to convene another. This marked a departure, in spirit at least, from Party bylaw no. 21 which stipulates that a Party congress should be held every four years, though 'the Central Committee may, where necessary, convene earlier or later than the four-year period'.[47] Kim's practice is reminiscent of Stalin's practice in his later years, and probably for the same reason: in conditions of total personal dominance of the Party, congresses become pointless gatherings. Moreover, unlike expressions of allegiance of the whole nation orchestrated through governmental institutions such as the CPC, there was little symbolic point in orchestrating such expressions from the Party.

THE INTERTWINING OF GOVERNMENT AND PARTY ACTIVITIES

The Leninist party system explicitly denies the autonomy of the governmental sphere and confines government institutions to policy implementation and symbolic activities. This outlook is usually expressed by institutions such as rubber-stamp parliaments and cere-monial heads of state, whose chief purpose seems to be to facilitate dealings with non-Communist countries. In the wake of the 1972 constitution, the DPRK sharply reduced this traditional distinction. This came about through the creation of government institutions which paralleled KWP structures and had overlapping membership with the KWP, such as the Presidency and the Central People's Committee. The KWP then treated these institutions as symbolic institutions, and associated them with the KWP in symbolic joint meetings, such as the February 1981 meeting on Non-Aligned Move-ment matters to emphasise the unity of purpose between government and Party.

NO FURTHER PURGES

Although senior Politburo members suffered demotion from time to time during the 1980s and early 1990s, at the time of Kim Il Sung's death it had been seventeen years since the purge of Vice President Kim Tong-gyu in October 1977—the last sudden, unexplained disap-pearance from public view of a senior cadre. This contrasts sharply with the regularity with which Kim purged high cadres in earlier times. For example, only five members of the fourteen-member Polit-buro elected by the Fourth KWP Congress Central Committee and incumbent in 1964 were reappointed in 1970, while the other nine disappeared altogether. Since in all other respects Kim Il Sung continued as a demanding autocrat in the 1970s, we must assume that by 1980 he had weeded out independently minded members of the guerilla generation, and had replaced them with either sycophants or with cadres who had been thoroughly moulded by the system to adhere to Kimist ideological parameters.

LACK OF GENERATIONAL CHANGE

Especially after 1980, commentators on DPRK affairs widely antici-pated a process of 'generational change' in politics, whereby younger

men with technocratic backgrounds and close links to Kim Jong Il
would be promoted into key positions formerly filled by the guerilla
generation.[48] However, while time has obviously thinned the ranks
of Kim's guerilla comrades, the KWP remained in the hands of a
gerontocracy. Moreover, the Party itself denied the notion of a
generational base for politics since this would conflict with the
monolithic, universalist character of Kimist ideology and party
organisation. The close identification of Kim Jong Il with the guerilla
generation has been a fundamental theme in the promotion of his
personality cult and, at the time of his father's death, no known
beneficiary of Kim Jong Il's patronage sat on the Politburo. Far from
allowing any process of generational change to proceed, the most
significant Politburo appointments made by Kim Il Sung in his last
years were reappointments of aging former guerilla colleagues whom
he had dismissed or demoted some years previously.

THE FAILURE OF THE TECHNOCRATS AND ECONOMIC PRAGMATISTS TO EMERGE AS SIGNIFICANT POLITICAL FORCE

During the 1980s, many foreign observers also speculated that control
of state policy had begun to pass into the hands of technocrats and
pragmatists. Party and government personnel changes in late 1983
and early 1984 were a particular focus of this speculation.[49] However,
in the light of overwhelming evidence of substantially unchanged
economic policies since 1984, it is clear that analysts have exaggerated the significance of these changes and overestimated the potential
power of cadres identified as technocrats or pragmatists. The rise of
a new generation within the Party has of course been inexorable, but
a change in outlook arising from the promotion of more pragmatically
oriented cadres has not taken place. While Kim lived, power
remained with the aging generalists and loyalist ideologues, most of
whom first entered the leadership ranks in the 1960s and early 1970s.

THE DECLINE OF THE MILITARY'S POLITICAL INFLUENCE WITHIN THE PARTY

It is a fundamental feature of Leninist party systems that Politburo
rankings reflect the power configuration within the ruling party.
While individuals may hold wide unofficial power—the cases of Jiang
Qing and Stalin's personal staff come to mind—the distribution of

power among different sectors by appointing select individuals from these sectors to the Politburo and Central Committee is a fundamental task of Leninist party leaders. For this reason, the decline in senior Politburo status of the DPRK military in the 1980s is striking. The Politburo elected at the Sixth KWP Congress contained six active military men among its nineteen members. They were (rankings in parentheses) O Chin-u (3), Ch'oe Hyon (7), O Paek-yong (10), Chon Mun-sop (13), O Kuk-yol (16) and Paek Hak-nim (19). Ch'oe Hyon died in 1982, O Paek-yong died in 1984, Chon Mun-sop and Paek Hak-nim were demoted in 1985, and O Kuk-yol was demoted in early 1988. The only active military officer promoted to the Politburo during this period was the elderly Ch'oe Kwang in mid-1988. This meant that from O Kuk-yol's dismissal until the death of Kim Il Sung, O Chin-u and Ch'oe Kwang were the only two full Politburo members who were active military officers, and both were aging former guerilla comrades of Kim Il Sung. No product of post-1945 military training became a member of the Politburo after the demotion of O Kuk-yol. Obviously Kim did not feel confident that the post-1945 generation wholeheartedly shared the guerilla ethos and mission, and so resorted to a pattern familiar to students of comparative Communism: he thoroughly controlled the gun. During the 1994–97 period of mourning, Kim Jong Il raised the public profile of senior military cadres once more, but since none of them has been appointed to the Politburo it remains to be seen how they will be formally integrated into the Party power structure.

Our survey of the Party and government institutions of the DPRK has described an elaborate network designed to promote the revolutionary missions of socialist construction and national reunification, as the leadership understands these missions. This structure is typically Leninist in the monopoly control exercised by the KWP, Stalinist in the personal autocracy and cult of personality of the leader, and Kimist in the application of the Manchurian guerilla ethos to Stalinism. The key characteristic of the KWP is that since the late 1960s it has functioned under conditions of extreme personal autocracy. Its forms and functions have become subject to that autocracy, and it has become remote, exclusivist, and untrammelled by demands that it be accountable to its citizens—even by the standards of other Leninist party systems. It holds itself unaccountable except by processes of reaffirmation and feedback ('going to the people') over which it exercises total control. It is triumphantly monolithic in outlook and aggressively dismissive of any need for self-corrective mechanisms within the Party.

Like all modern autocrats the Kims have been dependent upon bureaucratic institutions to carry out their orders, but checks on the Kims' effective domination of DPRK state and society have been insignificant. The political and governmental institutions of the DPRK are intricate, well organised, and they functioned in support of personal autocracy to a degree unparalleled in the history of Leninist party states. There is no evidence to suggest that competitive factional activity, whether based on sectoral, policy or personality grounds, has been significant under the Kimist personal autocracies. While the leader and senior Party cadres obviously discuss tactical options in some shape or form, they discuss them amid highly selective information flows, and in an atmosphere constrained by the existence of pervasive security surveillance and multiple ideological tripwires. By what is known of the personalities involved, and also by the accumulated record of policy outcomes over the years, we would not expect to find debate of even marginally differing opinions, let alone frank and open discussion of basic options, among the leading cadres. Thus the Party is without obvious means or motivation to adapt to societal change.

3

THE EMERGING
TYRANNY, 1958–70

In 1958 the indices of modernisation in the Democratic People's Republic of Korea (DPRK) were substantial. The DPRK state had decisively broken with the traditional political culture and was now directed by a new elite that was effecting a profound material and spiritual transformation. The effects of intense political and social mobilisation were felt throughout the country. Rapid urbanisation had brought many rural dwellers into contact with broader horizons, and marked progress in public health, literacy and, at least initially, technology likewise contributed to a pattern of growing industrialisation, and unprecedented social mobility. The creation of a large standing army likewise introduced many young men to new technologies, methods of organisation and work. The country was tightly linked as never before by a new communications network, by a pervasive print and electronic media, by a universal education system and by a web of Party-controlled mass organisations that drew agricultural and industrial workers, women, youth, professionals, the military, artists, writers and intellectuals into immediate and direct contact with the political centre.

However, this transformation differed from similar processes in other countries during the course of this century in at least two important respects: it was rigorously directed from the top through Party and government institutions and it took place in almost complete isolation from the international community. As a result, the commitment to modernisation was not open-ended, but firmly circumscribed by the ruler and his ideology. This ideology was profoundly anti-modern in many important respects, and increasingly it undermined the modernisation process. Economic and social development were not ends in themselves, but were the means of achieving political and military objectives determined by a leader whose visions of the ultimate purpose of life lay in the ever-receding past. This was not the past of Korean traditionalism but the revolutionary past, where core training and experience had left Kim deeply attached to the prewar guerilla style of revolutionary mobilisation and to wartime Soviet production methods. As the modernisation process gained momentum in the 1960s it further exposed this contradiction.

The Kimist ethos was a militarist ethos. Its ideology emphasised violent conflict as the mainspring of history, its world-view was of life as an unremitting struggle, and its actual experience of war was one of near-victory, followed by the bitter humiliation of defeat amid catastrophic material destruction. In this combination lay the seeds of re-dedication to the cause of independent national reunification that Kim had pursued since the early 1930s. Accordingly, in the aftermath of the Korean War the Kimists reconstituted the DPRK as a militarist society under the leadership of former guerillas whose major objective was the reversal of the verdict of the Korean War and who made an astounding material commitment to military production in order to achieve this.

The March 1958 Party Conference set the seal on Kim Il Sung's domination of the Korean Workers' Party (KWP), and public ideological debate ceased accordingly. The prime functions of the Party became increasingly organisational and devotional—to organise the people in pursuit of policies of industrialisation, modernisation and reunification, and to reinforce Kim Il Sung's growing personal dictatorship and cult of personality. In the first few years after 1958 the pursuit of these two tasks involved little contradiction for the Party elite. The expulsion of gradualists, doubters, and other independently minded cadres gradually left a Party elite bound by long-standing personal ties with Kim, accustomed to responding to his rigid discipline, and accepting of the firm Stalinist precedent for cult of personality leadership. There was little, if any, disagreement among the Party elite on the wholesale adoption of political and economic development strategies modelled closely on Soviet practices of the 1930s, and in the years immediately after 1958 the country mobilised on this basis.

But while the KWP elite may have seen compelling parallels between the developmental needs of the Soviet Union in the 1930s and those of the DPRK in the 1950s, there was one supreme difference between the two: Korea was still a divided nation and the DPRK was involved in a struggle to reunify it. This ensured that state ideology retained a strongly militarist character, and in time this caused Kim to fall out with a significant number of his loyalist colleagues, for what divided Kim from most of his colleagues during the 1960s was the extent to which he was prepared to use the country's growing economic resources for military ends. No one staked out a more radical stance in this area than Kim when, in December 1962, he established the Equal Emphasis domestic policy framework which placed equal emphasis on high economic growth rates and high levels of weapons production. The major slogan of the day 'Arms in the one hand and a hammer and sickle in the other!' describes its essence, and an estimated seven-fold rise in military expenditure as a proportion of annual state budget describes the substance of a policy which gave decisive shape to the DPRK economy and which, in its essentials, Kim pursued to the end of his life.[1]

The simultaneous pursuit of rapid industrialisation and rearmament imposed severe strains on the economy and led to severe unrest within the Party. This resulted in the convening of a second Party Conference in October 1966, at which Kim effected a sweeping purge of senior cadres not just in the area of economic management but across a range of portfolios and areas of expertise, including military affairs, ideology, education and party organisation. The diversity of policy areas involved in these dismissals signified that the underlying issue was leadership, and in particular the demand by Kim for a degree of unquestioning personal loyalty above and beyond what might be sanctioned by Party rules and practices. Then in May 1968 at the Fifteenth Plenum of the Fourth KWP Central Committee, Kim finally crossed the increasingly blurred line separating dominant authority within the Party from personal autocracy. Later on, Party historians were to describe this plenum as the time when Kim 'took the revolutionary step of establishing a monolithic ideological system in the whole Party in order to strengthen the unity of the ideology and purpose and solidarity of Party ranks' (*PT* 10 April 1993). This 'monolithic ideological system' was founded on the infallibility and universal application of Kim's ideology. From that point on unconditional loyalty to Kim became the essential prerequisite for political survival among the Party elite.

The DPRK's strategy for Korean reunification also evolved during the 1960s. In 1950 Kim and his colleagues had seen the solution to the problem in purely military terms, but in the 1960s Kim Il Sung began to acknowledge the need to combine military struggle with political and diplomatic campaigns. In 1964 he articulated this strategy of combined struggle in his Three Fronts strategy, a strategy which defined the Korean reunification as a task requiring revolutions on three fronts: within the DPRK, within the Republic of Korea (ROK) and internationally. Within the DPRK, the task of the KWP was to bring about a far-ranging political, military and economic transformation that would provide the material base for future reunification under Party leadership. Within the ROK the task was to establish a Marxist–Leninist party, support anti-government forces, and instill them with revolutionary consciousness by rallying them under the leadership of this party. Internationally, the major task was to encourage revolutionary forces with the object of bringing maximum pressure to bear on the United States to withdraw its armed forces from ROK territory.[2]

DPRK state policies during this period became closely linked to the Three Fronts strategy. Equal Emphasis itself was a policy designed to maximise the development of military production in the North, and to regiment politics and society in anticipation of future conflict. Within the ROK, the KWP claimed the establishment of a clandestine Revolutionary Party for Reunification in March 1964 by 'South Korean revolutionaries who are faithful soldiers of Kim Il Sung'.[3] More substantively, the DPRK sought to apply pressure to ROK and US forces through an acute military confrontation with the South during 1966–69. Internationally, the DPRK sought alliances based on a shared commitment to active confrontation with US imperialism and rejection of peaceful coexistence, and by 1970 it was involved with a broad spectrum of terrorist, guerilla and insurgency movements.

Pyongyang's radicalism placed it at odds with the Soviet Union, and Kim's refusal to take the Soviet side in the Sino–Soviet dispute led to an open rift with Moscow during 1961–65. Disappointment with Soviet foreign policy, and especially with the Soviet withdrawal of its missiles from Cuba in the face of US pressure in October 1962, marked a clear watershed in the evolution of DPRK foreign policy, and encouraged the evolution of an independent foreign policy. In this context the DPRK steadily became more active among newly independent countries and laid the groundwork for its active involvement in the Non-Aligned Movement during the 1970s.

The story of the 1960s in the DPRK, therefore, primarily relates how Kimist ideology came to dominate the politics of the DPRK. This period began with Kim Il Sung clearly the dominant figure within the KWP, but still ruling in conjunction with other ex-guerilla comrades. It ended with the Kimist personal autocracy firmly established. During this period Kim's emphasis on simultaneous and intensive economic and military mobilisation initially produced uneven, rapid economic growth and then severe distortions in the economy. The DPRK also became increasingly committed to militarist policies at home and to adventurist, radical policies abroad. The result was isolation and increasing obsolescence and backwardness on the technological, economic, cultural and social levels. The only exception to this trend was the military and its associated military-industrial complex, where continued high rates of investment and periodic access to advanced Chinese and Soviet weaponry and technology ensured that the DPRK maintained an advanced, modern force.

After the March 1958 First Party Conference confirmed Kim's authority within the KWP, he lost no time in laying the foundations of a new economic mobilisation system. Here the chief model continued to be the Stalinist model of the command economy of the 1930s. Kim, and many others, believed that this model had succeeded in bringing about a sustained process of rapid economic development and industrialisation, and had enabled the Soviet Union to emerge victorious in World War II as a leading world power without compromising its anti-Western, anti-capitalist and anti-imperialist ideology. The DPRK's post-1953 rehabilitation therefore proceeded from the rigid implementation of the classic features of the Soviet command economy of the 1930s. These included:

- state ownership of industrial enterprises, with little or no private ownership of business;
- collectivised agriculture with agricultural prices kept low in order to provide cheap inputs into the industrial sector;
- close Party and bureaucratic involvement in all aspects of economic planning, including the setting of national and sectoral economic targets, output and supply quotas, and prices and wages;
- little priority accorded to light industry, consumer goods production and the service sector;
- a growth strategy aimed at achieving rapid economic and social transformation and the establishment of a heavy industrial base;
- priority investment in the military-industrial sector; and
- an autarchic economy closed off from the international capitalist economy featuring little or no foreign investment, a government foreign trade monopoly and the widespread practice of barter trade.

The DPRK rapidly adopted these policies and practices. Extending state ownership over enterprises large and small presented little challenge in the DPRK after 1953, since the propagation of class warfare in the North during 1945–50, the destruction wrought by the Korean War and the radical policies of 1953–56 effectively destroyed the basis for private ownership. There was no need to deal with 'patriotic capitalists' since they were not significant, nor did the government have any use for them. By 1959 the government was able to claim that the industrial sector had been fully socialised.

The DPRK was no different from other industrialising countries in generating capital for industrial expansion from the agricultural sector, and Stalinist precedent mandated the strategy of agricultural collectivisation. The point of interest is therefore not so much that Kim opted for collectivisation but that he carried it out with exceptional speed and intensity, citing the Soviet precedent in support of this policy.[4] Moreover, from the 1960s on, he remained resolutely uninterested in attempts to reform the faltering collectivised agricultural sector elsewhere in the Socialist Bloc. Against opposition within the Politburo led by Pak Ch'ang-ok and Ch'oe Ch'ang-ik, in late 1954, Kim took the position that rapid collectivisation was the most effective means of modernising the agricultural sector without compromising the policy of absolute priority investment in heavy industry. In a radicalised polity where many landlords and larger farm owners had fled, where the Party had enrolled peasants in wholesale numbers, and where many peasants had been able to leave the rural sector for more prestigious town and city jobs in offices and factories, there was remarkably little opposition to collectivisation. The government was able to announce the completion of the collectivisation process by August 1958.

Kim had little reason to feel well disposed toward the peasantry. In the 1930s he had an exploitive relationship with farmers which was typical of the guerilla, extracting produce from the farms in his theatre of operations by a variety of means. In power, he viewed the agricultural sector as a source of manpower and food for the industrial sector, and as the home of ideologically suspect elements.[5] Wherever possible, agricultural workers were to be proletarianised and agriculture itself routinised to the level of factory work. Retreats from this ideal, such as the introduction of the sub-team system in the 1960s, were effected grudgingly as a result of production failures and loss of food self-sufficiency.[6]

In August 1958 the process of collectivisation was completed and in September Kim launched the first of his major mobilisation campaigns, Chollima Movement, an ideological mobilisation campaign named after the Korean folk image of a winged horse capable of covering vast areas at high speed and designed to increase production across all major sectors of the economy.[7] The major organisational feature of Chollima was the formation of work teams which performed Stakhanovite feats in increasing production. In its broad coverage of economic sectors, its collective mass competitiveness, its ideological purpose and its propaganda themes, at its most intense stage, between 1958 and 1962, the Chollima Movement resembled the Great Leap Forward, which began in May 1958. Unlike the Great Leap Forward, however, the Chollima Movement was never countermanded. To the end of his life Kim's major speeches contained references to the 'spirit of Chollima', and he continued to apply its central technique of intense, mass ideological mobilisation on a regular basis.

Chollima, the first major expression of Kim's vision of economic development, had as its central themes the primacy of ideological training and reliance on Stakhanovite methods of quantitative production. From Kim's point of view it was a triumph, but more objectively, this movement also resulted in the debilitating entrenchment of ideologically driven disregard and contempt for the science of economic management in economic policy. Alongside the ideological gains, the emphasis on the work team as a near autonomous unit dedicated to quantitative output brought about such economic problems as sector imbalances, production bottlenecks, and severe quality control problems. As a result, the current Five-Year Plan (1956–60) ceased to reflect the actual state of economic activity in the country and was set aside. The year 1960 was then designated a buffer year to correct the imbalances and to ready the economy for the next plan period (Joseph Chung 1974:96, Alexander Joungwon Kim 1965:262).

Kim established the politics-first line through the Chollima Movement and then intensified it through two further ideological campaigns. In February 1960 he enunciated the Chongsanri Method, which took its name from a village near Pyongyang which Kim Il Sung visited in February 1960 and closely scrutinised existing work practices. This method stressed the need for close supervision of local level activities by Party officials if assigned production tasks were to be fulfilled.[8] What began as an agricultural guidance technique then spread to other sectors, including the Party and the bureaucracy, and achieved canonic status in the revised DPRK Constitution of 1972.[9] In December 1960 the Taean Work System which took direction of factories and other industrial economic units away from a single technician-manager and vested it in the unit's Party political committee, became the norm for the operation of all industrial enterprises (Joseph Chung 1974:63–4). Again, these hallmarks of a politics-first economic mobilisation system were given the stamp of Kim Il Sung's personal approval and remained in place as integral features of the Kimist system until his death.

The Fourth KWP Congress reflected many of the trends noted above when it convened during 11–18 September 1961. The agenda consisted of four items—two reports on past activities, an outline of the proposed Seven-Year Plan (1961–67) and Party elections—and served as a suitable occasion for Kim to give an authoritative version of the Party's ideology, to rally the country to achieve the goals of the Seven-Year Plan, and to fill the many Central Committee (CC) places left vacant by the post-April 1956 purges. The reports and speeches at this 'Congress of Victors'[10] affirmed key Kimist beliefs concerning the efficacy of mass Stakhanovite campaigns and the necessity for close, direct Party guidance in the economic development process. They stressed the immediate economic success that had greeted the adoption of the politics-first line embodied in the Chollima, Chongsanri and Taean campaigns and presaged more of the same in the forthcoming years of the First Seven-Year Plan.

The effects of the political battles of the previous five years became clear when the congress announced the names of the new 135 (85 full and 50 alternate) Central Committee members. Of the 85 full members, only 28 survived from the 1956 Third Party Congress, and 12 were promoted from alternate membership. Forty-five were new members. Similarly, 32 of the 45 alternate members were also new. This meant that of the 116 (71 full and 45 alternate) elected at the Third Congress in 1956, 75 (64.6 per cent) disappeared from public view. A clear majority of the new members had strong affiliations to the prewar Manchurian guerilla movement, domestic Communists and those with either a Chinese or Soviet background largely disappeared, while a small number with no known record of prewar activism also appeared.[11] The Party elite was now predominantly Manchurian or of far northern rural background. Pre-1945 activists had little, if any, experience of life outside the ambit of the anti-Japanese guerilla movement, while the outlook of those who emerged after 1945 through the Party apparatus had obviously been shaped by the profound experience of the Korean War and the intense ideological struggles and mobilisation campaigns of the 1950s. Technicians and bureaucrats—indeed, 'specialists' or 'experts' of any description—were conspicuous by their absence.

Not only had all groups of the former Communist oligarchy other than the Manchurian guerillas disappeared, but Kim, himself 49-years old at the time of the Fourth Congress, was already beginning to show signs of an inability to appoint younger men to senior positions. Few post-1945 recruits achieved Central Committee status—a significant trend, especially when one considers the losses of the Korean War—but as the 1960s progressed the average age of Politburo members increased from 51.7 (1961) to 58.2 (end of 1969), reflecting the lack of promotion of the younger generation. By the 1980s this inability to share real power with a younger generation had become even more pronounced. At Kim Il Sung's death in 1994, Kim Jong Il, the youngest Politburo member at age 52, could survey the Politburo and find Prime Minister Kang Song-san the second-youngest at age 65. The remaining members were all in their seventies and eighties.

Foreign relations did not rate much attention at the Fourth KWP Congress, and this reflected the relatively stable international environment for the DPRK in the immediate post-Korean War years. For a country preoccupied with postwar rehabilitation and domestic political struggle, near-total economic and political dependence on the Soviet Union and China brought many advantages and few drawbacks. To the extent that if the DPRK thought of foreign relations apart from the Socialist Bloc, it had little room to manoeuvre. It had been declared the aggressor in the Korean War by the United Nations and was a staunch defender of the interests of Socialist Bloc members in their dealings with the world at large. Kim's policies during this period emanated from his major policy objective—the reunification of Korea. In his view, the militant pursuit of the anti-imperialist, anti-US struggle on a worldwide scale was most likely to lead to a withdrawal of US troops from the South, whereupon he confidently expected the ROK to collapse.

The Sino–Soviet split and the increasing Soviet commitment to peaceful coexistence had a major impact on DPRK strategy. The split began in earnest in 1959 with a series of disputes over the terms and conditions of Soviet aid to China, and was essentially a product of competing security concepts, ideological positions and national interests. During 1959–61 the Chinese rejected the Soviet Union's traditional position of leadership of the international Communist movement in favour of the full sovereignty of individual Communist parties. China also rejected the Soviet doctrine of peaceful coexistence in favour of strong commitment to the anti-imperialist, anti-US struggle,[12] and insisted on the right of each party to pursue its own path to socialist economic construction. The DPRK found much to agree with in the Chinese position, since increased independence would mean independence to pursue its armed struggle against the South, while on this point, the Soviet position offered them little encouragement.

The real significance of the split and the debates it generated for the DPRK lay in the extent to which it highlighted the growing policy divergence between a radical, Stalinist Pyongyang and an increasingly conservative, revisionist Moscow. As a small state heavily dependent upon aid from both the USSR and China, in the initial period of the split the DPRK did not openly take sides, and instead stressed the need for unity in the Socialist camp with a view to the re-adoption of a hard line on peaceful coexistence, and higher levels of commitment to the cause of Korean reunification. Moreover, as the DPRK's signing of Treaties of Friendship, Cooperation and Mutual Assistance with both China and the Soviet Union within a few days of each other in July 1961 makes clear, the Soviet Union and China themselves clearly had no expectation that Kim should deal with one to the exclusion of the other.

However, by 1962 the DPRK interest was no longer served by even-handedness. The KWP was heavily dependent on the Soviet Union for economic and military aid but, like the Chinese, Yugoslav, Albanian, and Vietnamese Parties, it did not rely on Moscow to enforce its domestic political authority. Impartiality was no longer possible. As Moscow applied more pressure on foreign Communist parties to accept Soviet leadership of the international Communist movement, many parties, including the KWP, became increasingly unwilling to accept the Soviet claim. Tensions between Moscow and foreign Communist parties were also exacerbated by the 'Khrushchev factor'—the attempt by Communist Party of the Soviet Union (CPSU) Secretary Nikita Khrushchev to emulate Stalin's leadership role in the international Communist movement. However, in the eyes of many foreign parties Khrushchev suffered badly by comparison to Stalin. Soviet claims to leadership of the international Communist movement suffered and nationalism accordingly emerged as a serious force in the movement. Thus when neutrality in the split became impossible, the KWP moved to a position of open support for the principle of full party sovereignty and independence. It first signalled this position in November 1961 when it sent a congratulatory message to Tirana to mark the twentieth anniversary of the founding of the Albanian Party of Labour, which at that time was openly defying the CPSU. The Soviets swiftly retaliated by insisting on payment for military supplies previously granted as aid, and in early 1962 relations between the DPRK and the USSR worsened substantially (Zhebin 1995:727).

The underlying issue in the DPRK's growing rift with the Soviet Union was the issue of militancy in the anti-imperialist, anti-US struggle. This was highlighted in October 1962 in the wake of the Cuban missile crisis, when the Soviet Union retreated from outright confrontation with the United States and removed its missile bases from the island. As a small, weak state, the DPRK's underlying strategy had been to rely on the Socialist Bloc for security and to anticipate that growing Soviet pressure on the US would lead to a US retreat from Northeast Asia. However, the Cuban missile crisis made clear that Soviet commitment to peaceful coexistence with the US was profound and that Soviet interest now favoured the continuing division of Korea. While Pyongyang was well aware of the general trend in Soviet policy toward peaceful coexistence, the DPRK made no attempt to conceal its keen disappointment at this outcome.[13]

Ideological and security issues in turn exacerbated an ongoing Soviet–DPRK dispute over DPRK economic policy. The Soviets disapproved of the DPRK's wholesale adoption of the Stalinist economic strategy of mass mobilisation for rapid heavy industrialisation and had applied pressure on Pyongyang to join the Soviet Bloc common market (Comecon), where the DPRK would focus on raw materials processing and light industrial production. The DPRK opposed the concept of economic integration with other Socialist Bloc countries since this would have compromised its economic autonomy and restricted its options in military-industrial production. As the First Seven-Year Plan (1961–67) began, Soviet economic pressure grew stronger, as did DPRK criticism of Moscow on this issue.[14]

Growing concern over Soviet policies provided the background for a radical change in DPRK economic policy. In December 1962 Pyongyang initiated a military build-up which, in relation to the scale of the human and material resources of the country, can only be described as staggering. Under the slogan 'Arms in the one hand and a hammer and sickle in the other!' the Fifth Plenum of the Fourth KWP Central Committee (CC) adopted the policy of Equal Emphasis, signifying that the country would place emphasis on economic development and military preparedness equally. Kim countermanded the original basic economic strategy under the First Seven-Year Plan (1961–67)—recovery from the excesses of the Chollima Movement

and moderation of the ongoing drive for rapid, heavy industrialisation—and reinstated the Chollima policies of far-reaching economic
and political mobilisation.

The December 1962 Plenum established four basic military policies: arming the entire population, extensive additional training for
existing soldiers, converting the entire country into a fortress, and
modernising of the armed forces.[15] Arming the entire population went
further than the norms of universal conscription: it established a
military basis for the daily life of the entire population with weapons
training, military drill and instruction from kindergarten to retire-
ment age.[16] Maximum use was also made of existing regular soldiers
by training them to perform the duties of their immediate superior
in the chain of command, thus enabling rapid expansion of the armed
forces in times of emergency and speedy replacement of command
losses in battle. Fortification of the entire country meant the establishment of substantial strategic stockpiles and the construction of
vast complexes of shelters, bunkers and underground facilities including whole armament factories. The modernisation process meant that
the proportion of total state investment devoted to military production rose from about 6 per cent to 30 per cent during the period
1964 to 1967 as the military-industrial sector expanded to roughly
four times the size of its Soviet model in proportional terms.[17] The
DPRK further signaled the intensification of its military commitment
to reunification by engineering an immediate rise in tension along
the Demilitarized Zone (DMZ) which marked the cease-fire line at
the conclusion of the Korean War.

Why did the DPRK adopt and then sustain measures equivalent
to wartime mobilisation at this time? The question is a crucial one
for our understanding of subsequent DPRK state policies, for it set
in place a strategic and policy framework that Kim pursued for the
rest of his life. Kim did not refer to the military policy decisions of
the Fifth Plenum until his speech to the Second KWP Conference
on 5 October 1966. There he stated:

> In recent years our Party has been compelled to direct special atten-
> tion to increasing our defence capabilities still more in the face of
> intensified aggressive moves by the imperialists. As you comrades all
> know, the US imperialists provoked the Caribbean crisis against Cuba
> in October 1962, thereby challenging the entire socialist camp and
> making the international situation extremely tense. After that, they
> embarked on a still more open aggression in Asia. They provoked the
> [Tonking] Gulf incident against the Democratic Republic of Viet
> Nam,[18] stepped up the war of aggression on a large scale in South

Viet Nam and further aggravated tensions in Southeast Asia, the Far East and other areas.

To deal with this situation, our Party set forth the line of carrying on economic construction in parallel with defence building at the Fifth Plenary Meeting of its Fourth Central Committee in 1962, and took a number of important measures for further increasing our defence potential while reorganizing economic construction. Subsequent developments have proved that the step taken by our Party was entirely correct. By greatly boosting our defence power through our efforts to carry out the Party's decision, we have become capable of defending the security of our country resolutely even when the imperialists are on the rampage.[19]

This statement is notable for its extreme perception of threat, and as such tells us a good deal more about the Kimist world-view than it does about the international situation facing the DPRK in 1962. Kim's explanation in terms of events in the region clearly involves considerable *post facto* justification, for in 1962 massive US involvement in the Vietnam War was still unlikely. Nor can we detect threats to the DPRK in events on the Korean peninsula or within the Socialist Bloc at large. A military coup in the ROK in May 1961 had brought Park Chung-hee to power, but from the start the new regime in Seoul directed its energies primarily toward economic reconstruction, not confrontation with the North. Within the Socialist Bloc itself, there was much tension throughout this period as a result of the Sino–Soviet split, but while the Soviet Union in particular brought considerable economic and political pressure to bear on the DPRK throughout this period, at no stage did this involve any suggestion of a threat to the DPRK state. Quite the contrary, as we have noted, in July 1961 both China and the USSR concluded Treaties of Friendship, Cooperation and Mutual Defence treaties with the DPRK.[20]

Rather, to understand the logic behind a policy that had such devastating consequences on the country, we need to consider not only the immediate factor of the Soviet backdown over Cuba but also the perspective of the DPRK leadership, and especially the extent to which militarism was embedded in the DPRK modernisation process. DPRK militarism arose from several factors. It was historical, in that militarism was deeply embedded in the state ideologies of all major powers in the first half of the twentieth century. More specifically, the DPRK leadership was influenced by the environment of both Japanese militarism during the 1920s and 1930s and Stalinism in the 1940s and 1950s, both of which believed in the efficacy of military force in pursuit of foreign policy objectives and in the need for a high degree of social mobilisation as a requirement for success in modern warfare. DPRK militarism was also situational, arising from geopolitical factors, including the size and nature of the country's human and natural resources, fears of encirclement, uncertain alliances, the experience of the Korean War, and the post-1945 regional military hegemony of the United States. It was also ideological, arising from a deep ingestion of the Leninist–Stalinist world-view, and it was psychological, arising from historical experience as refracted through the personal experience of Kim Il Sung in his guerilla days. This personal experience was, of course, profound, according with a common tendency of men under arms to see the experience of regimentation, fear, bravery, blood and sacrifice as among the most profound of their lives.

One may debate the relative importance of these factors, but by 1962 militarism exercised a profound and singular influence on DPRK state policy. The DPRK leadership consisted almost entirely of men who had been socialised primarily within the military brotherhood of the anti-Japanese guerilla movement and who had followed no other calling in their lives other than preparation for war and engagement in war. The characteristics of the military community have been described by various social anthropologists. Nisbet (1976), for example, lists these characteristics as follows:

- the consecration to violence, acceptance of the legitimacy of violence in pursuit of given ends, and willingness to engage in violence;
- emphasis on such qualities as physical strength, endurance, and adaptability that are necessary for effective aggression;
- release from accountability to the authority of the broader community, and especially from the religious and moral norms of that community;
- the centralisation of authority—'the authority of the warrior chief was prescriptive, centralized in him and his lieutenants, and applied directly, without qualification, to each and every individual in the war band' (Nisbet 1976:29); and
- the inculcation of discipline based upon the exact, unconditional and immediate execution of orders from superiors.

The implications of these outlooks for the later development of the Kimist system in the DPRK are obvious. But perhaps the most interesting and relevant characteristic highlighted by Nisbet is what Weber termed the warrior-communism of the military community, with its masculine, barracks-house life, its rough egalitarianism contrasting with the status-ridden world of the kinship community, its sharing of the spoils of victory and the aftermath of defeat alike, its dissociation from family and from all private economic ties, and its moral puritanism (Nisbet 1976:31–3). We have already noted the weak role played by Marxist–Leninist ideology in the development of the Korean Communist movement, and in the ethos of the military community we see the outlines of an ideological system that could compensate for that weakness. This ideology possessed many points of affinity with Marxism–Leninism theory and Stalinist practice, but it drew decisively upon the defining life-experiences of its leader for its innermost guiding principles.

The post-1945 preparation for war with the South and Kim's adoption of the Stalinist model in the immediate post-1953 period firmly entrenched the habit of quasi-military organisation in all major sectors of Party and society. As we have already noted, military imagery permeated the vocabulary of Stalinist politics. Shock troops of workers 'stormed' and 'captured' key economic heights; oppositionists, defeatists and empiricists were 'smashed' and 'annihilated'; and the country was turned into an 'impregnable fortress'. The role-model for every citizen became the anti-Japanese guerilla in his Manchurian hinterland encampment—inured to hardship and boundlessly loyal to the Supreme Commander. We have also noted how upon securing domination of the KWP in 1958 Kim almost immediately and instinctively resorted to quasi-military techniques of economic development such as mass mobilisation and Stakhanovite strategies. Now, as the state began to acquire some of the basic means of production, the deployment of a substantial proportion of these means to armament production in support of the task of national reunification, from Kim's perspective, was a logical step.

The country felt the consequences of the December 1962 Plenum decisions with its massive diversion of resources away from a still-fragile economy into military production almost immediately, and the process was further exacerbated as the Soviet Union began to withhold economic aid. The cutting edge for achieving independence in military production was the heavy industry sector, where rates of investment now soared, surpassing the figures of around 40 per cent typical during the 1950s and peaking at about 66 per cent of total state investment in 1965. The rest of the economy, especially agriculture and light industry, had enjoyed a brief respite in the period 1960–62 as the imbalances of the Chollima campaigns were ironed out, but now rates of investment again fell.[21] The economy as a whole proved unable to bear the weight of preponderant heavy industry investment, and severe bottlenecks began to appear, particularly in the extractive, energy and communications sectors.

Poor harvests and failure to adjust to lower levels of foreign aid also contributed to a severe downturn. In 1963, all major sectors fell below Plan targets, steel and textiles production dropped below 1962 levels, and statistics for agriculture were withheld. The statistical blackout spread to the entire economy in 1964, and at the beginning of 1965 Kim Il Sung acknowledged that the country would be unable to meet the targets of the Seven-Year Plan.[22] As the proportion of defence-related expenditure continued to rise, the economic situation steadily worsened to crisis point. Total industrial production, which rose by an estimated 17 per cent in 1964 and by 14 per cent in 1965, actually contracted by an estimated 3 per cent in 1966.[23]

At this point Kim's refusal to modify the Equal Emphasis policy produced a political crisis. The crisis was sparked by a debate on economic priorities, and it pitted Kim and supporters of Equal Emphasis against cadres who sought lower, but more sustainable, rates of growth.[24] Many of the details of this dispute are still hazy, but the outcome is clear. The debate triggered a Second Party Conference in October 1966, and when a revised leadership line-up was announced at the conclusion of the Conference, nine of the sixteen full and alternate members of the Politburo, had been replaced. The Conference resolved the economic debate by reaffirming Equal Emphasis and by dismissing six Politburo members who had occupied key economic positions. At the same time the dismissal of three other Politburo members at the Conference indicated that behind this policy issue lay the broader issue of Kim's authority within the Party. The three cadres not directly involved in economic administration who were purged at this point were Kim Ch'ang-man (military education), Ha Ang-ch'on (President of Kimilsung University) and Pak Chong-ae (party functionary) and they were joined by two further high-level victims in the first half of 1967—Pak Kum-ch'ol (career military man) and Yi Hyo-sun (civilian Party functionary), ranked at No. 4 and No. 5 in the Party respectively. Nor were the ructions confined to the Politburo level, for an estimated one-fifth of Central Committee members were also replaced at the Conference (Dae-Sook Suh 1988:220).[25]

In replacing the dismissed cadres Kim did not turn to other leading cadres with experience in economic administration but rather to former guerilla comrades in the military, which gained significantly greater representation in the Politburo at this time.[26] Kim's statements at the time further indicated that he saw the Conference as the culmination of a decade-long struggle to oust doubters and to establish his personal autocracy.[27] In this struggle he was successful as the Party underwent what was to be its final transformation under Kim. The scope for meaningful ideological and policy debate effectively disappeared under the influence of Kim's personality cult and its associated claims of infallibility. The Politburo purges during 1966–68 were the last of their kind and a notable stability in Politburo membership ensued as Kim refilled it with cadres willing to accept exclusive dependence upon his judgment as a basis for state policy.

The revision of the leadership line-up at the Second Party Conference foreshadowed an unprecedented display of militancy toward the South. As we have already noted, the DPRK first raised the level of confrontation along the DMZ in the immediate aftermath of the adoption of the Equal Emphasis policy in December 1962. Now Pyongyang applied further pressure, and significant DMZ incidents increased eleven-fold in 1967.[28] On 21 January 1968 thirty-one Korean People's Army (KPA) commandos launched an attack on the ROK presidential compound (the Blue House) in Seoul; on 23 January the DPRK navy seized the US surveillance vessel *Pueblo* in international waters off its east coast; and in October teams of guerillas landed on a sparsely populated section of the east coast of the ROK, apparently in an unsuccessful effort to establish a base for guerilla warfare in the hinterland.[29]

It is always difficult to account fully for the actions of leaders who are driven by dogmatic interpretations of ideology and who often pursue high-risk scenarios involving violence. In accounting for Kim's willingness to confront the ROK and the US and to invite retaliation, we should first of all note that military confrontation was consistent with the DPRK's broader strategies and past behaviour. We must also factor in Kim's strong conviction that under the right circumstances the populace of the South would rise up against the ROK government. He may well have calculated that a show of strength could demoralise the ROK government and encourage groups sympathetic to the DPRK. This in turn might open up new possibilities in the inter-Korean conflict, for which the DPRK was well-prepared militarily. Kim may also have assessed that the US was preoccupied with Vietnam, and that a display of resolute force by the DPRK might sap the ROK and US will to resist.[30]

Whatever the calculation, these operations achieved little. The *Pueblo* incident delivered a substantial propaganda victory to Pyongyang, but it caused new strains in the DPRK–Soviet relationship and, if anything, strengthened the determination of the US forces to remain in Korea. The DMZ incidents did not have any noticeable effect on morale in the South, and the east coast landings failed. Moreover, the entire militant strategy precipitated dissension within the senior ranks of the DPRK military, and in January 1969 this culminated in the purging of Kim Ch'ang-bom, Ho Pong-hak and Ch'oe Kwang, ranked sixth, fourteenth and sixteenth respectively in the Politburo. Again, while the precise reasons for the dismissals are unclear,[31] the dismissal of leading military cadres after an unsuccessful campaign suggests that they were called upon to take responsibility for failure. Accordingly, in 1969 the number and scale of DMZ incidents began to fall and the DPRK abandoned this phase of direct military pressure.

Kim Il Sung's domestic policies during this period resulted in significant and lasting changes to DPRK foreign policy. After DPRK–Soviet relations reached their nadir during 1962–64, Khrushchev's ouster in October 1964 and the advent of a new, cautious and conservative leadership in Moscow led to a significant improvement in bilateral relations. Soviet Premier Alexei Kosygin visited Pyongyang in 1965, and the Soviet Union resumed substantial economic and military relations.[32] However, although the Kosygin visit did much to remove immediate sources of irritation, the steady divergence of national interests meant that relations never returned to their former closeness. The Soviet Union's interests lay in institutionalising its political system at home and consolidating its international position as a super-power. It had publicly denounced what it termed the 'excesses' of the Stalin era and had substantially modified many hallmark Stalinist policies. It had accepted coexistence and business-like relations with the capitalist world, and its economic plans focused increasingly on the need to raise the average citizen's standard of living. The DPRK, on the other hand, reflected the Soviet Union's past. It preserved the personality cult leadership, mass mobilisation techniques and militant political rhetoric of the Stalin era, and it actively promoted confrontation with the capitalist world. Under these circumstances only limited rapprochement was possible.[33]

Improvement in DPRK–Soviet relations occurred just as DPRK–China relations underwent a marked deterioration with the outbreak of the Great Proletarian Cultural Revolution in China in late 1965. Although, as we have already noted, in the earlier stages of the Sino–Soviet split the respective interests of Pyongyang and Beijing strongly coincided. Within a year of the launching of the first attacks of the Cultural Revolution the Chinese began to pressure Pyongyang to match Beijing's criticism of Moscow on the basis that 'to oppose imperialism is to oppose modern revisionism' (Roy Kim 1968:721). The DPRK resisted these calls, and although it continued to criticise the Soviets during this period, most notably for pursuing an 'exploitative' foreign trade policy (Joseph Chung 1974:117), the major development in DPRK foreign policy at this time was the clear articulation of DPRK claims to complete independence within the international Communist movement (Paige 1967:28, Dae-Sook Suh 1988:205–6). This development did not please Beijing, and in January 1967 Red Guard wall posters criticising the DPRK, as well as Kim Il Sung personally, began to appear.

These attacks continued throughout 1967–68, reaching a crescendo in February 1968 (Ho-Min Yang 1988:60, Dae-Sook Suh 1988:191–2). The posters reflected Chinese leadership views at the time, and were accompanied by public criticism, such as by the Director of Information for the *Renmin Ribao* (*The People's Daily*) that the DPRK had been 'sitting on the fence' in the Sino–Soviet dispute (Scalapino and Lee 1972:641). On a more serious note, unofficial reports of military clashes between Chinese and DPRK troops along their common border in the vicinity of Paekdu-san began to circulate.[34] However, as government in China began to regain coherency, tension with the DPRK abated. In October 1969 the DPRK resumed the exchange of delegations, broken off in 1965, when it sent envoys to celebrations commemorating the twentieth anniversary of the 1949 revolution, and in January 1970 the two sides announced they had conducted 'friendly consultations' on border issues. The rapprochement process was consolidated with a visit to Pyongyang by Zhou Enlai in April 1970, the first leadership visit between the two countries in six years (Simmons 1971:105).

By the end of the 1960s the DPRK had completed its shift from close identification with the Soviet Union to a position of independence within the Socialist Bloc. The shift occurred firstly because Kim Il Sung ceased to believe that solidarity with the Soviet Union was a viable strategy for Korean reunification, and secondly because Kim developed an overweening belief in the capability of the DPRK to accomplish reunification by means of a thoroughgoing militarisation of its economy and society. In the years after 1962, DPRK foreign policy increasingly reflected these twin beliefs. It strove for a position of independence in the Sino–Soviet dispute and was successful in having this position accepted.

The scholarly literature often describes the DPRK's foreign policy toward the Soviet Union and China from the era of the Sino–Soviet split to 1989 as a 'balancing act', carried out with the object of playing one off against the other to secure maximum advantage in economic and military assistance.[35] However, this description suggests a level of pragmatism that is not otherwise apparent in the DPRK's external transactions, and also implies that Kim was able to manipulate DPRK–Soviet and DPRK–China relations toward this end. In fact, as seen previously, DPRK foreign policy, especially toward the Soviet Union under Khrushchev, was strongly driven by ideology, not pragmatism. Moreover, this description exaggerates the influence of Sino–Soviet rivalry on Chinese and Soviet economic and military decisions affecting the DPRK. This rivalry, while significant, was just one of a number of factors involved, including relations with the US, Japan and other regional and global powers. A situation where the Chinese and Soviets remained prepared to deal with the DPRK strictly in accordance with the perceived benefit to their own respective interests gave Kim little opportunity to exploit either relationship.

In fact, as the 1960s ended, the apparent success of the DPRK in achieving this independence concealed severe diplomatic handicaps. Kim obtained benefits from his patrons not as a result of adroit diplomacy but as the by-product of a situation in which the influences of Moscow and Beijing on Pyongyang offset each other and created room to manoeuvre. But more significantly, isolation and ideological dogmatism constantly warped Pyongyang's judgment and rendered it unable to assess situations except in ways that reinforced its ideology. In 1969 the DPRK moved away from the tactic of applying direct military pressure, but the continuing confrontation with the ROK and the US remained a national obsession, reinforced daily by rabid, crude propaganda depicting the ROK as a living hell and the US forces there as routine perpetrators of unspeakable atrocities against Korean civilians. This might have fired the resolve of North Koreans to bring about reunification, but it was of little concern to outsiders, who were mostly either unconcerned, unconvinced or else simply repelled at the crudity of DPRK propaganda. Accordingly, efforts to convince foreigners, especially countries in the Non-Aligned Movement, to share this obsession and to support its anti-US struggle met with little success.

The inability of the DPRK to establish a sustainable economic base in support of its claims of self-reliance and independence constituted a further serious handicap. Throughout the 1960s industrial output and foreign trade rose steadily, but the balance of trade remained in chronic deficit, and the country remained highly dependent on trade within the Communist Bloc (see Table 3.1 below).

Juche, irrespective of its utility as political rhetoric, provided no impetus toward economic self-sufficiency. The DPRK recorded more foreign trade deficits than surpluses and continued to rely on a variety of expedients to pay its way, including truculent acceptance of Soviet Bloc and Chinese aid, debt repudiation, smuggling and other predatory transactions. Moreover, its inability to reduce its high level of dependence on intra-Communist Bloc trade undercut its resistance to Comecon-style integration, since it was effectively held captive within the Comecon framework by its inability to trade in more sophisticated markets. In these circumstances, the large-scale diversion of resources to military production under the Equal Emphasis policy was largely an internal transaction which, over time, cannibalised the economy by siphoning off an ever-increasing proportion of resources from the non-military sector.

DPRK policies in the 1960s evolved from priorities established by Kim Il Sung and his colleagues in the aftermath of the Korean War. From the standpoint of a person who had spent his entire adult life constantly and directly involved in either military struggle or preparation for military struggle, the Korean War left Kim with the deeply unsatisfactory outcome of an armistice agreement and control of roughly one-third of the Korean population. It is hardly surprising, then, that he should have viewed the process of economic construction as inseparable from the process of rearmament and re-dedication to the cause of Korean reunification. Nor is it surprising that his concept of the modern state was that of a state whose central purpose

**Table 3.1   Estimated DPRK foreign trade 1960–69
(unit: US$ million)**

Year	Total Value of Foreign Trade	Balance of Trade	% Trade with Communist Bloc
1960	320.0	−12.0	96.3
1961	326.4	−6.4	93.5
1962	352.5	+95.5	96.2
1963	420.8	−39.4	93.8
1964	415.6	−28.8	89.1
1965	441.1	−24.5	88.9
1966	463.4	+25.0	86.0
1967	500.0	+30.4	86.3
1968	n.a.	n.a.	n.a.
1969	696.1	−82.7	72.7

Source: Joseph Chung (1974:105, 110–11).

was to conduct effective warfare against a very broad range of enemies.

This led Kim to implement a military build-up beginning in December 1962 in the wake of the Cuba crisis. The colossal proportions of this build-up and its enduring nature cannot be explained by any objective analysis of possible threats to the DPRK at the time, but rather as a reflection of the profoundly militarist nature of Kim Il Sung's world view. The vision itself was not eccentric, and its central theme of unending struggle against imperialist invaders until oppressed countrymen were liberated and the beloved motherland reunified would probably have appealed to many DPRK citizens in the 1960s. But the means of pursuing it were obsessive and strategically simplistic. Moreover, because this policy was rooted so firmly in the personal conviction of the autocrat only he could modify or countermand it. In time, the decisions taken in December 1962 gave the DPRK a definitive identity as a righteous war-making state. We can scarcely understand subsequent political, economic or foreign policy developments without reference to this context.

The 1960s also marked the transformation of Kim Il Sung from dominant Party leader to personal autocrat. The attrition rate among senior Party cadres in the period 1951–58 had been severe, but it had been followed by a period of relative stability which lasted from 1958–64. The attrition rate from 1964–70 again became severe, and resulted in the purging of twelve of the sixteen Politburo members elected at the Third KWP Congress in 1961—which, we may recall, had itself been dubbed the Congress of Victors. This time, however, the victims were not from different streams of the Korean Communist movement, but were Kim loyalists with records of association and support dating back to pre-1945 days. They included economic managers, military leaders, Party functionaries, and the President of Kimilsung University.

This wholesale purging of loyalists across a range of portfolios and areas of expertise, later revelations that Kim Il Sung's son began to play an active role in the Party Secretariat beginning about 1965 (See Chapter 4), and the glorification of Kim's family as a model revolutionary family at this time, indicated that the Party itself had undergone a transformation and had become an instrument of Kimist rule, directed by cadres willing to give Kim the degree of personal loyalty he demanded above and beyond what might be sanctioned by Party rules, procedures and practices. The actual transition was relatively swift and those who remained as members of the Party elite were those who adapted quickly to a polity in which policy decisions no longer issued from Party debate but from Kim's personal conviction.

And so a familiar pattern emerges. Direct, interventionist rule by an omnipotent leader could ensure vigour and consistency in policy, but without even the tenuous checks and balances of the Leninist party-state, the whims and prejudices of the leader assumed considerable importance. Under collective or bureaucratic rule, vigour and clarity of purpose tend to diminish but are compensated for by gains in stability and specialist input. We can only guess to what extent the Party restrained Kim before 1968, but some restraint obviously existed because the 1967–68 purges indicate that many loyalists were still prepared to argue their case and had not yet learnt the habit of docility and self-censorship. The loss of any semblance of debate among senior cadres meant that the Party now lost a vital source of restraint. A further consolidation of militarism and rigidity in the economic and cultural spheres resulted.

The nature of the DPRK regime always obliges us to pay close attention to the personality that has been so dominant in shaping it. To date, our discussion on the personality of Kim Il Sung has focused largely on the twin influences of the Manchurian guerilla campaign and wartime Stalinism, but now the corrupting effects of power without accountability begin to emerge. In 1970 Kim Il Sung was 58-years old, and had been the dominant Party leader for the best part of fifteen years. When we observe such key features of DPRK state policy in the 1960s as irrational use of economic resources, military adventurism, the genesis of plans for the eventual succession of Kim Jong Il, and the purging of many colleagues who had served him since the 1930s, we see signs of a fundamental loss of perspective, precipitated by hubristic national pride, isolation, selective information flows, and deep faith in the primacy of political and military power over economic power. The chief Kimist policy objective remained the reunification of Korea under KWP leadership, but Kim's chosen means had become increasingly anachronistic and counterproductive.

4

SETBACKS TO
SOCIALISM, 1970–80

A survey of the Democratic People's Republic of Korea's (DPRK) three revolutionary fronts in the struggle for Korean reunification in 1970 would have given Kim Il Sung considerable cause for encouragement. In domestic politics, he would have noted with approval that the political system of the DPRK had graduated through the collectivist, Leninist party stage to exclusive dependence on his personal authority and judgment. He was far beyond challenge, he had a group of unquestioning loyal lieutenants, and he was increasingly persuaded that the succession of his son would perpetuate Kimist ideology in the DPRK. In the economic sphere, fifteen years of intensive mobilisation had produced a solid foundation of heavy industry and a military-industrial sector capable of supplying most of the armed forces' basic needs. Serious shortcomings in the economic planning system had emerged during the First Seven-Year Plan period (1961–67), but the overall pattern was one of continuing growth in heavy industry and military-industrial production. The country was well on its way to becoming, as he frequently and ritually described it, an 'impregnable fortress of socialism'.

Developments within the Republic of Korea (ROK) would also have encouraged Kim. The Korean Workers' Party's (KWP) efforts to conduct effective espionage activities and to build a Marxist–Leninist Party within the ROK had failed, as had the direct military pressure of the 1967–68 period, but Kim convinced himself that this was not the result of any strategic miscalculation. Rather, it was the fault of the relevant cadres in charge of southern operations, and he punished them accordingly. Meanwhile, although ROK society showed few signs of harbouring significant revolutionary potential, Kim believed this was only a matter of time. In his analysis, the ROK political system was inherently unstable, and the society was experiencing considerable strain from the effects of ongoing rapid economic development. He did not see any threat in this pattern of economic growth as publicly (and probably privately) he judged it to be the achievement of a 'bubble economy', destined to collapse under the weight of its own contradictions.

On the international front, United States military support for the ROK remained the crucial factor blocking reunification, but in 1970 the US was in a substantially weakened position when compared with even five years previously. In 1968 Lyndon Johnson had been forced from office by the depth of anti-Vietnam War feeling in the US, and by 1970 there was evidence of widespread demoralisation in the US military in Vietnam. Also by 1970, the US was beginning to waver in its twenty-year-old policy of containing China. Combined with the Nixon Doctrine and US plans to sharply reduce troop levels in the ROK, these were substantial grounds for confidence that the US might withdraw from the ROK in the not-too-distant future.

Moreover, in contrast to the ROK's uncertainties with the US, the DPRK had the benefit of a pair of stable alliances that guaranteed its security. Neither the Soviet Union nor China would support another war in Korea, but the DPRK's policies of Equal Emphasis and self-reliance meant that they could no longer veto the war either. This gave Kim some room to manoeuvre, for if he did resume the Korean conflict and the tide turned against him, the Soviets and the Chinese would probably have to intervene diplomatically, if not militarily, to ensure that the DPRK did not disappear from the map. The alternative would be to forfeit a significant buffer state on their respective eastern borders. This meant that the DPRK could survive military defeat while the ROK could not—perhaps a dire calculation, but it was also a logical one that Kim had already seen borne out in 1950.

There were, of course, important gaps in this Kimist analysis, including much that was screened out by ideology, was too hallowed by past experience to invite close scrutiny, or was too abstract for Kim to grasp. These gaps caused him to grossly overestimate the strength of his own system, and to misread a number of growing challenges to the DPRK on all three revolutionary fronts. On the domestic front, the composition of the Party elite at last became relatively stable, but his overwhelming reliance on the Manchurian guerrilla generation meant that the steady aging process among the Party elite continued unabated. Little new blood appeared other than Kim Jong Il, who gradually emerged as a successor-designate groomed to rule in the interests of the guerrilla generation. The strict economic parameters of the 1960s remained in force, and the economy began to lose momentum. The government attempted a short-lived program during 1972–74 to effect technological innovation by importing significant amounts of Western and Japanese plant and equipment, but the economy was unable to either absorb these inputs or pay for them. As the country defaulted on its commercial debts, it acquired a reputation for commercial unreliability that largely excluded it from further access to foreign capital markets. Economic autarky increasingly became a necessity, not a choice, and stagnation set in.

In dealing with the ROK, the DPRK had no more success in its southern operations during the 1970s than during the 1960s. Pyongyang discontinued direct military confrontation with the South, partly under pressure from China and Moscow to reduce tension on the Korean Peninsula, and perhaps partly because Kim believed that military pressure alone would not be effective without a political campaign. In July 1972 the two sides initiated high-level negotiations on reunification. Within eighteen months, however, the dialogue was stalemated, and the years that followed were marked by the refusal of the DPRK to recognise the existence of the ROK Government, by a continuing, massive DPRK military build-up, and by strong evidence of the DPRK's continuing aggressive intent. Meanwhile, despite a substantial increase in political unrest in the ROK during the period of Park Chung-hee's restrictive Yushin Constitution (1972–79), the ROK economy continued its rapid expansion and by 1980 was nearly four times the size of its northern counterpart.

In the international arena the principal challenge to the DPRK came from the US. The Nixon Administration adjusted rapidly and effectively to the looming reality of defeat in Vietnam, and in 1970 it initiated substantial US rapprochement with China. Soon after, it also initiated a process of detente with the Soviet Union. The overall effect was to enhance greatly the commitment of the major powers to maintaining stability on the Korean Peninsula, and perforce this meant tacit recognition by the Soviet Union and China that the presence of US forces in the ROK was an integral part of that stability. Meanwhile, the DPRK was forced to confront the re-emergence of Japan as a major regional economic and diplomatic power. This development worked sharply against DPRK interests, for the revived Japanese state was influential as a strong US ally which had also begun to achieve rapprochement with the Chinese, and to play a rapidly expanding economic role in the ROK.

In the 1960s Kim Il Sung was concerned chiefly with erecting the Kimist system on the pillars of personal autocracy, a militarised economy and society, and independence within the international communist movement. As the 1970s progressed the DPRK encountered significant challenges in a number of domains, and the system proved to be rigid and ineffective in identifying and responding to them. The major questions for an understanding of the DPRK during the 1970s therefore revolve around the nature of these challenges and the reasons why the DPRK made such a minimal response to mounting evidence of unsuccessful state policies.

The full extent of the 1967–68 purges became clear when the Fifth Party Congress was convened in Pyongyang during 2–13 November 1970. After the events of the 1960s, it was not surprising to note a heavy turnover of cadres in the new Politburo, comprising eleven full members and four alternate members.[1] Some idea of this turnover emerges from a comparison with the Politburo elected by the Fourth Congress. Of the sixteen full and alternate members of the Politburo who were elected in 1961, only four survived the ensuing decade of intra-Party warfare (see Table 4.1 below). For their

Table 4.1 Comparison of Fourth and Fifth KWP Congress Politburos

The Fourth KWP Congress (1961) Politburo	The Fifth KWP Congress (1970) Politburo
1. Kim Il Sung	1. Kim Il Sung
2. Ch'oe Yong-gon	2. Ch'oe Yong-gon#
3. Kim Il	3. Kim Il#
4. Pak Kum-ch'ol*	4. Pak Song-ch'ol##
5. Kim Ch'ang-man*	5. Ch'oe Hyon#
6. Yi Hyo-sun*	6. Kim Yong-ju+
7. Pak Chong-ae*	7. O Chin-u##
8. Kim Kwang-hyop*	8. Kim Tong-gyu**
9. Chong Il-yong*	9. So Ch'ol#
10. Nam Il*	10. Kim Chung-nin##
11. Yi Chong-ok*	11. Han Ik-su**
12. Kim Ik-son*	12. Hyon Mu-gwang#
13. Yi Chu-yon*	13. Chong Chun-t'aek#
14. Ha Ang-ch'on*	14. Yang Hyong-sop##
15. Han Sang-du*	15. Kim Man-gum#
16. Hyon Mu-gwang	

Notes: * purged during the 1960s; ** purged during the 1970s; # died in office with state funeral; ## outlived Kim Il Sung; + disappeared from public view and official Party rankings in 1975 and re-emerged in 1993

Source: Dae-Sook Suh (1981:325, 329).

replacements, Kim turned again to the ranks of his former Manchurian colleagues and this time found a group willing to accept his personal autocracy. All the new members except Kim Chung-nin, Yang Hyong-sop, and Chong Chun-t'aek are believed to have fought in Manchuria with Kim Il Sung, while Kim Yong-ju was Kim's younger brother.[2]

With the election of the Fifth KWP Congress Politburo, the practice of rapid turnover ceased and the ranks of the senior Party cadres now became remarkably stable. All but two of the fifteen Politburo members elected in 1970 were still members at the time of Kim Il Sung's death in 1994. This onset of stability closely coincided with the establishment of Kim's personal autocracy and indicated that at last Kim succeeded in assembling a group of cadres who supported this autocracy. However, this stability did not extend to the Central Committee (CC) as a whole, for this body continued to experience rapid turnover. Eighteen of the top 30 were new appointees, 85 (72.2 per cent) of the 117 full members were newly appointed, while 48 of the 55 (87.2 per cent) alternate members elected in 1970 were also new appointees. Only 31 of the 85 full members elected at the 1961 Congress of Victors (or 26.5 per cent) were among the 117 full members elected to Fifth KWP Central Committee.

By now it was clear that while Kim's personal autocracy did not automatically exclude intellectuals and technocrats from membership of the party elite, it was practically impossible for such people to survive at the senior party level. An antagonistic relationship with intellectuals, for example, was implicit in the bloodline of the KWP, for the Manchurian guerillas had been young men of action, limited in education and of generally low socioeconomic background—in short, the type of people to whom intellectuals would have posed a threat. Moreover, when the guerillas emerged into open competition with other groups in the Communist oligarchy after 1945, the Communist intellectuals in the domestic and Yan'an groups were their rivals and were, from all accounts, openly contemptuous of their 'boorish' guerilla comrades. As the leaders of these rival groups were purged, the intellectual elements of the Party fell steadily by the wayside, and their passing in turn reinforced the anti-intellectual tendencies of the Manchurian guerillas who remained. By 1970, only two cadres among the top ranking fifty or so Party cadres, Hwang Chang-yop and Yun Ki-bok, had ever been identified as having worked for any length of time in an intellectual environment.

Nor was the Party generous to the technocrats spawned by the industrialisation of the 1950s and 1960s. Most members of this technocracy had belonged to the Soviet–Korea group and had opposed Kim's economic strategy of immediate and rapid industrialisation after 1953. Accordingly, within the KWP Kim Il Sung regarded technicians, or 'experts', with suspicion and always subordinated them to cadres in the Party organisation-military generalist mould. Like the intellectuals, many fell steadily by the wayside during the 1950s, leaving behind a new generation of economic managers who were accustomed to working within the ideological parameters of the Chollima Movement, the Chongsanri Method, and the Taean Work System. Typically, they were not experts in economic management per se, but were technically minded cadres capable of applying mass mobilisation techniques to the operation of the economy and extracting results from the system. Some of these cadres eventually advanced to the status of alternate Politburo member in the 1980s, but a solid phalanx of ex-Manchurian guerilla Party organisation and military men always remained above them in the rankings. At all times, the Party controlled not only the gun, but also the library, the science laboratory, the lecture hall, and especially the factory manager's office.

The slow, measured emergence of Kim Jong Il as a force within the KWP constituted the major development in DPRK domestic politics during the 1970s. Kim was born in the Soviet Union on 16 February 1942 to Kim Chong-suk, Kim Il Sung's first wife who died in 1949,[3] and graduated from Kimilsung University in 1964. We are almost entirely reliant on later hagiographic accounts for information on his activities before 1980, when he emerged publicly at the Sixth KWP Congress. Prior to this time he made no official public appearances, gave no official speeches, and the media did not mention him by name. According to his hagiographers, he spent this time working at the KWP Central Committee in an unspecified capacity, initially on ideological matters and then in literature and the arts.[4] Reports that the younger Kim was emerging as his father's successor first surfaced in the foreign media in 1974, but by this time he was already well known to Party members and, to a lesser extent, the population at large. They were aware of his activities chiefly through the activities of an entity called the Party Centre (*Tang chungang*), perhaps best described as the office which provided definitive ideological guidance to the Party as a whole. To the initiated, reference to the Party Centre or else to specific words and phrases in Party literature and the public media indicated ideological pronouncements whose authority emanated from Kim Jong Il.

We do not know how or when Kim Il Sung settled on the idea

of a dynastic succession. He may have always harboured it, for we see no sign of any mentoring or designating any other successor within the Party. To judge from later accounts, the preparation of Kim Jong Il for leadership began in the mid-1960s, with circumstantial evidence pointing to the period 1967–68 as crucial (Chong-sik Lee 1982:441). This was the period when Kim ceased to tolerate policy debate within the circle of former Manchurian guerillas around him in the Party and instead based his political authority on unconditional personal loyalty. As an ideological basis for personal autocracy Kim turned to Stalinist precedent and, as discussed in Chapter 2, employed elaborate kinship metaphors similar to those developed in the Soviet Union during the 1930s. In one respect he went further than Stalin, for beginning in the period 1967–68, selected members of his family, especially his parents, also began to be portrayed in the media as revolutionary heroes, suggesting that Kim had already decided on Kim Jong Il as the inheritor of the guerilla dynasty.[5]

Although the public media did not mention Kim Jong Il by name until 1980, a cult of personality began to form around him in 1973, featuring songs of loyalty and study sessions on his writings. At the Seventh Plenum of the Fifth KWP Central Committee in September 1973 Kim Jong Il was reportedly elected to the position of Party Secretary in charge of organisation, propaganda, and agitation; and at the Eighth Plenum in February 1974 he was elected to the KWP Politburo, though neither appointment was made public (Byung-Chul Koh, 1993:63). By 1975 his portrait hung in schools, uncaptioned magazine photos showed him in the company of top military leaders such as O Chin-u, Party cadres and government workers were well aware which senior Party figures were close to Kim Jong Il, and foreign diplomats were aware of his identity as 'The Party Centre' referred to in slogans, banners and media articles as delivering, for example, 'wise guidance' and 'embodying the teachings of the Great Leader'.[6]

Why did Kim Jong Il remain behind the scenes for such an extended period of time? The seeming coyness on the part of an absolute ruler who could have simply forced this issue might seem strange, but there were basic sensitivities involved, probably best illustrated by the fact that the 1970 edition of the DPRK Academy of Social Science's own *Dictionary of Political Terminologies* carried the general Marxist definition of hereditary succession as 'a reactionary custom practised in exploitive societies'.[7] Internationally, the marriage of Marxist–Leninist ideology with hereditary succession carried a price, for it gave the DPRK considerable presentational problems in dealing with fraternal parties and with more politically sophisticated members of the Non-Aligned Movement. Within the DPRK, Kim Il Sung might well have viewed the hereditary succession as essential for the preservation and continuation of his life's work, but the careful attention he devoted to building up his son's claims to political leadership suggests he did not believe that either senior cadres or the general populace would willingly and spontaneously accept his son as leader. In these circumstances, Kim Il Sung seems to have decided not to impose his son on the country from the top, but to portray Kim Jong Il's rise as an irresistible tide issuing from within the Party.

The second half of the 1970s was given over to building up that tide. Kim Jong Il became associated with the specific policy areas of literature and the arts, economic production 'speed battles', the glorification of Kim Il Sung's anti-Japanese guerilla activities, the strengthening of cadre study practices, and especially the direction of the Red Guard-like 'Three Revolution Teams'.[8] These Teams comprised groups of young Party zealots who were dispatched to various economic and administrative organs of the state with the mission of uncovering and correcting ideologically unhealthy practices. This activity gave them ample opportunity to test out the responsiveness and loyalty of local cadres, and in this manner Kim Jong Il was able to build up a power base founded on even more rigorous definitions of ideological correctness than had previously been tolerated.

However, even with this careful preparation plans for the succession did not proceed smoothly, and were in fact held in abeyance for two years from 1977 to 1979. For reasons that are still a mystery, the hitherto smooth pattern of references to the Party Centre in the KWP theoretical journal *Kulloja* was broken and references ceased almost entirely between April 1977 and February 1979, indicating a marked decline in the significance being attributed to the younger Kim's activities.[9] The break in this pattern suggested some form of dissatisfaction on the part of Kim Il Sung at his son's performance. Senior cadres may also have had misgivings about the hereditary succession at this time, because this development also coincided with the purging in 1977 of Politburo members Kim Tong-gyu, who was also a Vice-President, and Yi Yong-mu, and the demotion of Politburo members Yang Hyong-sop and Kim Chung-nin. Kim Tong-gyu and Yi Yong-mu made their last public appearances in September and October 1977 respectively. Yang Hyong-sop and Kim Chung-nin were dropped from the Politburo in May and September 1977 respectively (Dae-Sook Suh 1988:281). However, by 1980 the older Kim had surmounted these difficulties and his son finally assumed his place at the apex of the Party at the Sixth KWP Congress in October 1980.[10]

The justification for the Kim Jong Il succession centred on the need for a 'model revolutionary' to consolidate his father's ideological system. In the economic sphere his name was associated with policies and activities that were the antithesis of reform—uneconomic prestige constructions, Stakhanovite 'speed battles', and a further tightening of Party control over economic activity. In the ideological sphere, his consolidation of a power base within the Party through direction of the activities of the Three Revolution Teams helped to maintain the rigidity of the system. This meant that at a time when one might have expected the DPRK, as an industrialising society, to be manifesting increasing technological sophistication and specialisation, and moving in the direction of political pragmatism, the younger Kim emerged not as an embodiment of a new generation reflecting this trend but as an agent of the old revolutionary generation of his father. From the beginning, the role of Kim Jong Il was to perpetuate the ideology of the revolutionary generation and to forestall any attempts at revisionism by subsequent generations.

The effects of this new ideological orientation on the economy were severe. At the Fifth KWP Congress Kim Il Sung endorsed the country's economic performance during the 1960s by proclaiming the successful completion of the First Seven-Year Plan (1961–67) after a three-year extension (1967–70), and by promulgating the new Six-Year Plan (1971–76), which projected rates of state investment comparable to rates during the 1960s and unambiguously continued the emphasis on heavy industry. However, Kim's euphoria over the results of the First Seven-Year Plan was not justified by actual economic performance. Even from the sparse and selective statistics available there are clear indications that in many cases the First Seven-Year Plan did not meet its stated targets or, where it did, it needed three extra years of production to do so. Nevertheless, the outcome was clearly acceptable to Kim because, by 1970, the basic economic strategies of self-reliance and the rapid construction of a sizeable military-industrial sector gave the DPRK formidable military strength that would be crucial if the US forces in the ROK were to leave.

But by now the best years for the DPRK economy were over, and as the 1970s progressed the rapid growth rates of the 1960s gave way to economic stagnation. The policies of self-reliance, extreme administrative centralisation and mass mobilisation exhausted their potential and became liabilities. In theory, centralised management aided the rapid and efficient allocation of resources, but in practice it now brought about endemic bottlenecks in the supply of power, fuel and raw materials, and distorted the economic structure by intervening to withhold investment capital from the agriculture and light industry sectors. Similarly, mass mobilisation had enabled the rapid construction of the basic means of production, but the economy was now increasingly beset by continuing emphasis on quantitative production, and by poor quality control, declining productivity, growing machinery obsolescence and technological backwardness (Joseph Chung 1971, 1972).

The first indication of these limitations came in 1972–74 when the DPRK carried out a short-lived program of massive purchases of Western plant and machinery on credit. The purchases included a complete French petrochemical plant, one of the world's largest cement plants, a large fertiliser plant, Japanese textile factories and steel-making equipment, a Swiss watch factory, a Finnish pulp and paper mill, and substantial amounts of Swedish mining and smelting equipment.[11] As a result, trade with the West as proportion of total trade rose from 11.1 per cent in 1965 to 40.6 per cent in 1975 (Namkoong & Yoo 1994:132). Evidently, the DPRK planned to pay for these purchases with the export income they were expected to generate, but this plan proved unrealistic. In many cases economic sectors and units did not possess the planning capacities, building technology skills, infrastructural sophistication or managerial skills to absorb the purchases, while their Stakhanovite work practices were not adaptable to the precision construction and operating demands of plants using advanced Western technology.[12] Many plants remained inoperable or else made only a marginal contribution to the national economy, and in these circumstances, other setbacks such as the first oil crisis in 1973 and the depressed state of such international commodity markets as non-ferrous metals had a considerable effect. By 1974 these large-scale foreign purchases had almost ceased, though not before the DPRK had acquired a sizeable foreign debt.[13]

Efforts to address the major problem of declining productivity by means of the introduction of advanced Western technology provided clear evidence of a leadership that was now clearly out of touch with the realities and capacities of the DPRK economy. The government carried out the purchasing program in an ad hoc manner, so much so that at no time did it link the program to any facet of the existing Six-Year Plan. In essence it attempted to graft

89

a series of major industrial projects onto the existing primitive eco-nomic structure without corresponding adjustments in infrastructure and without reference to the levels of technical knowledge required to bring the new facilities into production. Moreover, the failure to achieve any significant economic result other than a sizeable foreign debt did not seem to make any particular impression on Kim. In the area of economic administration, one would naturally have expected the government ministers and Party officials responsible for what can only be described as a debacle to suffer demotion or dismissal, yet this did not occur. The Minister for External Economic Affairs during this period (1972–75), Kong Chin-t'ae, was in fact promoted to a Vice Premiership in 1975. Kong and the Minister for Foreign Trade during this period, Kye Ung-t'ae, both Politburo members, continued to play a major role in foreign trade and to enjoy high party ranking for many years afterward. Kim did not regard their actions as signifi-cant, let alone blameworthy. Even with the passage of time Kim did not seem to understand what had occurred. In a 20 June 1977 interview with a *Le Monde* correspondent he described the trade deficit as 'a passing phenomenon' and 'a temporary difficulty' which was the result of 'the economic difficulty of the advanced capitalist countries of the West caused by the fuel crisis . . . they are unable to purchase our goods' (Byung-Chul Koh 1978c:39).

Yet the significance of this failure was considerable. It reflected the extent to which the leadership had cut itself off from competent economic advice and management through its purges of the mid-1960s. It also provided clear evidence that the economy had become technologically backward and inefficient, and this had clear long-term implications not only for the economy as a whole but for the war-making potential of the state. Internationally, the erratic fashion with which the DPRK had gone about these purchases and then dealt with the resulting debt situation—frequent defaulting and reneging on repayment schedules—effectively cut the country off from further access to foreign investment and advanced technology with serious long-term consequences. While ignorance of what constituted accept-able international commercial practice is the most frequently offered explanation for the DPRK's actions in this sphere, this is too simple an explanation. The DPRK's attitude was more calculated than this, demonstrating a fixed view of the international economy as a preda-tory environment in which flouting the conventions of normal international commercial behaviour was justified.

Under these circumstances, it is not surprising to find that the increasing economic challenge of the ROK went unanswered, despite the serious implications this had for the DPRK's reunification strategy. Just as the DPRK's economic performance tapered off, the ROK underwent a process of rapid economic expansion in the 1970s (see Table 4.2 below). If we start with data on the respective sizes of the two economies, we find that during the 1970s the ROK economy began to pull sharply ahead of the DPRK. In 1970 its GNP was roughly twice the size of the DPRK's, which made the two economies roughly even on a per capita basis, but in 1980 the ROK economy was nearly four and a half times the size of the DPRK economy. In 1970 the ROK would have had to spend roughly 15 per cent of GNP on military-industrial production in 1970 in order to match the estimated total defense expenditure of the DPRK, which remained at about 30 per cent of GNP during the 1970s, but in 1980 this figure had fallen to 6.6 per cent.

The large-scale purchases of foreign plant and equipment during 1972–74 did not signal an opening of the DPRK economy or a relaxing of ideological parameters. Economic adjustments occurred only at the periphery of the command system,[14] and reliance on mass mobilisation became further entrenched in the mid-1970s with the onset of the Three Revolution Teams movement under Kim Jong Il. Except for the 1972–74 purchases, foreign trade remained insignificant, the general population remained without access to media, post

Table 4.2   Comparison of GNP for the ROK and the DPRK 1960, 1966, 1970–80 (unit: US$ billion, trade exchange rate)

Year	ROK (A)	DPRK (B)	A/B
1960	1.95	1.52	1.28
1966	3.67	2.41	1.52
1970	7.99	3.98	2.00
1971	9.37	4.09	2.29
1972	10.57	4.62	2.29
1973	13.50	6.27	2.15
1974	18.55	7.29	2.54
1975	20.85	9.35	2.23
1976	28.68	9.68	2.96
1977	37.42	10.64	3.52
1978	51.96	13.32	3.90
1979	62.37	12.40	5.03
1980	60.30	13.50	4.47

Note: Often the quality and quantity of statistics available on the DPRK economy does not permit precise calculations. These figures are drawn from Namkoong Young (1995a), who also provides a useful discussion on the methodological basis for quantitative comparative analyses of the two economies. We should also note that Hwang (1993) arrives at somewhat different figures, but both reveal a clear trend of DPRK economic decline relative to the ROK.

or telecommunications links with the outside world, and within the country the pervasive security and surveillance system strictly controlled internal movement, social intercourse and the dissemination of basic information. The government exercised a total monopoly over social, cultural and intellectual life and otherwise subjected its citizens to a degree of discipline and control that was unparalleled elsewhere in the communist world.

Meanwhile, important shifts in the strategic thinking of both Koreas' major big power allies were taking place. In June 1971, US National Security Advisor Henry Kissinger visited Beijing, formally inaugurating the process of Sino–US rapprochement that led to US President Richard Nixon's visit to Beijing in February 1972 and eventually to full normalisation of relations in 1979. Sino–US rapprochement had a substantial impact on the Korean peninsula, and especially on the ROK, because as part of this rapprochement both the US and China sought stability on the Korean Peninsula and so encouraged their respective Korean allies to engage in dialogue.

To the two Koreas, these moves emphasised the speed at which the regional balance of power could change, and also emphasised their vulnerability to changes in the interests of their respective patrons. The DPRK had already sought to eliminate this vulnerability with a policy of extreme self-reliance, and now the ROK leadership also began to reassess the extent of its military dependence on the US. In the space of five years Park Chung-hee had seen the US position in the region change from resolute prosecution of the Vietnam War to demoralisation and defeat in that war. By 1970 the US security role in Korea, always prone to displays of ambivalence, seemed especially fragile. Therefore, when on 26 March 1970 the US advised the ROK government that it was withdrawing 20 000 men, one-third of its total force in Korea, the ROK made no attempt to conceal its distress and anger at this development, and the acrimonious exchanges that followed precipitated some very deep and fundamental rethinking in Seoul about the shape of a future without firm US security guarantees.[15] Motivation to seek some sort of political settlement with the DPRK strengthened accordingly.

The situation had also changed for the DPRK, though not nearly to the same extent, because the underlying Chinese commitment to the security of the DPRK remained firm. However, in less than three years Kim Il Sung had seen Chinese foreign policy change from energetic confrontation with US imperialism to one of seeking dialogue. Kim interpreted the July 1971 announcement of the Nixon visit as 'a trip of the defeated that fully reflects the declining fate of

US imperialism'.[16] And, while he may have been less sanguine in private, he gave every public sign that he believed the tide was running against the US in the region and against the ROK in particular. In addition, Sino–US rapprochement came at a time when Kim was regrouping after the failure of his 1967–68 campaign against the South. Revolutionary violence had failed to produce the anticipated collapse on that occasion and had led to a period of reassessing tactics, though not strategy. He therefore had nothing to lose and everything to gain from negotiations in which he believed he was bargaining from a position of strength.

The net effect of Sino–US rapprochement was to stimulate the two Koreas to initiate dialogue. On 12 August 1971 the ROK Red Cross Committee proposed talks on humanitarian issues such as the reuniting of separated families, and on 14 August their northern counterparts accepted this proposal. A year-long process of liaison committee and preparatory committee talks followed, leading to full-scale talks in Pyongyang on 30 August 1972 and in Seoul on 13 September 1972. On the political level, in May 1972 the two sides exchanged top-level secret envoys and on 4 July signed an agreement to hold full political talks. Thus began what became a long, drawn-out process of sporadic contact and negotiation between the two Koreas. As the progress of this issue is a significant part of the history of both the DPRK and the ROK after 1972, we consider some of the basic characteristics of this dialogue here.

In the 25 years since 1972, the talks process has not been continuous. Almost all negotiation has been concentrated into three short passages of negotiation, each lasting less than two years: 1972–73, 1984–85 and 1990–91. The intervening periods have seen a resumption of traditional DPRK policies of military confrontation and sometimes outright terrorism against the ROK. Moreover, the achievements of these negotiations have been extremely meagre. Despite the convening of a variety of official, unofficial, open session and secret meetings to discuss political, economic, military, humanitarian, cultural and sporting issues, the two Koreas have rarely moved past procedural matters. Where they have signed communiques or agreements they have been unable to agree on ways and means of implementation. Meanwhile, the two sides have remained in a state of war, and their transportation and telecommunication links are confined to servicing the commercial links that began to grow in the early 1990s. No sanctioned, regular people-to-people contact takes place. The periods of negotiation stand out as interludes against an unchanging background of confrontation.

While the dimensions of major power rivalry and differing perceptions of regional security are significant for a full understanding of the inter-Korean dialogue, differences in political system and style have been the chief determinant of negotiation strategy. Here the DPRK has endeavoured to seek advantage by bringing its monolithic control system to bear against the pluralism of the South. As a closed, rigidly controlled, militarist system, the DPRK has always maintained that the resolution of fundamental political and military issues is the prerequisite to progress in other fields, though it has also made strictly limited, tactical gestures in other fields, especially on humanitarian issues. Pyongyang does not see progress on people-to-people and humanitarian negotiations as desirable policy objectives in themselves and, as it is unaccountable to popular pressure, has engaged in, or withdrawn from, negotiations at will. Moreover, as an isolationist polity, the DPRK is not interested in the effect of reunification negotiations on other countries. On the other hand, the relatively open, pluralist political system of the South has mandated a pragmatic, gradualist approach to the talks. For the South, confidence-building measures and progress on humanitarian issues are essential prerequisites for retaining domestic political consensus and ensuring continuing support from the ROK's foreign allies. The range and variety of the ROK's regional and international linkages also require it to adopt a more circumspect attitude to the interests of outside parties such as Japan. Because of its standards of domestic and foreign accountability, the ROK cannot move swiftly on military issues and remains vulnerable to sudden changes to the status quo.

These widely differing political systems have influenced not only the agendas of each party but also the fundamental tactical approaches of each side. Underlying the difference in tactics is the ROK adoption of many hallmarks of Western negotiation, most notably a predisposition to flexibility, compromise and concession; and the DPRK adoption of the Maoist view of negotiation as an integral part of a broader strategic struggle.[17] In its militant form, this view excludes the concept of lasting compromise or peaceful accommodation of interests, and assesses progress as that which brings closer the final defeat of the adversary.[18]

The three phases of inter-Korean negotiation (and, for that matter, the DPRK negotiations with another adversary, the Japanese political leader Kanemaru Shin, in September 1990) display a number of similarities. In each case, the two Koreas signed broad statements of principle, which in 1972 and 1991 took the form of actual written agreements, ostensibly to form the basis for subsequent substantive negotiation. Typically, such agreements were hailed internationally as positive outcomes of negotiation, not as starting points for nego-tiation. However, in each case the next step was not substantive negotiation within the framework of the agreement, but insistence by the North that the South accept a unilateral Pyongyang interpre-tation of the statements as a precondition to further talks. In each case the interpretation defined either the continued presence of US forces in the ROK or ROK internal security laws, or both, as incompatible with further negotiation. Stalemate ensued, with the DPRK bringing a unilateral halt to negotiations at a time of its own choosing amid charges of bad faith against the South.

The 1972–73 phase of talks proceeded in accordance with this pattern. They began with a pair of far-reaching umbrella agreements in both the humanitarian and political fields. On 16 June 1972 the Red Cross committees exchanged documents of agreement on an agenda for full-dress talks that included locating dispersed families, home visits, facilitating the reunion of dispersed families, and the free exchange of mail. On 4 July the two sides issued a joint communique which enunciated three fundamental principles for the achievement of unification: that it be pursued independently without outside interference, that it be pursued peacefully and that 'a great national unity, as a homogeneous people, shall be sought first, trans-cending differences in ideas, ideologies and systems'.[19] A number of other points of agreement related to such issues as the cessation of propaganda and armed provocation. The communique also estab-lished a South–North Coordinating Committee (SNCC) under the co-chairmanship of Lee Hu-rak (ROK) and Kim Yong-ju (DPRK) to give effect to the three principles.

Negotiations immediately assumed a rigid pattern. The ROK sought to address humanitarian issues before proceeding to the broader politico-military issues, while the DPRK had reverse priori-ties. The DPRK position was summed up at the third plenary session of the Red Cross talks held 22–26 October 1972 in the demand that 'the [political] climate should be so constituted in south Korea as to eliminate all social, political, and statutory obstacles to the talks' (Hakjoon Kim 1992:350), by which Pyongyang signified that talks could not proceed while ROK national security laws remained in force. This stance effectively deadlocked the Red Cross talks. Mean-while, by December 1972 Pyongyang had also revealed a similar across-the-board approach in political talks, when it advised: 'There cannot be such problems that intercourse and collaboration between the north and the south can be realised first in some fields and put off in other fields, and can be conducted in some fields and cannot be undertaken in some other fields' (Hakjoon Kim 1992:351).

By March 1973 the DPRK had drawn up this stance into a five-point proposal that included withdrawal of US troops, mutual troop reductions and weapons controls, all to be guaranteed by a peace treaty. The essence of the DPRK position was contained in the order of the agenda. Its first order of business was to negotiate a military withdrawal and peace treaty to replace the Military Armistice Agreement with the US as the real belligerent on the southern side. Upon the removal of what, among other things, was the cornerstone of the ROK's national defence structure without corresponding concessions of its own, the DPRK's second order of business was then to negotiate a political settlement with the ROK government. This order of business conflicted with the ROK agenda for the implementation of confidence-building measures as a prelude to substantive bargaining, and the talks stalled at this point. After a fruitless exchange of positions at the second plenary meeting of the SNCC in Pyongyang in March 1973, the DPRK resumed low-level military violence on the DMZ, and in August 1973 the talks effectively ceased altogether. The precise issue at this point was the refusal of the northern side to deal with the southern side co-chairman and head of the Korean Central Intelligence Agency (KCIA), Lee Hu-rak, in the wake of the abduction of prominent opposition figure Kim Dae Jung from Japan by, as was widely assumed at the time and eventually confirmed, KCIA operatives.[20] The two Koreas held a series of brief and insubstantial meetings in 1980 (see Chapter 5), but no further substantive negotiations took place until 1984.

To the North, the 1972–73 talks revealed little sense of disorganisation or demoralisation in the South, and this encouraged a resumption of its traditional policy of maintaining strong military pressure on the ROK. In breaking off dialogue Kim Il Sung demonstrated a conviction that he was dealing from a position of strength and could afford to wait. Here he was encouraged by the restored DPRK–Chinese alliance, under which China became Pyongyang's leading arms supplier by 1973, by a belief that the tide of international events, as measured by events in Indochina, the Middle East and in the Third World, was flowing against the imperialist camp, and by the capacity of his own ongoing military build-up to force the issue more effectively than negotiation.[21]

The evidence for DPRK preparedness to pursue a military option for reunification during the 1970s is substantial. First, there was a considerable build-up of offensive weapons such as tanks (750 in 1971 to 2650 in 1980), field artillery pieces (2300 to 4000), and armoured personnel carriers (192 to 1000). Second, this build-up was matched by the continued forward deployment of the bulk of the DPRK's combat divisions.[22] Third, analysis of DPRK population figures from the 1970s suggests that the size of the DPRK's armed forces also rose substantially during this period, from about 400 000 in 1970 to 700 000 in 1975 to nearly 1 000 000 in the late 1970s.[23] Fourth, beginning in November 1974, the South detected three elaborate infiltration tunnels entering the DMZ from the North whose construction is believed to date from 1972. Fifth, and most important, at no stage had the DPRK forsworn the policies of the 1960s. The same leader was in charge, surrounded by the same men who had fully backed him in 1967-68, the public rhetoric was the same, and there had been neither public redefinition of Pyongyang's strategy nor evidence of private redefinition.

The withdrawal of the US from an active role in the Indochina War and the accompanying emphasis on detente between the major powers had particular significance for the DPRK since, next to self-preservation, its overriding foreign policy objective was to bring as much international pressure as possible to bear on the United States to effect a withdrawal of US forces from Korea. In essence, Pyongyang sought to recreate the same kind of international situation that enabled it to go to war in 1950: a strong, international anti-imperialist coalition that would provide backing for its reunification strategy, and enable effective military action against the ROK without the threat of US intervention.

With the Sino-Soviet split and the growing Soviet commitment to peaceful coexistence with the US during the 1960s, the DPRK saw hopes fade of that coalition ever re-emerging and, by the early 1970s, US-Soviet detente had become a particularly alarming trend for the DPRK. Within the limits imposed by rivalry with China in the region, Moscow now actively sought to persuade the DPRK to acknowledge the larger web of national interests that made up the balance of power in Northeast Asia and especially to acknowledge the desire of the USSR to avoid military confrontation with the US. After the *Pueblo* incident in January 1968 and a further crisis caused by the shooting down of a US Navy EC-121 reconnaissance aircraft off the east coast of North Korea in April 1969, the Soviets dispatched high-level Politburo members to Pyongyang and publicly warned Kim that the defence of the socialist camp had to be 'collective', and that unilateral attacks on the US would not be sanctioned. While the Soviets continued to offer support for the DPRK stance on reunification, Kim's tendency to unilateral, unpredictable confrontation on the Korean peninsula meant that they did so with notably less enthusiasm than the Chinese. For example, in 1972–73 Moscow made a series of low-key but significant gestures toward the ROK which signalled their readiness to have dealings with the Park regime in the course of ordinary international sporting and commercial transactions.[24] They also withheld advanced weaponry from the DPRK while at the same time supplying this weaponry to Egypt and Syria.[25] Accordingly, relations with the Soviets remained cool, correct and low-key for much of the 1970s, with routine, non-political exchanges continuing, but no high-level political exchanges or visits.

DPRK–Soviet relations became further strained in the mid-1970s, first when the DPRK implicitly began to endorse Chinese criticism of Soviet 'dominationism', which referred to residual Soviet claims to a position of international leadership of the communist movement, and then in the aftermath of the August 1976 axe killings incident at Panmunjom.[26] This incident seemed to confirm the Soviets' worst fears about DPRK adventurism and, as a mark of displeasure, they refused DPRK requests for assistance in meeting initial payments on their recently acquired hard currency debts, precipitating both a rescheduling of the debt and a significant downturn in DPRK trade with the Soviet Bloc.[27] At the very end of the 1970s, however, relations again improved as the DPRK expressed support for the December 1979 Soviet intervention in Afghanistan, accepting the Soviet argument so widely rejected elsewhere that the ruling communist party in Kabul had requested the intervention.

In contrast to the tension of the Soviet relationship, the DPRK maintained warm, steady relations with the Chinese for most of the 1970s. There had always been a more solid basis for a friendly, pragmatic China–DPRK relationship than was the case with the Soviet Union. This was due to the DPRK's greater strategic interdependence with China, its closer ideological affinity with a China untainted by revisionism, and the strength of China's support for the DPRK position on reunification, which in no small part issued out of the Chinese need for consistency with China's own policy on the Taiwan issue.

Following Zhou Enlai's 1970 visit to Pyongyang there were continual exchanges at the highest level. As the Soviets grew increasingly reluctant to supply the DPRK with up-to-date military hardware, China stepped in and, as noted, by 1973 it had become Pyongyang's leading supplier. This phase of relations culminated in Kim Il Sung's April 1974 visit to China, his first official overseas visit in thirteen years. However, at the close of the 1970s, relations with China again grew more distant following the signing of the Sino–Japanese peace treaty in September 1978, the full normalisation of US–China relations on 1 January 1979 and the China–Vietnam border conflict in February 1979. While to some extent the DPRK had been able to rationalise away the first Chinese moves toward the US and Japan in the early 1970s, these subsequent events provided clear evidence that friendly relations with these two bitter enemies of the DPRK were now a central feature of Chinese foreign policy.[28]

The other major feature of the DPRK's international relations in the 1970s was its participation in the Non-Aligned Movement (NAM). After energetic lobbying, the DPRK was admitted to the NAM as a full member at the Lima Conference of August 1975. In joining the NAM, Kim seems to have genuinely believed that this movement would become a powerful force in international politics. In the avowed principles and especially in the rhetoric of the NAM, Kim thought he detected a valuable forum in which to promote an anti-imperialist and anti-revisionist agenda, to promote the DPRK's approach to economic development as a model for less developed NAM member states and, of course, to promote his own image as a significant international Communist leader.[29]

For about a year after the DPRK's entry, leading NAM members provided strong diplomatic support for the DPRK position on reunification, and in 1975 the First Committee of the thirtieth meeting of the United Nations General Assembly (UNGA 30) in New York passed a pro-DPRK resolution on the Korean Question for the first time.[30] At the NAM Summit Conference in Colombo in August 1976, the DPRK made a massive lobbying effort to have this meeting endorse its stance on Korean reunification, but while it achieved its objective, its methods of diplomacy proved counterproductive. An unprecedented number of countries recorded written reservations on the relevant resolution, while still more were reportedly offended by the DPRK's resort to bribery and physical threats to secure votes.[31] The DPRK had again been preparing for a campaign at UNGA 31 to seek the passage of a pro-DPRK resolution by a greater margin than the previous year, but events at Colombo and the international reaction to the Panmunjom axe killings, which occurred almost immediately afterward, seem to have persuaded Pyongyang that it was unlikely to achieve this. It therefore asked its supporters to withdraw a planned pro-DPRK resolution, perhaps to avoid offering evidence of declining international support. The DPRK's interest in the UN as a forum for generating pressure against the ROK and the US waned, and the Korean Question disappeared from the UNGA First Committee agenda.

Diplomatic support for the DPRK within the NAM also began to dwindle. To many influential NAM members such as Josip Broz Tito of Yugoslavia, the DPRK had initially seemed a hopeful sign of the future—a former close Soviet ally which now embraced non-alignment. However, once admitted to the NAM, the DPRK pursued a highly political agenda based on anti-imperialist ideology. It failed to perceive the diversity, disunity and multiple agendas within the NAM, and was especially out of touch with the agendas of the more moderate and diplomatically sophisticated members who had no interest in the adoption of a highly political, confrontationist agenda. Moreover, as the extent of the DPRK's foreign debt and its erratic way of dealing with this debt became clear in 1975–76, the DPRK lost credibility as a responsible member-state and also increasingly lost the means of pursuing political influence through foreign aid and economic diplomacy. The NAM did not, of course, become anything like the powerful anti-imperialist force Pyongyang had expected, but even in dealing with the Movement as it was, the DPRK reinforced the general international perception that it was out of touch with international political and economic realities to an often staggering degree.

By 1980 the situation on all three fronts of Kim Il Sung's revolution had begun to deteriorate. Within the DPRK his personal autocracy remained unchallenged and unchallengeable, and after some vicissitudes he managed to install his son as heir and successor, thus guaranteeing that, should he die before his time, the country would continue under 'correct' political leadership. Furthermore, he continued a substantial military build-up and maintained a credible military threat despite ever-diminishing economic resources. But per-versely, these apparent sources of strength were in fact weakening the state. The economy had stagnated, and a simple extrapolation of the respective growth rates achieved by the two Koreas in the 1970s suggested that whether or not the South eventually collapsed under the weight of its own economic contradictions as Kim believed, in the meantime the ROK would enjoy an alarming economic supe-riority over the DPRK. By 1980 the DPRK showed no sign of willingness to take responsibility for its sizeable foreign debt, and its international credit rating was at rock-bottom. This cut Pyongyang off from further access to international capital markets, foreign invest-ment, and hence from advanced technology. Self-reliance was no longer an option but a necessity.

Developments in the ROK were likewise unfavourable for the DPRK. Pyongyang remained optimistic of political and economic collapse in the South and had some grounds for optimism. The domestic political unrest that had continued for much of the decade culminated in the assassination of Park Chung-hee on 26 October 1979, and in 1980 the country faced an uncertain political future. On the economic front as well, the ROK economy entered into a deep recession in the wake of the 1979 oil shocks, and probably again raised DPRK hopes that the bubble economy prediction was well founded. However, wishful thinking and ideological dogma obscured the underlying reality that the ROK economy was immeasurably stronger in 1980 than in 1970. While industrial development had been uneven, the ROK had become a growing regional economic power. It possessed a substantial industrial infrastructure, including an international standard integrated steel mill, massive shipyards, vast and sophisticated metal processing, chemical, machine tool and electronics sectors, and an automobile industry that was about to launch the first Korea-designed and developed automobile on the international market. The implications of these developments for defence production were, of course, considerable.

But it was on the international front that the DPRK suffered its most serious reverses during the 1970s. The US recovered from its post-Vietnam War malaise and again became a stable regional presence. The Carter Administration's strong commitment to a withdrawal of US ground forces from Korea was overruled by a broad coalition of US legislative and military interests, with the result that in 1980 the US commitment to the defence of the ROK was strong, stable, and reaffirmed. The US also entered into a process of detente with the Soviet Union and effected diplomatic normalisation with China, giving both of the DPRK's chief military allies strong reasons for supporting the status quo in Korea. Finally, the hopes that Kim Il Sung had pinned on DPRK participation in the Non-Aligned Movement had proven to be illusory. The Movement as a whole was not interested in the DPRK cause, and individual members were interested strictly in proportion to the DPRK's provision of foreign aid or other material benefits. Increasingly, the hard-pressed DPRK economy could not compete with the ROK in economic diplomacy in this sphere.

Why, then, did the DPRK display almost total lack of interest in change or reform throughout this period despite the clear development of adverse economic and diplomatic trends? Several factors were at work. First, the DPRK response had a great deal to do with the manner in which its political system perceived the challenge. Whereas the major challenges to Kim Il Sung during the 1960s had been relatively straightforward, quantifiable and, to the military mind, susceptible to clear, albeit extreme, countermeasures, the challenges of the 1970s were of a different nature—more abstract, subtle and increasingly impossible to counter from within the corrosive simplicity of Kimist ideology. It is therefore not surprising that the DPRK had limited success in analysing these challenges and taking effective counter-measures. Second, Kim turned 60 in 1972, and as he aged his personal lifetime experience exerted an ever-stronger influence on state policy. Any reassessment of strategy would entail a reassessment of his life's work, and Kim gives no sign of ever having possessed the self-reflecting nature that might have permitted this. The cumulative weight of past decisions and practices lay heavily over his mind—all the more heavily for the elimination of all elements within the Party which might have been prepared to argue for alternative courses of action—and so he continued to apply rigid thought patterns to state and Party activities, and these produced increasingly eccentric and irrelevant ideas to the problems of the country.

Third, the haphazard plant and machinery purchases, the handling of the resultant foreign debt, the vainglorious promotion of Kim as an international statesman, and the manner in which the DPRK courted the Non-Aligned Movement provided further evidence of a leader out of his depth in economic and international political matters. As a consequence of the severity of his personal autocracy, Kim now had around him an inner circle of aging, poorly educated politico-military generalists, either blindly loyal by instinct or browbeaten into the semblance of absolute and unconditional loyalty. He had cut himself off from expert, effective counselling in matters beyond his direct, concrete experience and therefore had no means of approaching the international community other than by projecting the 'realities' he had fashioned at home onto the outside world.

Finally, no matter how much damage was done to the DPRK's international economic and diplomatic standing, Kim did not see this as constituting a clear and direct threat to the survival of the DPRK state. Kim continued to operate in a domestic environment that did not offer any immediate challenge or threat to his policies, and he did not seem to have made any logical connection between domestic and foreign policy. Dogmatic belief that he had correctly read the tide of history induced a string of failures abroad, but these made little impression alongside the daily evidence he saw of his power within his own domain.

The major challenge to Kim Il Sung's strategic objective was a failing economic base. The only economic models that Kim had experienced were the war-making states of Japan in the 1930s and the Soviet Union in the early 1940s, and he saw little value in economic activity that did not boost the war-making potential of the state. His ignorance of, and hostility toward, the capitalist systems of the US, Japan, the ROK and Western Europe was deeply ingrained, and this led him to underestimate their power and resilience. Thus he could not perceive the extent to which the economy was being cannibalised by a military-industrial sector that now operated as an almost separate economy, accounting for nearly half the country's total industrial output.

Kim also remained committed to the fundamental proposition that the DPRK economy could be run from a single command post by means of mobilisation that continually stressed the primacy of ideology in economic development. Core features such as the Chollima Movement, the Chongsanri Method and the Taean Work Systems, along with assorted 'speed battles' and other Stakhanovite work practices were therefore frequently reaffirmed in resounding terms throughout the 1970s. Likewise, he continued to believe that the inability of the DPRK system to foster significant technological innovation, to generate adequate investment capital, and to achieve rational deployment of the work force were ideological and organisational problems, not economic problems arising from the demands of a more complex, industrialising economy.

Kim's political blind spots were equally significant. As a deep article of faith he attributed all power to the state and to its ruling party. The people had no part in the equation other than as followers of the vanguard party's 'correct' leadership. Kim was capable of making the DPRK polity fit this formula by the pervasive application of persuasion and coercion, but it was useless as a revolutionary stratagem when applied to South Korean society. The traditional DPRK image of the ROK as a US puppet, mired in mid-1950s poverty and degradation, remained a staple feature of propaganda, but it engendered unrealistic, dismissive assessments of ROK economic and military power which suggested that the North had committed the fatal error of starting to believe its own propaganda.

In fact, ROK society was developing in a direction vastly different from anything Kim had ever experienced. A vigorous and strong civil society whose collective memories of the Korean War sustained sometimes virulent anti-communism was emerging. Kim's analysis could account for neither the vigour of a nascent capitalist society nor the widespread rejection by the South Korean masses of communist ideology, and he therefore continued to base his reunification policy on the conviction that the overwhelming majority of South Korean people harboured a deep dislike for their government and were innately well-disposed to reunification under the banner of the North. In fact, while many South Koreans were dissatisfied with their government on any number of grounds, reunification policy was not one of these. Any appeal the model of the North might once have exerted in the South had almost entirely disappeared by 1980.

The things Kim had done well in the past he continued to do well, though only by the standards of that past, and so he ended the decade of the 1970s with the same set of core ideological positions with which he had started. He remained a virulent opponent of peaceful coexistence, a firm believer in the unchanging nature of capitalism, a resolute advocate of an unending anti-imperialist, anti-US struggle, and a critic of modern revisionism. In both rhetoric and actual policy measures he was as firmly committed as ever to the reunification of Korea under the KWP, and just as firmly convinced that the North would prevail. Economically, he remained committed to Equal Emphasis and to the efficacy of Stalinist mobilisation policies that essentially had not changed since the beginning of the Chollima Movement in 1958. Meanwhile, beyond the country's borders a vast process of modernisation continued to transform the Asia–Pacific region, increasingly condemning the DPRK to political and economic backwardness and sterility.

5

THE CONFIRMATION OF KIM JONG IL, 1980–83

After exercising considerable power for many years without public mention of his name, Kim Jong Il became a public figure when he was elected to a series of high Party positions at the Sixth Korean Workers' Party (KWP) Congress in October 1980. Following this unveiling, Party cadres began to make open reference to the younger Kim's role as his father's successor and the Party moved swiftly to confirm Kim Jong Il's authority as his father's chosen successor. In 1981 Kim Jong Il began to make on-the-spot guidance tours, as his father had done since the 1950s, and the son's personality cult flourished as the media reported these activities in the same extravagant language previously reserved for his father. The final steps consolidating the hereditary succession came in 1982. On 15 February, the day before his fortieth birthday, Kim Jong Il was awarded the title of Hero of the Democratic People's Republic of Korea. On 31 March he published *On the Juche Idea*, the first of a series of treatises that identified him as the definitive interpreter of his father's ideology. By 1983 he was publicly designated as the future leader of Party and state, and widely portrayed in the media as being endowed with the same personal and political genius-leader attributes as his father.

Internationally, the public emergence of the younger Kim caused widespread speculation that he would lead a younger generation of political leadership, less wedded to revolutionary violence and more pragmatic in orientation. However, Kim Jong Il's treatises carried a different message: although he belonged to a younger generation, he was not the product of any specific generation, but would serve as a model for all generations in his absorption of the revolutionary spirit of the Manchurian guerillas. This vision was both universal and timeless, and it became the younger Kim's role to symbolise the unwavering attachment of successive generations to it. Accordingly, his emergence signified no change to basic policies and strategies.

In 1980 Kim Il Sung would have had every reason to be pleased with the successful manner in which he engineered his son's rise. However, his pleasure would also have been tempered by evidence that the regime had sustained significant setbacks on the economic and diplomatic fronts. As the Second Seven-Year Plan (1978–84) progressed, there were signs that yet another Plan was faltering badly. This continuing poor economic performance was thrown into sharper relief by the high economic growth rates of the Republic of Korea (ROK). The military dimension was especially worrisome, for the DPRK could no longer expect its high levels of expenditure to produce a decisive superiority over the ROK armed forces. Instead, this high expenditure was now necessary simply in order to keep pace with both ROK defence production and the deployment of new, advanced US weaponry. The only countermeasure that offered a long-term prospect of halting a further deterioration in the DPRK's military position was the development of nuclear weapons. Accordingly, in 1980 the DPRK began construction of a 5 MW reactor fuelled with natural uranium and moderated with graphite. Plutonium produced from this reactor would stand at the heart of the US–DPRK nuclear stand-off in 1994.[1]

Meanwhile, the 'revolutionary situation' in the South began to look increasingly unfavourable. The assassination of Park Chung-hee in October 1979 produced a power vacuum, but after a short period of vigorous, open political life, the ROK military again took control when General Chun Doo-hwan seized power on 17 May 1980. An enforced calm again descended on ROK politics and, after a severe slump during 1979–80, the South's economy recovered and began to grow rapidly again. This economic strength translated into substantial diplomatic gains, best symbolised in November 1981 by the awarding of the 1988 Olympiad to Seoul.

Pyongyang briefly resumed inter-Korean contacts in February 1980 in order to test out the new political environment in the South, but in September unilaterally broke them off, thus indirectly confirming that once again it was dealing with a solid, cohesive adversary. In the period 1980–83 no new formula for dealing with the ROK emerged as the DPRK watched Chun Doo-hwan consolidate his hold on power. On the contrary, its terrorist bombing attack on Chun and his entourage in Rangoon in October 1983, which took the lives of four ROK Cabinet Ministers and thirteen other senior ROK officials, was consistent with past patterns of intransigence and violence.

The international outlook was also unpromising. The close relations with China that Pyongyang had maintained for most of the 1970s came under strong pressure in 1978–79 with the signing of the Sino–Japanese Peace and Friendship Treaty in September 1978, the full normalisation of US–Chinese relations in January 1979, and the China–Vietnam border conflict in February 1979. The new reality for the DPRK in the 1980s was therefore an emerging China–Japan–US triangle of common policy interests in the region generally and on the Korean Peninsula in particular. Kimist ideology dictated a resolute confrontation with US imperialism and Japanese militarism, and this basic strategy continued, affected neither by the enormous economic power which Japan had acquired nor by the increasingly stable, long-term US political and military commitment to Northeast Asia. Only with China was the perception of common need strong enough to absorb ever-growing differences of outlook on regional developments, and so in 1982 Pyongyang and Beijing succeeded in a establishing a new, pragmatic basis for relations.

The major DPRK strategic countermove to these regional developments was to begin a process of major rapprochement with the Soviet Union. The Soviets shared DPRK fears about the consequences of an emerging China–US–Japan axis, which it viewed as an anti-Soviet alliance on its eastern flank. The Soviets had long-standing disputes with China and Japan, and relations with the US had worsened steadily since the high-point of detente in the mid-1970s. In these circumstances the Soviets began to see the strategic advantages of a closer relationship with the DPRK, and by late 1983 the two sides had taken preliminary steps to increase levels of military and economic cooperation.

The DPRK faced these issues at precisely the time that the KWP party elite was entering old age. Kim Il Sung turned 68 in 1980, and the average age of the Politburo elected at the Sixth KWP Congress was 61.2.[2] It is debatable whether a younger, more vigorous Party elite could have tackled the country's problems more pragmatically and creatively, but in addition to age, this elite had survived by reason of its willingness to give unquestioning obedience to an overbearing leader who had repeatedly evinced little understanding of major international economic and political trends.

By 1982 the net effect of these trends appears to have had some impact on the thinking of the leadership. In October 1982 Kim Jong

Il departed briefly from the usually extravagant optimism of the DPRK's public rhetoric to describe the state of the nation in the following terms:

> Today our Party has entered a new stage of development. Our revolution is assuming a protracted and arduous nature and generations are changing among our revolutionary ranks. The internal and external situation of our revolution is strained and complicated. Realities raise the establishment of the monolithic ideological system of the Party as a still more important problem [*PT* 19 October 1982].

In the increasingly esoteric language of the leadership, the younger Kim was acknowledging the severity of recent setbacks and admitting that the Party was no longer likely to lead the country to reunification in the near future. At the same time, however, he was reaffirming that 'the monolithic ideological system of the Party', that is, the system of unconditional loyalty to teachings of Kim Il Sung by which the Party had functioned since 1967, would provide the remedy for the situation. This statement illuminates the paradox of the DPRK in the 1980s as few others do. While acknowledging that the tide of events was running against it, the younger Kim advanced a response drawn from the now distant past: the country should rely even more on the man who had led them to their current difficulties. The statement also foreshadowed that the country's deteriorating economic, military and diplomatic situation would be addressed from within existing ideological parameters. It is therefore not surprising to see in the DPRK after 1980 a chronic, almost pathological inability to change and adapt.

The Sixth KWP Congress convened in Pyongyang during 10–14 October 1980. As already noted, by now the major purpose of KWP congresses was to celebrate the leadership of Kim Il Sung. The chief significance of the congress therefore lay in Kim Il Sung's lengthy report on the work of the Party since the Fifth KWP Congress in 1970, and in the election of office bearers including Kim Jong Il. Kim Il Sung's speech was ebullient and self-congratulatory—as of course the occasion demanded.[3] In his introductory remarks Kim acknowledged that since 1970 'the international environment of our revolution was very complex and our Party was confronted with many difficult and serious revolutionary tasks'. However, these trials had again found his judgment infallible, for 'at every stage our Party correctly analysed and judged the situation, put forward well-founded [policies] and strove for their implementation'. He gave particular prominence to the pursuit of the three revolutions—ideological, technical and cultural—which had won for the Party 'a brilliant victory in the building of socialism'. As a result, the Six-Year Plan (1971–76) had been successful and the Second Seven-Year Plan (1978–84) had already achieved 'great success'. On reunification the DPRK had achieved 'great progress', and the people of South Korea had delivered a 'serious blow to the colonial fascist rule of the US imperialists and their stooges'. In the international sphere the Party had 'strengthened the international solidarity of our revolution and considerably expanded our country's international relations'.

The speech provided a strong reaffirmation of the mass mobilisation techniques of the early 1960s, with the Chollima Movement, Chongsanri Method and Taean Work Systems receiving specific re-endorsement. Kim identified the primary ideological task as 'hastening the complete victory of socialism through vigorous promotion of the ideological, technical and cultural revolutions', and reaffirmed the primacy of ideology, stating that 'only when priority is given to the ideological revolution to remould the thinking of the people and call forth their revolutionary enthusiasm can all problems of revolution and construction be solved successfully'. In this connection, he evaluated the 1970s in a positive light as a time when the Party 'further stepped up the struggle for implementing the line of the three revolutions' because 'following the achievement of socialist industrialization our Party and people were confronted with the urgent tasks of accelerating the revolutionization and working class-ization of the whole society'. The principal means of achieving this was by the Three Revolution Team movement, launched by Kim Jong Il in 1975. Kim assessed the movement, which had dispatched Red Guard-like teams of young Party workers to oversee economic activity throughout the country as effective, noting 'Experience shows that the movement is an effective method of revolutionary guidance for further organizing and activating the three revolutions to fit in with the new stage of socialist construction'.

On economic matters, Kim revealed no doubts or qualifications on the success of the DPRK economic model. As had been the case in public speeches on economic matters since the early 1960s, Kim gave an extended, sector-by-sector account of successes claimed under the current Second Seven-Year Plan (1978–84), but disclosed no verifiable statistics. In a ringing endorsement of traditional economic policy parameters, he reserved his chief criticism for 'the self-centred tendency manifested among economic officials' which he defined as 'a vanity of egoism and an expression of love of fame. Self-centred persons are fame-seekers who work for their personal honour and career. Party organizations must wage a major ideological battle against the self-centred tendency among economic officials, so that they work responsibly in the overall interests of the revolution from a firm Party and state standpoint'. With no further elaboration forthcoming, it seemed that Kim was levelling criticism at any tendency to pursue economic goals and production targets other than by the politics-first methods dictated by the Party. Thus the only demons identified at the Sixth KWP Congress had an inclination toward economic pragmatism.

The continuing attachment to command economics was also evident in the announcement of the Ten Long-Range Goals of Socialist Economic Construction for the 1980s. Since this was the first congress that did not mark the beginning of a multi-year plan period, Kim did not have to outline plan targets. Instead, his description of the shape of the DPRK economy in 1990 was couched in the traditional language of production targets in sectors such as electricity generation, coal, steel, nonferrous metals, cement, chemical fertiliser, textiles, aquaculture, grain, and land reclamation.

Another major theme was Kim's conviction of the continuing relevance of his Manchurian guerilla experience to the Party. In a section titled 'Let Us Strengthen Party Work', the key passage was:

> During the period under review an epochal change took place also in improving the method of party work. The conventional work method had persisted in our Party for a long time, obstructing the development of Party work. Through a vigorous struggle to improve its work method, our Party eradicated the outdated bureaucratic work method and fully restored the work method of the anti-Japanese guerillas. The application of the anti-Japanese-guerilla method to all aspects of Party work brought a new look to the Party and fundamentally changed its way of work. The whole Party vibrates with revolutionary spirit, and all work is done with a strong drive and vigour. This is our Party's look and its way of work today.

The 'epochal change' was an allusion to campaigns of the Three Revolution Teams, and by 'outdated bureaucratic work' Kim meant the work of the large Party bureaucracy that had come into existence with the KWP's rebirth as a Stalinist mass Party in the 1951–53 period. Kim, like Mao Zedong before him, had sanctioned the development of this bureaucracy as a requirement for exercising effective political control, but nevertheless grew increasingly alienated from it.[4] If the task of the Party bureaucracy was to be, as he often described it, 'the General Staff of the Korean revolution', then it needed to have restored to it the revolutionary vision of the anti-Japanese guerillas—highly disciplined, unquestioningly obedient to their leader, loyal, persevering, mentally and physically tough, improvisatory and disdainful of material comforts and rewards. By the mid-1970s Kim was thirty-five years removed from the Manchurian campaign, but nothing had shaken the profound hold this campaign still exercised on his psyche. For him it was a step of the utmost necessity to recreate this world for his countrymen by means of the Three Revolution Teams under the direction of his son.

Finally, Kim Il Sung's 1980 congress speech was noteworthy as an illustration of the emerging protocol of the hereditary succession. Although he assigned a central role to the Three Revolution Teams movements as a means of strengthening ideological control over economic activity and praised them at length, he made no direct references to his son who had led this movement. Nor in fact would he ever refer to Kim Jong Il in public speeches. It was left for others to sing the younger Kim's praises, and of course in the months that followed they did, filling in and elaborating fulsomely on what Kim Il Sung had merely adumbrated at the congress.

The election of office bearers at the congress was notable chiefly for the public emergence of Kim Jong Il, who became the fourth-ranking member of the Politburo, fourth-ranking member of a new five-member Politburo Presidium, second-ranking member of the Party Secretariat and third-ranking member of the Party's Military Commission.[5] Since there was no other discernible reason for holding what had become a rare event—this was the only congress that Kim Il Sung would call in the last twenty-four years of his life—the chief motive for convening the congress was to publicly confer high Party office on Kim Jong Il.

The younger Kim was essentially co-opted into the ranks of the guerilla generation by virtue of his unique background and training, and so in the years after the Sixth KWP Congress the Party presented the hereditary succession as a process by which the anti-Japanese guerilla revolutionary tradition passed as intact as human agency could devise to a younger generation. Long before the demise of the last of the guerilla generation, the Party would entrust leadership to someone who was deeply imbued with its letter and spirit and would not significantly depart it. At the time of the Sixth Congress the media did not elaborate on this theme, but a February 1982 statement is typical: 'Comrade Kim Jong Il is an outstanding leader of our Party who is skilfully leading the struggle of our Party and our people to complete the revolutionary cause started by the respected leader

Comrade Kim Il Sung'.[6] The Party stressed the younger Kim's close identity with the guerilla generation in various ways, beginning with accounts of his early life. Although he was born in 1942, by which time most objective accounts place his mother and father in the Soviet Union, his official birthplace was designated as a guerilla camp on the slopes of Mt Paekdu, in the far northeast of the country. His hagiographers describe his earliest experiences as follows:

> When Kim Jong Il was born in the camp of anti-Japanese guerilla fighters in the thick forests, he had no home. For him, who was born and brought up on a battlefield, gun reports and the 'March of the Guerillas' were a lullaby, and the summit of Mt Paekdu towering above the sea of clouds gave a deep impression to the young Kim Jong Il as a symbol of his fatherland. Bugle notes for an advance spreading over the thick and dark forests and over the snow-covered fields, the log cabin and the red flag in the cabin white with snow, the figure of his father, General Kim Il Sung, drawing arrows on an operation map while elaborating strategy and tactics for fatherland liberation, the cap and the bullet band of his unforgettable mother, Madame Kim Jong Suk—all these made a deep impression on his mind, and through these he felt his fatherland [Tak, Kim & Pak 1985:10].

The regime was careful and consistent in not identifying Kim Jong Il as a member of a specific, younger generation possessing specific characteristics apart from those of the guerilla generation. For example, at no stage in his grooming did the regime publicly associate him with the Party's youth organisation, the League of Socialist Working Youth (LSWY). Thus when the Seventh LSWY Congress opened on 20 October 1981, it was Kim Il Sung, not Kim Jong Il, who gave the keynote address, and he made no direct mention of the Three Revolution Teams' campaigns directed by his son, despite their obvious resonance for youth. The following year Kim Jong Il himself specifically refuted the idea of generational politics when he stated: 'Our party gave special attention to building up the backbone of the revolutionary forces. It strengthened the ranks of cadres *on the principle of combining old, middle-aged and young people*, regarding loyalty to the Party and the leader as the basic criterion' (*PT* 19 October 1982, [*italics added*]).

The co-opting of the younger Kim into the ranks of the guerilla was the co-opting of an individual, not a group, and much less a generation. It was not surprising, therefore, that the Sixth Congress did not elect any other cadres raised wholly in the post-1945 period to the Politburo. At age 38 Kim Jong Il was nine years younger than the second youngest member of the new Politburo, O Kuk-yol, who was himself the son of a Manchurian guerilla comrade of Kim Il Sung. This suggested Kim Il Sung's intention that the guerilla generation should rule as long as possible in order to instill its traditions in the minds of younger generations.

The new Politburo demonstrated the stability that was characteristic of Kim's personal autocracy. In contrast to the high attrition rate among Politburo members between the Fourth and Fifth Congresses, when only four of sixteen were re-elected, eight of the eleven full Politburo members elected at the Fifth Congress in 1970 retained their full membership in 1980 (see Table 5.1 below). Moreover, seventeen of the nineteen cadres elected to full membership of the Sixth Congress Politburo had already entered the Central Committee in 1970. Kim Jong Il and Kim Hwan were the only members who attained Central Committee ranking after 1970. Changes were

Table 5.1   List of Politburo full members elected at Fifth and Sixth KWP Congresses (in order of ranking)

The Fifth KWP Congress Politburo (1970)	The Sixth KWP Congress Politburo (1980)
1. Kim Il Sung	1. Kim Il Sung (age 69)
2. Ch'oe Yong-gon*	2. Kim Il (69)
3. Kim Il	3. O Chin-u (71)
4. Pak Song-ch'ol	4. Kim Jong Il## (40)
5. Ch'oe Hyon	5. Yi Chong-ok+ (67)
6. Kim Yong-ju**	6. Pak Song-ch'ol (69)
7. O Chin-u	7. Ch'oe Hyon (73)
8. Kim Tong-gyu**	8. Im Ch'un-ch'u+ (66)
9. So Ch'ol	9. So Ch'ol (74)
10. Kim Chung-nin	10. O Paek-yong# (73)
11. Han Ik-su**	11. Kim Chung-nin (57)
	12. Kim Yong-nam# (56)
	13. Chon Mun-sop# (64)
	14. Kim Hwan## (52)
	15. Yon Hyong-muk# (58)
	16. O Kuk-yol# (49)
	17. Kye Ung-t'ae# (58)
	18. Kang Song-san# (53)
	19. Paek Hak-nim# (63)

Notes: * died in office with state funeral during the 1970s; ** not appointed to the Sixth KWP Congress Politburo in 1980; # elected to the CC at the Fifth KWP Congress in 1970; ## entered the Central Committee after 1970; + dismissed from the Politburo in the mid-1960s, reappointed in the mid-1970s.

Sources: The Fifth KWP Congress Politburo as listed by Dae-Sook Suh (1981:329); the Sixth KWP Congress Politburo as carried in *PT* 15 October 1980. Ages as given in Dong-Bok Lee (1981a).

therefore minimal and the composition of the Party elite was characterised by stability—and the increasing onset of old age. The new Politburo consisted almost entirely of two elements—the surviving core of Kim Il Sung's prewar Manchurian guerilla group, into whose ranks Kim Jong Il had now been drafted, and a collection of individuals typically ten to fifteen years younger than the former guerillas with no known links to each other, but bound by ties of either blood, marriage or patronage to the older group. As senior Party officials in their fifties, members of this second group had typically spent their entire working lives in the DPRK, had endured the Korean War, and had survived earlier purges.

At the same time, Kim Il Sung's practice of maintaining a high turnover in the Central Committee continued, with 175 of the 248 Sixth KWP Congress Central Committee new appointees. No doubt many of them were of a younger generation, but this did not mean they possessed a distinct outlook and policy orientation. First, throughout this period the Party insistently proclaimed the virtues of what it called the Party's 'monolithic ideology', and was clearly serious in enforcing discipline on this matter—significant differences of outlook within the Party were unacceptable as both an affront to the Leader and a potential threat to the Kim Jong Il succession. Second, as outlined in Chapter 2, Central Committee membership status was held fleetingly by the vast majority of its incumbents, and did not necessarily lead to higher office. In fact, only two cadres elected to the Central Committee for the first time in 1980 became full Politburo members during the remaining fourteen years of the Kim Il Sung era.[7] Third, no modification to basic policies occurred under the new Central Committee, suggesting that the younger generation has either been highly supportive of the leadership or ineffective in advancing any alternative views.

A closer analysis of the Politburo emphasises the point that the guerilla group began the 1980s with an almost total monopoly on power within the Politburo.[8] Eight of the ten most senior ranking figures were ex-guerillas—Kim Il Sung, Kim Il, O Chin-u, Pak Song-ch'ol, Ch'oe Hyon, Yim Ch'un-ch'u, So Ch'ol, and O Paek-yong—while Kim Jong Il had also been co-opted into their group. The only exception was Yi Chong-ok, who was the incumbent premier and who had exercised key roles in the management of the economy since the 1950s. Of the remaining nine Politburo members two more were ex-guerillas—Chon Mun-sop and Paek Hak-nim—and KPA Chief of Staff O Kuk-yol was the son of a former guerilla comrade of Kim Il Sung. Two other members had extensive intelligence and espionage experience—Kim Chung-nin, who played a key role in the conduct of military and espionage operations against the ROK throughout the 1970s, and Kye Ung-t'ae, whose formal government title was Minister for Foreign Trade, but whose ability to survive in that position despite the disasters of the 1972–74 period had a lot to do with his role in assisting the younger Kim to exercise control over the multiple, overlapping DPRK intelligence and surveillance agencies.[9] This left a total of five 'civilians'. In addition to Yi Chong-ok, three others—Yon Hyong-muk, Kim Hwan, and Kang Song-san—had spent most of their careers involved in the management of various sectors of the economy, while Kim Yong-nam served a Gromyko-like role as the Party's long-standing manager of foreign policy.

Since 1968 (and probably for quite a few years before that) these cadres had tendered unquestioning loyalty to Kim Il Sung and, in the course of twenty years of enforcing the ideological parameters of the Party, had probably acquired some of the characteristics of specialisation associated with the processes of modernisation and industrialisation in the DPRK. But there is no evidence to suggest that Politburo members with particular responsibility for the economy such as Kim Hwan, Yon Hyong-muk, Kye Ung-t'ae or Kang Song-san were specialists or technocrats in the sense of individuals who possessed particular specialised knowledge of the fields in which they worked. Rather, as seen in previous chapters, since the Fourth KWP Congress in 1961 the primacy placed by Kim Il Sung on ideological struggle favoured the promotion of cadres from the party bureaucracy. These cadres were adept at applying Kimist ideology, rather than specialist expertise, to specific economic problems.

The military–security–intelligence sector was overwhelmingly present, but with the single exception of O Kuk-yol, what is often termed the second generation of the DPRK military—the generation that was a product of formal training in the first few years after 1945 at the Mangyongdae Military Academy—was not represented. The military men that Kim felt at home with did not come from officer training schools, but were the product of irregular or conspiratorial modes of warfare, and as they grew old and died or else were demoted from the Politburo during the 1980s and early 1990s, Kim did not replace them with younger officers who were the products of postwar regular military training.

The Sixth KWP Congress stopped short of making public reference to Kim Jong Il as his father's successor, but Party officials and the DPRK media made it clear in the immediate aftermath of the

congress that he would fill this role.¹⁰ With broad Party authority
confirmed, all that remained was to confirm his authority in ideological matters as the only person qualified to interpret the works of
Kim Il Sung. This was not long in coming.

In the period immediately following the Sixth Congress, the
DPRK media carried almost daily commentaries elaborating on Kim
Il Sung's report to the Sixth Congress. The original speech was
lengthy and detailed but now became subject to further sustained
exegesis. The role of Kim Jong Il in dispatching the Three Revolution
Teams received particular attention. Although the younger Kim's
name appeared at No. 4 in the KWP hierarchy, the national media
still avoided direct reference to his name, preferring the customary
term 'the glorious Party centre'. The following description of his role
during the 1970s is typical:

> Especially, after its Fifth Congress our Party launched a dynamic strug-
> gle for implementing the line of the three revolutions. Upholding the
> lofty intention of the great leader, the glorious Party centre dis-
> patched the Three Revolution Teams composed of Party hard-core
> elements and young intellectuals to various branches of the national
> economy to strengthen the guidance of the three revolutions . . .
> [*PT* 15 November 1980].

By the beginning of 1981, the common formulation was '. . . our
Party centre which puts into effect the grand plan and intention of
the great leader with exceptional organizational ability and ambitious
revolutionary sweep' (*PT* 8 January 1981).

The final stage of Kim Jong Il's public emergence as a person
endowed with the same personal and political attributes as his father
and capable of performing the same role began in August 1981. In
that month he made his first publicly reported on-the-spot guidance
tours—of the Pyongyang circus, an ice rink and 1000-seat restaurant
complex on the banks of the Botong River in Pyongyang, and the
People's Palace of Culture (*PT* 22 August 1981, 28 August 1981).
He then inspected Moranbong Stadium and the Korean Film Studio
in December (*PT* 26 December 1981). These inspection tours, which
were reported with the banner headlines and heavy typeset usually
reserved for his father's activities, replicated the on-the-spot guidance
tours frequently undertaken by his father. The younger Kim was also
reported as giving the same kind of detailed technical guidance as
his father did, evoking the quality of omniscience that underpinned
Kim Il Sung's personality cult. On the other hand, the older Kim
tended to visit sites of major economic importance such as steel mills,

state farms and major infrastructure projects, while the younger Kim visited sites connected with cultural and leisure pursuits. In addition, while the media often described his father's inspection tours in vigorous, even quasi-military language, it described the younger Kim's visits in counterpoint softer language, stressing a benevolent, caring nature.

These reports were part of a build-up to a series of major events in 1982, when Kim Jong Il turned forty and his father turned seventy. These began on 15 February 1982, the day before Kim Jong Il's fortieth birthday, with the award of the title of Hero of the Democratic People's Republic of Korea along with the Gold Star medal and the Order of National Flag First Class. Shortly afterwards two Kim Jong Il treatises were published: *On the Juche Idea*, in March 1982 and *The Workers' Party of Korea is a Juche-type Revolutionary Party Which Inherited the Glorious Tradition of the Down-with-Imperialism Union* [hereafter *The Workers' Party . . .*], in October 1982. When the collected works of Kim Jong Il were published several years later, they contained speeches and articles going back to 1963, but none of these earlier works had received mention in the media at the time. These two 1982 works, the first to receive widespread media acclamation at the time of their publication, established definitively Kim Jong Il's role as the only person capable of fully interpreting Kim Il Sung's Juche ideology and carrying forward the revolutionary cause. They are vital to understanding the role assigned to Kim Jong Il in the hereditary succession arrangement.

The extended laudatory descriptions of *On the Juche Idea* which began to appear during the course of 1982,[11] and regularly continued in the years that followed, presented it as an authoritative exegesis of the Juche idea. One early description marvelled at how it 'deals with comprehensively the origin of the Juche idea, its philosophical principle, socio-historical principles, guiding principle and historical significance', making 'a total exposition of the origin of the Juche idea and its components'. Its publication was 'an everlasting ideo-theoretical exploit which clarified like a beacon light important philosophical tasks that had not been raised or solved in the history of human thought and the pressing theoretical and practical problems of our age'.[12]

Meanwhile, *The Workers' Party . . .* took as its inspiration the fifty-sixth anniversary of the Down-with-Imperialism Union, a society allegedly founded by Kim Il Sung in 1926 at the age of fourteen. The work contained three sections, which dealt respectively with the history of the KWP, the present-day characteristics of the KWP and the tasks for the future. Most of the content was indistinguishable from the speeches and writings of Kim Il Sung over many years, though, unlike his son, Kim Il Sung could not devote paragraphs of fulsome praise to himself. The principal significance of the work lay in how Kim Jong Il described the tasks of the Party at a time when, as he put it, 'the revolution is assuming a protracted and arduous nature'. The careful organisation of this treatise and the role it played in systematising KWP ideological education in the 1980s can hardly be underestimated. Kim Jong Il began by setting a scene of unremitting struggle:

> Even after communist society is built, the struggle continues to abolish the old and create the new in various spheres of social life. Through this struggle society keeps developing . . . As long as capitalism and imperialism remain on the globe, even after communism is realized in one country or some regions, we cannot be free from the danger of aggression from outside enemies and the resistance of internal enemies hand in glove with the former [PT 19 October 1982].

Under these circumstances the machinations of hostile forces can only be countered under the leadership of the Party, and the Party can only perform its leadership task when it is imbued with the Juche idea. Therefore 'imbuing [the whole] Party with the Juche idea means, in essence, strengthening and developing our Party for ever [sic] into a party of Comrade Kim Il Sung'. Accordingly, the younger Kim offered an extended paean of praise to his father, outlining how Kim Il Sung had founded and developed the Party and brought it to its current stage. Here Kim Jong Il introduced the theme of generational change:

> We must make not only the present generation but also the generations to come hold the Great Leader Comrade Kim Il Sung's ideology and theory as the eternal guiding ideology and theory of the Party, stoutly defend his revolutionary exploits, struggle experience, revolutionary method of work and popular style of work and splendidly carry forward and complete the revolutionary cause of Juche . . . We can never be satisfied with the successes achieved in the struggle for the unity and cohesion of the Party. Our revolution is not yet over and we shall have to continue with an arduous struggle. As long as imperialism remains, opportunism survives, and the class struggle continues, we should unremittingly intensify the struggle for the Party's unity and cohesion [PT 19 October 1982].

The major problem for the Party was, of course, to ensure that succeeding generations saw things the same way. As noted previously, one solution was to counter firmly the notion that a succeeding generation possessed specific characteristics that might set it apart from the guerilla generation. Now Kim proposed two additional measures. First, Party life should be strengthened through active participation in ideological struggle movements. As he put it: 'This is all the more important in view of the fact that generations are changing within the Party ranks today. The Party can be succeeded dependably only when Party life is strengthened. This is because the Party ranks are constantly replenished as the days go by with new generations who are lacking in Party tempering'. Second, the Party needed to avoid bureaucratism. Again, in his own words: 'We should decisively put an end to the old work method and style . . . if a working class party fails to overcome bureaucratic and administrative tendencies, it will be disqualified from leading the revolution . . .' (*PT* 19 October 1982).

The significance of Kim Jong Il's two works lay both in their content and in the way they were used to consolidate his personality cult. They presented him as the resolute upholder of the traditions of the guerilla generation and as the codifier who followed and consolidated the work of the genius-founder of the system. Some eighteen months after Kim Jong Il had emerged at the Sixth KWP Congress, and less than a year after he had begun a series of on-the-spot tours, the publication of the two works completed the process of associating him with the key attributes of his father: formal political authority, authority to give definitive guidance in all areas of the national life, and the spiritual aura of one who had mastered the ideology that validated that authority.

In a system that gave such primacy to ideological work, the assumption of this aura essentially completed the process of the younger Kim's emergence. The treatises were widely hailed and became the subject of intensive study. A typical passage described *The Workers' Party* . . . . as 'a precious fruition of the outstanding ideological, theoretical and practical activities of the dear leader Comrade Kim Jong Il who has wisely directed our Party with his extraordinary intelligence and leadership ability from his early age' (*PT* 30 October 1982).

Throughout the 1980s and beyond, overseas observers depicted the younger Kim in a number of stock and, frequently, misleading images. The more optimistic portrayed him as the harbinger of a new, technocratically oriented elite, fuelling hopes for the emergence of a more pragmatic outlook in Pyongyang, while more pessimistic assessments described him as an erratic, unstable personality inclined to more radical policies including the use of terror as he sought to emerge from beneath the shadow of a dominant father. Neither portrait is convincing or based on solid evidence. The overwhelming evidence of Kim's writings shows that he was anything but pragmatically-oriented. He continually insisted on the subservience of technology to ideology in much the same way as his father. Furthermore, no cadres of his generation—technocrats or otherwise—gained entry to the Party Politburo in his wake. There has also been consistent speculation on Kim's mental stability, often the result of second-hand lurid tales of a dissipated lifestyle. Here we may simply observe that DPRK leaders may often behave in a manner that does not seem 'rational' by external standards, but no convincing evidence has ever emerged of emotional or psychological instability, as opposed to mere eccentricity, on Kim Jong Il's part. Most significantly, there has never been evidence of erratic or capricious action in significant policy areas such as negotiations with the US on nuclear issues in the 1990s when Kim Jong Il was known to be involved.

Speculation continued throughout this period on resistance from unnamed members of the party elite to Kim Jong Il's succession. Commentators outside Korea speculated that the younger Kim's lack of military or governmental status to match his Party status was due to residual opposition to his succession, but this is unconvincing. Not only do we have no credible evidence of any member of the Party elite suffering demotion or purging for resisting the younger Kim's rise after 1980, but it is inconceivable that Kim Il Sung would have tolerated such opposition. Moreover, although the younger Kim did not begin to receive military titles until the eve of his fiftieth birthday in 1992 and did not receive any state titles before his father's death, there was no immediate need for him to assume these posts in the early 1980s. With particular regard to a government post such as a Vice Presidency (his father was State President), we have already noted in Chapter 2 the limited significance of governmental positions in a Leninist party state. If Kim Jong Il were to have become a Vice President this would merely place him on a par with a number of elderly, semi-retired cadres who no longer held any significant Party positions and who engaged in mainly ceremonial functions—hardly an appropriate office for a future leader. It is not clear what his opponents would have gained by blocking his accession to an insignificant, largely ceremonial government post.

While the DPRK remained absorbed in these ideological matters, the economic stagnation which had set in during the 1970s continued to deteriorate. This period was marked by a greater than usual reluctance to release statistics, an uneven pattern of foreign trade, and poor foreign debt management. Although concealing data on actual economic performance under an avalanche of stirring revolutionary rhetoric had been a staple of public commentary on economic matters since the early 1960s, in the early 1980s the DPRK established new benchmarks for concealment by withholding both the growth rate in total industrial output for 1981 and 1983, and the grain production figure for 1983.

Economic stagnation was reflected in the DPRK's two-way foreign trade, which declined by 38.4 per cent in the period 1980–83, from US$3.6 billion to US$2.9 billion (see Table 5.2 below). The balance of trade grew especially unfavourable during this period. The DPRK has suffered from chronic trade deficits throughout its existence, but in the early 1980s these deficits increased substantially. Analysis of the commodity composition of DPRK foreign trade during 1970–82 reveals a lack of structural change which reflects the lack of progress in industrialisation during the Six-Year Plan (1971–76) and the Second Seven-Year Plan (1978–84). This situation became more pronounced in the early 1980s as the DPRK continued to rely on fewer and fewer export commodities to earn the foreign exchange needed to pay for an increasingly wider assortment of imports (Joseph Chung 1987:130). This trend underlay the steadily worsening balance of payments situation at this time.

The average deficit for the four-year period 1980–83 of US$355 million compared with an average deficit for the four-year period 1976–79 of US$106.1 million.[13] In addition, severe fluctuations in trade with China, the Soviet Union and Japan occurred (see Tables 5.3, 5.4 and 5.5 below). The 1980s began with the impetus of a five-year trade agreement signed with the Soviet Union in 1981 and a similar agreement signed with China in 1982. These agreements produced a stronger trade performance in 1982 as bilateral trade recovered from a severe downturn in trade that had accompanied the DPRK's recent political problems with both countries. Trade with both China and the Soviet Union increased in 1982 after a decline in 1981. Total DPRK foreign trade rose 10.6 per cent in 1982.

However, by 1983 the immediate stimulus from a resumption of cordial ties with Pyongyang's two neighbours had exhausted itself, and the DPRK suffered a record trade deficit of US$551.2 million. In the case of China, exports fell by 9.3 per cent in 1983 despite cordial political relations and a new five-year trade agreement. Together with the withholding of basic economic data, these trade figures suggested poor DPRK performance over a range of the sectors

121

Table 5.2   DPRK foreign trade 1980–84 (unit: US$ million)

Year	Imports	Exports	Balance	Total	% increase
1980	1851.1	1694.5	−156.6	3545.6	20.6
1981	1532.0	1099.7	−432.3	2631.7	−25.8
1982	1596.3	1314.0	−282.3	2910.3	10.6
1983	1367.9	816.7	−551.2	2184.6	−24.9
1984	1313.0	1194.4	−118.6	2507.4	14.8

Source: Bon-Hak Koo (1992:160, 185). Adjustment made to correct mathematical error.

responsible for extracting, processing and transporting the DPRK's chief export commodities.[14] The substantial increase in the trade deficit also provided a strong rationale for reform in the area of foreign trade.

By the end of 1982 the DPRK also showed signs that it was experiencing difficulty in meeting its debt repayment obligations. It rescheduled its Western European debts in March 1980, but again rapidly fell behind on interest repayments. Concerning its Japanese debt, in the period 1979–82 the DPRK repaid ¥43.1 billion, but in 1982 it again sought rescheduling of principal payments due in December 1982. In February 1983 Japan agreed to DPRK repayment in six instalments between June 1986 and December 1989 (Kawai 1983:18).

Despite these growing difficulties, Kim Il Sung's re-endorsement of the Chollima Movement, Chongsanri Method and Taean Work Systems at the Sixth KWP Congress indicated that the DPRK econ-

Table 5.3   DPRK Trade with USSR 1980–83 (unit: US$ million)

Year	Total	Balance	% total	% increase
1980	925.4	−50.0	26.1	17.4
1981	774.4	−78.6	29.4	−16.3
1982	983.8	16.8	33.8	27.0
1983	788.3	83.9	36.1	−9.9

Source: Bon-Hak Koo (1992:160, 185). Adjustment made to correct mathematical error.

Table 5.4   DPRK Trade with China 1980–83 (unit: US$ million)

Year	Total	Balance	% total	% increase
1980	687.3	−135.9	19.4	5.9
1981	540.4	119.4	20.5	−21.4
1982	586.1	−32.9	20.1	8.5
1983	531.8	−69.6	24.3	−9.3

Source: Bon-Hak Koo (1992:188).

Table 5.5 DPRK trade with Japan 1980–83 (Unit: US$ million)

Year	Total	Balance	% total	% increase
1980	579.1	−248.9	16.3	29.6
1981	446.2	−192.2	17.0	−22.9
1982	481.6	−207.4	16.5	7.9
1983	475.9	−244.3	21.8	−1.1

Source: Bon-Hak Koo (1992:188).

omy would continue to operate under traditional ideological parameters. The accession of Kim Jong Il served to reinforce these
parameters, for his 1982 treatises stressed the ideology-first nature of
economic activity, chiefly by reference to the Three Revolution Team
movement. Moreover, the younger Kim imposed a further burden on
the economy in the form of the diversion of economic resources to
massive, prestige construction projects, which became sites for his
on-the-spot guidance tours beginning in 1981. These projects
included the Juche Tower, the Arch of Triumph, a string of sports
facilities including the Moranbong Stadium with a reported capacity
of 150 000 people, and numerous tourist hotels for the practically
nonexistent tourist industry.

Meanwhile, inter-Korean relations remained at a stalemate during
the period 1980–83. In the wake of the assassination of Park Chung-
hee, the ROK government acknowledged that the harsher features
of Park's Yushin system had died with Park, and adopted policies of
reconciliation such as the appointment of a liberal, civilian-domi-
nated Cabinet, the wholesale release of political prisoners and the
removal of civil rights restrictions on such political leaders as Kim
Young Sam and Kim Dae Jung. As a period of open, active politicking
ensued, this series of developments presented the DPRK with the
prospect of negotiating with an adversary under considerable domestic pressure, and so it proposed a resumption of the talks that had
been suspended in 1975. In proposing the talks, the importance that
the DPRK attached to this strategic opening was reflected in its
calling the ROK by its official name, The Republic of Korea, for the
first time, a gesture which the ROK reciprocated.

Pyongyang's initiative led to a series of preliminary talks from
February–August 1980 with the objective of laying the groundwork
for prime ministerial talks.[15] However, in May 1980 General Chun
Doo-hwan re-established military control over the ROK government.
By August 1980 the influence of liberal civilians in the ROK Gov-
ernment had again been marginalised, the civil rights of all leading

opposition politicians suspended, and Kim Dae Jung was awaiting trial on the capital charge of sedition. From the DPRK's point of view, the further pursuit of talks with an increasingly well-entrenched Chun Doo-hwan was counterproductive. Pyongyang could no longer effectively exploit political divisions within the ROK, while further negotiation would play into Chun's hands by implying DPRK acceptance of Chun as a legitimate negotiating partner. Therefore, almost immediately after Chun's inauguration as interim President on 1 September 1980, the DPRK signalled its conclusion that further dialogue was futile, first by resuming hostile loudspeaker broadcasts against the South along the DMZ (suspended since 1972), and then by withdrawing unilaterally from the preliminary talks process on 24 September.

Chun's consolidation of power and Pyongyang's withdrawal from talks provided the background for Kim Il Sung's elucidation of the DPRK's reunification policy in his report to the Sixth KWP Congress some three weeks later. Accordingly, Kim broke little new ground and was forthright in maintaining that the removal of the current rulers in the ROK was an essential precondition to progress.[16] If the rulers were unacceptable, however, the 'ideas and social system' of the South were acceptable in the context of a one-state–two-governments formula for a Confederal Republic. This would be achieved through 'the establishment of a unified national government on condition that the north and the south recognize and tolerate each other's ideas and social systems . . .'. Kim went on to describe in detail the characteristics of the proposed Confederal Republic including non-alignment, opposition to foreign forces, democratisation, freedom of speech, organisation and assembly. He also gave examples of joint activities between its two governments, including economic cooperation and exchange, joint exploitation of natural resources, scientific, cultural and education exchanges.

At various stages in the past, most notably in 1960 and 1973, Kim had raised the concept of a Confederal Republic as a possible interim measure for the two Koreas pending final reunification. In his report to the Sixth KWP Congress, however, he appeared to present the concept not as an interim measure but as the final form of a reunified Korea.[17] Through DPRK official pronouncements it is not possible to determine why this shift took place and what its significance was, but on the surface, the shift from confederation as interim step to confederation as final form seemed calculated to make the proposal more attractive. However, since Kim's speech was prefaced with explicit rejection of the Chun regime, it may best be described as a policy statement aimed past, not at, the ROK government, and underlined the DPRK's belief that talks would not achieve progress toward their objectives at this stage. This policy of eschewing contact with the Chun regime continued with a brusque rejection of Chun Doo-hwan's 12 January 1981 proposal that he and Kim Il Sung exchange visits in order to establish a greater degree of mutual trust and possibly a resumption of dialogue.[18]

The depth of DPRK commitment to preventing Chun Doo-hwan from becoming as entrenched in power as Park Chung-hee became clear on 9 October 1983 when DPRK commandos detonated a bomb that killed seventeen senior ROK officials, including four Cabinet ministers, at the beginning of an official ceremony at the Martyrs Mausoleum in Rangoon. The officials were accompanying Chun on the first leg of a tour of South East Asian nations and Australia. Chun, the intended victim of the bomb, escaped injury because the DPRK commando group evidently detonated the bomb prematurely. After an official investigation, on 4 November the Burmese authorities pronounced themselves satisfied that the DPRK was responsible for the bombing. The Burmese government then expelled the DPRK's Rangoon mission and withdrew diplomatic recognition of the DPRK.[19] Despite DPRK protestations that the ROK and the US were themselves the guilty party, the international community found the evidence of DPRK complicity convincing. In particular, China made it clear that it accepted evidence of DPRK guilt by publicising the Burmese government's findings.

There can be little doubt that the Rangoon operation was carefully planned at the highest level in Pyongyang with the intention of creating an atmosphere of fear, confusion and demoralisation in Seoul. In 1983 the DPRK was under the same leadership and publicly committed to the same set of policies that had led to similar acts against the ROK in the past, such as the commando raid on the Blue House in 1968. Moreover, Kim Il Sung had a world view of deep, permanent and desperate struggle between the Party and its enemies. He continued to glorify the guerilla tradition with its modes of irregular warfare and terrorism and had already shown a profound lack of judgment in international affairs in such areas of state policy as foreign trade management and relations with the Non-Aligned Movement. Kim was explicitly committed to a view that the ROK leadership was unrepresentative and that it played a major role in the suppression of progressive social forces in the South. In his view, the removal of Chun and many of his advisers would constitute a major step toward unleashing the revolutionary potential in ROK society while also going some of the way toward slowing the rate at which the ROK was now outperforming the DPRK economically and diplomatically.

Elsewhere, the DPRK's foreign relations were dominated by China and Russia. Relations with China deteriorated sharply in the immediate aftermath of the signing of major Sino–Japanese and Sino–American accords in 1978–79 and the Sino–Vietnamese border conflict in February 1979, but in late 1981 both China and the DPRK took steps to place relations on a pragmatic footing. Although Kim may have longed for a return to radical policies in China, there was little point in taking issue with the pragmatic economic policies emerging under Deng Xiaoping. Therefore, the DPRK accepted rapprochement with Beijing and the material advantages that came with it. A series of high-level visits took place, including a visit by Premier Zhao Ziyang to Pyongyang in December 1981, an unpublicised visit to Pyongyang by Hu Yaobang and Deng Xiaoping together in April 1982, and an official visit to China by Kim Il Sung during 16–26 September 1982.[20] There was a significant increase in the exchange of high-level delegations in 1983, and the unpublicised visit of Kim Jong Il to China during 2–12 June 1983—his first official foreign visit—was a highlight of this process.[21] These visits set the seal on a process of rapid rapprochement in which the two sides agreed to disagree on the nature of the US presence in the region and on their respective domestic economic policies.[22]

For the Chinese it was desirable to maintain DPRK goodwill and, as far as possible, to bring Kim Il Sung around to their outlook on the international situation and on the type of outward-looking economic policies they felt were appropriate to this outlook. In pursuit of this, the Chinese made a series of tangible gestures. They increased oil exports to the DPRK at the discounted 'friendship' price, they made Chinese-built MIG–21As available to the DPRK Air Force, they scaled down their growing indirect trade with the ROK and they adopted tougher rhetoric in support of the DPRK stand on reunification.[23] This level of Chinese support was useful to the DPRK, given its increasingly threatening geopolitical environment.

The major foreign policy development for the DPRK in the early 1980s was rapprochement with the Soviet Union. This made sense since both parties had much to fear from the emerging Japan–China–US axis in the region. The Soviets faced an emerging anti-Soviet entente on their eastern flank, spearheaded by three major powers with whom they had profound and seemingly intractable disputes.[24] They had long regarded Japan with a mixture of suspicion and antipathy, feelings reinforced by nearly three decades of dispute over the future of the Kurile Islands. Soviet failure to counteract growing Sino–Japanese cooperation was evident in the 1978 Sino–Japanese Treaty where a clause expressing mutual opposition to 'hegemonism', a code word for Soviet influence, had been inserted at China's insistence. Meanwhile, in China the legacy of the Sino–Soviet split was still strong and, after a brief thaw in relations during 1982, relations again became strained in the face of continued disagreement on the 'three obstacles'—Afghanistan, Cambodia and troop levels on the Sino–Soviet border (Kelley 1987:96; Ha 1983:220–1). After the high point of detente in the early 1970s, US–Soviet relations deteriorated during the Carter Administration (1976–80), especially after the Soviet invasion of Afghanistan in 1979. The Reagan Administration's deployment of significant new weaponry in the Northeast Asian region including cruise missiles and F–16 fighters (Zagoria 1986b:349), and the Soviet shooting down of a ROK civilian airliner, KAL Flight 007, in August 1983 further raised tension.

These developments set the stage for the major revival of the Soviet–DPRK relations. Despite the DPRK's international reputation, the Soviets saw significant military advantages in seeking closer ties. Moscow could bring greater pressure to bear on China's east flank, and the Soviets may also have calculated that they could help redress a growing military imbalance between the two Koreas. This would promote an indefinite stand-off which would pin down the US forces in Korea. Similarly, the Soviets could buttress their presence in the Sea of Japan if they gained access to ports on the DPRK's east coast. The DPRK's perception of the advantages of closer ties with the Soviet Union was no less compelling. It was experiencing increasing diplomatic, economic and military pressure in its competition with the ROK, and the continuing US military build-up in the Northeast Asian region was a major concern, particularly as this was reflected in the steady expansion of the annual US–ROK Team Spirit joint military exercises. These exercises began in 1978, and in 1981 expanded to a two-month exercise, mobilising a total of 161 500 troops (Koh 1984a:88–93). The DPRK made annual protests about these exercises but, judging from its official media, it was in February 1983 that Pyongyang began to display strong signs of alarm at Team Spirit.

The first steps toward a closer Soviet–DPRK relationship in the early 1980s were tentative, perhaps because the two countries had a history of twenty years' strained relations to overcome. The Soviets saw the DPRK as far closer to Beijing than Moscow on major ideological issues, and they still viewed Kim Il Sung as an unpredictable ally who was likely to involve it in unwanted crises. On the DPRK side, in 1982 Pyongyang was still reprinting Chinese articles accusing the Soviet Union of 'dominationism' (Zhebin 1995:727) and consolidating ties with China. In addition, the DPRK was irritated by a series of limited, low-key, but unprecedented gestures by Moscow toward the ROK in 1982. In September 1982 the former *Tass* chief correspondent in Japan and a director of the Cultural Preservation Bureau of the Soviet Ministry of Culture both sought and were granted entry visas to attend international meetings in Seoul, a gesture aimed at reminding the DPRK that Moscow was both prepared to, and capable of, advancing the international standing of the ROK at the DPRK's expense.[25] These actions brought forth a strong protest from the DPRK.

There were two major turning points in Soviet–DPRK rapprochement. The first came with the accession of Yuri Andropov as Soviet leader after the death of Leonid Brezhnev in November 1982, and the second came with the Soviet shooting down of KAL Flight 007 on 1 September 1983. Whether Brezhnev was naturally more cautious as a result of long experience in dealing with Kim, or whether it fell to Andropov to take actual concrete measures to counter recent unfavourable trends in the region, Soviet inclination to strengthen ties with the DPRK took shape during 1983 after Andropov's succession. The KAL incident and the strength of the international reaction to it was especially influential in exacerbating Soviet fears of a hostile and deteriorating security situation in Northeast Asia. In the aftermath, the Soviets cancelled plans to attend an Inter-Parliamentary Union meeting in Seoul in September 1983, and sent a high-ranking delegation to Pyongyang for the thirty-fifth anniversary of the founding of the DPRK.[26] In October the Soviets proved especially supportive of the DPRK in the aftermath of the Rangoon bombing, publishing only the DPRK version of events. This contrasted with the Chinese, who published the Burmese government's version, and also contrasted with Moscow's stand on a previous, comparable occasion, the 1976 Panmunjom axe killings, when it publicly criticised the DPRK. These displays of warmth and solidarity continued over into early 1984 when, for the first time, a senior Soviet official and Asian specialist, Deputy Foreign Minister Mikhail Kapitsa, attended a 16 February DPRK Embassy reception in Moscow to mark the birthday of Kim Jong Il. The death of Yuri Andropov later that month also afforded the opportunity for further tributes to the warmth in relations that had developed under his administration.[27]

In February–March 1984 the Soviets resolved their lingering doubts about the wisdom of engaging the DPRK in a major new relationship and gave final approval for Kim Il Sung to visit the Soviet Union and Eastern Europe in May–June 1984.[28] The understandings and formal agreements that flowed from this visit constituted a significant upgrade of relations, and from mid-1984 until 1988 Soviet–DPRK relations achieved a warmth and depth unseen since the Korean War. As we shall see, the economic and military benefits that flowed from this relationship significantly influenced DPRK thinking on ways and means to address its growing economic difficulties.

Meanwhile, the high-water mark of support for DPRK policies within the Non-Aligned Movement passed in 1981 when at the Seventh NAM Conference of Foreign Ministers held in New Delhi, India, the DPRK was unsuccessful in its efforts to place the Korean question on the conference agenda (Koh 1984a:221). Previous NAM Heads of State summits and Foreign Ministers' meetings had regularly passed pro-DPRK resolutions. The declining level of NAM support for DPRK policies was further confirmed in June 1982 when a meeting in Havana of the foreign ministers of the Coordinating Committee of Non-Aligned Countries declined to support a DPRK-sponsored resolution calling for the withdrawal of US troops from Korea and the dissolution of the UN Command. The awarding of the 1986 Asian Games and 1988 Olympics Games to Seoul, and the disappearance of pro-DPRK resolutions from NAM agendas during a seventeen-month time-span from February 1981 to June 1982 marked significant diplomatic gains for the ROK outside the orbit of its traditional Western allies and, consequently, marked a significant setback for the DPRK in its international rivalry with the ROK.

By the early 1980s the Stalinist–Maoist doctrine that a modern economy could be built by an isolated and highly regimented population, devoted primarily to military production and hero-worship, was not only outmoded but had been set aside in the Soviet Union and China. In the DPRK, however, Kim lived on in isolation as an activist, interventionist ruler, and so the doctrine remained intact. Accordingly, he maintained a clear priority of ideology over economic development. Domestically, the economy had reached its limits and could not increase output without significant changes to long-standing policies. Abroad, the continuing economic rise of the ROK meant that, barring a sudden collapse in the South, the North would have to bear the economic burden of maintaining high levels of military production and preparedness indefinitely, and the DPRK state did not have the means to do this. Moreover, the changes in Chinese domestic and foreign policy in the late 1970s and early 1980s had profound and far-reaching consequences for Pyongyang, for without a major power also committed to the anti-imperialist struggle, DPRK policies had no realistic prospect of success.

Obsessive pursuit of reunification blinded Kim to many things, but it was especially in the international sphere, where the growing international prestige of the ROK and changing priorities in Chinese foreign policy were eroding the DPRK's diplomatic position, that his limitations continued to be exposed. Fixed, doctrinaire assessments of the international situation prevented the DPRK from adjusting to change in the region. It was not Kim Il Sung's intention to secure the growing diplomatic isolation of his country, but this was the result of an approach that equated diplomacy with pursuit of the anti-US, anti-imperialist struggle and which equated gains in DPRK security with the increased insecurity of a wide range of adversaries. Kim's gross over-assessment of the political significance of the Non-Aligned Movement likewise issued from a belief in the primacy of politics over economics, while the cavalier fashion in which the country treated its foreign debt issued from a cynical, predatory approach to international dealings. The repeated involvement of DPRK diplomats in smuggling and other nefarious activities, intermittent support for international terrorism and, of course, the Rangoon bombing itself underlined the primitive expediency that increasingly drove DPRK foreign policy.

The rise of Kim Jong Il accelerated the DPRK's decline. Far from symbolising the rise of a new generation of technocratically–minded cadres oriented toward pragmatic policies, the younger Kim himself emphasised that his role was to ensure that the Party safeguarded the revolutionary tradition of the anti-Japanese guerillas. The Kim Jong Il succession was his father's means of guaranteeing that such traditional parameters as command economics, mass mobilisation, profound militarism, and uncompromising confrontation with the ROK and the US would guide future policy.

6

SIGNS OF REFORM, 1984–86?

In late 1983 the Democratic People's Republic of Korea (DPRK) adopted a number of measures aimed at countering the economic and diplomatic reversals of the early 1980s. As the Second Seven-Year Plan (1978–84) drew to an unsatisfactory conclusion, the Party adopted a more liberal attitude to foreign trade and investment, culminating in the promulgation of a Joint Venture Law in September 1984. In a related move, it also placed a greater emphasis on production in the light industry sector. In the inter-Korea dialogue, a DPRK proposal for tripartite talks involving the two Koreas and the US in January 1984 seemed to herald a moderation in the long-standing refusal of the DPRK to recognise the existence of the ROK. During 1984, the two Koreas also initiated talks on sporting, economic, parliamentary and humanitarian cooperation. A DPRK shipment of flood relief goods to the South in September 1984 and the first-ever exchange of home visits between the two Koreas in August 1985 marked the high points of a process that seemed to herald a breakthrough in negotiations. Also beginning in 1984, the DPRK carried through a major process of rapprochement with the Soviet Union, restoring bilateral relations to a level of closeness and agreement unseen since the late 1940s. Kim Il Sung's 45-day tour of the Soviet Union and Eastern Europe in May–June 1984, his first official visit to the Soviet Union since 1961, brought about increased cooperation, especially in the economic and military sphere.

To a number of outside observers it seemed logical for the DPRK to take measures to address both recent economic and diplomatic setbacks and more fundamental issues of reform. This was, after all, the course that China had recently adopted with some success. Observers also saw these changes as the result of a 'generational change' in politics, whereby younger, pragmatic men with technocratic backgrounds and close links to Kim Jong Il had been promoted into key positions formerly filled by the aging guerilla generation. However, this perception of pragmatic change flowed from a misperception of the nature and extent of personnel changes at senior levels of the Party and government during the period 1982–85. As we shall see, these changes were confined almost entirely to the relatively powerless governmental sphere, and left the Politburo almost untouched.

In fact, DPRK state policies displayed a noteworthy consistency with past practice throughout this period. Political developments did not follow from a conscious process of 'generational change' in the political leadership, nor from significant modifications to traditional policies. Rather, they followed from tactical shifts within long-established ideological parameters for the pursuit of a stable set of long-term goals—the building of socialism in the North and the reunification of Korea under the leadership of the Korean Workers' Party (KWP). In domestic economic policy the DPRK considered the adoption of measures based on Chinese experience to enhance foreign trade performance, but it quickly abandoned them as closer ties with the Soviet Union opened up alternative economic opportunities which entailed less contact with capitalist economies and minimal ideological impact on existing economic policy.

Similarly, in the inter-Korean talks process, the DPRK negotiated for tactical advantage in pursuit of traditional objectives. The tripartite talks proposal broke no new ground and seemed designed to distract attention from the Rangoon bombing three months earlier. Likewise, the various dialogues with the South did not involve senior Party cadres and did not produce any breakthrough. Just as the high point of the August 1985 home visits exchange was reached, momentum disappeared, and at the end of 1985 the inter-Korean dialogue re-entered an extended period of stalemate.

There were three signs of Party reaction to the Rangoon operation at the Eighth Plenum of the Sixth KWP Central Committee (CC) convened in Pyongyang during 29 November–1 December 1983: the demotion from full to alternate Politburo membership of Kim Chung-nin, a wide-ranging reshuffle of DPRK ambassadors, and the promotion from alternate to full Politburo membership of Foreign Minister Ho Tam. Kim Chung-nin had had a long involvement in espionage and terrorist operations abroad as head of the KWP's Reunification Front Bureau, which carried responsibility for anti-Republic of Korea (ROK) operations in foreign countries. His demotion was consistent with a reaction to the failure of the mission. The diplomatic reshuffle was almost certainly a face-saving measure related to the Rangoon operation, since appointing new ambassadors to many of the DPRK's posts would relieve the pressure on the incumbent ambassadors to explain and defend their country's action. It also suggested Pyongyang's desire to put Rangoon into the background.

The promotion of Ho (then 56 years old), a deputy premier who had held the post of Foreign Minister since 1973, entailed a rise from No. 19 to No. 10 in Party ranking. Upon receiving this promotion he was replaced as Foreign Minister by an older cadre, Kim Yong-nam (then 60 years old), a full Politburo member. Kim Yong-nam had been in charge of foreign policy matters at the Party level for the previous ten years as chairman of the KWP's International Committee. Ho remained a deputy premier, and in January became the ailing Kim Il's successor as chairman of the Committee for the Peaceful Reunification of the Fatherland (CPRF), the umbrella organisation that oversaw the DPRK's united front strategy for reunification. This minimal response to Rangoon was, of course, to be expected since it would have made little sense for the DPRK to protest its innocence abroad and then publicly designate scapegoats.[1]

Apart from these moves, the substance of the Eighth Plenum was not political, but economic. The plenum heard reports on a strategy for improving performance in the light-industry sector, and especially in foreign trade, where the trade deficit had widened substantially in the early 1980s. In anticipation of action at the governmental level, the Party promoted three cadres with economic management experience, Kim Pok-sin, An Sung-hak and Hong Song-yong as alternate Politburo members. The ramifications of the Eighth Plenum for government soon became clear. The third session of the Seventh Supreme People's Assembly (SPA) was called into session in Pyongyang during 25-7 January 1984, three months prior to the usual April sitting. The timing reflected the need for early SPA ratification of the decision of the Central People's Committee (CPC) and the SPA Standing Committee at a joint sitting on 10 January to officially propose tripartite talks with the US and 'the south Korean authorities' (see page 146), but the sitting also passed a resolution titled 'On strengthening South–South cooperation and external economic relations and further developing foreign trade' which established a set of general principles for the conduct of foreign trade.

The January 1984 SPA sitting also attended to such routine governmental business as approving the 1984 State Budget and personnel changes. First Deputy Premier Kang Song-san replaced Yi Chong-ok as Prime Minister and three new deputy premiers were added to the Administration Council: Cho Se-ung, Kim Pok-sin, who was concurrently Chairman of the Light Industry Commission, and Kim Chang-ju, who was concurrently Chairman of the Agricultural Commission. Former Prime Minister Yi Chong-ok was appointed to a largely ceremonial position as the country's third Vice President, alongside the elderly duo Pak Song-ch'ol and Im Ch'un-ch'u. This did not affect his Politburo ranking. Like Kong Chin-t'ae and Kye Ung-t'ae, who likewise retained their Politburo ranking after presiding over economic disasters in the 1970s, Yi had overseen the implementation of the largely unsuccessful Second Seven-Year Plan (1978–84), but did not suffer demotion, presumably because he had always acted within the ideological parameters set down by Kim Il Sung. But now, as the economy entered an inter-plan period of economic stabilisation, it made sense to effect a change at the top. Kang Song-san was a relatively younger man aged 56 and, like Yi, had a background in administration of the economy.[2]

Many foreign commentators saw these new appointees as key figures in bringing about change,[3] and cited the new tripartite formula for peace talks with the ROK and the US, the resumption of the inter-Korean dialogue, economic policy statements that placed a new emphasis on the role of foreign trade, and the promulgation of a Joint Venture Law aimed at inducing foreign investment as examples of departures from past policies. However, this perception cannot be sustained by a closer examination of developments in the DPRK during this period. With regard to personnel, some of the changes in Party and government have already been noted. Discussion of this topic begins by drawing together a full list of significant personnel changes in the period between the full public emergence of Kim Jong Il as Kim Il Sung's successor in 1982 and the Ninth Plenum of the Sixth KWP CC in December 1985.

In the highest ranking political body, the Politburo:

- Ho Tam was promoted from alternate to full membership in December 1983.
- So Yun-sok and Ch'oe Yong-nim, two long-time Central Committee members who had been alternate Politburo members since

1980, were promoted to full Politburo membership in 1982 and 1984 respectively.

- Kim Chung-nin was demoted from full to alternate membership.
- In late 1985 two veteran ex-guerillas, Chon Mun-sop and Paek Hak-nim,[4] were also demoted from Politburo status but retained Central Committee status.
- A total of seven cadres were appointed to alternate membership over the period in question: Kang Hui-won, Hong Song-nam, Chon Pyong-ho, Kim Tu-nam, An Sung-hak, Hong Song-yong and Kim Pok-sin.
- Kim Il (aged 75), the nominal No. 2 behind Kim Il Sung, died in March 1984, and O Paek-yong (aged 71), a leading military cadre ranked No. 10 in the Politburo, died in April 1984.

In the Party Secretariat:

- Five new Party Secretaries were appointed at the Seventh Plenum of the Sixth KWP held June 15–17 1983: Hyon Mu-gwang, Ho Chong-suk, Son Kwan-hui, An Sung-hak, and Ch'ae Hui-jong. In February 1984 they were joined by Kim Yong-sun.

In the Administration Council:

- A new Minister for Foreign Affairs, Kim Yong-nam, was appointed in December 1983 with an unchanged Politburo ranking.
- A new Prime Minister, Kang Song-san, was appointed in January 1984, while outgoing Prime Minister Yi Chong-ok was appointed to the mainly ceremonial position of Vice President. Yi's Politburo ranking remained unchanged, while Kang rose from the nominal No. 11 to No. 5 in the hierarchy, and then to No. 4 after the death of the No. 2 cadre Kim Il in March 1984. As noted in Chapter 2, this promotion was customary for the incumbent Prime Minister after 1980.
- In January 1984 the Supreme People's Assembly also named four new deputy premiers: Ch'oe Yong-nim, Kim Chang-ju, Cho Se-ung and Kim Pok-sin.

In the course of our examination of the DPRK party and government institutions in Chapter 2, we discussed the institutional history of the KWP Politburo and Secretariat. We shall now examine the changes during 1982–85 in the light of this discussion in order to determine their significance.

CHANGES TO FULL MEMBERSHIP OF THE POLITBURO

Ho Tam had been Foreign Minister since 1971 and an alternate Politburo member since 1970. The change was not unusual, especially as it was accompanied by another periodic exercise affecting the Foreign Ministry, namely, a broad reshuffle of ambassadors. The government appointed a replacement for Ho with minimum disturbance: Kim Yong-nam, four years older than Ho and the long-term Chairman of the KWP International Committee, took up the position. Moreover, a replacement was required for Kim Il, who had been too ill to appear in public since early 1982, as Chairman of the Committee for the Peaceful Reunification of the Fatherland. Ho now possessed the senior Politburo rank traditionally associated with this position.

Other moves did not involve generational change. So Yun-sok (then 58) and Ch'oe Yong-nim (then 56), the two cadres promoted to full membership status, were veteran Party officials, and neither Kim Chung-nin nor the former Manchurian guerillas Paek Hak-nim and Chon Mun-sop were replaced by younger military men.

PROMOTIONS TO ALTERNATE MEMBERSHIP OF THE POLITBURO

The new appointees to alternate Politburo membership came from a variety of backgrounds and there is no pattern to connect them. On the whole, they were younger than the incumbent Politburo members, but Kang Hui-won, for example, was a Party veteran. Of more significance is the fact that only one of their number, Chon Pyong-ho, proceeded to achieve full member status in the Politburo (in 1988), though Hong Song-nam achieved this status fleetingly in 1987–88. An Sung-hak and Hong Song-yong were promoted while the Party was considering measures to improve foreign trade, and demoted when this ceased to be a priority. Kim Tu-nam was also soon demoted. The cadres promoted during this period therefore were not all of the same generation, were not rising stars and had little subsequent impact upon the Politburo.

THE PARTY SECRETARIAT

We discussed the significance of the Party Secretariat and the pattern of appointments to it in Chapter 2 and concluded that it functioned as a personal secretariat for Kim Il Sung and Kim Jong Il. Appointments to it were routine and usually comprised a mixture of veteran cadres whose best years were probably behind them, and younger cadres of relatively junior Politburo or Central Committee rank. There are no examples of the Secretariat serving as a springboard for rising young cadres in the Party. The five appointments to the Party Secretariat in June 1983 conform closely to this analysis. They were a mixture of veterans, such as the septuagenarians Hyon Mu-gwang and Ho Chong-suk, and younger cadres. Of the three younger cadres only An Sung-hak proceeded to enjoy alternative membership status in the Politburo (1984–86) before again being demoted. Similarly, while Kim Yong-sun, appointed in February 1984, was a younger man who played a highly visible role in DPRK diplomacy with the US in the years that followed, he did not receive Party status commensurate with this role. Prior to the death of Kim Il Sung he enjoyed Politburo alternate member status for less than two years (1992–93). None of the appointments to the Secretariat, therefore, had any lasting significance.

THE PRIME MINISTER

The appointment of Kang Song-san as Prime Minister was a routine change. Since the 1970s the DPRK had followed the practice of appointing new prime ministers to administer new economic plan periods. Yi Chong-ok's incumbency coincided with the period of the Second Seven-Year Plan and now a further change was made as the government entered an inter-plan period. Kang was younger than Yi (56 versus 71), but was not of Kim Jong Il's generation. The post of Prime Minister remained in the hands of aging senior Politburo members, a point later emphasised by Kang's two successors, Yi Kun-mo, who was 66 when appointed in 1986, and Yon Hyong-muk, who was 64 when appointed in 1988, and by Kang himself, who returned to the position in 1994 at the age of 65.

THE NEW DEPUTY PREMIERS

The comments made above concerning the Party Secretariat also apply to the deputy premier appointments. The Administration Council has always appointed several deputy premiers who hold the position in conjunction with their ministerial portfolios. The purpose is not clear, but there are no grounds for assigning particular significance to government appointments in the DPRK unless they are accompanied by significant moves for the individuals concerned in the Party hierarchy. The appointment of Ch'oe Yong-nim, Kim Ch'ang-ju, Cho Se-ung and Kim Pok-sin had little effect on their Party ranking.

In sum, change in the DPRK leadership during the period 1983–86 amounted to minor adjustments within the Politburo and largely routine changes in the Party Secretariat and Administrative Council. Analysis of these changes does not support either the perception of widespread personnel changes, nor the advancement of any significant group of technocrat cadres linked to Kim Jong Il. Policy formulation and execution in the key areas of ideology, the economy and foreign policy remained in the hands of veteran cadres and this obviously constituted a severe retardant on any moves toward reform.

During this period the Party continued to enhance the public image of Kim Jong Il as a devoted cadre, working to carry out policies determined by his father, with special emphasis on culture, the arts and propaganda. The DPRK media portrayed Kim Jong Il as growing in public stature during this period, especially in the international sphere, where reports of him receiving official messages from friendly foreign governments and fraternal communist parties began to appear in the media during 1983. He paid an unofficial visit to China during July 1983, and personally invited Chinese Communist Party (CCP) General Secretary Hu Yaobang to visit Pyongyang in May 1984. However, there was little scope for the further projection of the younger Kim as an international statesman, especially after the Rangoon bombing. The Chinese and Soviets were unwilling to receive him on official visits, especially in view of Pyongyang's insistence that he should receive head of state protocol on foreign visits (Zhebin 1995:734), and this left only minor Third World countries as possible destinations.

The younger Kim also continued to give 'working guidance' in various localities in 1984 (*PT* 4 March 1984, *PT* 18 April 1984, *PT* 25 April 1984, *PT* 5 May 1984, *PT* 26 May 1984, *PT* 27 June 1984, *PT* 7 July 1984). During these visits, as on various other occasions, he continued to offer strident, ringing endorsements of long-established ideological campaigns such as the Chollima Movement, the Chongsanri Method, the Taean Work System, speed battles, and the Three Revolution Teams movement. Kim Jong Il was left in de facto charge of the country for six weeks during May–June 1984 while his father was abroad. The increased range and importance of reported activities after his father's return indicates that the younger Kim's performance met with his father's approval. He therefore retained a good portion of the administrative authority he had exercised in his father's absence.

Meanwhile, the leadership evolved a twofold response to the country's poor economic performance in the early 1980s. On the one hand it continued to uphold the absolute supremacy of the Party's ideological parameters to economic activities and left the hallmark features of the DPRK economy—extreme centralisation of manage-ment, reliance on ideological incentives, reliance on Stakhanovite mobilisation campaigns, continuing high levels of military expendi-ture—intact. On the other hand, the leadership sought to seek new economic inputs through adjustments in the area of foreign trade.

In foreign trade, the DPRK announced a willingness to trade with capitalist countries and to seek investment capital from abroad. In January 1984 the SPA carried a resolution to this effect, and there were further indications of a policy shift in the form of praise (for the first time) for China's Four Modernisations program, evidence of DPRK interest in the operation of China's Special Economic Zones (SEZs), and the enactment of a Joint Venture Law in September.[5] The Party also began to pay greater attention to the light industrial sector. This sector, comprising 4500 small economic units, accounted for more than half total industrial output, but had suffered due to the overwhelming priority accorded to the heavy industry sector. Now the Party reappraised the role of light industry as a foreign exchange income earner, and the campaign to highlight the significance of this sector became prominent during 1984 as Kim Il Sung and Kim Jong Il frequently toured light industry sites.

In particular, Kim Jong Il raised the profile of the light industrial sector with a visit to a light industry goods exhibition on 3 August 1984, where he exhorted officials to 'clearly grasp the Party's intention and more vigorously push ahead with a light industry revolution and a service revolution . . .' (PT 8 August 1984). This visit initiated a major new campaign to produce consumer goods at the local level known as the 'August 3 Consumer Goods Production Campaign'. Its purpose was to boost the production of consumer goods by devolving a major part of the responsibility for the production of daily necessities such as clothes, household goods and processed food products to local authorities using local raw materials and employing local labourers working in their spare time. The state provided a distribution network, non-material incen-tives and, according to Soviet sources (see EIU 1995–96:67), also extracted considerable revenue from these activities. In so doing, it largely absolved itself of the need to factor light industry into central planning. By 1996 a reported 600 000 workers were engaged in the campaign (*VP* vol. XIX, no. 8).[6]

Nevertheless, there are a number of indications that the DPRK had in mind only very limited policy changes at this stage. First, the full title of the relevant SPA agenda item, 'On strengthening South–South cooperation and external economic relations and further developing foreign trade', indicates that the DPRK was not seeking a radical departure from previous policy, but rather placed the development of foreign trade within the context of its existing trade policy and structure, which emphasised economic ties with the socialist bloc and the Third World. The Party emphasised this point at its Ninth Party Plenum of the Sixth KWP CC, held in Chongjin during 6–9 July 1984, when its major references to foreign trade policy gave clear emphasis to ties with the Socialist Bloc and did not contain any reference to trading with capitalist countries (*PT* 14 July 1984). Second, while there is evidence that the Administration Council took steps to streamline the administration of foreign trade within individual ministries at this time,[7] there is no evidence in the form of follow-up public announcements, campaigns or commentary of sustained efforts to give effect to any major new policy direction. For example, the lengthy report of the Ninth Party Plenum contained no references to recent developments such as the January SPA resolution on further developing foreign trade (*PT* 14 July 1984).

Third, there is no evidence of trade-related diplomatic activity in 1984. For example, a crucial first step would have involved serious negotiations on the DPRK's Western European debt since the confidence of the international banking community would have been crucial to future trade financing. This did not take place. After the DPRK failed to comply with a 1980 debt rescheduling agreement, it reached a routine rescheduling agreement with debtors in May 1984, involving the repayment of principal and interest on debts acquired in the period 1974–77. However, the DPRK did not act on this agreement. No principal repayments were ever made and interest repayments actually ceased immediately after the signing of the agreement.

Fourth, there was no amelioration in the policy of not releasing even basic economic data. Whatever the role envisaged for foreign investors, the DPRK clearly assumed that they would invest without access to even basic economic data such as GNP and sector output figures. Fifth, in any coherent foreign trade strategy, the upgrading of the DPRK's primitive economic infrastructure would have been highlighted, but the government made no significant reference to it during this period. The country's telecommunications system, transport network and power grid were all exceptionally primitive, and this had been a significant factor in nullifying the effect of the DPRK's purchases of Western plant and machinery in the early 1970s. Despite the lessons of the 1970s, the DPRK still clearly expected that new foreign trade inputs could be handled by the existing national infrastructure.

Finally, the extent to which the September 1984 Joint Venture Law represented a new departure has tended to be magnified by an exaggeration of the extent to which the DPRK had hitherto isolated itself from the international economy. In fact, the DPRK had conducted significant trade with Japan for a number of years before 1984, trade with capitalist countries had accounted for 20–30 per cent of total DPRK trade during the 1970s and in 1979 totaled US$970 million (Koo 1992:187). In the early 1980s the DPRK had also sought out Western European and Japanese partners to set up joint mining ventures and had accepted substantial aid from the United Nations Development Program (UNDP).[8] Moreover, on the ideological level, while the leadership held deep convictions on the predatory nature of international trade, it had never advocated complete economic isolation. Already in 1982 Kim Jong Il had noted in his treatise, *On the Juche Idea*: 'Building an independent national economy on the principle of self-reliance does not mean building an economy in isolation. An independent economy is opposed to foreign economic domination and subjugation; but it does not rule out international economic cooperation' (Kim Jong Il 1982:48).[9] The measures contemplated by the Party in late 1983 and early 1984 seem even less significant when considered against this background.[10]

We cannot be sure where the DPRK's foreign trade measures might have led, because within months of the December 1983 Eighth Party Plenum and the January 1984 SPA session, relations with the Soviet Union became a decisive factor in economic policy counsels. As we have seen, as late as March 1984 the Soviets had misgivings about Kim Il Sung's scheduled May visit, but finally decided to receive him. The visit seems to have been an outstanding success and brought in its wake a series of economic and military agreements.[11] The tempo of economic exchanges rose sharply, and in 1985 two-way trade with the Soviet Union increased 94.2 per cent over 1984 (see Table 6.1 below).

The Soviet link gave Kim Il Sung a real alternative to the uncertainties of expanded contact with capitalist trading partners. First, the DPRK had founded and developed its industry with

Table 6.1   DPRK trade with the USSR 1983–86 (unit: US$ million)

Year	Total	Balance	% of total DPRK foreign trade	% increase
1983	788.3	83.9	36.1	−9.9
1984	909.2	23.4	36.3	15.3
1985	1766.1	−300.4	62.5	94.2
1986	1720.6	−436.6	53.1	2.6

Source: Bon-Hak Koo (1992:188).

extensive Soviet input, and almost all major economic units functioned according to Soviet blueprints, organisational methods,
machinery, spare parts and market requirements. Second, the disastrous efforts to import Western plant and machinery in the early
1970s demonstrated that it was beyond the capacity of the economy
to absorb more advanced technologies. Third, in dealing with the
Soviets, Pyongyang need not deal with the threats posed by intercourse with open societies but instead could deal with closed,
compatible political systems within the Socialist Bloc. Fourth, and
most importantly, the new Soviet relationship led directly to a
renewed flow of up-to-date weaponry and military technology.[12]

As the massive scale of Soviet assistance became increasingly
clear, the DPRK retreated behind traditional economic policies. The
communique of the Tenth Plenum of the Sixth KWP Central Committee, held during 4–10 December 1984 did not suggest an economy
in a state of transformation. It gave a routine endorsement to the
Taean Work System, and noted that 'tremendous successes were made
this year in attaining the targets of the Second Seven-Year Plan and
the ten long-range objectives of socialist economic construction for
the 1980s through the acceleration of production and construction
at the speed of Chollima plus the 'speed of the eighties' in all
economic sectors' (*PT* 15 December 1984). The bulk of the communique was given over to detailing tasks in the designated priority
areas for 1985 of mining, railway transport and the metal industry.
References to foreign trade were minimal, reflecting the de-emphasis
which had now taken place.

On 17 February 1985, the Government announced that the
Second Seven-Year Plan (1978–84) had attained production targets
in all sectors, but the circumstances of this announcement suggested
a disappointing economic performance. Unlike previous economic
plans, the DPRK did not publish a formal document summarising the
details of plan fulfillment. Instead, it announced completion by means
of a routine news release from the Central Statistics Bureau. Kim Il

Sung had made no reference to it in his New Year Address some six weeks earlier, and the announcement itself contained even less useable economic data than previous announcements of plan completion.[13] Moreover, when the Third Seven-Year Plan was announced in 1987 it adopted 1986 figures as base figures for targets—thereby acknowledging that the second plan had become a de facto nine-year plan. After the announced completion of the Second Seven-Year Plan, the economy passed into a transitional period of indeterminate length prior to the next plan period. There were no announced production targets for this period, only annual guidelines. The general purpose of this device was to correct imbalances between the various sectors that arose in the course of rigid centralised economic planning.

By the end of 1986 the most salient aspect of the DPRK economy was the forthright manner in which Kim Il Sung had reaffirmed and reinforced traditional policies of rigid orthodoxy in economic matters. In his speech to the inaugural session of the Eighth SPA on 29 December 1986, there were no references to material incentives, decentralised planning, independent accounting, or other aspects of economic liberalisation (*PT* 3 January 1987). While the process of economic reform was well entrenched in China, and cautious debates on the need for reform had begun in the Soviet Union and Vietnam, in the DPRK tendencies toward reform remained under strong attack in a forceful reassertion of the need to pursue fundamental ideological objectives.

There is little reason to dispute the analysis later offered by Soviet economists that the DPRK began to enter into a serious and prolonged economic crisis beginning in the early 1980s (Trigubenko 1991:108). Self-enforced scientific, cultural and educational isolation, the glorification of self-sufficiency, and the alienation of world capital markets through debt delinquency had resulted in low levels of technological input and very little capacity to produce value-added exports. Roughly 70–80 per cent of the DPRK's exports were either raw or semi-finished products such as minerals, agricultural and marine products, cement, pig iron and precious metals. Tiny pockets of high technology excellence continued to exist in defence-related industries, but quality problems plagued the DPRK manufacturing industry to the extent that Chinese officials routinely cited the quality factor as a major impediment to expanding trade. The products themselves were all but unsaleable except in captive Third World markets.[14] Thus, as the DPRK stood poised to announce a new multi-year economic plan, it faced a formidable array of problems.

The country possessed a stagnant economy, high foreign debt, an enormous burden in military expenditure, few value-added exports, little access to foreign technology and capital, few students or technicians with foreign training or experience, rapidly aging and inefficient plant, machinery and infrastructure, and an obsolete, highly centralised command system of economic management. The new Plan would now proceed in strict accordance with the traditional ideological parameters that had produced these outcomes.

Kim Il Sung gave even stronger evidence of the limited, tactical nature of DPRK policies during this period in December 1984 and June 1985 in interviews with foreign media representatives, which provide a clear, detailed exposition of his economic and political world view.[15] In the interviews, Kim painted a characteristically dire picture of an international economy locked in desperate conflict:

> As for the world's economic situation today, we can say that the economic sphere, too, as is the case with the political sphere, is characterized mainly by antagonism and struggle between the developed countries of the Western world and the newly-emerging nations, and between billionaires and the working masses. In an attempt to get out of the chronic economic crisis, the imperialists are now obstinately manoeuvring to maintain the old international economic order while internally intensifying the exploitation of the toiling masses and externally increasing economic pressure upon the socialist countries and stepping up their neo-colonialist plunder of the third world countries [PT 20 February 1985].

He also gave forceful expression to his belief that capitalist countries were facing a serious, systemic crisis:

> Recent Western press reports say that the economy in some capitalist countries is recovering, but this is only a local and temporary phenomenon. Available information shows that the rate of growth of the capitalist economy which showed a sign of recovery will again drop next year. Many capitalist countries still suffer a serious shortage of raw materials and fuel, the difficulty of marketing, increased deficits in budget and foreign trade, inflation and unemployment [PT 20 February 1985].

Kim saw the predicament of capitalism issuing out of its very nature:

> Basically, there can be no universal, lasting economic stability in a capitalist society. It is a rule that a chronic economic crisis ensues in a capitalist society when anarchy prevails in production. Furthermore, now that the system of plundering the resources of the third world

144

countries, the lifeline of the capitalist economy, is crumbling, the capitalist countries can never develop their economy smoothly nor can there be a way for the imperialists to completely free themselves from economic crises [*PT* 20 February 1985].

This contrasted with the socialist economy:

The socialist economy is a planned and people-oriented economy. In a socialist society the country's natural and manpower resources are used rationally and in a planned way, and all economic activities serve the promotion of the people's material and cultural prosperity. This fundamental advantage of the socialist economic system enables the socialist countries to increase production steadily, develop science and technology rapidly and promote the people's material and cultural standards systematically [*PT* 20 February 1985].

It is hard to think of another Communist leader who would have been so prepared to offer such textbook views at length in the mid-1980s, but given that these represented views which had been held with considerable tenacity since the early 1930s it is not surprising to see the 73-year old Kim well satisfied and unflinching in his defence of traditional policies of self-reliance. By July 1985, thought of introducing joint venture capital were far from his mind:

We shall never bring in foreign capital. An economy which is built on foreign capital is bound to become a dependent economy. The economic independence of a country is as important as its political independence. If a country is subordinated to another country economically, it will also be subjugated politically. Our country will not be like south Korea which is burdened with 50 000 million dollars of debts [*PT* 17 July 1985].

This last sentence fits so neatly into Kim's analysis that one almost overlooks its unintentional irony. Yet in Kim's words there is also a significant key to the DPRK's attitude to its own foreign creditors—namely, that Kim simply could not see indebtedness to foreign banks as a factor in his country's international economic relations. We may surmise that in the Manchurian guerilla mind-set international bankers were themselves predators, and he had merely got in first and taken what he wanted from them.

In the *Sekai* interview we also gain further evidence of the extent to which Kim Il Sung was isolated from the economic reality of his country. Arguably, it is an integral part of a political leader's role to portray the country's economic achievements in a positive light. However, Kim reaffirmed not only the solid state of the nation's economy, but again enunciated in detail an unchanging economic strategy for raising capital to finance the next multi-year economic plan through the export of raw materials.

> The situation in our economy which is continuing to develop on an independent basis, is good at present, but its future will be even brighter. Our workers in the economic sector are now making preparations for a new long-term plan . . . The main thing in obtaining the money needed to carry out the new long-term plan is self-reliance . . . If we mine and export lead, zinc, copper, gold, silver and other nonferrous metals, the deposits of which are enormous in our country, we shall be able to solve the problem of the funds needed for the new long-term plan on our own [PT 17 July 1985].

If the economy could satisfy its capital and investment needs from the mining sector, this obviously marginalised the significance of foreign trade, and Kim's references to the Joint Venture Law accordingly did not go beyond the generalities first enunciated by Prime Minister Kang Song-san eighteen months previously.

The chief significance of the two interviews is that they were given during an eighteen-month period during which the DPRK was frequently perceived as undergoing a significant process of change. It is hardly necessary to repeat that the interviews do not support this interpretation. Rather, it is important to observe that throughout this period the DPRK's economic policies continued to be held in place by a tightly interlocking set of long-held ideological convictions.

Unchanging ideological parameters were decisive in shaping the course of the renewed inter-Korean talks during 1984–86, for despite active engagement on a number of levels the two Koreas were unable to achieve significant progress. This phase began when Chinese Premier Zhao Ziyang visited Washington on 10 January 1984, and hand-delivered a letter from Kim Il Sung to United States President Ronald Reagan proposing that the DPRK, the US and the ROK hold tripartite talks on matters relating to the reunification of Korea. Domestically, the DPRK announced the proposal the same day as a communique after a joint meeting of the Central People's Committee and the Standing Committee of the Supreme People's Assembly on 10 January 1984 (PT 14 January 1984).

The key section of the relevant CPC–SPA resolution read: 'The joint meeting decided to propose to hold tripartite talks by letting the south Korean authorities, another party responsible for the mounting tension in Korea today, participate in the talks between us and the United States this time'. Although references to the role of the South in the proposed talks were few, the communique stated:

'The south Korean authorities should not keep the US troops in south Korea, but make them withdraw, not incite north–south confrontation but take practical measures for relaxing the tensions between the north and the south; they should be prepared for consultation of such problems at the tripartite talks'. While the DPRK stressed that the participation of the ROK was 'on an equal footing', the scope of initial ROK participation was therefore severely limited by the nature of the proposed agenda. The first item of business involved the bilateral negotiation of a peace treaty and troop withdrawal between the DPRK and the US, and the two Koreas would negotiate only after the US withdrawal.

Both the South and the US found the proposal unacceptable since it conflicted with their joint position that the North should negotiate directly with the South from the outset, but a period of intensive diplomacy nevertheless followed in an attempt to clarify the North's proposal.[16] The ROK's immediate response was therefore to restate its position that any talks on a peace treaty should be bilateral, and in this it was supported by the US. Since the North's proposals had included the ROK in negotiations without defining its role or position at any stage of the proceedings, the South also sought further details from the North. An exchange of letters between the DPRK and ROK Prime Ministers followed, in which DPRK Prime Minister Kang Song-san stated on 7 March: 'The South Korea authorities with no real power can in no way settle military problems through the talks with us without the approval of the United States' (*PT* 7 April 1984).[17]

Headlines notwithstanding, the proposal did not so much break new ground as reformulate some of the many ambiguities latent in the North's basic two-tier bilateral talks policy, whereby the North proposed to negotiate a peace treaty with the US bilaterally with the South on hand as a clearly inferior participant, and then negotiate the shape of a post-treaty political settlement with Seoul.[18] Upon clarification of this point all momentum to proceed with the tripartite formula was lost. The proposal remained on the table, but Ronald Reagan did not raise it when he visited Beijing in late April 1984, nor did Kim Il Sung make public reference to it during his May 1984 visit to the Soviet Union.[19] In the years that followed the DPRK, made only occasional, passing references to it.

Why, then, did the DPRK take this initiative? It was inherently unlikely that the DPRK would offer concessions to the ROK in the wake of a major terrorist operation, and in fact Pyongyang's rhetoric remained uncompromising in the immediate aftermath of Rangoon.

As for the proposal itself, in September 1983, prior to the Rangoon attack, the US had already approached the DPRK through Beijing intermediaries with an offer to participate in any talks in which the ROK was represented on an equal footing.[20] This was, of course, unacceptable to the DPRK, but indirect contact continued after Rangoon, and the gist of the DPRK's tripartite talks proposal was conveyed to Washington through Beijing in October and December 1983.[21] The key to the dynamics of this passage of negotiation was therefore the fact that the US, not the DPRK, initiated the tripartite concept. Primarily as an expression of goodwill toward the US, the Chinese then played a role in convincing Kim Il Sung that it was worth responding to. In the aftermath of Rangoon the DPRK may have felt the need for a diversionary tactic, or perhaps it felt that it had struck a psychological blow against the South even though it had not achieved its principal objective. In the circumstances, with the US possibly prepared to offer concessions, or at the very least offering an opportunity for the DPRK to drive a wedge between the US and the ROK, it was a sound negotiating tactic to respond with a tactical ploy designed to see how far the US might be induced to go. The DPRK's proposal therefore seems to have been Pyongyang's concept of a probe for weaknesses in the joint US–ROK position on reunification talks. More than anything else, Pyongyang had been seeking out such weaknesses, for these had the potential to undermine, perhaps fatally, the ROK's negotiating position.

Since Rangoon was also a *failed* major terrorist operation, the DPRK may also have felt the need to direct some mollifying gesture in the direction of its chief allies, especially China. There is little doubt that the Chinese were surprised and appalled by the Rangoon operation, and they had shown this by openly publishing the Burmese Government's findings of DPRK perpetration. The role of Zhao as intermediary also indicated that the Chinese were applying pressure to the DPRK to take some initiative. However, the offer to act as go-between in establishing contact with the US does not necessarily mean that the Chinese saw the tripartite formula as one that might lead to a breakthrough, let alone a settlement. Given their experience of dealing with the DPRK they would almost certainly have been pessimistic on this score. Limiting their role to go-between was therefore not only realistic but also served broader objectives. It demonstrated basic Chinese commitment to resolving the Korean problem and to maintaining positive relations with the US, and perhaps it also reflected the Chinese conviction that isolating the DPRK only increased the danger of more Rangoons occurring.

Although the tripartite talks proposal faded from the agenda by mid-1984, the two Koreas generated new momentum in the inter-Korean dialogue when they began a series of negotiations relating to sport, flood relief, economic exchanges, and parliamentary talks during 1984–85. These talks constituted the most active phase of inter-Korean negotiation since 1972–73. The first negotiations took place over the issue of joint sporting teams. The awarding of the 1986 Asian Games and the 1988 Olympiad to Seoul in December 1981 elevated the political significance of sport in the inter-Korean rivalry for international recognition and prestige. This issue came to the surface on 30 March 1984 when the North proposed to the South that a unified Korean team be formed for the 1984 Los Angeles Olympiad. The issue soon became moot when Pyongyang withdrew entirely from the Games as part of the Soviet boycott. After the Los Angeles Olympiad, on 17 August 1984 the South approached the North with an unconditional proposal to reopen talks on sporting ties. The North rejected this approach and sporting contacts left the talks agenda.

A second avenue for negotiation opened up in the humanitarian field in early September. After widespread floods entailing loss of life and substantial property damage in the South, on 8 September the DPRK Red Cross offered supplies of rice, textiles, cement and medicine to aid victims. Seoul had previously declined other international offers, but for political reasons accepted the North's offer on 14 September.[22] The flood relief shipment led to the reopening of the direct Red Cross telephone link on 28 September, cut off by the North some years previously, in order to coordinate the delivery of supplies and, while Seoul officials saw nothing in the DPRK's actions to suggest that the shipment was anything but a one-off exercise,[23] a routine proposal by Seoul on 4 October to reopen the Red Cross Talks, which had been suspended unilaterally by the North in 1973, received positive public comment in Pyongyang. On 29 October the DPRK agreed to a resumption of the talks, thus opening a humanitarian avenue of contact for the first time in nearly twelve years.

Meanwhile, a third avenue for talks opened in the economic sphere. On 20 August 1984 Seoul had proposed talks on trade and economic cooperation but Pyongyang had responded negatively. On 12 October Seoul made a further proposal and this time a positive response from the North led to a vice-ministerial level meeting on 15 November at Panmunjom. As an export-oriented economy, the ROK's basic view of the economic talks was to stimulate complementary trade, with the ROK purchasing anthracite coal, iron ore, magnesite, lead ingots, and food products in exchange for such manufactures as electronic products, textiles and pharmaceuticals. It also sought to initiate talks on possible joint ventures and technology transfer, and because of the apparent DPRK interest in developing foreign trade, the South hoped that this might prove to be a sustainable point of contact between the two governments. However, the statement of positions at an initial meeting on 15 November revealed the North's preference for negotiating the establishment of a high-level joint economic committee to deal with economic collaboration measures over the South's preference for more specific agreements to promote trade links as a prelude to broader agreements. The talks were therefore inconclusive.[24]

An exchange of small arms fire during the defection of a trainee Soviet diplomat at Panmunjom on 23 November 1984 led to a postponement by Pyongyang of the second set of trade talks set down for 5 December. The DPRK proposed a resumption of the economic cooperation talks for 17 January and of the Red Cross talks for 23 January 1985 (*PT* 19 December 1984), but then suspended all talks indefinitely on 6 January 1985 as a protest against the annual ROK–US Team Spirit military exercises, which the North claimed were contradictory to the spirit of inter-Korean cooperation.[25] Then on 4 April 1985, the North agreed to resume both sets of talks in the latter half of May. The timing of this agreement reflected primarily the completion of the Team Spirit exercise, but with senior level talks scheduled with the Soviets in late April and China in early May, Pyongyang may also have calculated that a promise of resumption of the inter-Korean dialogue would contribute positively to the atmosphere of those talks. As we have already seen, Soviet and Chinese discomfort at DPRK adventurism was a constant factor in relations.

At this point another avenue of negotiation began at Pyongyang's initiative when on 9 April at the Fourth Session of the Seventh SPA the North proposed that a joint conference of parliamentarians be held with a view to making a joint declaration of non-aggression.[26] The South's response to this proposal, delivered on 3 June, was lukewarm, and at subsequent meetings on 9 and 23 July, agreement on an agenda for discussion proved elusive. The South refused to conduct substantive political negotiations with a rubber-stamp counterpart and would not go further than a suggestion that the two legislatures form a joint committee to discuss the possible shape of a constitution for a united Korea. The North swiftly rejected this (*PT* 15 June 1985, *PT* 27 July 1985).

Meanwhile, the resumed Red Cross talks were more productive, and at the eighth round of talks in Seoul during 28–30 May 1985, the two sides reached unprecedented agreement on an exchange of visits by members of families divided since the Korean War, and also on an exchange of folk-art troupes (*KH* 28 May 1985, *PT* 1 June 1985). Subsequent working-level negotiations finalised arrangements for these exchanges, but the ninth round of talks were ill-fated. Held in Pyongyang during 27–29 August 1985 with an agenda of realising further humanitarian exchanges, they encountered an unexpected obstruction in the shape of a walk-out by the South Korean delegation from a mass demonstration and gymnastics display held for their benefit. The delegation maintained that the political content of the display was offensive to the ROK and intensely political in contravention of bilateral Red Cross agreements.[27] This generated considerable ill will and effectively prevented any further progress from being made at the talks, but did not prevent the hometown visits negotiations from coming to fruition. During 20–23 September the exchanges, the first of their kind, took place.[28]

However, these exchanges marked the high-point of the 1984–85 passage of negotiation, and the tenth round of talks, held in Seoul on 3 December, quickly reached an impasse. The North rejected a South proposal for exchanges over the Lunar New Year on the grounds that this was no longer a significant holiday in the North. It also rejected a proposal to initiate mail exchanges between the family members involved in the September exchange of visits, and declined to discuss a number of proposals to institutionalise the Red Cross link, such as by establishing a Joint Red Cross Committee, a projects office in Panmunjom or liaison offices in each other's capitals. Instead, the North concentrated on the modalities of travel, proposing that delegates travel to each other's capitals by air (which the South rejected on the grounds of the opportunity it might give for aerial military surveillance), and that family members from the North or their proxies be allowed to move freely throughout their South in order to locate southern relatives. The South was reportedly puzzled as to why the North was demanding a degree of freedom of movement that it did not give to its own citizens at home, and remained suspicious of the opportunity this might give for Northern agitation and espionage.[29] The two sides could not find room for compromise, talks were adjourned and then unilaterally suspended by the North in protest against the Team Spirit exercises.

The economic and trade talks also reached stalemate at this time. The two sides had resumed talks on 17 May 1985 after the Team

Spirit hiatus and, after intense negotiation, the two parties endorsed the North's concept of a high-level joint-committee on 20 June 1985 (*PT* 26 June 1985). The South's endorsement was without enthusiasm as it had earlier rejected the concept as an unnecessary impediment to direct trade. It now agreed to the committee proposal largely to deny the DPRK grounds on which to discontinue the dialogue. However, with a leader so far removed from a grasp of the economic realities of both the North and the South, it was always unlikely that the DPRK could identify any common ground on economic exchanges. This was underlined by Kim Il Sung in his June 1985 *Sekai* interview. In an extended, somewhat rambling historical discourse on the issue, he noted that in 1972 he had proposed that South Korean labourers work in North Korean mines,[30] and that South Korean fishermen work in North Korean waters.[31] he also proposed that North Koreans go south to construct irrigation works.[32]

Kim also saw an essential continuum between his 1972 and 1985 proposals and the present and drew pessimistic conclusions:

> At the recent economic talks our side proposed that the north and the south should cooperate in line with what we had proposed on the previous occasion. However, the south Korean side suggested that the north and the south should confine themselves only to trade, treating the north-south economic talks as though they were something like talks between delegations of trading companies. Their attitude cannot be regarded as intended to promote the interests of both sides by effecting economic cooperation between the north and the south in the true sense of the word. It can only be considered as a scheme to delay the talks [*PT* 17 July 1984].

Despite dismissive rhetoric from Kim, the talks nevertheless staggered on, with the ensuing months taken up with the task of reconciling differing draft proposals for the operation of a high-level cooperation committee.[33] This avenue reached an effective impasse in late 1985 as it became clear that the North's predilection for immediate, wide-ranging negotiations on economic cooperation was incompatible with the South's preference to work through relatively minor issues in order to establish whether a basis for high-level negotiations existed.

On 20 January 1986, Pyongyang unilaterally suspended all talks, initially for the duration of the annual US–ROK Team Spirit military exercises (February to mid-April). Unlike the previous year, however, the completion of the Team Spirit exercises did not lead to a resumption of talks. Instead, in a statement issued on 24 April 1986,

Pyongyang laid down a number of wide-ranging preconditions to a resumption of the dialogue. These related chiefly to the holding of military exercises such as Team Spirit and to the South's anti-Communist security laws, and they effectively brought the 1984–85 period of negotiation to an end. The rest of 1986 saw both Koreas revert to aiming proposals past, rather than at, each other. Yet another refinement of the North's tripartite strategy for achieving dialogue with the US emerged on 17 June 1986 with a proposal that military talks be convened involving the defence ministers of both North and South Korea and the Commander of the UN Command (UNC) in Korea, the latter a position held by the Commander of US Forces in Korea. The talks were presented as a means of reducing military tension on the peninsula and, in fact, a resumption of dialogue with the South in other spheres was made contingent upon such talks taking place. However, the proposal was summarily rejected by both the South and by the UNC, foremost on the grounds that in seeking to circumvent the existing Military Armistice Commission machinery, the North's proposal stood to undermine the only existing instrument for maintaining the armistice. Another round of skirmishing occurred in late 1986 with a South Korean call for joint water-resources control talks, but the proposal, made on 28 November 1986 after revelations that North Korea was building a potentially menacing dam not far north of the DMZ, was rejected the same day.[34]

A high-level, secret round of talks involving Chairman of the DPRK Committee for the Peaceful Reunification of the Fatherland Ho Tam and senior ROK representatives was another casualty of the North's retreat from dialogue. Despite denials from both sides that such an avenue had been opened, persistent and informed reports portrayed these talks as an attempt by the North to encourage the South into the grand gesture of a summit meeting between President Chun Doo-hwan and Kim Il Sung (Kwak 1986:2). Such a meeting had been on offer from the South for some time, but the position adopted by the North in the various talks to date and, one must assume, the details of Ho's proposals, seemed to give Seoul little or no encouragement that the North had anything meaningful to offer.

The balance sheet for the 1984–85 period of inter-Korean negotiation was meagre. First, the only tangible achievements were in the humanitarian fields of flood relief shipments and the exchange of hometown visits. However, although Seoul attached particular importance to confidence-building measures the DPRK did not, and so these humanitarian gestures did not signal wider forms of agreement. In other areas, all negotiations stalled at the preliminary level of discussion on procedure. Second, with the exception of the Ho Tam talks, at no stage did the level of representation on the northern side remotely approach the level of the 1972–73 talks. Negotiations were typically handled by DPRK government officials who had little room to manoeuvre and who routinely and regularly sought instructions from their superiors over even minor procedural issues. Third, with the exception of the tactical dimension already noted, there was no sign of any strategic change in the wider picture of DPRK state policy. Fourth, as we have also seen, throughout this period there were no significant changes within the DPRK leadership, and it is intrinsically improbable that an aging, doctrinaire revolutionary leadership would undertake a significant rethink of reunification strategy following the Rangoon bombing.

The North's objectives issued from an ideology which gave the DPRK an unshakable faith in the revolutionary potential of the South Korean people, provided its 'puppet' government could be removed. Accordingly, Pyongyang sought to appeal to the interests of non-government groups and to portray the ROK government as the chief obstruction to more people-to-people contact. It also sought access to non-Communist dissident groups with the objective of organising more effective united front activities. Toward this end, the North deployed the substantial assets of a stable leadership and a population under tight control. This meant that it was not answerable domestically for its actions, and could enter or withdraw from the talks process with political impunity. Wherever possible, it sought to apply pressure to, and undermine the standing of, the Seoul government in order to sap the will of the South to resist northern pressure.

This was a crucial time for inter-Korean negotiation. Had the DPRK been able to adopt a more gradualist agenda, then it may well have found that the Chun administration was more than usually anxious to see progress in inter-Korean talks. Not only was Seoul looking for success in inter-Korean talks to offset political liabilities such as the lingering effects of the 1980 Kwangju massacre and various political corruption scandals, but its prestige was heavily invested in the successful holding of the 1986 Asian Games and the 1988 Olympic Games. On a number of occasions the ROK was skeptical and reluctant to accept DPRK proposals, such as in the case of the flood relief and the parliamentarian talks, but it frequently responded positively out of a sense of domestic political weakness.

However, the North was unable to modify its traditional tactics, and its commitment during this period remained highly tactical. It sought to tease out any weaknesses in its adversaries' positions, and may also have calculated that the appearance of renewed negotiations might help to mute memories of Rangoon, thus making it easier for the Soviet Union and China to extend diplomatic support. Given past Soviet misgivings about Kim's tendency to adventurism, a resumed dialogue may have eased Moscow's abiding fears and facilitated the flow of economic and military assistance. It may also have helped to secure for the North a hearing in international forums such as the International Olympic Committee that it otherwise might not have received.

The conservative nature of DPRK policy during 1984–86 was also evident in its foreign relations, and in particular in the revitalisation of its relations with the Soviet Union. The trend toward closer DPRK–Soviet relations in 1984 culminated in Kim Il Sung's 47-day tour of the Soviet Union and Eastern Europe (16 May–1 July), his first official visit to the Soviet camp in twenty-three years. Something of the significance Kim attached to the visit may be gauged by the size of his entourage (reportedly 250-strong) and the number of key cadres that accompanied him, including those in charge of the economy (Kang Song-san), the military (O Chin-u) and foreign policy (Kim Yong-nam). Kim's numerous visits to plants at the cutting edge of Soviet and East European technology in the fields of precision machinery, automobile manufacture, semiconductors and electronics emphasised his interest in expanding economic relations with the Socialist Bloc. At this stage Kim did not sign any major agreements, but in the wake of the trip, Moscow and Pyongyang began to exchange delegations of working-level officials at a rapid rate and over the next eighteen months it became clear that neither side viewed the substantial strengthening of ties as merely a short-term, tactical expedient.

The next major step in the new relationship occurred with a two-week visit to Pyongyang by Soviet Deputy Foreign Affairs Minister Mikhail Kapitsa in November 1984, primarily to discuss strategic cooperation in detail. Within a year the DPRK had received up to 52 MIG–23 fighters, SA3 SAM and SCUD-B surface-to-surface missiles in substantial quantities (Huh and Jeung 1994:157, Pfaltzgraff 1986:334, Zhebin 1995:729–30). Upon Kapitsa's departure, Kim Il Sung paid a three-day unofficial visit to Beijing during 26–28 November, suggesting that he appreciated the need to advise the Chinese personally about what had transpired, especially since the DPRK was about to give Soviet military aircraft permission to overfly DPRK territory in intelligence gathering missions that would take them close to the east coast of China (Suck-Ho Lee 1986:30).

In 1985 the Soviet Union and the DPRK demonstrated their commitment to an expanded, substantial long-term relationship through an exchange of high-level visits led by senior party officials, the signing of major border-transit, consular and economic-assistance treaties, and frequent, strong, public expressions of warmth and solidarity. The visit of a Soviet air squadron in May 1985 for celebrations of the fortieth anniversary of VE Day, the visit of Soviet First Deputy Premier Geydar Aliyev in August 1985 for the fortieth anniversary of the liberation of Korea in 1945 and an associated naval visit—the first-ever in peacetime—were especially noteworthy. A significant upgrade in military cooperation also took place. The Soviets gained use of Chongjin harbour in the northeast, were granted permission to make port calls at Nampo on the west coast, and obtained permission for Soviet military aircraft to use DPRK air space. The two sides also agreed to coordinate strategic weapons systems and to conduct joint naval and air force manoeuvres.

In 1986 the two sides reached the high point of their restored relationship. The year began with a visit to Pyongyang by Soviet Foreign Minister Edvard Shevardnadze in January, the first such visit by a Soviet Foreign Minister, and during the visit the two countries signed a number of intergovernmental agreements. During December 1985–January 1986 the two governments also reached agreements covering economic cooperation for 1986–90, Soviet assistance for the construction of a nuclear power plant, the surveying and exploitation of maritime economic zones, and civilian travel between the two countries.

The tempo of DPRK–Soviet exchanges continued to be brisk in the wake of Shevardnadze's visit. Kang Song-san visited Moscow in February 1986 for the Twenty-Seventh CPSU Congress, and to commemorate the twenty-fifth anniversary of the signing of the DPRK–Soviet Treaty of Friendship, Cooperation and Mutual Assistance. In July 1986 the two countries exchanged naval fleet visits, with Soviet ships visiting Wonsan and a DPRK fleet paying an unprecedented call to Vladivostok. Throughout this period, the DPRK also publicly mentioned the role played by the Soviets in the liberation of Korea for the first time in many years, a seemingly minor point that had nevertheless been a long-standing point of irritation for the Soviets.[35] High-level exchanges in 1986 culminated in the visit of Kim Il Sung to Moscow during 22–27 October 1986, when both sides confirmed their commitment to continued cooperation (Boulychev 1994:96–7).

Yet even as the two sides reached this high point in 1986, there were signs that the relationship was beginning to exhaust its possibilities. The differences between the two political cultures and the manner in which they set about pursuing their policy goals had induced a relationship 'marked by dualism, a lack of openness and an absence of real mutual confidence' (Zhebin 1995:733). The Soviets remained uneasy at the DPRK insistence on constant deference to Kim Jong Il, at the almost total disappearance of references to Marxism–Leninism in DPRK ideology and at the persistent slighting of the Soviet role in the liberation of Korea. Although the Soviets had the evidence of Rangoon before them, they continued to be surprised and dismayed at the extent to which the DPRK engaged in brinkmanship with the US and the ROK. After the high point of 1986, there was little scope for further development. The Soviets could extract little benefit from their investment in the DPRK economy, and while large numbers of Soviet and Eastern European technicians worked side by side with North Korean counterparts, DPRK politics and society remained closed to its socialist neighbour.[36] Mikhail Gorbachev reportedly contemplated a visit to Pyongyang but his advisers persuaded him not to go, and while the Soviets were prepared to receive Kim Jong Il on an official visit, the two sides were unable to agree on an appropriate level of protocol (Zhebin 1995:733).

By 1987 the processes of *perestroika* and *glasnost* had begun to undermine the Soviet Union's strategic premises in its restored relationship with the DPRK. As the 1988 Seoul Olympiad approached, Soviet thinking on security matters in Northeast Asia underwent a significant change, stressing improvement of relations with China and economic development of the Soviet Far East. The DPRK, with its fixed policy of maintaining a high degree of military tension on the Korean peninsula, was a useful ally when it came to confronting the US military presence in Northeast Asia, but it had significantly less to contribute to these two new policy objectives. Moreover, while the DPRK adopted a pro-Soviet slant on a number of issues such as arms control, and the Soviet proposal for an Asian security conference (Suck-Ho Lee 1986:22), its utterances on aspects of Soviet policies in Asia such as Afghanistan continued to display equivocation—doubtless to avoid damage to Pyongyang's Non-Aligned Movement credentials.[37]

The DPRK's expanded relationship with the Soviet Union during this period did not occur at the expense of relations with China. In May 1984, on the eve of Kim Il Sung's departure for the Soviet Union, CCP General Secretary Hu Yaobang visited Pyongyang and spent some ten hours with the leadership discussing the results of the visits of Japanese Prime Minister Yasuhiro Nakasone and US President Ronald Reagan to China in March and April respectively. China appeared to be reasonably at ease with the growing DPRK–Soviet relationship and when Premier Kang Song-san visited China in August 1984, he found declarations of friendship and support for the tripartite-talks proposal undiminished (*PT* 15 August 1984). Leadership contacts were further consolidated in late 1984 with an unofficial visit by Kim Il Sung to Beijing 26–28 November 1984 (*PT* 5 December 1984). In January 1985 the DPRK and China concluded a major joint economic agreement, while Kim and his son, in turn, played host to a Chinese Communist Party General Secretary Hu Yaobang during 4–6 May.

Nevertheless, evidence of China's changing attitude toward the ROK also began to emerge in 1984 with unprecedented gestures in the sporting and humanitarian field. Sport was a particular focus of interest in the light of the forthcoming 1986 Asian Games and the 1988 Olympic games in Seoul. China began adjusting to the need to have sporting ties with the ROK in February 1984, when it allowed the ROK national tennis team to enter China for a Davis Cup tie in Kunming. Sporting contacts continued with the dispatch of a Chinese team to the Eighth Asian Youth Basketball Championships in Seoul and an invitation to ROK soccer administrators to attend a sports conference in Canton. For the first time, China allowed two ROK journalists to accompany them. Another sign of change was the Chinese announcement in March that ROK citizens would be permitted to travel to China for the purpose of family reunions (*EIU Quarterly Economic Review of China and North Korea* 2/1984:25).[38]

China needed to come to some accommodation with the ROK as a consequence of its expanding international ties, especially with Japan and the US. The Beijing leadership was further helped toward this conclusion when in May 1983 it was forced into bilateral negotiation with the ROK government over the hijack of a Chinese civilian airplane to Seoul in May 1983. Subsequent direct negotiations secured the return of the aircraft and crew, though not the hijackers, but demonstrated the increasing awkwardness for both parties of Beijing's policy of non-recognition. This issue arose again in March 1985 when crew members of a Chinese torpedo boat mutinied and diverted the boat to ROK territorial waters. Again, direct negotiations secured the return of boat and crew, this time including the mutineers (Chae-Jin Lee 1996:108–10).

The success of both these negotiations contributed to the development of mutual trust between China and the ROK, and in a broader sense illustrated how the DPRK's isolationism and China's ongoing process of economic reform were weakening the traditional DPRK–Chinese relationship. This relationship was disproportionately based on an ideological bond that was rapidly becoming obsolete. Now that China was increasingly prepared to develop a broad array of pragmatic relationships in pursuit of economic development, state policies, especially as they related to regional stability, contrasted more and more sharply with the DPRK's continuing intransigence and extremism in pursuit of the anti-imperialist, anti-US struggle. This naturally tended to put distance between the two countries.

DPRK diplomacy also concentrated on its demand to co-host the 1988 Seoul Olympiad. Pyongyang had initially opposed awarding the Games to Seoul, maintaining in an open letter to the President of the International Olympic Committee (IOC) that Seoul was not a fit place to hold the Olympiad on the grounds of the existing tensions on the Korean peninsula and the internal political situation in the ROK (*PT* 22 December 1984). In July 1985 it modified this position to a proposal for a joint 'Pyongyang–Seoul, Korea, Olympiad' (*PT* 3 August 1985), but after official talks held in Lausanne under IOC auspices in October 1985 and January 1986, Pyongyang rejected a counteroffer by the IOC covering table-tennis, archery, soccer and cycling events in June 1986. The DPRK campaign against the Seoul Olympiad continued but with little success: 152 countries, including all East European bloc countries attended the April 1986 meeting of the Association of National Olympic Committees in Seoul. Only nine minor countries were absent and some of these absences were reportedly not linked to support for Pyongyang. In a similar vein, DPRK lobbying at the Eighth Summit of the Non-Aligned Movement, held in Harare from 26 August–7 September 1986, failed to secure any expression of support for its proposal to co-host the Olympics.

Examination of DPRK domestic and foreign policy during 1984–86 does not bear out the proposition that significant personnel moves occurred among the DPRK political elite aimed at advancing a younger generation associated with Kim Jong Il. As we have seen, personnel changes were of a routine nature, no significant new faces entered the inner counsels of the leadership during this period, and ideological parameters remained unchanged. Nor is the proposition tenable that significant, pragmatic policy changes relating to the economy and the inter-Korean dialogue occurred during the period. Not only do actual events during this period indicate minimal change, but this is what one would in any case anticipate from an unchanging, aging, doctrinaire leadership.

In 1983 the DPRK appeared to recognise the need to redress a foreign trade deficit that had widened alarmingly during 1980–83. In 1983–84 it made adjustments to foreign trade administration and emphasised the importance of the light industrial sector in addressing the foreign trade problem, but beyond these steps, it limited its reforms to minor tinkering with budget structures and accounting systems, much as it had done since the early 1970s. At no stage did the government show signs of any sustained efforts to adopt Chinese economic reform practices or to otherwise 'open' the economy. On the contrary, in his public statements Kim Il Sung continued to flatly reject any significant role for foreign capital, and the economy as a whole was untouched by reform.

Moreover, within months of the first hints of these adjustments, the pace of Soviet–DPRK rapprochement picked up unexpectedly. The key event was Kim Il Sung's trip to the Soviet Union and Eastern Europe, and the communique of the Ninth Plenum, held on his return, evinces a marked re-emphasis on economic ties with the Socialist Bloc. By the end of 1984 renovation of the existing command economy structure under Soviet auspices had become a preferable alternative to the opening of the economy to more contact outside the Socialist Bloc. The latter option would have directed Kim Il Sung away from a lifetime of commitment to commandism toward unfamiliar ground, while Soviet-sponsored renovation offered the prospect, however illusory, of achieving an economic breakthrough through familiar methods. The Joint Venture Law remained enacted but, rather than providing a framework for the introduction of Western capital and technology, it became a vehicle for repatriating funds from pro-DPRK Koreans in Japan (Namkoong 1995b:468), and as long as the restored Soviet relationship remained strong, the DPRK leadership saw no need to readdress the issue of reform. It was to take the fall of the Soviet Union to reassess this attitude.

DPRK strategy in the inter-Korean dialogue likewise did not change during the period 1984–86. The tripartite talks proposal and an active phase of inter-Korean negotiation suggested a new, pragmatic attitude in Pyongyang and aroused hopes of substantial progress toward Korean unification. However, the tripartite talks proposal broke no new ground and gestures such as the DPRK's flood relief and the exchange of home visits did not of themselves create momentum or reveal any shift in long-held positions. The DPRK controlled the pace and direction of talks and, from its point of view, the talks on such 'minor' issues such as Red Cross-sponsored exchanges, economic cooperation and interparliamentary contacts which dominated the 1984–86 agenda had tactical value, but they did not address the North's agenda. Moreover, these talks did not reveal any disunity in the ROK, nor did they bring the DPRK any closer to its goal of direct negotiations with the US. Above all, many of the significant gestures toward the South occurred in the aftermath of the Rangoon bombing, and any coherent view of policy making in Pyongyang must assume that the sudden change from terrorist attack to negotiation was highly tactical.

DPRK foreign diplomacy showed little change during this period. The rapprochement with the Soviet Union was a major step, but it was a conservative option based on shared economic and military interests. This was a singularly unfortunate decision for the DPRK, for it led Pyongyang to attach itself to a system which was about to enter terminal decline. On the other side of the coin, when one looks at the Soviet decision to invest massive resources in an economy such as the DPRK's, one must wonder at either the paucity of plausible options open to the Soviets or else at the poor judgment of the Soviet decision-makers at the time.

In the DPRK prior to 1984, the record is clear that the leadership was consistently extremely hostile to even the notion of debate on possible reform. In the political sphere, Kim Il Sung maintained an unflinching personal autocracy and unambiguously asserted the Stalinist doctrine that class struggle intensifies as the socialist revolution proceeds. Any shift in this attitude would have had major ideological ramifications. However, analysis of the DPRK media and contemporary interviews such as the June 1985 *Sekai* interview show no evidence of any shift from these positions at this time. From his isolated vantage point, Kim had no perception that he was facing anything other than minor setbacks and irritations. At most, he felt only the need for small adjustments in order to reduce the trade deficit. His opportunistic behaviour toward the Soviets was not that of a drowning man grateful for a lifeline but rather that of the eternal optimist, convinced of the righteousness of his cause and forever confident that all setbacks were temporary because, whatever the situation, the tide of history was on his side.

While it was true that the DPRK was now no longer able to compete economically with the ROK and that its geopolitical position had declined significantly in the early 1980s, the full impact of these developments seems to have been screened from the leadership by ideology and selective information flows, and screened from the general population by the control and repression apparatus. Thus, Kim operated in an atmosphere largely free of pressure to adjust to external developments. Any adjustments, were they to be made, would have had to emerge primarily from his personal conviction that they were necessary, and the evidence is clear that he did not see any need for change during 1984–86. In theory there were, of course, a range of policy options open to him, all relating to modification of the degree of centralisation in economic planning and the size of the military economy. In practice, however, pursuit of any serious alternative demanded that an elderly Kim undergo a basic reassessment of the significance of his life's work and strike out in a different direction.

Why, then, did so many external commentators perceive change during this period? As even a cursory review of the literature reveals, expectations of reform tend to base themselves on pragmatic premises, with perhaps the most common theme being that the regime needed to embrace reform in order to arrest its decline. Less common are attempts to turn this argument around the other way, and see the failure of the DPRK to embrace reform as suggestive of a polity that obviously lacked such key prerequisites for pragmatism as openness to influence from the social effects of industrialisation and from participation in international economic and political structures. Extreme isolation produced a regime that was almost entirely unaccountable to its population. The challenges of the 1980s underlined a core dilemma for would-be reformers within the DPRK: how could change be generated from dogmatic ideology by elderly cadres from within an unchanging set of state and Party institutions?

7

THE DEMOCRATIC PEOPLE'S
REPUBLIC OF KOREA AND
THE COLLAPSE OF
THE SOVIET BLOC, 1987–91

The renewed Democratic People's Republic of Korea (DPRK) commitment to close military and economic relations with the Soviet Union in 1984 proved disastrous. While the military ties brought major benefits, especially in the form of new, advanced weaponry, Pyongyang bound itself to a system which was approaching a terminal crisis and which could do little to slow the pace of the DPRK's own economic decline. By the late 1980s, the DPRK faced unprecedented challenges from the continuing rapid economic growth in the Republic of Korea (ROK), the collapse of the Soviet Bloc, and the cumulative effect of its own policies.

The challenge from the ROK was severe. In September–October 1988 Seoul successfully staged the Seoul Olympiad and proceeded to make substantial inroads into Pyongyang's diplomatic support base by establishing closer ties with both the Soviet Union and China. The collapse of the Soviet Bloc in 1989 compounded the challenge. Soviet Bloc trade and aid fell away as the Soviets increasingly lost interest in assisting the DPRK economy, and this seriously undermined the DPRK's traditional economic, military and diplomatic support base. Meanwhile, even before the final collapse of Soviet Bloc power, there were signs of serious economic difficulties.

To the end of his life, whenever asked his views on international matters, Kim Il Sung unfailingly began with a vivid description of the desperate, Manichean nature of the global struggle between socialism and imperialism, and the importance of the Korean conflict in that struggle. We have no reason to doubt either the depth of his conviction or the effectiveness with which he communicated his vision to the Party and to the masses. Nor have we reason to doubt the DPRK's material commitment to this struggle for, as we have seen, beginning in the early 1960s, the leadership had consistently pursued policies intended to maximise the effectiveness of the DPRK's participation in this struggle. Therefore it does not surprise that the DPRK's response to the setbacks of the late 1980s was conservative and defensive. This response expressed itself in various forms, beginning with a succession of treatises and rescripts from the Kims, couched in increasingly extreme and uncompromising rhetoric, which attacked the notion of economic reform and defended Kimist ideology. The DPRK media reflected this commitment by continually highlighting long-standing ideological parameters such as the Chollima Movement, the Chongsanri Work Method, the Taean Work System and the Three Revolution Movement. Within the Politburo, Kim continued to promote aging members of the guerilla generation. No members of the postwar Kim Jong Il generation advanced to full membership of the Politburo during 1987–91.

The essence of the DPRK response was the use of tactical compromise to defend strategic intransigence. This was noticeable mainly in selected areas of the economy, where the rapid retreat of the Soviet Union caused the DPRK to accept trade with the ROK and to display some renewed interest in aspects of China's economic reforms. This interest culminated in the designation of the Rajin–Sunbong area in the remote northeast of the country as a Free Economic and Trade Zone (FETZ) in December 1991. However, though in a DPRK context, this might have constituted a significant development, it was almost meaningless in the overall context of the DPRK's economic problems. The economic situation continued to deteriorate, and by 1990 the ROK GNP totaled $237.90 billion, more than ten times larger than the DPRK GNP figure of $23.10 billion. In fact, the annual increase in GNP in the ROK now exceeded that of the entire DPRK economy.

Tactical compromise also occurred in the inter-Korean dialogue and in foreign policy. After almost five years of stalemate, in July 1990 Pyongyang agreed to talks with the ROK at the prime ministerial level, and in December 1991 these talks culminated in the conclusion of an Agreement on Reconciliation, Nonaggression, and Exchanges and Cooperation Between the South and the North. This Agreement set in place a substantial framework for negotiation on many issues of contention between the two Koreas, especially military issues. In other signs of adjustment, on 31 October 1988 the DPRK and the US initiated the first of a series of unofficial diplomatic contacts in Beijing. In September 1990 the DPRK also appeared to reach a breakthrough in its relations with Japan with an agreement to hold talks on the normalisation of relations. In May 1991 Pyongyang reversed long-standing policy and accepted the separate entry of the two Koreas into the United Nations.

Whether these tactical moves might have developed into broader strategic compromises remains moot, for as the DPRK absorbed manifold external shocks to its system, its leaders appeared to gain new confidence in their ability to continue the traditional struggle against the ROK, the US and the forces of imperialism. The key factor here was faith in the country's nuclear weapons program, for as the DPRK's major adversaries became aware of the extent of the DPRK nuclear weapons program, they forced the DPRK to choose between the continuation of dialogue and the acquisition of nuclear weapons. Despite some encouraging signs in the second half of 1991, such as agreement with the International Atomic Energy Agency (IAEA) on the signing of a safeguards agreement, and the signing of the December 1991 Agreement with the ROK, Pyongyang opted to continue its nuclear program and, as 1992 began, still occupied its customary isolated position in the region.

Kim Il Sung made few significant moves affecting the Politburo between late 1986 and the end of 1991. At the first session of the new Eighth Supreme People's Assembly (SPA) on 29–30 December 1986, Yi Kun-mo succeeded Kang Song-san as Prime Minister and Hong Song-nam succeeded Yon Hyong-muk as First Deputy Prime Minister. The government made these changes on the eve of the announcement of the Third Seven-Year Plan (1987–93) in accordance with the now customary practice of appointing a new prime minister at the start of each plan period with the responsibility for its implementation. Yi and Hong were given party status commensurate with their new administrative responsibilities, and became full Politburo members at the Twelfth Plenum of the Sixth Korean Workers' Party (KWP) Central Committee (CC) on 27 December 1986. At the same Plenum Kang Song-san, Yon Hyong-muk, Chong Pyong-ho and Ch'oe T'ae-bok were appointed to replace Yi Kun-mo, Kim Hwan and Pak Nam-gi in the Party secretariat.[1]

In other Politburo changes, full Politburo member Ch'oe Yong-nim was dropped from the Politburo during 1986 and spent four years in unexplained obscurity before emerging again as an alternate member in 1990. During 1987, the Party dropped An Sung-hak and Hong Song-yong from alternate Politburo membership. They were specialist economic administrators who had been appointed in December 1983 at a time when the DPRK was contemplating new policies to address its foreign trade deficit. However, the swing toward the Soviet Union seems to have left them without a significant role to play. An Sung-hak disappeared entirely from the Party and government hierarchy, but Hong regained his alternate membership status in 1993 when the leadership began to display renewed interest in foreign trade reforms.

The most significant move affecting the Politburo during this period came with the dismissal on 21 February 1988 of O Kuk-yol (then 57) from the Politburo and from his position as Chief of General Staff of the Korean People's Armed Forces. As the No. 2 ranking active military cadre in the Party, O was heir apparent to the top job of People's Armed Forces Minister, a Party post with Cabinet ranking then occupied by the aging and ailing O Chin-u (no relation). The Party gave no explanation for the dismissal,[2] and O, who was not of the guerilla generation, was then replaced by a considerably older man, the ex-guerilla Ch'oe Kwang (then 72). This appointment reflected the lack of new blood around Kim Il Sung as Kim had originally dismissed Ch'oe from the same position in 1968.

O Kuk-yol's dismissal was highly significant as a revelation of Kim Il Sung's complete command of the military, for O was not only the son of a former guerilla comrade of Kim, but the only representative in the Politburo of the post-1945 generation of military cadres. This generation was the product of a standard military academy training at Mangyongdae Revolutionary School after 1945. In replacing O with Ch'oe Kwang, Kim ignored the claims of this younger generation in favour of a substantially older man who was the product of irregular guerilla warfare and not regular military training.[3]

The determination of Kim Il Sung to ensure that the country remained under the control of the guerilla generation for as long as possible was also illustrated by the fate of the then third-youngest full Politburo member Kim Hwan. Some time during 1987 Kim, an economic administrator and the only member of the Politburo to enter the Central Committee after 1970, also disappeared from Politburo listings. According to the account of a former member of the Pyongyang elite who defected to Seoul in 1994, Kim was dismissed for his sponsorship of a group of pragmatically-minded cadres in the agricultural sector who advocated reducing the size of agricultural work teams from 30–40 households to a single household. In so doing, he had overlooked the fact that somewhere in the detail of Kim Il

Sung's many pronouncements on rural policy, the Great Leader had endorsed the 30–40 household policy.[4]

The Thirteenth Plenum of the Sixth KWP CC, held during 7–11 March 1988, restored Kye Ung-t'ae to full Politburo membership six years after his demotion to candidate membership (*PT* 19 March 1988). Ostensibly a Party cadre in the field of foreign trade, Kye played a key role in coordinating the operation of the country's multiple and overlapping security organisations.[5] At the Fourteenth Plenum, held during 28–30 November 1988, Chon Pyong-ho advanced to full Politburo membership after six years as a candidate member, while Han Sok-yong, an economic affairs cadre, was elevated to candidate membership (*PT* 10 December 1988). However, Kim Il Sung must have soon had second thoughts about what he heard at the meeting, for he convened a further plenum two weeks later on 12 December 1988 to discuss a Politburo proposal 'to relieve Yi Kun-mo of the premiership of the Administration Council, at his request since he found it difficult to carry on economic organisation and external activities for health reasons' (*PT* 17 December 1988). Full Politburo member Yon Hyong-muk replaced Yi, who then left the Politburo. This was the first time Kim had removed a Prime Minister early during an economic plan period, a clear indication that the Third Seven-Year Plan was already in trouble.[6]

The tendency of Kim Il Sung to seek the company and counsel of old comrades in arms rather than younger men, already noticeable in the O Kuk-yol affair, now became more pronounced. In June 1988 Kim appointed his guerilla comrade Chon Mun-sop who, along with Paek Hak-nim, had been demoted from the Politburo in late 1985, as a Vice Minister in the Ministry for the Korean People's Armed Forces. Then at the Eighteenth Plenum of the Sixth KWP CC, held on 23 May 1990, Ch'oe Kwang, O Kuk-yol's replacement, received promotion to full membership status in the Politburo (*PT* 26 May 1990). Ch'oe thus joined O Chin-u as the only active military officers with full Politburo membership. At this time Kim also re-appointed Kim Ch'ol-man to candidate Politburo membership, marking the restoration of status lost in 1981. Again, the pattern of appointments emphasised the pre-eminence of the guerilla generation.

The personality cult around Kim Jong Il intensified during 1987–91. The media portrayed him as standing at the centre of the artistic, educational and cultural life of the country as a solicitous leader deeply concerned with solving the food, clothing and housing problems of the nation, and as a dynamic technician directing such huge construction projects as the 105-storey Ryugyong Hotel in

Pyongyang, begun in July 1987. In addition, during 1987 his ties to the anti-Japanese guerilla movement received emphasis by the dedication of a number of 'historical sites' in the far north of the country, including the 'secret camp' on Paekdu-san that was designated as his official birthplace. Speeches and commentaries that accompanied the opening of the 'restored' secret camp on 11 February 1987, five days prior to Kim Jong Il's forty-fifth birthday, stressed the identity of the camp as 'a base area where General Kim Il Sung, brilliant commander of the anti-Japan war and legendary hero, led the military and political activities of the Korean People's Revolutionary Army', drew attention to the preservation of 'a simple log cabin where dear Comrade Kim Jong Il was born', and noted: 'He grew in the midst of the severest ordeals of anti-Japan war, a record unparalleled in the world practice of war' (*PT* 14 February 1987).

Father and son continued to work effectively together throughout the period 1987–91. The continuing vitality of Kim Il Sung was evident in an often punishing round of on-the-spot guidance tours, including a nineteen-day tour of North Hamgyong Province during 16 August–3 September 1990 at the height of the hot and humid Korean summer, and the younger Kim was regularly portrayed in the media as working to give effect to the teachings of his father. The older Kim obviously still possessed strong reserves of stamina and enthusiasm, and gave every appearance of acting as the final arbiter on matters of state policy. Kim Jong Il did not compete with his father for the public limelight, and was absent from public view for extended periods of time. Whether this was due to a more reclusive personality, or whether it was by conscious arrangement with his father is not clear.

On 15 July 1986 the *Rodong Shinmun* published another major treatise by Kim Jong Il, *On Some Problems of Education in the Juche Idea*. In it we find Kim Jong Il chiefly concerned with elaboration of a pre-existing metaphor of DPRK political society as a 'living political organism', whereby people received their biological life from their parents but could only realise their full human potential when they lived in organic socio-political unity with the Great Leader and the Party. In this work, and in the sustained exegesis in the media that followed its publication, we find the leadership keen to press its categorical denial of any need to look outside the Juche system or indeed to find new, flexible interpretations of Juche in order to meet a changing situation. Rather, new, more stringent definitions and elaborations on Juche's characteristic themes of unconditional loyalty and obedience became the new staple of party ideology during this period. The key argument ran as follows:

> The socio-political organism needs a focal point which has unified command of the activities of the social community. Just as a man's brain is the centre of his life, so the leader, the top brain in a socio-political community, is the centre of the life of this community. The leader is called the top brain of the socio-political organism because he is the focal point which directs the life of this organism in a unified manner . . . Since the leader is the centre of the life of a socio-political community, revolutionary duty and comradeship must also be centred on the leader. Revolutionary duty and comradeship find their most noble expression in the relationship between the leader and his men. Loyalty to the leader and comradeship towards him are absolute and unconditional because the leader, as the top brain of the socio-political organism, represents the integrity of the community [PT 1 August 1987].[7]

As the crisis in the Soviet Bloc unfolded, Kim Jong Il did not publish any further treatises on ideological matters though, as we shall see below, his father made periodic references to these events. It was not until January 1992 that Kim Jong Il offered a detailed, public analysis of these events.[8]

In economic affairs the inter-plan period 1984–87 finally came to an end in April 1987 when the DPRK announced its Third Seven-Year Plan (1987–93) at the Second Session of the Eighth SPA.[9] Analysis of the plan targets revealed more modest expectations than for previous plan periods, but from the outset there were signs that the Plan was unrealistic.[10] Given the state of the DPRK's industrial infrastructure, the projected 10 per cent per annum increase in industrial production was extremely high, and compared, for example, with the 7.5 per cent sought by the Chinese under their Seventh Five-Year Plan (1986–90). In specific areas, it was intrinsically unlikely that the DPRK could raise steel production by 4 million tons per annum over seven years with no significant new sources of capital and with only a limited input of Soviet technology to improve the performance of obsolete plants. The construction of hydroelectric power facilities with a capacity of 4 million kilowatts was likewise unrealistic,[11] while the figure of 15 million tonnes of grain production would have required a 50 per cent increase on the stated 1984 figure of 10 million (Komaki 1987:14–15).[12]

By now it was clear that multi-year economic plans were serving as fantastic ideological rallying points rather than as sober economic planning documents. Under these circumstances, to assess DPRK performance by the stated targets and achievements of such plans is not a very helpful exercise. However, other signs suggest that by the late 1980s the DPRK economy had drifted into a state of semi-permanent crisis. The replacement of Prime Minister Yi Kun-mo after only two years in charge of the plan (see page 167), continuing and uncharacteristic minor changes of structure and personnel in the economic ministries and commissions, public Soviet criticism of the quality of DPRK steel exports (Kongdan Oh 1990:79), and public DPRK acknowledgments that agricultural production had been significantly affected by weather patterns since 1984—the last year that a grain production figure had been announced—all indicated a deteriorating economy.

Perhaps the clearest sign of the DPRK's reversion to traditional economic methods came in the Third Seven-Year Plan's section on foreign trade. Here the new DPRK priorities received clear expression in the statement that 'the socialist market shall be given continued prominence and during the new long-term plan, trade, cooperation, joint venture and technical cooperation with socialist countries shall be developed extensively' (PT 2 May 1987). References to trade with non-aligned, developing countries and with 'capitalist countries which respect our sovereignty and are friendly towards our country' were brief and couched in general terms.

Despite continuing tactical measures aimed very specifically at earning foreign exchange, such as continuation of the 3 August 1984 consumer goods movement, no evidence emerged during this period to suggest that the DPRK was prepared to make the ideological concessions necessary for a substantial freeing up of its economy. On the contrary, throughout this period the official media continued to reaffirm both the primacy of capital and heavy industrial construction and the relevance of traditional ideological parameters, including the Chollima Movement and speed campaigns (PT 16 February 1989), Kim Il Sung's Rural Theses (PT 25 February 1989), the Taean Work System (PT 17 June 1989), the Three Revolutions (PT 13 January 1990), and the Chongsanri Method (PT 10 February 1990). The official communique of the Seventeenth Plenum of the Sixth KWP CC, held 5–9 January 1990, highlighted many of these themes and provided a forthright description of the Party's economic policies for the 1990s when it noted that 'the most shining success in socialist economic construction in the 80s is that a great victory was achieved in heavy construction'. Foreshadowing more of the same, the Party leadership attributed these achievements to 'the invincible might and superiority of our socialist system', and saw three major requirements for continued strong performance—maintaining the Taean Work System, establishing 'a serve-the-people style of work throughout the Party', and pursuing this style through the Three Revolutions Red Flag Movement. There was no hint of changed economic strategy and, as always, the primary stress lay on ideological incentives, best summed up in the closing call for 'all party members and other working people [to] turn out as one in hearty response to the Party's militant call and launch a vigorous mass innovation movement for increased production and economy to bring about a new upswing in socialist construction' (*PT* 13 January 1990).

It is not easy to account for such a forthright reaffirmation of traditional policies in the face of continuing and overwhelming evidence of economic decline, and again we must turn to the leadership perspective for explanation. We have already observed the disastrous effect of implementing the Equal Emphasis policies in the 1960s and evidence of serious economic mismanagement dating from the early 1970s. We have also noted that, far from being punished for these outcomes, the economic managers throughout this period in fact received promotions within the Party hierarchy. Kim Il Sung was an exacting leader, but he was tolerant of economic failure in a manner that can only suggest that he did not perceive it as failure. With his incessant on-the-spot guidance tours and almost limitless power to intervene in economic matters, we cannot account for this tolerance by assuming his ignorance of the actual situation. Rather, we must assume that the problem lay with the stringent ideological world-view with which he interpreted what he saw. Kim seems to have measured economic progress by his Stalin era perspective—endless projects of major capital construction and heavy industry produced by labouring masses under strict, centralised Party control—and was effective in ensuring that the country as a whole adopted this standard of measurement.

The result was a deeply idiosyncratic attitude toward economic management which had catastrophic effects on the country. The DPRK economy manifested an extraordinarily unsophisticated gigantism, including the spectacle of billions of dollars lavished on an essentially meaningless World Youth and Students Festival in 1989, the unfinished and unfinishable 105-storey Ryugyong Hotel, scores of other empty hotels built for non-existent tourists, the 150 000-seat Moranbong Stadium, the broad, empty streets, and the expressways leading nowhere. The follies also affected major industries. Moiseyev (1991:73), for example, describes the case of the Ryonsong Bearing Plant, completed with Soviet assistance in 1985, which was designed for annual production of 10 million bearings. Only upon completion did the Soviets learn that there was neither the steel feed to produce the bearings nor any demand for the product.

Within this economic policy framework the DPRK was forced to confront dual crises in the late 1980s. The first was the result of a long drawn-out process of economic decline that had first set in during the mid-1960s. In any circumstance, the cumulative effect of economic decline and ideological rigidity would eventually have had serious repercussions, but the economy now encountered the further, major setback of political turmoil and economic collapse of the Soviet Union.

At this time the Soviet Union was the source of about half of the DPRK's foreign trade (see Table 7.1 below), a substantial proportion of its oil imports, and almost all of its new technology inputs. As the relationship with the DPRK became an increasing liability to the Soviets, Soviet–DPRK trade began to decline in 1989. In September 1990 Soviet Foreign Minister Shevardnadze officially informed the DPRK that Moscow would suspend further large-scale Soviet investments in the DPRK, cut military aid sharply, and insist that future bilateral trade be conducted in hard currency (Boulychev 1994:103–5). These new conditions for bilateral trade combined with the sharp decline in the Soviet Union's production and export capacity which accompanied political and economic turmoil. The result was a sharp contraction in DPRK–USSR trade in 1991. In particular, Soviet oil exports to the DPRK were badly affected, with the 1992 figure amounting to only 10 per cent of the 1990 figure of 410 000 tonnes (Komaki 1992:168).

From their public statements during this period, it is clear that the Kims continued to believe that this setback was temporary, that the contradictions of the capitalist system were serious and that 'the end of contemporary imperialism was nigh'.[13] In this situation the

Table 7.1   DPRK trade with the USSR 1986–91 (unit: US$ million)

Year	DPRK-USSR trade	Balance	% total trade	% increase
1986	1720.6	−436.6	53.1	2.6
1987	1947.6	−582.2	51.2	13.2
1988	2809.0	−850.0	56.1	35.0
1989	2531.8	−750.4	55.2	−9.1
1990	2715.3	−620.5	56.7	7.3
1991	1421.0	−295.0	40.4	−47.7

Source: *EIU Country Report*, 2nd quarter 1995, p. 55.[14]

most persuasive course of action was to make tactical adjustments to find new economic inputs until the final battle was won, and the Party made no radical moves to counter the loss of Soviet economic support. Instead, during the period 1988–91, while neither public statements of policy nor personnel movements within the leadership gave any clear indication of change, a distinct economic strategy aimed at defending, not reforming, the economic system began to emerge.

The most visible sign of this strategy was the designation of the Rajin–Sunbong Free Economic and Trade Zone (FETZ) in the far northeast of the country in December 1991.[15] Previous attempts to induce foreign capital by means of the Joint Venture Law of September 1984 had been half-hearted and had rapidly receded into the background when the opportunity for massive Soviet re-entry into the DPRK economy occurred shortly afterwards.[16] As late as August 1989 government spokesmen still routinely dismissed the need to establish a FETZ, but the DPRK then reassessed its attitude, especially in the light of growing regional interest in establishing a multinational Special Economic Zone in the Tumen River estuary region.[17]

A further indication of change was a rapid increase in trade with the ROK (see Table 7.2 below). As late as 1988 this had totaled only $1 million, but 1991 it rose to $111.27 million, making the ROK one of the DPRK's major trading partners.

The balance of trade ran heavily in the North's favour. In many cases ROK firms entered the northern trade not for immediate profit, but as a bridgehead for the future,[18] while in other cases they found themselves under direct government pressure to accept North Korean commodities and products despite quality problems. ROK firms were limited in their capacity to export to the North because Pyongyang's lack of foreign exchange largely restricted trade to barter arrangements.

Also significant was a further relaxation of controls on border

Table 7.2　DPRK trade with the ROK 1989–92 (unit: US$ million)

Year	Exports	Imports	Balance
1989	18.66	0.07	+18.59
1990	12.28	1.19	+11.09
1991	105.72	5.55	+100.17
1992	162.86	10.56	+152.30

Source:　ROK National Unification Board figures quoted in Kwang-Yong Kim (1994:100).

trade with China in the far northeast. In this region the Korean province of Ryanggang and the Chinese Yanbian Korean Autonomous Prefecture shared economic problems such as sparse population, poor communications, rough terrain and harsh climate. They also shared a legacy of development as one economic unit under the Japanese as well as strong cross-border family and personal ties. Despite these affinities, however, political disputes between the two countries limited cross-border contacts until the signing of a border trade agreement between the two sides in February 1982. Contact then gradually expanded during the 1980s with a number of measures aimed at facilitating the flow of people and goods.[19] As the 1990s began, the region's status as the most convenient crossing point between the two countries led to a rapid increase in the economic penetration by Chinese–Koreans into the DPRK province of Ryanggang, chiefly by means of cross-border smuggling.[20]

These tactical measures took as their first principle the defence of the country's socialist system. As a result, long-standing ideological parameters and practices continued in force, no public debate was permitted, and an important criterion for new forms of economic activity became the extent to which these could be concealed from the population at large. This could be accomplished either geographically by confining them to remote areas such as the northeast, or else procedurally by allowing, for example, foreign investment and merchandise to enter the country with their point of origin concealed. Thus inter-Korean trade could flourish as long as the goods involved did not overtly display their southern origin and as long as capital investment from the south remained concealed.[21]

The full dimension of the DPRK's predicament becomes clearer through a comparison with the ROK economy (see Table 7.3 below). While the two Koreas were in some respects roughly equal in the state power which they could project during the 1960s and early

Table 7.3 Comparison of ROK and DPRK GNP 1985–90 (unit: US$ billion)

Year	ROK	DPRK
1985	83.40	15.14
1986	102.70	17.40
1987	128.40	19.40
1988	169.20	20.60
1989	211.20	24.00
1990	237.90	23.10

Source: Namkoong (1995a:6).

1970s, from the mid-1970s high growth rates in the ROK and stagnation in the DPRK soon rendered the DPRK grossly inferior in all sectors except the military.[22] By 1990 ROK annual GNP exceeded the DPRK's GNP tenfold, and the annual increase in ROK GNP was greater than the entire DPRK GNP. This disparity had obvious and severe consequences for their military rivalry and for the economic and political influence that the two countries could exert regionally and globally. ROK economic performance had, for example, been a prime reason for awarding the 1988 Olympiad to Seoul, and had also been a principal reason why China and the Soviet Union had entered into relations with Seoul.

Could any protagonist that allowed such a trend to develop without effective response be called 'rational'? Although ROK economic growth was rapid, the DPRK had ample warnings. As we have seen, by 1980 the ROK economy was already approximately four times the size of the DPRK economy and any reasonable projection would have predicted dire consequences for the DPRK if, as seemed likely, the trend continued. The failure of the DPRK to respond to this trend is therefore all the more striking, and affords two key conclusions about the perspective of its leadership. First, the leadership was deeply convinced of the fragility of the ROK economy. This conviction did not result from rational analysis, but from an ideology which placed no intrinsic value on capitalist economic achievement. Kim did not understand the concept of a market economy, but instead viewed economic activity as an entity that could be entirely controlled and directed by ideology and genius-leadership. He was supremely confident of the DPRK's intrinsic superiority over the ROK system, and was dismissive of any evidence to the contrary. Second, Kim placed major stress on military production, and a major criterion for judging the effectiveness of economic policies was whether or not these policies could continue to achieve appropriate levels of production. In the process he seems to have become largely oblivious of the destructive effect the military-industrial sector had on other sectors of the economy.

The tactical nature of increased inter-Korean trade flows from the North's point of view meant that there was no improvement in the broader inter-Korea relationship. After the DPRK unilaterally withdrew from existing dialogues in January 1986, the inter-Korean dialogue entered a new phase marked by low-level official contact, occasional high-level secret contacts, and an active exchange of talks proposals. This phase lasted until July 1990 when high-level official talks began, culminating in the signing of an Agreement Concerning

Reconciliation, Non-aggression, Exchanges and Cooperation between the South and the North on 13 December 1991.

In his speech before the first session of the Eighth Supreme People's Assembly on 30 December 1986, Kim Il Sung reiterated his June 1986 tripartite military talks proposal, to which he added an offer to combine such talks with high-level political discussions (*PT* 3 January 1987). Since Seoul and Washington remained opposed to any talks formula that would reflect adversely on ROK sovereignty, they rejected the proposal.[23] On 14 March 1987 the ROK attempted a compromise tack in linking the resumption of the established dialogue to the holding of prime ministerial talks, presenting this resumption as meeting 'minimum conditions for mutual trust', which would lead to higher-level talks.[24] On 30 March, the North accepted the principle of prime ministerial discussions but ignored the ROK condition of prior progress in the established dialogues (*PT* 4 April 1987). A further barren exchange took place in April, with the ROK proposing dates for reconvening the stalled talks on 10 April, and the DPRK rejecting the proposal on 24 April.

Pyongyang returned to military issues on 23 July 1987 with a troop reduction proposal under which both sides would reduce troop strengths to 100 000 by 1992. As a first step, the North planned a unilateral cut of 100 000 by the end of 1987 (*PT* 1, 8 August 1987). However, both Seoul and Washington rejected the proposal on the grounds that it was tied to a complete US troop withdrawal by 1992, and also to a modified tripartite talks structure whereby the ROK, the DPRK and the US would negotiate disarmament with the four members of the Military Armistice Agreement Neutral Nations Supervisory Committee present as observers. Seoul and Washington assessed the offer to unilaterally cut Korean People's Army (KPA) forces as unlikely to alter KPA strength because large numbers of DPRK troops were already surplus to requirements and involved in non-military construction work. On 3 August the ROK essentially abandoned all hope of reverting to the 1984–85 talks process by proposing talks at the foreign minister level at the UN in September with an open agenda. In its response the DPRK immediately inserted a tripartite condition in asserting that such discussions would also have to involve the US Secretary of State (*PT* 15 August 1987). The proposal lapsed.

The year 1988 began with detailed and convincing evidence of DPRK complicity in the destruction of KAL Flight 858 over the Andaman Sea on 29 November 1987 with the loss of 115 lives. At a press conference in Seoul on 15 January one of the agents captured in a sequel to the incident stated that, acting on official DPRK orders, she had planted a bomb on the aircraft.[25] The DPRK vehemently denied complicity, maintaining as it had in the case of the Rangoon bombing that the ROK itself had planted the bomb to embarrass the DPRK (*PT* 30 January 1988). However, a wide spectrum of governments and political parties around the world found the evidence detailed and convincing and, amid another chorus of international condemnation, once again applied diplomatic sanctions to the DPRK.

The year also began with a proposal by Kim Il Sung that the two Koreas hold a 'north–south joint conference attended by persons in authority of both sides and the representatives of all the political parties and social organizations and people of all social standings' (*PT* 2 January 1988). The ROK rejected the proposal as another attempt to highlight what Pyongyang viewed as the unrepresentative nature of the ROK government by appealing to non-governmental groups in the South. Nevertheless, with the potential for further acts of DPRK terrorism during the lead-up to the Seoul Olympiad in mind, the ROK was keen to maintain contact with the North, and in June the ROK press reported that a secret round of contacts had taken place in April between the newly elected administration of Roh Tae-woo and representatives of the North. The agenda had focused on economic assistance from Seoul in return for a pledge from the North not to disrupt the Olympics, but the DPRK was not satisfied with Seoul's offer of $900 million against its demand for $4 billion, and seized on the 1 May defection of a DPRK trade official to break these talks off (*KH* 5, 14 June 1988, Byung-Chul Koh 1989b:43). Nevertheless, the fact that the DPRK did nothing further to disrupt the Olympics, and inter-Korean trade began to grow sharply with a heavy surplus in the DPRK's favour within a year suggests circumstantially that the two sides reached an understanding on these issues at this time.

By now developments in ROK domestic politics were beginning to have a significant impact on inter-Korean relations. In February 1988 President Roh Tae-woo was inaugurated as President of the Republic of Korea after an improbable series of events. In June 1987 the ruling Democratic Justice Party (DJP) nominated Roh as its candidate to succeed Chun Doo-hwan in the scheduled December 1988 presidential election. Under the constitution of the Fifth Republic (1980–87), this election would have been carried out through an indirect electoral college system that ensured success to the ruling party nominee. However, the holding of the DJP nomination convention also triggered off widespread anti-government demonstrations which brought about the downfall of the Fifth Republic shortly afterwards. This led to the promulgation of a new constitution which provided for the election of the president by direct popular vote. The election took place in December 1987 and, due to the splitting of the opposition vote in the first-past-the-post system, Roh was successful despite gaining only 36 per cent of the vote. Thus Roh, who had been poised to become president under the old system, became president under the new system.

Roh entered office weakened and carrying considerable political baggage. This was immediately underlined in National Assembly elections in April 1988, where the electorate further expressed its distaste for the DJP and the Fifth Republic politics it symbolised, by giving it a mere 25 per cent of the vote. In an effort to counterbalance this liability and to deflect domestic political pressure, Roh sought a breakthrough in inter-Korean relations and also concentrated on improving relations with China and the Soviet Union in a policy that became known as Nordpolitik. In adopting this strategy, he perceived and acted upon the diplomatic dividend accruing to the ROK through continuing rapid economic growth, the now-imminent Seoul Olympiad, and the ongoing process of economic reform in both the Soviet Union and China. The background to inter-Korean relations during this period is therefore not only one of a drastic decline in the level of diplomatic support for the DPRK, but also one of the emergence of a flexible, confident, activist ROK increasingly capable of dictating the terms of inter-Korean negotiation.

Roh's first major initiative toward the North came in the form of a Six Point Declaration, which was announced on 7 July 1988 with the support of all major political parties.[26] In this declaration Roh defined the DPRK not as an adversary but as part of 'a single nation community' and sought to develop relations on this basis. Accordingly, the ROK would promote a broad program including exchanges of visits, concerted action via Red Cross talks to resolve humanitarian issues affecting separated families, and the opening of trade relations. It would also drop its objections to other nations trading with the North in non-military goods, end diplomatic rivalry, seek to cooperate with the DPRK internationally, and assist the DPRK to improve its relations with ROK allies such as Japan and the US. In October 1988 Roh expanded further on these themes in an address to the United Nations General Assembly, and in September 1989 made a further detailed policy statement in which he proposed that the two Koreas work toward final unification via an interim, loose union to be called a Korean Commonwealth (Hakjoon

Kim 1992:594–7). This proposal was essentially an elaboration on a number of themes that had long been an established part of ROK policy.[27] Its basic assumptions were gradualist in the recognition that reunification would be a long drawn-out process requiring some interim structure to oversee the process, integrationist in its expectation that the Commonwealth would aim to lay the groundwork for the emergence of a single social and political system, and democratic in its advocacy of full reunification validated through a general election.

In putting forward the basic concept of an interim governmental structure, the ROK invited comparisons with the DPRK's own concept of a Democratic Confederal Republic of Koryo (DCRK), a concept first aired in 1960 and then revived by Kim Il Sung at the Fifth KWP Congress in 1980, but the two proposals differed substantially.[28] The DPRK proposal was precipitate in its precondition of a withdrawal of US forces and the repeal of ROK national security laws, and separatist in that the DCRK proposal saw one Korea containing two different social and political systems as the final form of reunification. Moreover, the DPRK's concept of 'people's democracy' saw no value in expressions of 'bourgeois democracy' such as general elections. Not surprisingly, the DPRK rejected the Roh proposal. It also rejected the ROK's single system proposal as fundamentally antagonistic to the socialist system of the North, condemning it as a two-Korea formula in disguise on the grounds that since neither party in any interim joint governmental structure would be willing to yield to the other, the result would be stalemate and indefinite division (*PT* 23 September 1989).

Between July and December 1988 the two Koreas also attempted to resume interparliamentary talks. On 18 July the Speaker of the ROK National Assembly transmitted to Pyongyang the text of a 9 July resolution calling upon the DPRK to allow its athletes to compete in the Seoul Olympiad. In turn, on 21 July the DPRK Supreme People's Assembly proposed interparliamentary talks and a draft declaration of non-aggression between North and South (*PT* 30 July 1988). Representatives from both sides met at Panmunjom on 19 August, but at this and subsequent sessions, they failed to agree on either a talks format or an agenda.[29] The South wanted a meeting of twenty representatives from each side, while the North initially sought a full meeting of the 950-odd representatives of both parliaments (the SPA contributing 655, the National Assembly 299), plus 50 non-parliamentary representatives from the South. Again, acceptance of the latter point would have effectively acknowledged

Pyongyang's claim that the South's National Assembly was unrepresentative. Since the North declined to discuss matters of agenda until the matter of format had been decided, the talks swiftly deadlocked after three further sessions. On 26 August, talks were suspended until 13 October where, despite concessions by both parties, the deadlock remained. The two sides then came close to agreeing on a formula whereby all law-makers would attend an opening and a closing session, but substantive negotiations would be carried out between delegations consisting of fifty from each side. Eventually, however, this initiative petered out on 8 February 1989 with the DPRK unilaterally suspending all talks for the duration of the annual ROK–US Team Spirit joint military exercises.

The overall balance sheet for inter-Korea talks in 1988 showed limited achievements. ROK, Japanese and US policy changes had created a sense of movement, while the Olympics had also expanded links between the South and the Socialist Bloc, but there were no signs of DPRK reassessment of its approach to dialogue. Its reasons for resuming the interparliamentary talks when it had nothing new to offer remain unclear. Pyongyang may have hoped to exploit the situation in the ROK National Assembly brought about by the April 1988 elections which had underlined the electoral weakness of the DJP and produced legislative stalemate with none of the four major parties able to command a majority. The North's proposal also probably owes something to external pressure from countries such as the Soviet Union and China to make some gesture during the Olympiad period. If so, then it became clear from the first two sessions of talks that the North's response to this pressure was perfunctory.

The period 1989–90 was a period of further barren manoeuvring. The various proposals and counterproposals proved significant more for what they said about each side's negotiating strategy than for what was actually discussed or achieved. ROK media attention focused on various people-to-people contacts in the wake of President Roh Tae-woo's 7 July 1988 Declaration, which had made such contacts much easier for ROK citizens. For example, the government-authorised visit of Hyundai founder Chung Ju-yong to Pyongyang from 23 January to 1 February 1989 led to the signing of a private commercial agreement on tourist development in the Kumgang-san (Diamond Mountains) region and joint economic projects in Siberia. The main avenue of official contact in 1989 remained a series of officials' preparatory talks to bring about a high-level governmental meeting.[30]

Meanwhile, in January 1989 Kim Il Sung issued a public invitation to seven prominent South Korean individuals, including the leaders of the four major political parties, to a 'north–south political consultative meeting' in Pyongyang (*PT* 1 January 1989). This approach again sought to highlight Pyongyang's assertions about the unrepresentative nature of the ROK Government and the ROK instructed the seven to decline the invitation. Only one of the seven, the dissident pastor Moon Ik-hwan, defied the instruction and made an unauthorised trip to Pyongyang from 25 March to 3 April. His arrest on 13 April upon returning to Seoul led Pyongyang to suspend unilaterally all talk activity, including talks on a unified Korean sports team for the 1990 Asian Games in Beijing (*PT* 18 March 1989).

The heavy DPRK propaganda barrage against the ROK over Moon's arrest then gave way to a sudden proposal on 31 May 1989 to negotiate a second hometown visits exchange. This proposal in effect picked up a long-standing ROK proposal to the same effect, and so the South reacted positively. Negotiations late in 1989 raised hopes of a second round of home visit exchanges under Red Cross sponsorship, but efforts to repeat the 1985 exchange foundered in November after Seoul rejected a series of DPRK preconditions. Among these was permission to stage a Seoul performance of the revolutionary opera *Flower Girl*, with its savage and anachronistic parody of life in the South.[31]

Elsewhere, contacts of a mainly symbolic significance took place during 1989. Kim Young Sam, President of the opposition Reunification Democratic Party (RDP) had an informal meeting with Politburo member and former DPRK Foreign Minister Ho Tam during a visit to Moscow on 6 June, and reported that he had found little common ground.[32] Meanwhile, the North scored a major propaganda coup when a representative of the radical South Korean student group, Chondaehyop, managed to reach Pyongyang for the 13th World Youth and Student Festival in July 1989. More substantial was the reported secret visit of ROK First State Minister for Political Affairs, Park Chul-on, to Pyongyang in July 1989.[33] Park's visit seemed less remarkable than it otherwise might have after revelations in the ROK media during July of a number of recent secret contacts between the two sides.

In February 1990 the DPRK again broke off all talks on the eve of the annual joint ROK–US Team Spirit military exercises. One immediate casualty was an attempt to send a single Korean team to the 1990 Asian Games, and on 14 April 1990 the DPRK, after having demanded that the South commit itself to either a joint team or not go at all, announced its intention to send a separate team.[34] Another casualty was Hyundai's Kumgang-san tourist development agreement, which was unilaterally nullified by the North on 16 May 1990. Against this unpromising background, an announcement by the South on 3 March that an ongoing intensive search under the DMZ had located a fourth invasion tunnel did not attract much attention.[35] Nor did Kim Il Sung's references to reunification in his speech at the inaugural session of the Ninth Supreme People's Assembly on 23 May contain anything of note.[36] The February–April 1990 talks hiatus, which also affected interparliamentary talks and preparatory officials' talks for a high-level ministerial meeting, continued well into July when, in another characteristic display of mercurial behaviour, the North vehemently dismissed a routine Seoul call for a resumption of dialogue on 13 June, and then proposed a similar plan on 20 June. The immediate result was a 3 July agreement to hold prime ministerial-level talks, initially in Seoul in early September 1990.

With this agreement a new phase of high-level talks began. DPRK motives in agreeing to talks at this time can only be surmised, but they followed closely on the collapse of a succession of Eastern European communist states in 1989. The DPRK media soon attributed this collapse to over-reliance on the Soviet Union and failure to develop indigenous socialism, but the December 1989 collapse of Romania by internal insurrection was of a different order, for here was a state and leader that had developed an indigenous ideology consciously modelled on the DPRK (Nelson 1992:3, Chirot 1994:240). Almost certainly, this was a considerable shock to Kim Il Sung and must have suggested the various ways in which he himself was vulnerable in an age when the Soviet Union had descended into chaos and was insisting that its former clients put their own houses in order.

The first session of prime ministerial talks, held between DPRK Prime Minister Yon Hyong-muk and ROK Prime Minister Kang Young-hoon, took place in Seoul during 4–7 September 1990.[37] The symbolic significance was for outside observers to debate, but the fact remained that neither head of government possessed any independent power or authority within his own government, nor had either party brought anything substantially new to the talks. Each side concentrated on presenting its own agenda for dialogue, and these agendas contained little if any overlap.[38] Nor were the atmospherics very encouraging, with the Pyongyang print media reporting the proceedings with the ministerial titles of ROK delegation members placed in inverted commas.

The North advanced three preconditions to substantive discussions: no separate UN entry, the suspension of the Team Spirit exercises, and the release of people who had been arrested for making unauthorised visits to the North. Otherwise, it reiterated long-standing positions, as did the South. This confined the meeting to non-substantive discussions, though Seoul provided some comfort by agreeing to discuss the UN entry issue with Pyongyang before taking any further action. However, a subsequent session on 18 September failed to identify any common ground on the UN issue. Seoul adhered to its position that simultaneous entry did not pose a barrier to future reunification, while the North presented an intriguing proposal whereby each government would occupy the one seat on monthly rotation.

The two sides held two further unproductive sessions of prime ministerial talks in 1990, on 17 October in Pyongyang and during 11–14 December in Seoul. Then, conforming to the ritual pattern of previous years, the talks entered their customary winter freeze. In his New Year Address Kim Il Sung again rejected the concept of confidence-building measures,[39] and in February 1991 the North unilaterally suspended the talks on the eve of the annual Team Spirit military exercises. After a five-month hiatus marked by uncompromising DPRK rhetoric, on 11 July 1991 the North proposed a resumption of talks for 27 August. After failing to agree on an agenda for the August meeting, the two sides made unexpected progress at the fourth round of the prime ministerial talks, held in Pyongyang during 22–25 October, and produced an agreement to negotiate what was to be officially titled an 'Agreement Concerning Reconciliation, Non-aggression, Exchanges and Cooperation between the South and the North'.[40] Somewhat unexpectedly, the two sides produced a mutually acceptable text for the Agreement, which the two parties signed at the fifth session of talks in Seoul during 10–13 December 1991 (PT 21 December 1991).

The Agreement foresaw the setting up of a number of civil and military committees to give effect to its provisions. These included a South–North Liaison Office, a South–North Political Subcommittee, and a South–North Exchanges and Cooperation Subcommittee within the framework of continuing prime ministerial talks. As 1991 drew to a close, the North–South talks had passed through the first stage of negotiation and established machinery to deal with inter-Korean reconciliation. However, at this point it was by no means clear that the two sides were closer to sustainable dialogue than in 1971–73 and 1984–85.

Meanwhile, in the late 1980s, the basis for relations between states in the Northeast Asian region underwent fundamental change as a result of far-reaching changes in the international economic and political order. Soon after becoming Communist Party of the Soviet Union (CPSU) General Secretary in March 1985, Mikhail Gorbachev began to articulate the principles of a radical change to traditional Soviet policies of global ideological and military rivalry with the US, most notably via his Vladivostok speech of 28 July 1986. By the end of 1988 he had enunciated a radical new basis for foreign policy. This included the freeing of international relations from ideology, the acceptance of greater political freedom in Soviet Bloc countries, and an end to the arms race. As the Soviet Union put these principles into effect during 1989, the Cold War effectively ceased, global ideological competition effectively ended, many regional disputes which had been sustained by Cold War exigencies became more susceptible to negotiated settlement, and the economic crisis afflicting the Soviet Union and Eastern Europe became a major focus of Western diplomacy.

The Soviet retreat from ideological and military contention with the West and its emphasis on economic issues inaugurated a new era in the East Asia region. US–Soviet confrontation in the region gave way to measures of cooperation including unilateral arms cuts. Similarly, Gorbachev's Vladivostok speech inaugurated a renewed process of Sino–Soviet rapprochement. The Soviet Union backed up the new priority accorded to the economic development of the Soviet Far East by a significant expansion of Soviet economic diplomacy in the region (Roy Kim 1987:382–3). This in turn underscored the need to revise its policy on non-recognition of the ROK. Meanwhile, much of the same economic logic applied to China, and as a result Beijing opted to seek a significant improvement in its relations with the ROK.

By 1987 it was already clear that the forthcoming Seoul Olympiad would also have a substantial impact on regional politics by offering the Soviet Union and China a major opportunity to address the emerging reality of the ROK as the dominant state on the Korean peninsula. The result would of course be a significant dilution of international support for the DPRK's policy of non-recognition of the ROK as a legitimate dialogue partner. Accordingly, during 1987, significant changes in Chinese and Soviet policies toward the ROK began to occur. In the past both countries had allowed non-government contacts with the ROK, but now they began to show signs that they were prepared to expand trading and semi-official contacts.

In June 1987 China began to refer to the ROK as 'Hanguo', the term preferred in the South instead of 'Nan Chaoxian', the term preferred in the North. More substantial changes lay behind this symbolic gesture, however, and in the summer of 1987 Deng Xiaoping made a public and specific commitment not to support the DPRK in the event of a military contest on the Korean peninsula (Hua 1991:30). This statement stimulated and gave focus to unofficial China–ROK relations, especially in the economic sphere. Chinese journals and periodicals began carrying articles analysing the ROK economy in an unprecedentedly serious and objective fashion, (Ilpyong J. Kim 1988:268–77, Chae-Jin Lee 1988:19–20), the number of visitors to each other's country rose from one thousand to nineteen thousand between 1987 and 1989 (Chae-Jin Lee 1996:166), in 1988 the first ROK–China joint venture began production, and a rapid increase in bilateral trade took place (see Table 7.4 below).

Changes in Soviet policy toward the ROK emerged more slowly because of Moscow's ongoing strategic and economic stake in the DPRK. However, non-official relations, especially economic relations, with the ROK underwent rapid expansion as Gorbachev's policies began to take effect. As with China, 1987 was a pivotal year in this process, and in 1988 trade almost doubled over the 1987 figure (see Table 7.5 below).[41]

Table 7.4   ROK trade with China 1979, 1983–90 (unit: US$ million)

Year	ROK to China	China to ROK	Total
1979	4	15	19
1983	51	69	120
1984	229	205	434
1985	683	478	1161
1986	699	621	1290
1987	813	866	1679
1988	1700	1387	3087
1989	1438	1705	3143
1990	1553	2268	3848

Source: Chae-Jin Lee (1996:146).

Table 7.5   ROK trade with the USSR 1986–90 (unit: US$ million)

Year	ROK to Soviet Union	Soviet Union to ROK	Total
1986	49.9	63.9	113.8
1987	67.2	133.1	200.4
1988	111.6	178.3	289.9
1989	207.7	391.7	599.4
1990	519.1	369.7	888.8

Sources: Young-Suk Oh (1992:190).

However, neither China nor the Soviet Union attempted to downplay relations with the DPRK at this stage. In April 1987 the Soviet Union stressed its close ties with the DPRK by awarding Kim Il Sung an Order of Lenin, a long-coveted award, on his seventy-fifth birthday. The Soviet Union also published selected works by Kim and the DPRK reciprocated with a publication of selected works by Gorbachev (Zhebin 1995:729). Otherwise, DPRK–Soviet exchanges during 1987 were most active in the military sphere with the exchange of several high-level military delegations, the continuing delivery of advanced Soviet weaponry including MIG–23s, MIG–29s, and SU–25 ground attack aircraft, anti-aircraft artillery and anti-aircraft missiles, and the holding of joint naval military exercises in the Sea of Japan that reportedly involved up to one-quarter of the DPRK navy's vessels (Zhebin 1995:729–30, Segal 1990:98).

China–DPRK relations were also active during this period. In March 1987, a Chinese Communist Party official, Zhu Liang, visited Pyongyang to personally brief Kim Il Sung following US Secretary of State George Shultz's visit to Beijing. In May, Kim Il Sung paid a largely ceremonial visit to Beijing. He was not accompanied by any leading cadres in the economic or military domains and did not raise substantive issues, probably because by this stage both sides had tacitly agreed not to dwell on their increasingly divergent stands on ideological issues such as basic economic policy and Chinese contact with the ROK.[42] Nevertheless, relations remained warm, and high-ranking DPRK officials who also paid official visits to China during this period included Prime Minister Yi Kun-mo in October 1987, KWP International Affairs Committee Chairman Hyon Chun-guk in April 1988, and O Chin-u in May 1988.

Olympic Games diplomacy also figured prominently in the DPRK's diplomatic activities during 1987, but its efforts to gain International Olympic Committee (IOC) approval to stage some of the events of the 1988 Seoul Olympiad failed. The key meeting between the two Koreas and the IOC took place in Lausanne during mid-July 1987. With the ROK's approval, the IOC added women's volleyball and the men's cycling road race to its standing offer of archery, table tennis and one of the four soccer-qualifying groups. It set September 1987 as the final deadline for a DPRK response, but when the DPRK would not modify its demand for eight full sports programs including the entire soccer tournament, the IOC withdrew the offer and talks ceased.[43] The DPRK then concentrated its efforts on persuading countries to stay away from the Seoul Olympics, but energetic lobbying managed to secure the withdrawal of only Cuba and Ethiopia from among the medal-contending countries.[44]

Pre-Olympiad diplomacy by the ROK and its allies was aimed at reducing the incentive for DPRK disruption of the Olympiad either by military incident or terrorism. Therefore, in April 1987 the United States made a tentative gesture toward Pyongyang by relaxing its policy on contacts with DPRK diplomats,[45] and in July followed this up with a public speech by a leading State Department official, Gaston Sigur, in which he urged the DPRK to adopt more outward-looking policies in the region. Sigur backed up the mild tone of this speech with use of the term 'Democratic People's Republic of Korea', which marked the first public use of this term by a US official.

The Seoul Olympiad took place without incident from 17 September to 2 October 1988 and, as the ROK anticipated, the event gave substantial impetus to the ROK's drive for acceptance by the Soviet Bloc and China. Accordingly, Mikhail Gorbachev's Krasnoyarsk declaration in September 1988, in which he signalled Moscow's preparedness to develop economic relations with the ROK,[46] while in November the Soviets initiated direct commercial contacts between the quasi-official Soviet Chamber of Commerce and Industry and ROK foreign trade bodies (Boulychev 1994:99), thus foreshadowing formal trade relations with Seoul. More serious for the DPRK, however, was the announcement on 13 September that Hungary and the ROK would exchange ambassador-level permanent missions with negotiations on full diplomatic recognition to follow. This brought forth a particularly angry public reaction from the North (*PT* 24 September 1988). Meanwhile, China also undertook a fundamental reassessment of its policy toward the ROK, which involved establishing parameters for moving toward diplomatic relations.[47]

The DPRK moved swiftly to seek clarification of the changes in Soviet policy. Foreign Minister Shevardnadze visited the DPRK in December 1988, but while the joint communique at the end of his visit affirmed that the Soviet Union had no intention of recognising the ROK, other speeches made by Shevardnadze in Pyongyang and the import of Gorbachev's Krasnoyarsk statement made it clear that DPRK and Soviet interests would continue to diverge sharply (Zhebin 1995:735). The Soviets now began to develop active commercial, cultural and scientific contacts with the ROK; Soviet economic investment in the DPRK began to taper off, weapons shipments effectively stopped after 1988, and joint military manoeuvres ceased after 1989 (Huh & Jeung 1994:157).

ROK relations with the Soviet Union and Eastern Europe expanded further in 1989. In April 1989 the ROK and the Soviet Union exchanged trade missions and a steady increase in business visits ensued. Then, as a succession of Eastern European communist regimes collapsed in late 1989, their successor-governments moved rapidly to establish diplomatic relations with the ROK. In June 1990 Gorbachev and Roh Tae-woo held talks for the first time, and on 30 September 1990 both sides announced the establishment of full diplomatic ties. Earlier that month Soviet Foreign Minister Shevardnadze effectively altered the basis for Soviet policy in the DPRK when he officially notified his counterpart, Kim Yong-nam, that large-scale Soviet investments in the DPRK economy would be suspended, that military aid would be cut sharply, and that future bilateral trade would have to be conducted in hard currency. The DPRK reacted strongly to this development and openly threatened to proceed with the production of nuclear weapons since the Soviet nuclear umbrella afforded by the 1961 mutual defence treaty was now useless.[48]

Meanwhile, throughout the year Soviet criticism of many aspects of DPRK economy and society increased in visibility and intensity via a series of electronic and print media commentaries. The general purpose seemed to be to apply pressure to Pyongyang to begin a liberalising process, but it also indicated Moscow's displeasure at the extreme language now being used by Pyongyang to denounce Soviet policies.[49] The DPRK had ample opportunity to employ a similar level of rhetoric during 1991 when Mikhail Gorbachev paid an official visit to the ROK in April, and announced Soviet support for Seoul's position on separate UN entry. DPRK–Soviet relations in all fields contracted sharply and reached their nadir when the DPRK gave overt support and encouragement to the leaders of the abortive August 1991 coup against Gorbachev.[50]

While Pyongyang's relations with the Soviet Union deteriorated steadily from late 1988, relations with China followed a less precip-itate trajectory. The DPRK drew immense and public comfort from the June 1989 Tiananmen Square massacre and the Chinese were grateful for this support. Chinese concern at the speed with which Communism had collapsed in Eastern Europe during 1989 also caused it to reappraise relations with the DPRK. Thus, for a while Pyongyang was not simply a fractious client, but a partner in socialist solidarity at a time when fraternal parties were collapsing everywhere. This renewed closeness was expressed in increased exchanges of delega-tions at various levels between the two countries, and also in a number of low-level gestures aimed at slowing the pace of the developing relationship between Beijing and Seoul. After Kim Il Sung himself visited Beijing in November 1989 (*PT* 18 November 1989), Chinese Communist Party (CCP) General Secretary Jiang Zemin visited Pyongyang during 14–16 March 1990, some five months after his appointment to office (*PT* 17 March 1990). Kim sought to be received again in Beijing in September on the eve of the Beijing Asian Games, (22 September–7 October), but was reportedly requested by the Chinese to proceed to the northeastern city of Shenyang where he met Jiang on 11 September (Huh and Jeung 1994:153).

However, as the Chinese began to put the events of 1989 into a longer term perspective, the cogency of the policy of improving relations with the ROK reasserted itself. Accordingly, the tempo of contacts between the two countries began to pick up in 1990. In civil aviation, direct charter flights had already begun to operate between the two countries in mid-1989, and the first scheduled air link, a weekly Aeroflot service between Shanghai and Seoul began operation in July 1990. This was followed by the opening of a trans-Yellow Sea ferry service in September 1990. In the governmental sphere, in June 1990 the Chinese Auditor-General visited Seoul for an international meeting. At that time he was the most senior Chinese official to visit the ROK and, by making a courtesy call on President Roh, became the first Chinese Minister to meet a ROK President.

On 20 October 1990 the two governments announced that they would exchange semi-official trade offices with consular functions. The ROK office in Beijing opened in February 1991, but this did not produce any public protest from the North, no doubt partly due to its conviction that China, unlike the Soviet Union, was not about to seriously undermine basic DPRK interests. Accordingly, senior bilateral exchanges between the DPRK and China continued at a steady rate. Chinese Premier Li Peng visited Pyongyang from 3–6 May 1991, where he apparently reaffirmed support for Pyongyang's Confederal Republic formula for reunification but also advised the DPRK that China would not veto Seoul's application for full UN membership, thus ensuring the success of the ROK's application. Prime Minister Yon Hyong-muk and a team of economic portfolio ministers visited Beijing from 23–27 November 1990 and Kim Il Sung himself visited China from 4–15 October 1991. The length of the visit (twelve days) and the size of his retinue (over one hundred) attracted attention, but although he gained some economic concessions from the Chinese, he did not succeed in slowing the pace at which China was moving toward recognition of the ROK.[51]

The international situation in 1988–89 held opportunities as well as dangers for the DPRK. The rapid reversal in its fortunes had resulted in large part from broader economic and political transformations in both the Soviet Bloc and Northeast Asia. However, for the US and Japan these transformations rendered the continuing isolation of the DPRK undesirable, and both countries now sought to engage Pyongyang in productive dialogue. On the DPRK side, the swiftness of the reversals to its strategic position also counselled tactical adjustments, and this led to the initiation of bilateral talks with both the US and Japan. The major, immediate objective of both Japan and the US was, of course, to secure an unequivocal DPRK acknowledgment of the ROK as a legitimate negotiating partner and an irreversible commitment to the resolution of the Korean conflict by negotiation.

The chief impediment to DPRK dialogue with Japan and the US was ideology. The Kimist world view identified US imperialism and Japanese militarism as immutable, sworn enemies of the Korean revolution, and it adopted a rhetorical intensity toward them that often beggared belief. While these views were often expressed in a more understated manner in some quarters of the DPRK government, there had never been any doubt that they represented the deep personal conviction of Kim Il Sung. Nor was there any doubt that over time the constant repetition of this conviction deeply influenced the attitudes of the Party, the bureaucracy and the society. This rendered the conceptualisation, let alone the discussion, of less extreme views exceedingly difficult. The DPRK was deeply convinced that the re-emergence of Japanese militarism was only a matter of time and that the US controlled the decision-making process in Seoul. It approached negotiations accordingly.

In dealing with the US the DPRK carried heavy historical and ideological baggage. It had suffered immense physical damage during the Korean War, primarily through intensive US bombing raids, but Kimist ideology had greatly exaggerated the very real dimensions of that suffering. Harrowing stories of US war atrocities, including claims of chemical and biological warfare, featured heavily in the ideological education of all North Koreans, and for decades the DPRK media, had portrayed the US as perpetrators of heinous crimes on a daily basis and on a global scale. It would always have been difficult for the DPRK to make a calm, steady appraisal of so threatening a presence, but propaganda excesses blurred truth to the extent where it is doubtful that the perpetrators could maintain a clear, rational perception of where the national interest lay. To offer just one example, the crude invective that they habitually directed toward the US, and the blood-frenzy they displayed toward US forces in a long list of military incidents, culminating in the Panmunjom axe killings in 1976, may have served to stiffen DPRK morale, but gains in this direction were undoubtedly more than cancelled out by the arguably greater stiffening effect they had in Washington. In an era when the value of US commitments in the Asian region was routinely and deeply questioned in the US, a broad domestic consensus on the US role in Korea held firm, not the least because of DPRK behaviour.[52]

After the preliminary US gestures in 1987 described above, on 31 October 1988 the US State Department announced another series of measures covering diplomatic contacts (suspended after the KAL Flight 858 bombing), relaxation of visa regulations and a review of currency and commerce regulations.[53] Regular diplomatic contact—the first-ever such contact—began at counsellor level through each country's Beijing mission in December 1988. Officials met on average every three or four months in the years following 1988. The issues for the US were progress in the DPRK's dialogue with the ROK, other confidence-building measures on the Korean peninsula, DPRK disavowal of the use of terrorism, and return of MIA remains. Nuclear transparency and the sale of missile technology were soon added to the list. For the DPRK the issues remained, as always, the withdrawal of US forces from Korea and the negotiation of a DPRK–US peace treaty.[54] However, despite periodic positive gestures, such as in 1990 when for the first time the DPRK handed over the remains of US MIAs from the Korean War, throughout this period it remained clear that the DPRK had no intention of moderating its long-standing demand for direct negotiations with the US on troop withdrawal. Productive negotiation in the face of this policy was no more possible between the DPRK and the US than it was between the two Koreas, and the US had no interest in further improving relations with the DPRK when no reciprocal benefit was forthcoming.

The Japanese effort to initiate a dialogue with Pyongyang was more substantial. In addition to supporting the ROK's Nordpolitik initiatives,[55] Japan also felt the need to support broader post-Cold War diplomatic strategies in the region by contributing to a settlement in Korea. The continuing situation where the two neighbouring countries had virtually no communications links of any kind and no mechanisms for resolving trading, consular, fishing and other disputes was not only anomalous but dangerous, given the DPRK potential for posing a military threat to the Japanese islands. Like all of the DPRK's would-be dialogue partners, Japan hoped that expanded diplomatic contacts might contribute to a more realistic Pyongyang perception of international trends. Moreover, the Japanese wished to close the books on the 1910–45 era by reaching agreement on compensation, as it had done when it normalised relations with the ROK in 1965. In addition to the burden of history, the issue of relations between the two countries was complicated by the DPRK detention since 1983 of two crew members from a Japanese fishing vessel *Fujisan-maru* in an attempt to secure the return of a DPRK soldier who had sought asylum in Japan after stowing away on the same vessel during an earlier voyage. The humanitarian issue of consular access to the Japanese wives of Korean residents in Japan repatriated to the DPRK was a further significant issue.[56]

Tokyo first signalled its willingness to open talks with the DPRK by allowing a KWP delegation to enter Japan to attend the national convention of the Japan Socialist Party in February 1989. However, although Japan then made a series of minor conciliatory gestures toward the DPRK such as substantially downplaying the *Fujisan-maru* issue in public, and referring to the DPRK by its official title of 'Democratic People's Republic of Korea', it did not achieve an immediate breakthrough in relations. The major breakthrough came in September 1990 when an unprecedented joint parliamentary mission, led by senior Liberal Democratic Party figure Kanemaru Shin and Japan Socialist Party Vice Chairman Tanabe Makoto visited Pyongyang for talks with the KWP. Discussion revolved principally around the issue of Japanese compensation for the colonial occupation of Korea 1910–45, and the visit was also notable for the strong personal relationship forged between Kim Il Sung and Kanemaru in the course of extended public and private discussions (Byung-Chul Koh 1994:216ff). This led to the signing of an eight-point joint declaration by the three political parties on 28 September 1990 which covered compensation not just for the colonial period but also for what were termed 'abnormal relations' in the post-1945 period. The declaration also endorsed the concept of one Korea, the need for peaceful reunification, and urged the two governments to hold talks on diplomatic recognition.[57] Separate-track negotiations on the *Fujisan-maru* issue secured the release of the crew members soon afterwards.

However, the Joint Declaration provided a flawed basis for the pursuit of DPRK–Japanese rapprochement. While Kanemaru was a senior Liberal Democratic Party (LDP) figure, he did not represent the full range of Japanese political, business and bureaucratic interests. When a significant number of his LDP colleagues, as well as sections of the bureaucracy including the Ministry of Foreign Affairs, examined the text of the Joint Declaration, they concluded that Kanemaru had exceeded his brief in signing a declaration unduly favourable to the interests of the DPRK, especially in the open-ended acknowledgment of Japanese responsibility for post-1945 events. Moreover, while the US and the ROK did not oppose outright the terms of the declaration, they also expressed reservations on the size of possible compensation on this basis (Hong-Nack Kim 1994a:675). The net effect was that when the talks on normalisation of relations began, DPRK expectations were tied to the Kim–Kanemaru–Tanabe declaration, but the Japanese government was pursuing a significantly modified agenda.

On 30–31 January 1991 the first round of intergovernmental talks on the normalisation of DPRK–Japan relations was held in Pyongyang. These talks soon exposed major disagreements, with the Japanese rejecting the principle of postwar compensation and insisting that the DPRK sign a nuclear safeguards agreement. The two sides continued to state their divergent views during a second round of talks in Tokyo during 11–12 March. The talks then achieved stalemate after a third session in Beijing during 20–22 May amid DPRK objections to the Japanese raising the issue of the alleged DPRK abduction of a Japanese national in 1978.[58] This was a relatively minor matter compared to compensation and nuclear inspection, but it raised a number of other issues, including the DPRK's record of support for terrorism, its denial of consular access to Japanese nationals living in the DPRK, and Japanese perceptions of the human rights situation in the DPRK. In view of growing international concern over the DPRK's nuclear program, the Japanese interest lay in slowing the pace of negotiations in this way. Tokyo therefore persisted on this issue and the atmosphere of the talks deteriorated sharply. The two sides met for a further five sessions without result and the talks eventually discontinued after a DPRK walkout over the abduction issue at the eighth session, held in November 1992.[59]

The limitations of DPRK diplomacy were also exposed at the United Nations in 1991 when the ROK succeeded in its long-standing policy of separate, full UN membership for the two Koreas. The North had opposed this as an unacceptable manifestation of a two-Koreas policy and in the past had been supported by the threat of a Chinese and/or Soviet veto should any application reach the Security

Council. As late as November 1989, the DPRK appeared to have firm Chinese backing for its stance (Samuel S. Kim 1994:35). However, as China moved to establish official relations with the ROK, this position became untenable, and Li Peng confirmed the withdrawal of the Chinese veto during his visit to Pyongyang in May 1991. After waging a vigorous campaign in which it warned of unspecified dire consequences if simultaneous UN entry were to go ahead, North Korea then bowed to the inevitable with an announcement on 27 May that it would also seek separate UN admission (*PT* 1 June 1991).[60]

While there were various strands of tactical compromise in the DPRK's foreign policy, especially after 1989, the underlying strategic intransigence gained its fullest expression in Pyongyang's program to acquire nuclear weapons. The concern here is what is known about the development of the program up until the end of 1991, and with the counterpoint it provides to DPRK diplomatic activities in other spheres.

The DPRK began a modest program of nuclear research under Soviet auspices in the 1960s, but the foundation of its weapons program was laid in 1980 when construction commenced at Yonbyon on a 5 MW reactor fuelled with natural uranium, moderated with graphite and capable of generating 20–30 MW of thermal power.[61] This reactor, which was capable of producing small amounts of plutonium, began operation in 1986. Meanwhile, construction of a second reactor at Yonbyon with a capacity of 50–200 MW began in 1984 with a scheduled completion date of 1995 (Oh and Hassig 1994:235). International concern over Pyongyang's nuclear intentions were initially allayed when the DPRK acceded to the Nuclear Non-Proliferation Treaty in 1985 and the program appeared to be under Soviet control and supervision. However, beginning in 1989, US and ROK sources began to express concern about the Yonbyon complex. The major sources of concern were the suspicious nature of specific buildings and facilities at Yonbyon;[62] the fact that the DPRK had not signed a Nuclear Non-Proliferation Treaty (NPT) safeguards agreement with the International Atomic Energy Agency (IAEA), and so was not subject to international inspection; and the fact that the DPRK possessed all the natural resources necessary to make weapons-grade plutonium.

As concern about the DPRK's nuclear program began to grow during 1989, concentration focused on persuading the DPRK to sign a safeguards agreement. In response to this pressure, the DPRK advised the IAEA in February 1990 that it would sign a safeguards agreement if the United States gave legal assurances that it would not resort to a nuclear threat against the DPRK. By Pyongyang's definition, this involved withdrawal of nuclear weapons from the South, removal of the US nuclear threat to the North, simultaneous inspections in the South and in the North, and no further international pressure on the DPRK over the nuclear issue. However, the IAEA rejected this linkage, and throughout 1990 international pressure on Pyongyang built up steadily. In particular, future economic and diplomatic gains that the North hoped to make with Japan, the US, and other Western nations became unambiguously contingent on its signing the safeguards agreement and allowing inspection.

At this stage the DPRK faced a complicated international situation. It had begun its nuclear weapons program years before the collapse of the Soviet Bloc could ever have been imagined, but now that this had occurred the acquisition of nuclear weapons acquired a special significance in Pyongyang. The announcement of the establishment of full diplomatic relations between the ROK and the Soviet Union in September 1990 was of particular importance since it meant that the 1961 DPRK–Soviet mutual defence treaty became ineffective. In public statements and official meetings with the Soviets on the eve of the Seoul–Moscow announcement, the DPRK stated that it would need to take measures to obtain 'weapons for which we have so far relied on the alliance', a clear reference to nuclear weapons (Mack 1991:89). The second half of 1990 also saw the build up to the Gulf War following the Iraqi invasion of Kuwait in August 1990. With the launching of Operation Desert Storm in January 1991, the DPRK had the opportunity to observe the power and reach of US diplomacy and military technology when it was unchecked by global competition with the Soviet Union.[63]

DPRK nuclear policy in 1991 showed signs of uncertainty and contradiction. Chinese Premier Li Peng reportedly urged the signing of a safeguards agreement when he visited Pyongyang in May 1991, and the DPRK stance then began to change. On 15 July the DPRK appeared to moderate its demand that US nuclear weapons stocks in the South be subject to international inspection when it informed the International Atomic Energy Agency (IAEA) that it would agree unconditionally to sign a safeguards agreement in September 1991. However, the issue remained confused by DPRK statements that they intended to sign the agreement but would not permit inspections until their demands on the US nuclear threat to their country were addressed. The DPRK was similarly noncommittal in its initial response to US President George Bush's 27 September 1991 announcement on the global reduction of US nuclear weapons, which included the withdrawal of US tactical nuclear weapons from the Korean peninsula. Eventually, Pyongyang stated that this move, coupled with assurances by Roh Tae-woo, was sufficient to warrant the signing and implementation of a safeguards agreement (*PT* 28 December 1991).[64] On 31 December 1991 the DPRK signed a Joint Declaration for the Denuclearisation of the Korean Peninsula with the ROK and followed this with the signing of a safeguards agreement with the IAEA on 7 January 1992. As 1992 began, these agreements were hopeful signs, but it was not clear where they stood in the DPRK's overall strategic vision.

No convincing account of the rationale behind the DPRK decision to acquire nuclear weapons exists. The setting of an obsessively secretive state and an isolated, eccentric leadership has naturally placed stringent limitations on the information base available and has led to various interpretations of Pyongyang's strategy.[65] Sufficient attention has already been drawn to DPRK leadership calculations in such other domains as economic management and foreign policy to make the argument clear that we should predicate answers on the assumption of a mind-set dominated by notions of life-as-struggle in a predatory international environment. In this setting, the acquisition of nuclear weapons, however unclear Kim may have been on their place in overall DPRK military strategy, offered a means of continuing the Korean struggle with greater hope and purpose than would otherwise have been possible. How much greater hope and purpose this option gave Kim may be judged from the spectre of the DPRK continuing to confront its southern neighbour throughout the 1980s and 1990s as the ROK established vast superiority in all major indices of state power. In this context, Kim clearly expected a nuclear weapons capacity to act as a counter to this superiority, to serve a broader intimidatory purpose, and to become a valuable export commodity in the continuing global fight against imperialism.

Moreover, in accounting for the DPRK's strategic objectives, we should remember that the nuclear program was the centrepiece of a wider program that included other weapons of mass destruction such as chemical and biological weapons, appropriate delivery systems and strategic relationships with customer countries.[66] The key here was the development of expanded military influence within the region through developing tactical and longer range missiles capable of reaching beyond the Korean peninsula to the Japanese islands, and outside the region by the sale of these weapons to Middle East countries such as Iran, Iraq, Syria and Libya. This trend became especially apparent after 1987, when the DPRK began domestic production of SCUD missiles with a range of 300km, while reportedly continuing developmental work on a 500–700km version.

Both the anti-Japanese guerilla tradition and DPRK state ideology underscored the historical necessity of unbending militant struggle against the ROK and its allies. Whereas Kim Il Sung's military strategy in the 1960s and 1970s aimed at forcing a final outcome to the Korean conflict by conventional means, by the beginning of the 1980s the nuclear-backed US defence umbrella in Northeast Asia meant that the Korean conflict was effectively stalemated. Since the option of a negotiated settlement involved unacceptable compromise with DPRK strategic goals, this left a continuation of military confrontation as the only option. For confrontation to be feasible, the DPRK would need to employ non-conventional means, and in this context a nuclear option became not simply desirable but necessary. But it was more than a defensive measure. DPRK military strategy derived from Kim's guerilla experience with an overlay of Stalin-era Soviet military strategy and was strongly offensive in orientation. While tactical retreats and defensive postures may occasionally be necessary, for the guerilla the purpose of warfare is to take the fight to the enemy, not to defend secured ground. Acquiring nuclear weapons was a matter of state survival but conceptually it enabled far more than mere survival. The very identity of the state was inextricably bound up with continuation of the struggle to reunify the country, and possession of nuclear weapons created an environment in which that struggle could continue. This outlook provided the driving logic behind the DPRK's nuclear policy in the 1990s.

Any account of DPRK diplomacy during this period of major transformation would be incomplete without recording the interpretations of events placed on record by Kim Il Sung and Kim Jong Il. In October 1988, in the wake of Gorbachev's Krasnoyarsk Declaration and the decision by Hungary to extend diplomatic recognition to the ROK, the DPRK highlighted the contents of a talk given by Kim Jong Il to senior officials of the KWP Central Committee on 25 September 1987.[67] The text of this talk affords a detailed account of the Kimist interpretation of international affairs as the implications of the Gorbachev reforms were beginning to become clear.[68]

Kim Jong Il began by describing a 'very complicated' situation which poses 'serious problems concerning the destiny not only of our revolution but also of the world revolution'. After noting that an understanding of 'the real features of contemporary imperialism and its fate' was essential, Kim proceeded to give a potted version of world history since World War II. Here he drew attention to the resilience of capitalism. This resilience, he explained, was due to the internationalisation of capital and the development of new forms of cooperation between capitalist nations, centering on the US. As a result, 'capitalism has survived its imminent doom and made rapid economic and technological progress'. However, this did not mean that capitalism had reinvented itself, for 'the basic contradiction of capitalism has never been settled, nor had the predatory nature of imperialism ever changed'. The result was 'today the contradictions of the capitalist world have been exacerbated still further, and imperialism finds itself in serious political and economic trouble'.

Kim proceeded to elaborate on the economic and social implications of this crisis. His description of capitalist society is especially noteworthy for its revelation of the depth of Kimist alienation from modernity:

> Outwardly, the developed countries seem to be prospering, but inwardly they are rotting due to ever-worsening contradictions. [Capitalists] are manufacturing a variety of things to stimulate extravagance, corruption and dissipation to paralyse the human body and mind, with the result that the number of drug addicts, alcoholics, as well as degenerates pursuing abnormal desires is growing rapidly and people are becoming mentally and physically deformed. Even the defenders of the bourgeoisie are lamenting and calling this phenomenon an incurable disease of modern capitalism . . . A decadent material life, a poor mental and cultural life and a reactionary political life—these can be said to be the main characteristics of capitalist society, and they show the anti-popular nature and corruption of modern imperialism.

The contrast with socialism could not be greater:

> There is a great gulf between life under socialism, where the masses of the people equally enjoy independent and creative activities to the full as masters of the state and society, and that under capitalism, where people become the slaves of money and seek only their own pleasure. A man whose mind has been paralysed by capitalism cannot see the difference.

With this observation, Kim proceeded to offer criticism of the Socialist Bloc with a severity of language not seen in the DPRK media since the early 1960s and the height of the Sino–Soviet split:

> Of course, we cannot say that so far socialist countries have brought the superiority of the socialist system fully into play. Frankly speaking, they have deviated sometimes to the 'Right' and sometimes to the

'Left' in managing the new social system. Deviations occurred in the process of establishing the socialist system, but in particular, grave mistakes were made in finding answers to new problems as to how the revolution and construction should be promoted after the establishment of the socialist system. A series of serious deviations were also made in dealing with the mutual relations between the socialist countries which carry on the revolution and construction in different historic conditions. All this has tarnished the image of socialism.

The younger Kim was equally clear on the causes of these deviations. They 'have nothing to do with the intrinsic nature of the socialist system. They are due totally to the fact that those who administer the socialist system are not experienced and fully prepared politically and ideologically'. When one considers the depth of experience available throughout most of Eastern Europe—Ceausescu, Honecker, Husak et al—the reference to Gorbachev is clear.

Nevertheless, Kim had no intention of dwelling on negative aspects, and he quickly returned to more familiar themes with a rousing statement of confidence in ultimate victory:

> The struggle between socialism and capitalism is the struggle between the new and the old. That the new emerges victorious and the old perishes is an immutable law of historical development. This law will never change, though the victory of the new may be attained only after experiencing twists and turns . . . Our era by no means suits imperialism; it is an era of historical change in which imperialism is on the brink of ruin and the people of the world are marching forward boldly along the road to socialism, the road of independence.

Some weeks earlier he had also reached the conclusion that the crisis in the Soviet Bloc was a passing phase:

> Many changes are now taking place in the world . . . Generally speaking, this can be called a passing historical vortex which has appeared in the course of mankind's advance towards a new world of independence. In order to form a correct view of the present age it is necessary to see the process of historical development in its full context and to identify its essence, not phenomena alone. To my regret, some people are interpreting the end of the cold war between East and West and the frustration of socialism in some countries as the victory of the old over the new and as a change in the direction of the historical tide. They are mistaken. There may be setbacks in the course of historical progress, but its direction cannot change [PT 16 November 1991].

But wishful thinking and overblown rhetoric could not conceal the fact that at the beginning of 1992 the DPRK looked out on a world that had changed drastically in only five years, and almost uniformly these changes had seriously weakened its capacity to continue the struggle against the South. The DPRK economy was contracting, its diplomatic strategies were ineffective, its alliance system had been seriously undermined, and its capacity for the future procurement of advanced weaponry was uncertain. Even worse, in many instances the zero-sum nature of the inter-Korean conflict meant that every reversal for the DPRK was a commensurate gain for the ROK.

Signs of potential adjustment to these changes were not entirely absent. At the beginning of 1992 the two Koreas stood on the threshold of a new phase of engagement—as they had in 1972 and 1984. The DPRK was also displaying new interest in elements of Chinese economic reforms—as it had in 1984. But to the leadership, these were system-defending, tactical expedients. Otherwise, the DPRK still faced the post-Cold War world with Party and government institutions, senior personnel and ideology essentially unchanged since the 1960s.

The deterioration of the DPRK's diplomatic and security situation was especially severe. While some sources view the DPRK as a practitioner of pragmatic diplomacy during this period,[69] in reality the fixed world view of the Kims caused them to seriously misread a number of situations. First, in offering immediate, enthusiastic support to the Soviet generals behind the abortive August 1991 coup in Moscow, Pyongyang evinced an ideological conviction that these generals represented the future, not the past of Soviet politics. It ignored the possibility that the coup might fail and that it would have to continue to live with a reforming Soviet Union. Second, in dealing with radical movements within the ROK, the North did little to support the strategies of such groups as the Chondaehyop, whose programs for reunification closely coincided with those of the North. On the contrary, the continuing projection of uncompromising hostility to the South undermined political support for pro-North radicals in the ROK and prevented them from becoming a more significant political force.

Third, the DPRK likewise failed to exploit the Japanese dialogue. It was clear from the start that Japan was prepared to conclude a financial settlement as reparations for the colonial period, but with billions of dollars waiting to flow from this source, the DPRK demonstrated inflexibility by insisting on holding Japan responsible for postwar events as well. Kim placed too much faith in personal diplomacy and failed to see that Kanemaru Shin had been out of step with his home government in agreeing to the September 1990 Joint Declaration. It should have been immediately clear to the DPRK that the Japanese Government would not accept the principle of postwar compensation under which Kanemaru had negotiated, but the DPRK opted to stand its ground, rather than return to negotiation.

Fourth, by any measure, reliance on nuclear weapons as a viable means to redress the grossly uneven nature of the military contest was an appallingly unsophisticated option to take, for while it could serve the security needs of the state, it could only do so on terms that locked the DPRK into its existing policy framework—the very framework that had produced economic backwardness and diplomatic isolation. Strategically, the nuclear weapons option not only painted the DPRK further into a corner but, more importantly, it allowed the DPRK the unaffordable illusion that it could continue to ignore the role played by a modern, efficient industrial base in the projection of state power.

Finally, Pyongyang was ineffective in countering the erosion of its diplomatic support base, especially in handling the UN entry issue. Over a long period of time the DPRK's cynical, predatory outlook on foreign relations and its disdain for the niceties of diplomacy left it without any reservoir of goodwill with which to counter the rush to establish relations with the ROK. Consistent with its outlook, Pyongyang resorted to ultimatums, threats and pleas to erstwhile allies not to recognise the ROK, but otherwise displayed a fatalistic inca-pacity to develop fall-back positions when it was clear that it could not achieve its major objectives. Kimist foreign policy remained committed to the aggressive view that identified increases in the insecurity of its adversaries as gains in the security of the DPRK. This outlook could only draw its adversaries into a commitment to pursue the same strategy in reverse, and in a contest that the DPRK was steadily losing, the persistence of aggressive diplomacy was a poor strategy. As the DPRK entered the 1990s, it stood in a position of gross economic inferiority vis-a-vis the ROK. It also sustained adversarial relationships with the two largest global economic powers with no strong compensating alliances of its own. However one defines or measures pragmatism, it is hard to point to a single diplomatic issue on which the DPRK manoeuvred successfully to either maximise gains or minimise losses during this period.

Obviously, a leader capable of self-reflection and ripe for self-correction would have handled the crises of the late 1980s more effectively. But Kim Il Sung could not provide this leadership.

Instead, he remained supremely confident that his chosen path was correct—politically, ideologically and historically. Kim's hold on reality had been weakened by megalomania, such that in a 1991 interview with a Japanese publisher we see him soberly likening ROK anti-tank traps on the southern side of the DMZ to a ROK equivalent of the Berlin Wall designed to prevent southerners coming north and vice versa,[70] while in formal meetings with the Chinese leadership we also see him offering exaggerated figures on DPRK economic performance which the Chinese knew were false.[71] Clearly, Kim began the task of convincing his countrymen by convincing himself and, in reading the treatises and interviews of the two Kims during this era and in observing policy outcomes, we find no grounds for doubting the sincerity of their constant professions of faith in ultimate success, which seemed to grow more and more shrill as the material base for achieving reunification on their terms dissipated.

Such self-deception did not make the DPRK's crisis any less real. By 1992 those in the party and government elite who so chose could see that the DPRK was in a state of profound crisis from which there seemed no way out. An unreformed DPRK could not sustain itself, but the process of reform elsewhere had been inexorable, forcing regimes well beyond the limited measures originally intended. Communist reformers had invited criticism and sought disavowal of a few unintended side effects of authoritarian Party rule, but instead had induced the people to reflect upon the very foundations of political power in their countries, on the core features of the dictatorship of the Party and on the policies that flowed from them. In turn, the people had served a log of claims on their political masters that included the right of open debate on social and political issues, the right to complain and register dissent, the right to be treated with respect by those in authority, to have access to petty privileges, to exercise autonomy within the immediate family group, to be better informed, to have more consumer goods and access to information both frivolous and serious from the outside world, and to travel and see foreign sights for themselves. The experience of the now-fallen Soviet Bloc was of the impossibility of repudiating select parts of an ideology for which the regime has long claimed monolithic truth, and of the futility of acknowledging even limited forms of accountability where the regime had long been unaccountable.

Despite the manifest futility of continued confrontation with the ROK and its allies, the KWP could not countenance reform, for this meant abandoning the goal of reunification under KWP leadership. Reform would undermine the legitimacy of the Party and bring about a severe identity crisis, for the ideology and the policies which had emerged in the pursuit of reunification gave decisive shape to almost every aspect of DPRK state and society. To depart from this ideology would threaten the DPRK's very self-definition as a state.

8

A MATTER OF SURVIVAL,
THE 1990s

To the ex-guerillas in the Democratic People's Republic of Korea (DPRK) leadership who had grown to maturity amid a protracted fight for survival with the Japanese and who had come to power under the tutelage of Stalinism, the Cold War vision of a desperate, immutable global struggle between the forces of socialism and imperialism made profound sense—far more so than to the cadres of more educated, cosmopolitan background scattered through the Politburos of other socialist states. Consequently, when the end of the Cold War placed the DPRK under enormous diplomatic and military pressure, this was not an unfamiliar situation for Kim Il Sung and the elite cadre he had fashioned. In many ways his glorification of the guerilla ethos had fashioned a state and society that could withstand these pressures—that could accept life in an isolated, hostile environment, embrace rigid Party discipline, endure prolonged privation, improvise and seize whatever advantages might arise, prize only what was within grasp, and above all accept the ethos of unremitting struggle.

The speed at which ordinary people in the Soviet Bloc had abandoned the regimes to which they had given every outward show of loyalty was an alarming revelation to the DPRK, and this intensified Party resolve to maintain the isolation of its people from capitalist 'contamination'. Accordingly, in the wake of the collapse of global communism, the Party continued to maintain tight ideological control over the population. System-defending economic policy measures were also an important element in the pursuit of economic survival, and so the government continued to implement these at a slow and steady pace, as was appropriate to their limited objective. Policy in the inter-Korean sphere and in foreign relations more generally also remained fixed on the principle that the DPRK would seek whatever advantage it could from its various dialogue partners, but that it would not rely on outcomes from these dialogues for the safeguarding of its national security.

Instead, Pyongyang would continue to rely on its own military strength, especially its nuclear weapons program. During 1991–94 the DPRK came into increasing conflict with the International Atomic Energy Agency (IAEA) over the issue of on-site inspections, and in June 1994 this led to a serious confrontation with the US. A compromise engineered by former US President Jimmy Carter resolved the immediate crisis and led to the October 1994 Geneva Framework Agreement, under which the DPRK agreed to cap its nuclear program in return for the US-brokered provision of fuel oil and the construction of two light-water nuclear reactors, but the underlying conflict remained.

The economic and diplomatic consequences of the DPRK strategy were, of course, considerable. The DPRK's major adversaries were fearful of the growing possibility of an economic and political collapse in the North, and so had acquired a vested interest in promoting economic growth, manageable political change and continuing social stability in the North. They were prepared to offer substantial material incentives to achieve this. The Republic of Korea (ROK) offered massive economic investment, Japan stood poised to negotiate a multibillion dollar settlement for reparations arising from the 1910–45 colonial era, and the US was prepared to relax long-standing restrictions on trade and other contacts with the DPRK. However, none of the three could give the DPRK what it wanted, which was the right and the means to safeguard its identity as a guerilla state and, as the ubiquitous Party slogan put it to 'live in our own way'. To the Korean Workers' Party (KWP) this meant identity as a militarist, socialist, anti-imperialist country that sought to free its compatriots in the South from capitalist and imperialist control and to reunify the country under its leadership.

This was the situation when Kim Il Sung died of a heart attack on 8 July 1994 at age 82. Upon Kim's death the DPRK entered into a self-proclaimed three-year period of state mourning, and with many normal public Party and government activities suspended it became difficult for outside observers to detect movements in policy and personnel matters. It was clear, however, that arrangements for the succession of Kim Jong Il went smoothly, and by the time the younger

Kim assumed the position of KWP General Secretary in October 1997, it was also clear that he would do little to change the hallmark policies of his father. He would rule by cult of personality, avoid any substantive economic reform measures, and continue his father's reunification strategy.

At the conclusion of the period of mourning the country was in serious economic disarray. Beginning in 1995, floods and then drought combined with the cumulative effect of decades of doctrinaire agri-culture policies to produce widespread famine conditions. Conservative estimates placed the number of famine deaths at two to three million people and Pyongyang became chronically reliant on international relief agencies to feed its people. As a result, the food issue became increasingly linked with other issues in the DPRK's external relations, as the DPRK demanded food as a precondition to talks and its adversaries demanded political concessions as a precon-dition to the provision of food in the quantities sought.

While the leadership continued to reject the option of reform, economic crisis forced compromise on traditional policies of isolation and economic autarky on a number of fronts. Most notably, it admitted representatives from various food aid organisations, it admit-ted ROK construction teams to build the two light-water nuclear reactors, it continued to promote, though ineffectually, the Rajin–Sunbong Free Economic and Trade Zone (FETZ), and it accepted an ever-expanding role for the DPRK in manufacturing goods on con-signment for ROK and Japanese companies. Toward the end of the decade, as the scope of these compromises grew and as Kim Jong Il's skills and energies remained dedicated to the maintenance of a failing system, a major systemic crisis seemed inevitable.

In his last years Kim Il Sung remained alert and vigorous, the father–son duumvirate operated smoothly, and Kim Jong Il continued to expand his role in Party and government. As had been the case on the younger Kim's fortieth birthday, the Party used the occasion of the younger Kim's approaching fiftieth birthday on 16 February 1992 to award him further high honours and praise. At the Nine-teenth Plenum of the Sixth KWP Central Committee (CC), convened on 24 December 1991, the younger Kim was named Supreme Commander of the Korean People's Armed Forces, marking yet one more stage in the gradual transfer of power from father to son. Then, during January 1992, the DPRK media gave wide publicity to a lecture Kim Jong Il delivered to senior Party officials on 3 January, titled *The Historical Lesson in Building Socialism and the General Line of Our Party* (PT 8 February 1992). Finally, on his fiftieth birthday the Party further emphasised the younger Kim's authority and charisma through the publication of a joint message of congratulations from the KWP Central Committee, the KWP Military Commission and the DPRK Administration Council (*PT* 22 February 1992).

Kim Jong Il's lecture afforded a significant insight into the mindset of the DPRK leadership. It was his first detailed public response to the collapse of the Soviet Bloc. In it he analysed reasons for the collapse, explained why the DPRK was not in danger of a similar collapse, and set forth parameters for domestic and foreign policy in the 1990s. Kim began with a forthright description of recent events:

> Socialism has suffered a setback and capitalism has revived in some countries in recent years; a short time ago the Soviet Union broke up and ended its existence. As a consequence of this, the imperialists and reactionaries are claiming that capitalism has 'triumphed' and socialism has 'come to an end'. This is causing ideological confusion among some people who do not understand the situation properly, and [is] seriously affecting the development of the world revolution. Now it is an urgent historical task to learn a lesson from the prevailing situation, reconstruct the socialist movement on a new basis and lead the cause of socialism to an upsurge.

Kim's faith in the theory and practice of socialism was, of course, unshaken. Not only was it 'an inexorable law of historical development that mankind advances towards socialism', but also since 1917 'socialism has spread worldwide, and the socialist countries have, in a short period of time, attained greater socio-economic progress than would have been possible even in hundreds of years under capitalism'. Where, then, had things gone wrong? Again, Kim was to the point:

> In short, the basic reason for the frustration of socialism in some countries is that they did not put the main emphasis on strengthening the motive force for building socialism; they failed to understand the essence of socialism, of centring on the popular masses, the makers of history . . . The basic way to promote the building of socialism successfully is to strengthen the motive force of the revolution by educating the popular masses in a communist way by giving priority to the transformation of the people and by rallying them fully behind the Party.

It was by no means the least of the contradictions of Kimist ideology that Kim, writing as the designated future leader in what was by general assessment the most highly centralised and repressive state in the world, professed to set little store by the political and economic conditions established by government. Instead, the decisive role in promoting the development of socialist society was played by the masses. Countries where socialism had fallen:

> had believed that socialism could be built merely by hastening the progress of economic construction while keeping control of state power and the means of production . . . They did not put their primary effort into the transformation of the people to raise their ideological and cultural levels rapidly and prepare them fully as the driving force of the revolution and construction.

Other factors were at work. Some socialist parties had 'failed to recognise the qualitative differences between socialism and capitalism' and had not adhered consistently to the fundamental principles of socialism. They had introduced 'revisionist policies [where] the degeneration of socialism was further accelerated by the introduction of "pluralism", on the pretext of the "reform" and "restructuring" of society'. Others had failed to adhere to the principle of independence between fraternal Parties and had 'yielded to the pressure of the great powers and acted under the baton of others and the result of this was that they meekly accepted revisionism when the big countries took to revisionism and accepted "reform" and "restructuring" when others did so'.

What of the future, then? It followed logically from Kim's analysis that there could be no flirting with compromise:

> In order to accomplish the socialist cause we must consistently maintain socialist principles in the revolution and construction . . . This is a revolutionary principle which must never be compromised. In the course of building socialism one can commit minor errors, but the working-class party that is responsible for the destiny of the popular masses must on no account abandon the fundamental principles of socialism.

Above all, the Party needed to avoid revisionism and reform at all costs:

> 'Pluralism' can never be tolerated in a socialist society. 'Liberalism' in ideology, a 'multiparty system' in politics and 'diversity' in the form of ownership which 'pluralism' advocates are the mode of politics that is characteristic of capitalist society in which competition for survival dominates, based on individualism and liberalism . . . Permitting liberalism in ideology and a multiparty system in politics in a socialist society is, in the long run, to open a road to counter-revolutionary manoeuvres that are aimed at demolishing the foundation of socialist society and overthrowing the people's government . . . Single conces-

sions and a gradual retreat from socialist principles have resulted in ten- and hundred-fold concessions and a full retreat until, finally, the grave consequences of the ruin of the working-class parties themselves was incurred.

In short:

Historical experience shows that when people, steadily strengthening the driving force of the revolution with a strong conviction in socialism and a correct guideline, hold fast to socialist principles in all circumstances and strengthen comradely unity and cooperation on the basis of independence, the socialist cause will advance along the road of victory; otherwise it will suffer setbacks and frustration. This is a serious lesson mankind has learned on its road to socialism [PT 8 February 1992].

These were, of course, the long-established hallmarks of the KWP, now validated through the downfall of the socialist regimes which had failed to observe them.

Kim Jong Il's range of responsibilities grew further in the early 1990s. Not only did his fiftieth birthday messages allude to his leading role in a wide range of Party and state activities, but when the first volumes of Kim Il Sung's autobiography *Reminiscences with the Century* began to appear in early 1992, the older Kim himself alluded to his son's ever-expanding leadership role in the preface: 'Many people, including celebrated foreign statesmen and well-known literary men, urged me to write my reminiscences, saying that my life would serve as a precious lesson for the people. But I was in no hurry to do so. Now that a large part of my work is done by [KWP] Secretary for Organizational Affairs Kim Jong Il, I have been able to find some time' (Kim Il Sung, 1994b).

Public statements by the Kims, and actual policy outcomes confirmed that until the death of his father, Kim Jong Il continued to rely on the same power base as his father—the unquestioning loyalty and obedience of the Politburo backed up by the operation of pervasive and overlapping security bureaucracies. Over the years commentators have identified various cadres as being close to Kim Jong Il, but while Kim Il Sung lived no such cadres entered the Politburo. No doubt Kim Jong Il sought advice from a select few behind the scenes but, again to judge from policy outcomes, these advisors were either in total agreement with all major policies or else, where they differed, were powerless to influence the course of events. Accordingly, periodic reaffirmation of key ideological movements continued, including the Three Revolution Team Movement (PT 28

March 1992, *PT* 28 November 1992), and the Rural Theses (26 February 1994).

The father–son leadership team continued to dominate a loyal, aging Party elite. Politburo changes reflected either the promotion of younger cadres to alternate Politburo status as a reflection of the transient significance of the policy area for which they were responsible, or else the reappointment of veteran cadres who had been dismissed earlier by Kim Il Sung. The Twentieth Plenum of the Sixth KWP CC, held on 10 December 1992, afforded an example of the former tendency when it appointed, as alternate Politburo members, two relatively younger men, Kim Tal-hyon and Kim Yong-sun. Both men were then playing prominent roles in DPRK economic and diplomatic strategy respectively. Kim Tal-hyon had been closely involved in the DPRK economic planning process for much of the 1980s as a Vice Minister and then Minister in the Administration Council. He had impressed the Soviets as a pragmatic administrator (Trigubenko 1991:132), and made a similar favourable impression on ROK officials when he visited Seoul for economic talks in July 1992 and, reportedly, first proposed inter-Korean cooperation in the building of light-water nuclear reactors for power generation. Kim Yong-sun had been one of the Party's leading foreign affairs administrators since 1980 and had been prominent in handling negotiations with the US and Japan. Some saw these appointments as indicating a new, more pragmatic line but they did not stand for long. A year later at the Twenty-First Plenum in December 1993, both men were dismissed from the Politburo in a move that probably reflected the declining significance of the policy areas with which they were associated. By that time economic relations with the ROK and dialogue with Japan and the US had fallen on Kim Il Sung's list of priorities.

The tendency to reappoint veteran cadres was evident at the Fourth Session of the Ninth Supreme People's Assembly (SPA), held on 11 December 1992, when Kang Song-san replaced Yon Hyong-muk as Prime Minister. For Kang it was a return to the position he had occupied between 1984 and 1986, and the reappointment took place under similar policy auspices. In January 1984, Kang's appointment as Prime Minister coincided with signs of interest in the selective adoption of Chinese economic reform measures, and he was replaced when the leadership discarded this option in favour of closer economic relations with the Soviet Bloc. He now returned to this office as the DPRK again began showing signs of interest in the Chinese experience.[1] With these changes Kang returned once more to the position of No. 4 in the hierarchy, and at the Twentieth Plenum of the Sixth KWP Congress CC on 10 December, Yon Hyong-muk was demoted from full to alternate membership of the Politburo. The Twenty-First Plenum on 11 December 1993 afforded two further examples of Kim Il Sung's tendency in his last years to reinstate aging former comrades who had been demoted or dismissed years previously. After seventeen years spent living in obscurity, Kim Yong-ju, Kim Il Sung's 72-year-old brother, again entered the Politburo, occupying the No. 7 position in the Party hierarchy. Kim Yong-ju was also appointed as one of four vice-presidents. Kim Il Sung also reappointed Yang Hyong-sop to alternate Politburo membership, having dismissed him from full membership in 1977.

These were the last Politburo personnel changes effected by Kim Il Sung. Seven months later, on 8 July 1994, he died of a heart attack at age eighty-two. His death brought no immediate change to state policies, especially on the nuclear issue. The early stages of the prearranged succession of his son, Kim Jong Il, proceeded smoothly, and no purges, dismissals or demotions of senior cadres or other signs of a power struggle in Pyongyang took place. The fact that Kim Jong Il did not immediately take up the posts of State President and KWP General Secretary left vacant by his father's death aroused speculation about limits placed on Kim Jong Il's authority by other forces within the Pyongyang hierarchy, but this line of speculation did not explain why these posts were essential to the exercise of effective political control in Pyongyang. Nor did it satisfactorily explain the juxtaposition of a serious power struggle with the consistent public media emphasis on Kim Jong Il's virtue and authority, including the unambiguous public designation of Kim as 'Supreme Leader of the Party, State and Army'.[2] The notion that Kim could project his cult of personality through the media but not have effective control of the reins of power was, of course, a dubious proposition in the setting of the DPRK.

A noticeable development after Kim Il Sung's death was the expanded public profile of the Korean People's Armed Forces. The media devoted considerable energy to praising the KPAF, its leaders received promotions and at gatherings of the country's leaders, the KPAF were given the unprecedented honour of being listed higher than the alternate members of the Politburo. Observers also noted that in October 1995, the DPRK began to use the military term 'the command post of the revolution' in describing the source of major policy decisions, giving rise to speculation that in the political and governmental void of the period of mourning, an ad hoc committee composed of members of the Politburo and a group of military leaders was functioning as supreme organ of power (*VP* July 1997, p. 2).

There were both immediate and historical reasons for this development. The immediate reasons were that Kim Il Sung died in the midst of an ongoing international crisis precipitated by the DPRK's nuclear weapons program, and this tended to highlight the role of the military. Moreover, Kim Jong Il's own personality cult relies on a deep identification with his father's anti-Japanese guerilla comrades, and he obviously shares with the survivors of this era a belief in the efficacy of toughness and force in confronting the Party's adversaries.

The historical reason was that, as we have seen, after 1980 Kim Il Sung did not admit any military figures to full membership of the Politburo, mainly because of an unwillingness to fully trust soldiers who lacked a guerilla background, and thus produced a de facto 'civilianisation' of the Politburo. His death opened up opportunities for senior military officers to assume political power commensurate with their military rank, but whether it represented a true expansion of military influence within the Party or just an adjustment to the previous situation in which military representation in the Politburo had fallen from eleven to three in the period 1980–95 remained debatable. Certainly, the massive interpenetration of the Party and the military under the Kimist garrison state ensured that military cadres did not possess even the vestige of an independent power base. The effective political power of senior military officers has always derived from the Party and, as happened to O Kuk-yol in 1987 and as has happened to others over the years, military leaders suffered dismissal if they did not adhere strictly to the Party's policies.

The three-year period of mourning brought few other changes of note to the Party hierarchy. No new appointments were made to the Politburo, which continued to shrink with the death of elderly members such as O Chin-u in February 1995 and Ch'oe Kwang in February 1997. With Ch'oe's death the last surviving cadre of the Kim Il Sung guerilla generation still actively exercising power passed from the scene. Also in February 1997, Hong Song-nam replaced Kang Song-san as Prime Minister. No reason for the change was made public, although Kang's recent lengthy absences from public view in 1996 had already caused speculation on his health. Change of a different sort occurred on 12 February 1997 when Hwang Jang-yop, a long-standing member of the KWP Secretariat defected to Seoul. This and other important defections suggested a Party and government elite in disarray and also gave the North's adversaries access to significant information about the decision-making process in

Pyongyang. The picture that emerged was of a nocturnal, secretive leader who rarely convened meetings, dealt with cadres individually by telephone as much as in person, and had no clear confidantes or court favorites.

On 8 October 1997, Kim Jong Il finally assumed the position of General Secretary of the KWP, a largely symbolic move since he had clearly exercised absolute authority over the country since his father's death. Otherwise, the end of the self-proclaimed three-year period of mourning for Kim Il Sung on 8 July 1997 brought no immediate change to either Party or government. Meanwhile, the position of State President remained unfilled and despite, though some would say because of, the country's multiple crises, there was no sign of any intention to either convene a Party congress or else hold long-over-due elections for a new Supreme People's Assembly.

During the period of mourning, policy objectives, especially in the ongoing nuclear crisis evinced strong continuity. Kim Jong Il continued to release his periodic rescripts on ideology, and almost every issue of every major publication in the DPRK continued to extol the virtues of the younger Kim in characteristically extravagant terms. Since his father's death, the major themes in promoting Kim Jong Il's personality cult have included:

- his supreme leadership of the Party, state and army;
- his co-responsibility with Kim Il Sung for the Korean revolution—'a great leader who has steered the revolution and national construction to victory together with the great leader Comrade Kim Il Sung';[3]
- his role as the formulator of Juche into an integral system, 'taking it over and developing it fully';[4]
- the theory of the Leader: 'For the first time in the history of the international communist movement, Comrade Kim Jong Il has advanced the unique idea of building a working class into a party of the leader, thus creating a model ruling party of socialism';[5]
- his role in transforming the KWP, into 'the Party of Comrade Kim Il Sung';[6]
- his omniscience and outstanding qualities as leader and motivator: 'He gets in motions [sic] operations on a world-wide scale and rallies billions of masses as one, galvanizing them into action with his dynamic leadership and bringing about miracles and innovations in all fields';[7]
- his continuing commitment to Korean reunification: 'All [his]

revolutionary activities are coupled with his sacred struggle for the achievement of national reunification . . .'[8]

Political and ideological continuity contrasted with chronic, severe economic hardship for the DPRK, with declining production in practically all sectors and widespread food shortages. By 1998 the economy had shrunk by as much as one-third since 1990, and many parts of the country were experiencing famine. The trigger was the natural disaster of widespread flooding in August 1995 which affected as much as 30 per cent of the country and destroyed an estimated 2 million tonnes of an estimated 5.67 million tonne harvest. This severely damaged an already fragile agricultural base and left the countryside vulnerable to further floods in 1996. Drought conditions in 1997 brought about outright famine conditions with widespread deaths due to starvation. As images of malnourished children in the North became common in the international media and as international appeals for famine relief became annual events it became increasingly unlikely that the DPRK would be able to feed its people adequately without radical changes to its economic policies.

In December 1993 the DPRK publicly announced that the Third Seven-Year Plan (1987–93) had not met its targets. Although this stated the obvious, and it is doubtful that the DPRK had ever achieved anything like the stated targets of previous economic plans, the announcement was nevertheless noteworthy because it was the first time Pyongyang had ever publicly admitted to economic failure. The government further announced that the economy would enter a three-year period of economic adjustment during which emphasis would be placed on agriculture, light industry and trade. This formalised an ad hoc procedure that the DPRK had regularly followed since its multi-year plans first began to fall short of their stated targets in the 1960s but when this period expired at the beginning of 1997 the government announced no further economic plan, thus effectively leaving the economy without a central planning mechanism.

Important shifts in the DPRK's foreign trade patterns also occurred in the early 1990s. In the wake of the 1991 shift to hard currency transactions, trade with the Soviet Union Russia fell to only 6.6 per cent of the DPRK's total foreign trade by 1994. In the period 1985–90 the Soviet Union had accounted for over 50 per cent of the DPRK's total foreign trade. In particular, imports of Soviet oil fell from 440 000 tonnes in 1990 to less than 40 000 tonnes in 1991, producing widespread dislocations in industry, key parts of which reportedly fell back to operate at about 30 per cent of capacity. China and, to a lesser degree, Japan filled this gap to some extent, but the decline in foreign trade remained marked (see Tables 8.1, 8.2, 8.3 below).

A further significant step forward in Pyongyang's relations with the international economic community occurred with its expressions of interest in joining the Asian Development Bank and the World Bank/International Monetary Fund. In September 1997 the ROK reiterated its full support for the move and the IMF dispatched an investigation team to the DPRK to examine Pyongyang's qualifications for membership. A key motivation for the North was access to aid funds and soft loans, but it remained unclear whether it could be induced to lift a statistical blackout which has existed since the early 1960s.

Table 8.1   Foreign trade of the DPRK 1990–94 (unit: US$100m)

Year	Exports	Imports	Total
1990	20.2	26.2	46.4
1991	9.5	16.4	25.9
1992	9.2	15.5	24.7
1993	9.4	15.4	24.8
1994	8.4	12.7	21.1

Source: Namkoong (1996:229).

Table 8.2   Major trading partners of the DPRK 1990–94 (unit: %)

Year	Russia/USSR	China	Japan	Other
1990	37.2	15.7	15.5	31.6
1991	14.1	23.6	19.7	42.6
1992	11.7	27.8	19.2	41.3
1993	8.6	34.1	17.9	39.4
1994	6.6	29.6	23.5	40.3

Source: Namkoong (1996:230).

Table 8.3   DPRK trade with China 1990–95 (unit: US$100m)

Year	Exports	Imports	Total
1990	1.37	3.05	4.42
1991	0.86	5.25	6.11
1992	1.55	5.41	6.96
1993	2.97	6.02	8.99
1994	1.99	4.25	6.24
1995	0.64	4.86	5.50

Source: Keum (1997:99).

Meanwhile, the DPRK continued to move at a steady pace to develop the Rajin–Sunbong FETZ. Unlike the Joint Venture legislation of 1984, which was largely unsupported by supplementary legislation and received little publicity as the government lost interest, in 1992–93 the DPRK enacted or revised a number of laws covering economic activity in the Rajin–Sunbong FETZ, and also began to actively promote it by means of seminars in China, Japan, the United States and other countries. Notwithstanding, the government lacked the commitment and the expertise to emulate the growth pattern of the Chinese Special Economic Zones, and by 1998 most commentators concluded that the FETZ was no longer a serious government priority. While many foreign companies surveyed the zone, the bulk of foreign investment mirrored that in the economy at large, consisting almost entirely of small-scale ventures by pro-Pyongyang Korean residents of Japan.

The Rajin–Sunbong FETZ represented one of the few instruments available to the DPRK for generating the foreign investment and technology flows that are essential to any reform process. However, foreign investor interest in the FETZ was limited by a number of major obstacles. These included perception of the sizeable political risks involved in investing in a DPRK while it is still strongly hostile to Japan, the US and the ROK; the lack of a strong legal basis for doing business in the DPRK in accordance with normal international commercial procedure; the degree and nature of government control over economic activity; and poor commercial and industrial infrastructure including the lack of reliable maintenance services, power supply, transport and telecommunications.

But while the argument for economic reform in the DPRK encountered hostility at the leadership level, this did not mean that the system was entirely devoid of reform characteristics. Even if Kim Jong Il still rejected economic reform as a viable strategy on ideological grounds, he did not rule out the tactical use of elements of reform as a means of supporting and defending the socialist economic system. This tactic of system-defending reform became pronounced during the 1990s. Its major hallmarks were:

- the maintenance of the present hallmark features of the command economy;
- the maintenance of collectivised agriculture;
- the maintenance of other basic DPRK state policies, including its nuclear weapons program;

- continuing experimentation with Free Economic and Trade Zone (FETZ) strategies in the north-east region;
- the continuing search for international sources of soft loans and capital investment;
- substantial relaxation of controls on border trade in the north-east;
- the continuation of trade with the ROK, but the exclusion of major ROK investment;
- concerted attempts to limit public awareness of experimentation and a continuing prohibition on public or semi-public debate on economic reform; and
- continued reliance on ideological incentives for the work force.

Under these policies, the DPRK presented a more or less unchanged profile to the regional and global economic system. Self-reliance, long abandoned in practice, continued to be subject to an increasingly elastic interpretation of maintaining control over foreign transactions, rather than excluding them. The DPRK's foreign debts remained barely acknowledged, much less addressed to the satisfaction of its major creditors, and the DPRK's international credit rating remained extremely low.[9] Combined with the factor of its nuclear weapons program, this meant that most potential foreign investors remained extremely wary of the DPRK.

This in turn meant that efforts to seek out funds for capital investment through foreign trade continued to be dominated by raw materials, semi-processed materials or low value-added items; that rates of capital investment remained low; and that the economy remained technologically backward with low rates of productivity, chronic energy problems and severe transport and communications bottlenecks. Meanwhile, the policy of screening the effects of economic experimentation from the general public resulted in an unchanging workforce, unfamiliar with other than the traditional highly centralised DPRK management methods, increasingly out of touch with advanced technology in industries such as electronics and vehicle building, and drilled to participate in the Stakhanovite speed campaigns and other forms of extensive, rather than intensive production.

As the 1990s progressed it became clear that the ROK would play an expanding role in the DPRK economy. However, growing ROK trade and investment did not immediately impact upon the broader issues in inter-Korean relations, and the DPRK's reunification strategy remained unchanged. As a result, the December

1991 Agreement was no more effective than the 1972 Joint Communique. Whereas the South interpreted the Agreement as a specific framework for confidence-building measures, the North interpreted it as a broad agreement that could accommodate its two-tier talks strategy of negotiating a peace treaty and troop withdrawal with the US and then negotiating a political settlement with the ROK. The wording of the agreement was vague enough to accommodate these widely differing interpretations, and without consensus on more fundamental issues the Agreement was incapable of providing a framework for sustained, productive negotiation.

There were three broad strands to inter-Korean negotiation in the wake of the December 1991 Agreement. The first strand addressed inter-Korean economic cooperation, the second sought to establish the administrative structures required to put the Joint Agreement into effect, and the third and most difficult strand sought ways and means to implement the Agreement. Inter-Korean economic relations expanded in the immediate aftermath of the signing of the December 1991 Agreement. In January 1992 a group of leading ROK businessman, led by Daewoo Group Chairman Kim Woo-choong, paid an unprecedented visit to Pyongyang. Kim Woo-choong stated that he had reached agreement with the DPRK authorities in three areas: on joint ventures in resource exploration, business ventures in third countries and light industry, the latter by means of a complex of light industry factories to be established at Nampo, near Pyongyang. Discussions continued, and Seoul received Deputy Premier and economy specialist Kim Tal-hyon on a seven-day visit to the South in July for discussions on the complex (*Korea Newsreview* 25 July 1992). However, Kim received a blunt message during his meeting with President Roh Tae-woo that progress in economic relations depended on progress in resolving the nuclear issue. As the North continued to be unyielding on the nuclear issue during the autumn of 1992, the South postponed further action on strengthening economic relations. The postponement then became indefinite in 1993 in the wake of DPRK threats to withdraw from the Nuclear Non-Proliferation Treaty (NPT). While the ROK and the DPRK continued to have non-government economic contacts with each other, economic cooperation became largely limited to trading in foodstuffs, and to processing on consignment, whereby DPRK labour assembled goods, mainly garments, for ROK companies (Kwang-Yong Kim 1994:99–106).

Meanwhile, the two sides initially made rapid progress toward establishing administrative structures under the Agreement. At the seventh session of the prime ministerial talks held in Seoul on 5–8 May 1992 they announced a detailed committee structure for the implementation of the Agreement.[10] However, the two sides quickly reached deadlock on implementation. Once more the North favoured the immediate and comprehensive implementation of the Agreement, while the South pressed its usual gradualist agenda of confidence-building measures. The North went part of the way toward accommodating this part of the South's agenda by agreeing to an exchange of visits between Seoul and Pyongyang in August covering one hundred elderly people from divided families, seventy artists and seventy journalists. In a forthright speech at the prime ministerial talks on 6 May, DPRK Prime Minister Yon Hyong-muk made clear the North's attitude when he stated that 'the north–south agreement signed between us is not an agreement of the sides each having an axe to grind but a document of agreement which confirms the common will of the north and the south to remove antagonism and confrontation of the past and hew the path of an independent, peaceful reunification of the country through reconciliation, peace and cooperation' (*PT* 9 May 1992). The DPRK could therefore not accept 'dealing with one thing preferentially and putting off another, construing their importance and priority in one's own way'. In particular, therefore, the ROK precondition that implementation of the Agreement should await a nuclear inspection in the North was unacceptable. Yon went on:

> If it was to reserve the fulfilment of the north–south agreements on account of the precondition of nuclear inspection, your side should not have signed the agreement. We cannot understand why your side is trying to reserve their implementation raising a totally unreasonable question at this time when your side had the agreements approved even by your chief executive . . . If your side has in mind nuclear inspection by the International Atomic Energy Agency, it is not a matter in which your side should interfere. We are now working smoothly with the IAEA for receiving nuclear inspection without problem. If 'the nuclear inspection' mentioned by your side is nuclear inspection between the north and the south, it is now under discussion between the two sides at the nuclear control joint committee [*PT* 9 May 1992].

Yon further took the ROK to task over what the DPRK saw as three major obstacles to progress: the presence of US forces in the ROK, the ROK National Security Law and the ROK's insistence on government-to-government negotiations.[11]

Contrary to the spirit of the north–south agreement, your side [not only] refuses to recognise a series of essential matters which have been made clear, but tries to avoid them. We consider that herein lies the seriousness of the matter. If one values the spirit of national independence specified in the North–South Agreement, one must effect a new turn in one's relations with the United States and the withdrawal of the US troops from south Korea. Under this condition, if your side is unable to seek the total withdrawal of the US troops right away, it should at least make clear such will and attitude. Secondly . . . we consider that your side should not try to maintain the 'National Security Law' under the pretext of respecting the other side's law system but do away with it without hesitation in the spirit of national reconciliation and the agreements on respecting the other side. Thirdly . . . we recognise that not only the authorities of the north and the south but all members of our nation—the party in power or out of power, the ministerial and opposition camps—are the driving force of national reunification, and that the reunification issue can be settled only by the united might and role of the nation, its master. To attempt to hold dialogue on reunification through 'unified channels' and to exclude and bar all parties, groupings and people of different social strata from the discussion of and negotiations on this matter can never be supported by anyone [*PT* 9 May 1992].

By the end of May 1992, the atmosphere of negotiations had cooled considerably. In a wide-ranging statement on 2 June 1992 the ROK accused the DPRK of a series of actions that placed the talks in jeopardy. These included the infiltration of armed troops into the DMZ on 22 May, attempts to circumvent the established intergovernmental channels and bring political pressure to bear in Seoul by organising a 'pannational rally' of youth and students in Pyongyang with the joint participation of DPRK students and ROK dissident students, and the issuing of numerous invitations to ROK businessmen to visit the North and undertake individual joint ventures.[12]

In June 1992 the two sides reached an effective impasse on the key issue of joint nuclear inspection. The two countries had signed a Joint Declaration for a Non-Nuclear Korean Peninsula on 31 December 1991 which declared that neither side would store or possess either nuclear weapons or the means to produce them. They also stated their commitment to establishing an inspectorate to verify by mutual observation the absence of such weapons and facilities (*PT* 25 January 1992) and established a South–North Joint Nuclear Control Commission (JNCC) to carry out this function. Military tension in the peninsula then eased considerably when the ROK announced the suspension of Team Spirit 1992 on 7 January. On the same day the DPRK announced that it accepted ROK assurances that there were no longer any nuclear weapons on ROK soil and that it would therefore sign an IAEA nuclear safeguards agreement (*PT* 11 January 1992). This was duly ratified at the Third Session of the Ninth SPA held 8–10 April 1992.[13]

However, despite a series of meetings in March–May 1992, the two sides could not agree on regulations to govern mutual nuclear inspections. The two sides reached an effective impasse at the fifth meeting of the JNCC on 27 May when they could not agree on issues such as the protocol for challenge inspections and inspections on twenty-four hours notice.[14] As the ROK applied pressure by linking progress on the nuclear issue to progress in other areas of the relationship, so too the DPRK applied pressure on this issue with a demand for a joint, unilateral North–South nuclear inspection of alleged US nuclear weapons and nuclear bases in the South (*PT* 4 July 1992). The nuclear inspections impasse spread to other areas when the ROK subsequently made the August family reunion, artist and journalist visits program subject to progress on bilateral inspection proposals.[15] In August, Pyongyang unilaterally suspended the visits program, and though the two sides met again for an eighth round of talks in Pyongyang 15–17 September, they could not narrow the widening gap between the two sides. Although at this meeting the two sides signed and put into effect various protocols that stemmed from the December 1991 Joint Agreement, they failed to make any progress on the visits issue or the nuclear inspection issue.[16]

In October 1992, lack of progress in the military talks, the exposure of a major DPRK spy ring in the South, and growing international suspicion that the DPRK was still actively pursuing its nuclear weapons program led to an announcement that the ROK and the US would resume the Team Spirit exercises in 1993 after their suspension in 1992.[17] The North reacted by advising that all dialogues would be stalemated and the implementation of all South–North agreements would be suspended for the duration of the exercises (*PT* 7 November 1992). Pyongyang duly kept its word, and the ninth round of prime ministerial talks, scheduled for Seoul on 21 December 1992 did not take place.

The level and frequency of inter-Korea negotiation sank to a ten-year low in 1993. The DPRK announced its intention to withdraw from the NPT in March and thereafter made bilateral discussions with the US the chief focus of its diplomacy. The prime ministerial talks did not reconvene, and the two sides reverted to sporadic official contact at junior levels. The Team Spirit exercises went ahead, accompanied by the ritual declaration of a semi-war footing in the DPRK. Then at the Fifth Session of the Ninth Supreme People's Assembly on 5 April, Pyongyang proposed a Ten-Point Program for Grand National Unity in Kim Il Sung's name, which essentially repackaged a series of demands that the South had previously rejected (PT 10 April 1993). On 20 May the ROK counterproposed that preliminary contacts take place with a view to resuming the suspended prime ministerial talks. On 25 May the North proposed as its own formula a meeting of presidential envoys of deputy prime minister rank. The South eventually agreed to the envoy idea on the condition that the nuclear issue remain on the agenda, but the North refused to discuss what it called the 'fictitious nuclear issue' (PT 3 July 1993). The two sides then entered into an extended period of stalemate.

Contact during 1994 was reduced to working-level contacts at Panmunjom between officials to arrange the meeting of presidential envoys. The major sticking point continued to be Pyongyang's insistence that Seoul cease efforts to seek international involvement in the nuclear issue. Negotiations reached a new low point on 19 March when the DPRK delegation leader walked out of negotiations, declaring 'If a war breaks out Seoul will be turned into a sea of fire'.[18] In this context Kim Il Sung's agreement during talks with former US President Jimmy Carter on 16–17 June to a summit meeting with ROK President Kim Young Sam was a surprising development which seemed at odds with established DPRK policy toward the ROK. Whether the talks would have achieved anything or even taken place became moot when Kim's death on 8 July brought about the temporary suspension of any inter-Korean negotiations. The DPRK took umbrage at Kim Young Sam's tactful but qualified statement of condolence on Kim's death, and its outright rejection of Red Cross talks proposed by Seoul on 15 August 1994 displayed a lack of interest in renewed dialogue in the immediate post-Kim Il Sung period.

A series of incidents during the period of mourning led to a continuing deterioration in inter-Korean relations. A DPRK request for 150 000 tonnes of rice in the wake of the September 1995 floods initially raised hopes of a breakthrough, but actual delivery in January 1996 took place in an atmosphere of tension and truculence when the DPRK detained a South Korean crewman on spying charges. In April 1996 the DPRK effected three armed incursions into the Panmunjom Joint Security Area. The incursions took place less than a week before National Assembly elections in the South and resembled similar military pressure brought to bear by China in the lead-up to Taiwan's presidential election in March 1996. However, as in the Taiwanese case, far from rattling Kim Young Sam's electorally embattled New Korea Party and its supporters, the incursions were generally credited with swinging votes to Kim. Finally, in September 1996 a DPRK submarine ran aground off the east coast of the ROK, evidently while on an espionage and infiltration mission. On 10 January 1997 Pyongyang expressed 'deep regret' over this incursion, but this apology did not foreshadow reconciliation as the South had insisted on an apology as a precondition for further food aid talks. On 16 July 1997 a DPRK incursion and exchange of fire in the DMZ once again emphasised the continuing stand-off, and although inter-Korean economic exchanges continued and expanded during 1997, political and military tension remained high.

Meanwhile, a new phase of negotiation opened in April 1996, when the US and the ROK jointly proposed four-party peace talks, involving China (as one of the original signatories to the Armistice Agreement), the US and the two Koreas. Pyongyang did not respond directly to this proposal, but in July obliquely rejected it by again stating its long-standing position that moves toward peace should begin with bilateral negotiations between the DPRK and the US on a US troop withdrawal. However, the extent to which the DPRK was hobbled by its food crisis became clear in 1997 when it reversed course and attended a 'briefing session' on the four-party talks concept in New York in April. It also attended a preliminary meeting on 7 August, also in New York, which aimed at setting an agenda for a formal meeting at the foreign minister level. However, this meeting produced little more than a reiteration of long-standing and well-known policies. When Pyongyang's position remained unchanged at an ensuing meeting on 18 September, the US advised that it would not attend further talks unless the North dropped its two preconditions of massive food aid and the inclusion of negotiations on a US troop withdrawal as a specific talks agenda item.

The broader picture of DPRK foreign policy during the 1990s concerns efforts to pursue its nuclear program as an absolute priority, to test the limits of international acceptance of its nuclear program, and to use this program to force the US into bilateral negotiations aimed at isolating the ROK. As the DPRK became more and more convinced that its security was best served by the development of nuclear weapons, its interest in dialogue with the ROK, Japan and the US waned, and in mid-1992 these dialogues effectively ceased. In the case of Japan, after five inconclusive meetings in 1991, DPRK and Japanese officials met in January and May 1992 without notable results. Japan then postponed what was to have been the eighth meeting in July due to lack of progress in the inter-Korea nuclear talks. Pyongyang insisted that the nuclear inspection issue should not impede progress toward normalisation, while Japan remained adamant that resolution of the nuclear issue was fundamental to progress. The talks broke down completely in November 1992 over Japan's persistent requests for information about the Japanese citizen employed as tutor to Kim Hyun-hui, one of the terrorists responsible for the bombing of KAL Flight 858 in November 1987. In December 1993 the DPRK rejected subsequent Japanese overtures to resume talks (Hong-Nack Kim 1994a:677–8).

Relations with the US likewise remained hobbled by the nuclear issue. After the results of an initial high-level meeting held on 22 January 1992 in New York between KWP International Bureau Chairman Kim Yong-sun and US Under-Secretary of State for Political Affairs Arnold Kanter were deemed satisfactory by the North (*PT* 1 February 1992), the US essentially placed further meetings on hold until evidence of DPRK responsiveness on the nuclear issue was forthcoming.[19] In addition, the US continued to place a series of other conditions on the improvement of relations including improvements in human rights and the cessation of SCUD missile exports to the Middle East. In this atmosphere, counsellor-level talks in Beijing remained the prime channel for communication.

Pyongyang's last remaining big power patron, China, established diplomatic relations with the ROK in August 1992, and Pyongyang accepted this with considerably more grace than it had displayed when the Soviet Union recognised the ROK. Otherwise, Chinese policy toward the DPRK remained cautious and low-key during this period.[20] Meanwhile, the dissolution of the Soviet Union in December 1991 had little immediate impact in the DPRK. The Russian Federation became the Soviet Union's legal successor in the former Soviet Far East and, with memories of DPRK support for the August 1991 coup still fresh, Moscow initially assigned a low priority to finding a new basis for stable bilateral relations. This attitude began to change in mid-1992 when Moscow announced that it would renew its 1961 mutual defence treaty with the DPRK for a further five years. This came despite energetic lobbying from the ROK, which was concerned at the implications of the automatic intervention implications of Article 1 of the treaty (Seung-Ho Joo 1996:34–5). This move also occurred amid the continuing Russian dispute with Japan over the Kurile Islands, and the dispute seems to have persuaded

Moscow of the wisdom of seeking influence in Northeast Asia wherever it could. A steady swing back to a more evenly balanced Russian policy on the Korean Peninsula began to emerge, culminating in a visit to Pyongyang by a Russian delegation headed by Deputy Foreign Minister Georgy Kunadze in January 1993 for wide-ranging talks aimed at improving bilateral relations.[21] During his visit Kunadze confirmed that the 1961 treaty would be abrogated in 1996 and that bilateral economic relations would continue on a purely commercial basis. On the nuclear issue, Moscow added its weight to international pressure on the DPRK, but the collapse of the previous Soviet–DPRK relationship left it with little leverage.[22] The cool and formal state of relations was perhaps best illustrated when the Russian Prime Minister—and not President Yeltsin—sent condolences to his opposite number after Kim Il Sung's death in July 1994.

The DPRK's nuclear program continued to attract international attention during the 1990s. The year 1992 opened positively after the 31 December 1991 signing of a Joint Declaration for a Non-Nuclear Korean Peninsula with the South, which the DPRK maintained cleared the way for its signing an IAEA safeguards agreement containing provision for international inspection. The DPRK duly signed the agreement on 30 January and the Supreme People's Assembly ratified it in April.[23] However, DPRK behaviour during inspection visits by the IAEA in May, June and September, and repeated stalling in inter-Korean military talks continued to raise considerable suspicions concerning Pyongyang's long-term objectives.

In March 1993 the nuclear issue became the centre of an international crisis when the DPRK announced its intention to withdraw from the NPT altogether. The immediate issue was the refusal of the DPRK in January to allow an IAEA inspection team access to two sites, believed to be wastepiles that might have revealed evidence of plutonium reprocessing. On 10 February 1993 the IAEA requested a special inspection which the DPRK again rejected, maintaining that the site was a military site, and had no connection with the nuclear program. A 25 February 1993 IAEA resolution took 'serious note of the significant inconsistencies between the [DPRK's] declarations and the Secretariat's finding resulting from ad hoc inspections and sample analysis which remain unresolved despite extensive discussions'.[24] It gave a one-month grace period for the DPRK to comply with the special inspection demand. This precipitated advice from the DPRK to the UN Security Council on 12 March that it was withdrawing from the NPT, the first country ever to do so. The DPRK maintained that the IAEA's resolution was 'an encroachment on the sovereignty of the DPRK, an interference in its internal affairs and a hostile act aimed at stifling socialism in our country'.[25] It further alleged that the resolution was the work of 'some officials . . . and certain member nations of the IAEA, following the lead of the United States', acting on the basis of fabricated US intelligence (*PT* 20 March 1993). Pyongyang maintained that the military sites had no connection with its nuclear program and that to allow the special inspection would constitute the thin end of the wedge because 'It is an old method of the United States to satisfy its demands one by one, that is, to demand the opening of one military site today and another tomorrow' (*PT* 20 March 1993).

When the IAEA formally referred the matter to the Security Council on 1 April 1993, the DPRK alleged that the IAEA was acting as the catspaw of the US, and maintained that negotiations should take place between Pyongyang and Washington (*PT* 10 April 1993). On 2 June 1993, the Security Council passed a resolution calling on Pyongyang to reconsider its position and honour its commitments under the NPT and the attendant safeguards agreement. At this point, ten days before the date when the DPRK withdrawal was to take legal effect, talks began between the DPRK and the US in New York. After four sessions of talks the North displayed characteristic brinkmanship by agreeing to suspend its NPT withdrawal on 11 June, one day before it was due to take effect.

By means of this agreement the DPRK at last gained the status of bilateral dialogue partner with the US, while for the moment the US forestalled a potentially serious blow against the NPT regime. The latter achievement was dubious at best, given public statements from Pyongyang that it would now proceed to resolve the nuclear issue outside the NPT by negotiating its demands directly with the US. Bilateral talks began in Geneva on 19 July 1993 and produced a joint agreement whereby the US undertook to consider ways and means of assisting the DPRK to replace the graphite-moderated reactor at the centre of the debate with a light-water moderated reactor. In language that avoided any commitment to altering its existing policy stances on dialogue with either the IAEA or the ROK, the DPRK stated its readiness 'to begin consultations with the IAEA on outstanding safeguards and other issues as soon as possible' and its preparedness 'to begin the North–South talks, as soon as possible, on bilateral issues, including the nuclear issue'. Both sides also 'reaffirmed the importance' of the implementation of the North–South Joint Declaration on the Denuclearization of the Korean Peninsula (*PT* 24 July 1993).

The two sides agreed to meet for a third round of talks in two months time, but the US insisted that it would require evidence of substantive dialogues with the IAEA and the ROK before conducting further negotiations. These dialogues did not eventuate. Continuing disagreement with the IAEA led to a 1 October 1993 IAEA resolution expressing 'grave concern that the DPRK had failed to discharge its safeguards obligations and had recently widened the area of non-compliance by not accepting scheduled Agency ad hoc and routine inspections as required by its safeguards agreement with the Agency'.[26] Meanwhile, a ROK proposal on 4 August 1993 to reactivate the Joint Nuclear Control Commission, which had lain dormant since January 1993, received a dismissive response from Pyongyang. However, working-level contacts between the US and the DPRK continued, and in December the two sides reached agreement on a means of resolving these two issues. After negotiations in January 1994, on 15 February the DPRK reached agreement in principle with the IAEA for a full IAEA inspection of its seven declared nuclear sites, and this led to the joint US–DPRK announcement on 1 March of a package of four simultaneous steps involving US endorsement of the ROK suspension of Team Spirit 1994, a full IAEA inspection according to the 15 February agreement, resumption of ROK–DPRK working-level negotiations on the exchange of special envoys proposal, and the holding of the third round of US–DPRK talks in Geneva on 21 March 1994.

However, far from contributing to a resolution of the issue, this agreement led directly to a major crisis. The IAEA carried out its inspection on 3–14 March but on 21 March pronounced the result unsatisfactory. This was because the DPRK had imposed on-site restrictions that prevented the team from verifying that no nuclear material had been diverted for reprocessing into weapons-grade plutonium since the last inspection in February 1993.[27] In the light of the IAEA report, the US discontinued bilateral negotiations with the DPRK and referred the matter to the UN Security Council. On 31 March the President of the Security Council issued a statement urging the DPRK to comply with the IAEA inspection regime. Pyongyang rejected the request, and the issue began to move towards a further crisis point in early May when it announced that it would soon begin unloading spent fuel rods without IAEA supervision, thus destroying evidence of suspected weapons-grade plutonium conversion. On 31 May the UN Security Council moved closer to approving economic sanctions against the DPRK, when it unanimously approved a statement by the President of the Security Council warning Pyongyang that unloading the rods without IAEA supervision might lead to further Security Council action. The DPRK quickly rejected the letter, stated that the application of economic sanctions would amount to 'an act of war', and threatened to convert its unilateral suspension of its NPT membership into outright withdrawal.

Confrontation with the US seemed inevitable until the visit of former US President Jimmy Carter to Pyongyang on 15–19 June for talks on the nuclear issue. Carter visited Pyongyang as a private citizen at the DPRK's invitation, and he obtained Kim's agreement to a freezing of the unloading process in return for cessation of sanctions talk and a return to negotiations with the US. After a delay caused by Kim's death, negotiations resumed on 13 August, and in October 1994 the two sides signed what is known as the Geneva Framework Agreement, whereby the DPRK agreed to remain in the NPT and to return eventually to the IAEA inspection regime.[28]

The US agreed to broker the provision of two light-water reactors (LWRs) for energy production in the North, take steps to normalise diplomatic relations, and reduce barriers to trade and investment. In effect, by the terms of the agreement the US accepted that it was now impossible to determine the extent of the DPRK's past diversion of nuclear material for reprocessing into weapons-grade plutonium, and so concentrated attention on ensuring future transparency. Pyongyang got to keep whatever plutonium it already had, but for the moment agreed to forgo further reprocessing.

Negotiations on implementation inched forward in 1995 with Pyongyang's refusal to accept LWRs of ROK design being a particular source of delay, despite its commitment under the Geneva accords to accept a nominated ROK supplier. Under considerable duress the DPRK finally accepted the ROK LWRs and in August 1997 construction began on the first of the two 1000 megawatt LWRs. The project, managed by the Korean Peninsula Energy Development Organization (KEDO), a US-led consortium, may take up to ten years to complete. Meanwhile, the North would gain some relief from its energy shortages through the KEDO-sponsored delivery of 500 000 tonnes of fuel oil per year. However, this represented partial relief at best from the estimated 1.5 million tonnes decline in oil imports since 1989.

The events described above lead to several observations about the DPRK's nuclear policy. First, we can safely dismiss any element of bluff on the nuclear issue in Pyongyang. Regimes like the DPRK may build Potemkin villages but they do not build Potemkin nuclear facilities. Beginning in the 1980s the DPRK mobilised substantial human and technological resources at Yongbyon and pursued a nuclear weapons program as rapidly as circumstances permitted.[29] Second, while the decommissioning of the Yongbyon reactor has proceeded smoothly under the Geneva Framework Agreement, the DPRK will continue to hold an unverifiable amount of plutonium for several years. It is not compelled to allow verification of its current stock nor has it been prepared to discuss ways and means of preserving a record of past plutonium production with the IAEA. Third, Pyongyang may or may not have worked out the full tactical ramifications of nuclear deployment,[30] but it has been developing nuclear weapons in support of its basic three-front strategy for reunification. From Pyongyang's perspective, as the conventional warfare option faded in the 1970s, nuclear weapons became a sheer necessity. If the North were ever to prevail over the South it needed an equaliser against the growing conventional weapons superiority of the South and a means of neutralising the US nuclear threat. Failure to develop some counter to these two strategic weaknesses would have condemned the DPRK to an unacceptable status of permanent weakness and inferiority.

Fourth, in the DPRK calculation nuclear weapons provide a means of driving a wedge between the US and the ROK. The DPRK operates from a deep ideological conviction that the US is the real power in the ROK, and attaches considerable importance to engaging the US in bilateral peace treaty negotiations. On the model of the Indochina War, the calculation appears to be that if the DPRK can induce the US to conclude that the defence of the ROK is not worth the cost, then Pyongyang will have won an important victory. In this scenario the achievement of a bilateral channel of dialogue with Washington would in itself increase the chances of driving a wedge between the ROK and the US. In short, disdainful of economic prosperity as an end in itself, inured to hardship and isolation, and patiently willing to accept small and piecemeal concessions from the US along the way, by 1998 the DPRK would have had every reason to be satisfied with the results of its nuclear program.

In 1992 the DPRK also began a series of steps which have effectively dismantled the 1953 Military Armistice Agreement (MAA). For the first time since the Korean War, in May 1992 the DPRK boycotted a Military Armistice Commission meeting, called as a result of an armed infiltration incident by three Korean People's Army (KPA) soldiers on 22 May 1992. Then in April 1994 an official DPRK communique explicitly stated the DPRK intention to seek the repeal of the MAA (PT 7 May 1994). Subsequently, in October 1994

China, one of the three signatories to the MAA along with the United Nations Command and the DPRK, advised that it was withdrawing from it at the request of the DPRK.[31] In May 1995, the DPRK expelled the Czech and Polish representatives on the Neutral Nations Supervisory Committee and closed the Neutral Nations Supervisory Committee office in the northern half of the Joint Security Area at Panmunjom. These actions were designed to put pressure on the US to negotiate a bilateral peace treaty with the DPRK to replace the MAA. However, the joint US–ROK position remained that the matter of a successor to the MAA should be negotiated between the DPRK and the ROK as the substantive parties to the conflict.

The collapse of Communism in the Soviet Bloc drastically altered the economic and military basis on which the DPRK had pursued the objective of Korean reunification. As a small, economically weak country deficient in all indices of state power except military, Pyongyang had relied heavily on China and the Soviet Union to apply pressure to the US and complement the DPRK's own military challenge to the South. When the Soviet Union withdrew from global competition with the US, the DPRK lost its last remaining strategic ally in the region and was thrown almost entirely upon its own resources. Its strategic response was to seek tactical accommodation through dialogue with its adversaries, to address its economic problems by adopting some system-defending economic measures, and to press ahead with its nuclear weapons program.

The simultaneous pursuit of dialogue and nuclear weapons development was, of course, a contradictory stance, and as this contradiction became clear the dialogues stalemated and confrontation resumed. The speed with which the December 1991 Agreement with the ROK effectively became a dead letter is particularly noteworthy. The DPRK concluded the Agreement in the wake of Operation Desert Storm in January 1991, and the final collapse of the Soviet Union during August–December 1991, both of which would have contributed to a sense of immediate threat. As this sense of threat diminished during 1992 and as the DPRK faced a clear and uncompromising ROK stance over the nuclear inspections issue in the early months of negotiations under the Agreement, Pyongyang effectively abandoned the Agreement and concentrated on its underlying strategy of seeking to engage the US in bilateral negotiations.

The DPRK's lack of interest in substantive reform during the 1990s showed itself in domestic policies and in particular in the leadership's profound attachment to the production of nuclear weapons, for this program effectively precluded serious action to address the country's economic difficulties. Not only did the DPRK's nuclear weapons program perpetuate an atmosphere of continuing crisis and lock the state into a defence of the ideology for which the nuclear weapons program was undertaken, but pursuit of a nuclear option also persuaded Pyongyang that the DPRK could remain a credible military threat without addressing its underlying economic problems. Moreover, the DPRK cannot establish a political environment that would induce foreign participation in any economic reform process unless it gives satisfaction to its neighbours and to the US on the nuclear issue. The notion of substantial foreign economic investment in a nuclear-armed DPRK is as unlikely as it sounds.

Extricating itself from this impasse will be difficult for the DPRK, because possession of nuclear weapons is the chosen panacea for a rapidly deteriorating strategic situation. Any extrication would thus involve a rather one-sided process of disarmament, and a substantial loss of potential to influence military affairs on the Korean Peninsula, not to mention loss of morale. The nuclear option attracts Pyongyang because it enables the leadership to pursue, for the moment, the policy goals that have become fundamental to the DPRK's identity as a state, but this option also gives Pyongyang the limited bargaining power of the perpetrator of a hostage situation.

The initiative for calculated change in North Korea remains with Kim Jong Il, and the 1994–97 period of mourning ended with strong evidence that he had become the effective ruler in the DPRK. Many analysts outside the DPRK initially viewed the younger Kim as a transitional figure who could not hope to control the Korean Workers' Party and the country in the same manner as his father, but after three years in charge there was no hard evidence to suggest that he was in less than full control. This smooth transition was perhaps due as much to the tight web of Party organisation that covers all aspects of life in the North as to the younger Kim's political acumen, but this in itself emphasised a relevant point for the DPRK's future: the Kimist system, rather than Kim Jong Il as an individual, now ruled the DPRK.

But Kim Jong Il now leads a state in distress—profound, mostly self-inflicted, and unacknowledged in public by the leadership. The roots of its predicament go far back into the past to the formation of a dogmatic ideology by which his father sought fundamental economic, political, diplomatic and social objectives such as modernisation, prosperity, security and reunification but instead achieved economic backwardness, international pariah status and a perpetuation of the division of the country well into the next century. Kim Jong Il is not only a product of this system, he has been intensively trained within it and knows no other. His skills and experience are therefore relevant only to the maintenance of a failed system and he shows no sign of offering dynamic leadership to address the country's systemic crises. As he continues to operate under increasing pressure from an array of forces he can neither control nor, seemingly, understand, the DPRK continues to drift toward a major systemic crisis.

9

CONCLUDING REMARKS

The revolution which began in North Korea in 1945 displays a blend of generic and specific characteristics. The generic lies in the lessons Kim Il Sung and his colleagues drew from the universal laws of Marxism, the revolutionary organisational and tactical framework developed chiefly by Lenin, and the practical experience of Communist parties in power, most notably the Communist Party of the Soviet Union (CPSU) in power under Stalin. The specific emerged in the course of their efforts to apply this body of knowledge, as they understood it, to the concrete conditions in their country. These latter characteristics—militarism, isolation, extreme centralisation and mobilisation, personal autocracy, cult of personality leadership and the hereditary succession—are obvious enough but the question of their origin and development is less obvious. In this work we have considered a number of influences on the life-experience and outlook of Kim Il Sung and have emphasised the role Kim's early life and experiences as an anti-Japanese guerilla and his practical experience of the Stalinist state have played in the development of Kimist ideology. As we revisit and re-examine these influences in the light of the events described in the preceding chapters, we begin by placing them in the generic context of Leninist revolutionary movements.

Typically, Leninist revolutionary movements have started as small study groups and cells led by young intellectuals. Their political strategies and tactics vary depending upon the political environment in which they operate, but common to the early period of all movements is the initiation of predominantly young revolutionaries into a situation of prolonged, almost constant political warfare. The pre-revolutionary period is a time when the leaders lay down the foundations of the Party's organisation, ideology and revolutionary mythology, and it is also a time when they form close and often durable personal and political relationships within the movement. The elitism of the leadership core, the exclusive, revelatory nature of Party ideology, the pattern of illegal, underground activities and state repression develop the revolutionary movement's organisational framework as a highly disciplined political combat team. In turn, ruthless political combat shapes the mythology of the movement, emphasising desirable qualities for followers such as perseverance, loyalty, self-sacrifice, militancy, and courage, and attributes of the leader such as prescience, wisdom and humanity. Meanwhile, the atmosphere of conspiracy, danger and ideological ferment has a profound impact on the revolutionaries' political and personal lives, and imparts an intensity to their relationships and experiences that often acquires considerable significance when the movement gains power. It is not surprising to find that the political dogma of revolutionary regime leaders is often strongly influenced by their pre-revolutionary experience, nor to find that this dogma, which has taken shape in conditions of hardship, adversity, danger, and isolation from the general populace, exerts a strong influence on their behaviour in power.

If the movement is successful in attaining power it becomes subject to a further complex array of forces. The nature of leadership in Leninist revolutionary movements—elitist, personalistic, conspiratorial, visionary, militant and monopolistic—remains a major factor in shaping the revolution, but to this factor we must now add the precise historical circumstances in which the party first comes to power, the legacy of the pre-existing political culture, the stage of economic and social development reached under the previous regime, the models of other revolutionary traditions with which it identifies, and the international environment at the time. In the light of these influences the Leninist party begins the process of role transformation from political combat team to promoter of modernisation.

The Leninist blueprint, which is above all else a prescription for the seizure of power, has less relevance for the party in power, and so while Leninism remains a powerful ideological tool, the party is increasingly thrown back on its own intellectual resources in pursuit of effective policies. The concerted attack on existing state institutions and the atmosphere of intense political and economic mobilisation brings to the fore the qualities of personal leadership.

At this point one member of the revolutionary elite typically assumes the role of a hero-leader and begins to exercise power on a personalistic basis with little reference to legally defined checks and balances. This marks the beginning of the Stalinist stage of the revolution in which the new hero-leader is the decisive adjudicator in matters of ideology and state policy. Ideological debate, formerly the life-blood of the movement, becomes muted, and the leader relies on a subservient cadre of officials to carry out his orders. Wide societal expectations of rapid social and economic transformation, and the demands of personal dictatorship produce a strongly mobilised, increasingly interventionist and repressive state. Meanwhile, the external environment remains a key factor, both in geopolitical and in ideological terms. The regime typically universalises its experiences, defines itself in terms of a broader, international struggle between imperialism and socialism, and regulates foreign dealings accordingly. It attaches a high priority to re-educating its citizens to accept its world view, and this process usually results in a substantial withdrawal from the international system as well as stringent state control over contacts with the outside world.

However, charismatic leadership becomes increasingly incompatible with the needs of the modernising state. The militant, visionary, millennial Leninist party ideology sanctions the drive to seek monopolistic control over civil society, and the classic economic institutions and practices that evolve from this—central planning, heavy oversight of basic industrial development, collectivised agriculture, suppression of consumer demand, economic autarky, encouragement of self-sufficiency and regimentation, restrictions on freedom of information and a pervasive security apparatus—give rise to elaborate bureaucracies. The hero-leader is typically antagonistic toward the emergence of bureaucratic politics, whose concern with stability, precedent and routine runs counter to his objective of continuing revolutionary mobilisation. However, despite strategies such as extensive intervention to assert authority in policy matters, or else sustained attacks on the phenomenon of bureaucratism itself, it is a characteristic of Leninist polities that the charismatic leadership of the revolutionary generation—a Lenin, Mao or Ho—should give way to efforts to bureaucratise and institutionalise the revolutionary objectives.

The seeds of the eventual downfall of the charismatic form of leadership are usually sown by economic policy. Leninist parties have usually come to power in countries where the economic base is relatively low, and have therefore geared the country's economic life to rapid industrial transformation. Because of the low base and because the initial inputs are strong, the party usually achieves an initial breakthrough in the form of rapid, uneven economic growth. This process poses further dilemmas for the party as the high degree of centralised planning becomes increasingly incompatible with the demands of a modernising economy. In particular, the drive for monopolistic social control restricts information flows, and inhibits the development of non-military science and technology. Increasingly, economic planners confront the limitations of their inputs and face the need for decentralisation, especially in economic planning and decision-making.

In this context, external economic and political relations assume greater significance. Leninist doctrine rules out indefinite coexistence with capitalist states and predicts their downfall, but when this does not occur tactical accommodation becomes necessary. Socialist internationalism replaces proletarian internationalism, and the regime accepts ever-receding time spans for the collapse of capitalism. The doctrine of the impossibility of continued coexistence with capitalist countries is then proven ironically valid as the continuing development of the country's socialist economic system increasingly forces international competition for investment capital and technology. As a result, the socialist economy becomes incapable of withstanding the pressures for structural reform generated by the comparative economic performance of capitalist economies. The pressure grows to accept decentralised economic decision making, and to allow a free market sector alongside the inefficient state-owned enterprise sector. Nor can the repressive political system withstand comparison with more open systems. It cannot enforce ideological conformity and loses its capacity to repress all non-approved political activity. The Leninist party may fall completely or else remain as a carapace for established central authority. The ideological rhetoric insists that the revolution continues, but to all intents and purposes the revolutionary phase is finally over.

A consideration of the specific characteristics of the DPRK revolution begins, of course, with Kim Il Sung himself, and here our first observation has been that Kim Il Sung owed little to, and drew little from, traditional Korean political culture. This is not surprising, for Kim lived outside the country from the age of seven. He had virtually no exposure to the norms and practices of a political culture which, in any case, offered no meaningful role to a young man of limited education and low socio-economic background. Later, as a political leader, he demonstrated the extent of this alienation in such regime traits as dynamic and charismatic leadership, political authoritarianism, the cult of the fatherly leader, militarism, the destruction of local elites, the suppression of traditional art, literature, music and folk culture, and pervasive government intrusion into what was previously the highly self-regulatory realm of clan and family life. These features are usually, and quite erroneously, associated with Korean political 'tradition', but in fact all represented radical departures from 'tradition'.

Some observers have also argued the DPRK polity has 'traditionalist' features such as ascriptive recruitment, the setting up a hero-figure as the focus of collective identity, legitimation of power based on canonical texts either written or inspired by the hero-figure, comparative lack of differentiation and specialisation in organisational structures, and lack of popular political participation. However, these features are not specific to the Korean tradition. Rather, they are features associated with traditional societies in general, and with many modern authoritarian regimes. More particularly, they are present in the neo-traditionalism that emerged as an integral part of Stalinism in the 1930s, and they emerged in the DPRK for the same reason that they emerged in the Soviet Union under Stalin: a highly conservative social system was an essential part of the DPRK's Stalinist model of development.

In virtual exile from the age of seven, Kim grew up in chaotic times in an isolated, rural environment and carried little in the way of a framework of traditional beliefs and social conventions into adulthood. As an adult, he displayed little intellectual curiosity or interest in Korean history or arts. His instincts remained profoundly anti-cosmopolitan, his mistrust of intellectuals and technocrats was deep, and his understanding of the processes of economic and social development was limited. A self-made, self-reliant man, he practised politics accordingly and found in his own life all he deemed necessary for the lives of others. He drew little from the Korean past, but his membership of the military community of the Chinese Communist Party (CCP) anti-Japanese guerillas had a profound and lasting effect on his social and political values. Clearly intelligent and highly self-disciplined, he was socialised in a harsh environment among ruthless and violent men. His experience in the Manchurian guerilla campaign seems to have rendered him extraordinarily callous and indifferent to suffering. Traits and values of the guerilla community, which later emerged as core features of Kimism, include a hostile, predatory attitude toward external transactions; the promotion of violence as a means to an end; belief in the overriding efficacy of a direct, centralised chain of command; an emphasis on unconditional obedience and loyalty; austerity; dissociation from family and from all private economic ties; indifference to the norms of a civil society; and moral puritanism. Many, if not all, of these traits were compatible with the traditions of the Leninist party, and it is not surprising that Kim should have later developed an ideology which related the theoretical framework of Marxism–Leninism to the intense, direct experience of nearly fifteen youthful years under arms.

A further important key for our understanding of the features of the mature Kimist system is that Kim did not pass directly from military leadership in a small-scale guerilla war to dominant political leadership in Korea. When he abandoned the guerilla campaign and entered the Soviet Union in 1941 at age 29, he began a seventeen-year period in which his authority was submerged in the Stalinist military, political and economic system. During 1941–45 he was exposed to the Stalinist model of military mobilisation, and from 1945–58 he observed and participated in the implementation of fully-blueprinted Stalinism in the North. Out of the experience of some twenty-five years came the grand synthesis of Stalinist state-building and the guerilla ethos that gave Kimist ideology its distinctiveness.

The basic program of the Korean Communist oligarchy in 1945 was Stalinist, and it was implemented with the assistance of a considerable number of Soviet–Korean CPSU Party members, many of whom had been active cadres in the Stalinist system in the Soviet Union in the 1930s. Simply put, Korean Stalinists implemented a Stalinist system in the North under the close direction of Soviet Stalinists. DPRK policies and practices that exemplify this influence include a mass communist party, a high degree of political mobilisa-tion, adherence to the doctrine of the intensification of class struggle, economic autarky, the collectivisation of agriculture, rapid heavy industrialisation through mass economic mobilisation, Stakhanovite work practices, and a heavy reliance on ideological motivation. In time this polity produced a political leader who modelled himself closely on Stalin in such features as a strongly interventionist working style, the pervasive use of terror and coercion, a heavy and constant turnover of cadres in the Party's Central Committee, and reliance on a personal autocracy reinforced by a cult of personality. We may surmise that Kim's debt to Stalin arose partly because of his experi-ence of war-time Stalinism, partly because to be a good Communist in the 1940s and early 1950s was to be a good Stalinist, but most of all because, unlike Lenin, Stalin provided Kim (and many others) with what was then a widely revered and successful role model for directing socialist economic development and militarisation under the dictatorship of the Party and in conditions of personal autocracy. Small wonder, then, the amazing detail with which Kim applied Stalinist norms, and the tenacity with which he adhered to them.

The Soviet role in Kim's rise can scarcely be underestimated for, without it, substantial political power and eventual political control of the country would not have passed to an obscure, patchily educated 33-year-old member of a tiny guerilla splinter group within an exclusivist, Leninist political subculture, who had not seen the settled areas of his country during his entire adult life. Kim owed his political success in the immediate postwar period mainly to Soviet patronage, which was based on the Soviet assessment of Kim as a young, able, personable, experienced Korean military officer who impressed the Soviets with his command of men, who had no vestige of a local power base, and who was highly amenable to a Stalinist chain of command. This assessment was extremely self-serving and flawed in a manner that would periodically return to haunt Moscow, but in at least one respect the Soviets were not deceived: Kim *was* a reverent Stalinist who would retain the Stalinist command-system and world-view long after the Soviet Union had abandoned them.

The transition from Communist oligarchy to Kim Il Sung's domination of the Korean Workers' Party (KWP) and then to personal autocracy required further catalysts in the form of the Korean War, the death of Stalin and the operation of a Leninist party political culture. Military defeat and widespread chaos during the Korean War destroyed the existing Party infrastructure and produced the conditions in which Kim could resurrect the KWP and use it as an instrument to isolate and destroy his opponents. The death of Stalin brought policy changes in the Soviet Union during 1954–56 aimed at reducing the extreme commandism and levels of repression under the Stalinist system. In a DPRK context these changes led to an internal struggle in the KWP between would-be emulators of the new Soviet line and the Kimists, who advocated close retention of the Stalinist mobilisation system. This conflict ended in total victory for unreconstructed Stalinism, and resulted in Kim's rise to dominant leadership in the Party in 1958. Meanwhile, Leninist party culture, with its personalistic, elitist, conspiratorial tradition, contempt for bourgeois legality, and disdain for institutional checks and balances played a key role in this victory, for in the setting of monopolist party control, the North Korean Communists were no more able than their Soviet or Chinese counterparts to check the drive of an individual who was determined to subvert the party and establish a personal autocracy.

As dominant leader of the Party in 1958, Kim Il Sung was ill-equipped by training, experience and temperament to deal with the practical problems of governance. These shortcomings were further exacerbated by the purges of the 1950s which effectively removed the resources of Soviet–Korean and Yan'an group expertise and left Kim surrounded with fellow ex-guerillas who mirrored his own background, strengths and weaknesses. Kim's leadership style became increasingly marked by pronounced dogmatism, extreme commandism, constant economic and political mobilisation campaigns and intolerance for pragmatic or flexible solutions. Such campaigns and practices such as the Chollima Movement, the Chongsanri Method and the Taean Work System attacked the very bureaucratic structures he needed to harness for effective government.

Chalmers Johnson's observation that a state's first priority will define its essence is a useful perspective from which to view the radical change in state policies that overtook the DPRK in the 1960s (Johnson 1982:306). In the broadest context, a world dominated by Japanese imperialism, Stalinism, militarism, nationalist struggle and crude violence provided both context and models for the political education of the DPRK leadership. It was under these auspices that the DPRK founding oligarchy came together, and imported and constructed the infrastructure of a modern state. It was the Kimist contribution to wrest power from this oligarchy and infuse this infrastructure with a world view that mandated a militarist order to society, an overriding commitment to the reunification of Korea under KWP leadership, and a blind faith in the necessity of unrelenting anti-US, anti-imperialist struggle.

This became evident in December 1962, when dissatisfaction with the outcome of the Cuban missile crisis, the Soviet trend toward peaceful coexistence, the increasing availability of the means of military production and the ideological conviction of the necessity of high levels of military production led Kim to effect a thoroughgoing militarisation of the DPRK economy and society through the adoption of the Equal Emphasis policy. As the 1960s progressed, evocation of the spirit of the anti-Japanese guerillas became more pronounced as a propaganda theme, and the state supported both increasing levels of military violence along the DMZ and an expanded commitment to revolutionary violence internationally. The economy faltered under the strains imposed by these policies, and dissent rose within the Party. During 1967–68 Kim responded with sweeping purges which removed the last traces of dissent from within the Party and completed the establishment of his personal autocracy. After this, the country could change only if Kim changed, and the strengths and limitations of Kim Il Sung became the strengths and limitations of the DPRK.

The strengths were basic—self-discipline, resilience, mental toughness, and a strong work ethic—but the weaknesses were far more significant. They began with Kim's intellect, which was formed under the influence of limited schooling, extended military struggle, and political combat within the oligarchy. As a result, he could not frame effective policies to pursue economic development and modernisation, nor was he able to seek the advice of those who could. Convinced of the universality of Stalinism, he was not interested in any further refinements or revisions, and his concept of modernity increasingly became frozen in the past: a 1940s-style economy and society drawing on the guerilla ethos for social organisation and cohesion, anti-Japanese and anti-collaborator invective for moral validation, and Stalinist industrialisation for national strength. Conservatism and reaction were deeply embedded in his avowedly revolutionary outlook, and the key to the country's stagnation lies foremost in the static, self-indulgent and retrospective character of Kim's vision.

A significant conservative force was militarism. Militarism was embedded in Kim's own past, in his ideological role-models, and in the Korean War experience. These factors impelled him to a worldview and a policy framework in which arms and the projection of military force were the main coinage. Like many nineteenth century European statesmen and like the pre-1945 Japanese militarists, Kim held, albeit with greater intensity and far less sophistication, the belief that the purpose of the state, no less than the purpose of the guerilla detachment, was to wage war effectively. The purpose of economic activity was to produce the means of waging war, the purpose of education was to produce soldiers for war, and the purpose of ideology was to convince people of the social and historical inevitability of war. War for Kim meant war to reunify Korea under the leadership of the KWP, but the US role in Korean affairs caused Kim to embrace a highly literal interpretation of the Leninist-Stalinist world-view, which mandated a continuing global anti-imperialist, anti-US struggle.

Militarism became an organising principle for both DPRK society and its economic activity, and from 1962 onward the DPRK economy developed essentially as a war economy. We cannot precisely determine the full dimensions of the DPRK's military-industrial production, but the evidence of former Soviet officials and high-ranking defectors leaves little doubt that from the mid-1960s the military, in effect, ran a separate economy responsible for up to half of all industrial production. It enjoyed priority access to raw materials, first call on the nation's power grid and transport infrastructure, and was not accountable to the cabinet-level State Planning Commission. A number of factors have contributed to the destitution of the DPRK, but the sustained, highly military purpose of economic activity has been most important. DPRK experience bears out Weber's observation that the war economy, with its overwhelming sense of contingency and its rough, inefficient methods of resource allocation, inherently tends toward bankruptcy (Weber 1964:209).

Kim's domination of the Party in the 1960s brought about the degeneration of ideology within the KWP and a decline in the intellectual life of both the Party and the country as a whole. Ideological truth became self-evident, to be accepted and acted upon with blind obedience by the people. The key factors in this development were Kim's anti-intellectualism and pronounced militarism, and the key characteristic was an atmosphere of incessant mobilisation and struggle in which emulation of the Manchurian guerillas became the dominant role-model. From the mid-1960s, the Party slogan 'Live, work and study the way the anti-Japanese guerilla did!' described the central tenet of a system whose claims on the allegiance of its citizens grew more and more insistent and all-embracing as time passed and the country's resource base diminished.

However, apart from enforcing the values of cohesion and discipline, this Spartan, anti-bureaucratic, anti-intellectual ethos contributed little to the process of rapid economic and social transformation. The construction of an elaborate mythology around Kim's Manchurian activities and the insistence that this mythology be accepted and acted upon as literal fact by the entire nation buttressed Kim's personal authority and gratified his ego, but the constant insistence that the guerilla encampment represented an ideal model of social community for the entire citizenry contributed greatly to a numbing sense of uniformity and regimentation. In this manner Kimist ideology profoundly devalued intellectual activity, traduced economic and political thought, and stifled scientific and technological innovation.

A particular facet of Kim's personality which compounded the stultifying effect of ideology was his pervasive mistrust. The purges, the elaborate, multiple overlapping security agencies, the continuing high levels of repression, the near-paranoid avoidance of all unnecessary foreign contact, the shrill insistence on unconditional loyalty and the torrents of self-righteous abuse heaped on domestic and foreign adversaries reflected a world-view that discounted trust, equality or interdependence as a viable basis for relations between individuals as well as nations. Kim viewed all other currents of Korean nationalism, socialism and communism as threatening, and did not cease purging colleagues until he had surrounded himself with unconditional personal loyalists and sycophants. He found it impossible to share real power with any members of the postwar generations other than his son. In turn, this reliance on a single generation meant that the DPRK was especially prone to the Leninist party characteristic of gerontocracy. As the guerilla generation grew old and died together, the Party became ossified, highly resistant to change, and capable only of applying increasingly dysfunctional, obsolete ideological formulae in the face of mounting problems. No agents except illness, incapacity and death existed to break the grip of these men on the political leadership of the country.

The activities of Kim Jong Il did further significant damage to the economic and social fabric of the country. In the 1970s, when one might have expected the DPRK's industrialisation process to be manifesting increasing technological sophistication and specialisation, and perhaps as a result, moving in the direction of political pragmatism, the younger Kim emerged not as an embodiment of a new generation but as an agent of his father's old revolutionary generation. Activities such as the construction of expensive prestige monuments, the continuing stress on 'speed battle' production campaigns, and the tightening of ideological control over economic activity by means of the Three Revolution Teams movement meant that the DPRK remained frozen in the revolutionary mobilisation stage. Insistence on economic autarky in an age of interdependence, and belief in the primacy of ideology in an age of increasing pragmatism, contributed substantially to economic decay and obsolescence.

Rigorous, self-imposed isolation compounded the effect of ideological training. To his own people Kim presented himself as a major international figure, but while the KWP adopted the rhetoric of proletarian internationalism, Kim clearly perceived the threat to his system posed by interaction with even other socialist countries, let alone the wider international economic and political system. He saw even less value—and more danger—in external contacts than Stalin or Mao ever did, and was successful in minimising them. However, success in this domain could only be measured in self-defeating terms of material impoverishment and intellectual sterility.

Militarism, self-imposed isolation and a fixed ideological world-view formed the basis of a foreign policy marked by strategic rigidity, broken only by occasional tactical expediency. Strategic rigidity derived primarily from Kim's deep conviction of the historical neces-sity of continuing the anti-US, anti-imperialist struggle. When developments seemed to support his view Kim welcomed them, but when they contradicted his view he largely dismissed them as tem-porary aberrations. In the Sino–Soviet split, for example, Kim consistently aligned himself with forces likely to reverse the trend toward peaceful coexistence, but when subsequent events and trends such as Sino–US rapprochement, Sino–Japanese rapprochement, ROK economic development, economic dynamism in the Asia–Pacific region, and the collapse of the Soviet Bloc, called into question the wisdom and efficacy of confrontationist policies, the DPRK response was minimalist.

An index of the failure of DPRK diplomacy was that its friend-ships with significant allies therefore remained tepid while its adversaries retained a high degree of cohesion in their containment of the DPRK throughout a period of exceptional change and flux in the region. The basic reason for this was that Pyongyang succeeded in convincing all comers that its determination to prosecute an ideologically driven civil war meant that it could not be accommo-dated by the ordinary practices of *realpolitik*. For this reason the projection of Kimist ideology into the international arena was rarely effective. On many occasions the DPRK displayed a crude, predatory outlook on foreign relations, embracing support for international terrorism, bribery, petty forms of coercion, smuggling, and widespread abuse of diplomatic privileges including arms, drugs and currency dealing. Within the Non-Aligned Movement and in many Western countries as well, the DPRK persistently alienated all but the most committed of supporters with its rigid insistence on the unsophisti-cated pursuit of its own self-interest. In other cases it displayed tactical ineptitude, especially over simultaneous UN entry and rec-ognition of the Republic of Korea (ROK) by Soviet Bloc countries, when its refusal to either compromise or establish fall-back positions led to humiliating outcomes. Irrespective of ideological considera-tions, a foreign policy which renders a country isolated and widely reviled cannot be considered either well-conceived or well-executed.

In almost any conceivable modern polity these outcomes would have long been grounds for a radical reassessment of policy, and attempts to understand the DPRK must ask why this did not occur in Pyongyang. Part of the answer lies in the manner in which the leadership evaluated policy outcomes. The country declined into economic backwardness in the 1970s, but the leadership perceived an economy still able to support a huge military establishment with a military-industrial sector capable of producing a wide array of armaments. The DPRK did not succeed in creating conditions in which it could confidently go to war again, but the Party could tell itself that this was due to ephemeral factors such as restraint from within the Socialist Bloc and the level of deterrence offered by the US and the ROK, which discouraged even limited warfare for fear of massive retaliation. And the leadership could still envisage a time when these inhibitions might no longer apply. The country steadily became an international pariah, but the DPRK has never set any store by effective participation in an international system which it regarded as inherently unjust and doomed. Another part of the answer lies in the accumulated weight of past policy decisions. Whatever private doubts key figures in Pyongyang might have had about the wisdom of Kimist policies, the concept of substantial economic and/or political reform remained anathematised, for it meant breaking with the ideology and past achievements that had given shape to the regime and to their personal and professional lives for more than forty years.

But the major part of the answer lies simply in the extent to which Kim Il Sung lost touch with reality. Physical isolation, paranoia, an overbearing, browbeating personal manner, the corrupting effects of power without accountability, the cumulative effect over decades of daily exposure to extravagant flattery, growing megalomania, unsophisticated adherence to an ideology that consecrated revolutionary violence and stressed the historical inevitability of global victory over imperialism, and blind insistence in a manifest destiny that gave him a significant role in this victory, all combined to give Kim the illusion of control over events and deprive him of any real capacity for self-reflection and self-correction.

What, then, will be the Kimist legacy? The most striking fact about the DPRK in the 1990s is its very survival. It shared the same political system and looked out upon the same international economic and political environment as both the Soviet Union and such independent Stalinist states as Romania and Albania, yet it has not shared their fate. Moreover, unlike Vietnam and China, it has not introduced any significant measures of reform. Rather, it has chosen

245

to face the world with its Stalinist political culture and ideological framework intact. Despite strong inducements, there is no sign of early change to this framework. Kim Jong Il remains in charge, at least for the foreseeable future, and Kimist ideology continues to determine policy. Kim is unlikely to be an agent of change, both because he continues to embrace the ideology and policies of his father and because this is the major source of his legitimacy. His treatises vehemently insist that this ideology has universal validity, and his behaviour over a long period of time suggests that this belief is sincere and profound.

Substantive reform from within is unlikely. As a political party the KWP is itself a dysfunctional body, and has degenerated to the situation where it is little more than an instrument for exalting its Great Leader. Under Kim Il Sung its bylaws were often set aside, Party Congresses and Supreme People's Assembly (SPA) elections became irregular, and the distinction between Party and government became heavily blurred. In the absence of regular, substantive Party meetings, we may assume that many of these cadres, long used to court intrigue as a substitute for politics, are extremely suspicious and wary of each other. A consideration of the actual people involved suggests that they are products of long, intense ideological training which must affect the extent to which they could conceptualise a process of reform, for it is inherently unlikely that cadres could initiate and direct processes and procedures of which they have had neither intellectual nor practical experience.

Hopes for the development of pressure for substantial reform from outside the Party focus on the considerable compromises the DPRK has made to its traditional policies of physical isolation and economic autarky during the 1990s. Border trade, activities in support of the Rajin–Sunbong FETZ, the growing scale of production on consignment for ROK textile, clothing, footwear and electronics firms, ROK construction of the light-water nuclear reactors, the operations of international food relief agencies and the expanding nature of unofficial markets and second economy activities have not only undermined belief in the socialist economy but have shown the existence of alternatives to the general populace. These developments present a growing challenge to the authority and credibility of the regime which over time must be answered. But in assessing the toughness and resolution of the regime in the face of this challenge we should remember that by 1998 seven years of continuing economic contraction and three years of famine had induced neither compromise with Kimist dogma nor substantial civil unrest. Moreover, such answers as Kimist ideology possesses would not have much of an impact on the systemic difficulties of the DPRK economy and would not arrest the steady economic decline, nor remove the need for a fundamental break with Kimism.

North Koreans themselves will salvage little from Kimism. The central paradox remains that while the overwhelming majority of the population still appears to direct its loyalty to the state, large sections of this population are destitute, malnourished, exhausted and cynical. Their education is largely inappropriate to the modern world, they have no sense of rights as a citizenry, and they continue to be indoctrinated with a harsh, fearful, often utterly mendacious view of the modern world outside the DPRK's frontiers. Politically they are schooled only in obedience and economically they have only known an extreme version of economic commandism. The regime has done enormous damage to the national psyche and has given its citizens little in the way of intellectual or material resources with which to make their way in the modern world. Its archaic and primitive economic infrastructure is almost useless as a basis on which to develop an economic system which can serve even the basic needs of the country. There are no exile movements, no dissidents, and no models for building new social and economic institutions except those in the demonised ROK.

The Northeast Asian region and the world as a whole will feel the consequences of Kimism for many years to come. Geopolitical consequences, many of them largely unforeseeable at present, will flow from the non-viability of the DPRK state in its current form, for this non-viability presages instability and convulsive forms of change. This in turn will pose a serious economic and demographic threat, foremost to the ROK, but also to other neighbouring countries. In the long term, the overwhelming pull toward a reunified Korea in both Korean states will eventually prevail in some form or other, but meanwhile there will be other consequences of a more immediate kind. In particular, the DPRK's neighbours will feel the consequences in the form of continuing high degrees of tension and high levels of military expenditure. Moreover, it is by no means clear that sound management will produce a peaceful end to the ongoing nuclear crisis because never before has a regime so indissolubly identified state survival with the possession of nuclear weapons.

The KWP, despite its extraordinary incompetence and irresponsibility on many levels, insists that its survival is inextricably linked with state survival. The political and institutional void that Kimism has created and the fact that the state has never known any other effective regime lends cogency to this perception, and this is a fundamental reason behind the continuing survival of the DPRK as a dysfunctional state. But it is also a fundamental reason why there are no obvious means at hand for the state to regenerate itself, and this is an unprecedented situation for a partly industrialised state with major military resources, which may still have its outcome in further violence. Yet even if the principal parties manage to avoid outright conflict, the human cost of the guerilla dynasty will continue to be felt for generations to come.

NOTES

CHAPTER 1—THE ORIGINS OF THE GUERILLA TRADITION

1   For English language accounts of Kim Il Sung's early life see Scalapino and Lee (1972:203–6), Dae-Sook Suh (1967:261–6), and Yang (1981:79–87). Also see Seiler (1994:7–41) for a discussion of the various accounts of Kim's pre-1945 career. The standard DPRK biography of Kim is by Baik Bong (1969). See also Kim's autobiography, the first volumes of which began to appear in 1992.

2   See Dae-Sook Suh (1967:49): 'The habit of tightly organized regional groupings of the Koreans at home was reflected abroad in the Nationalist as well as the Communist groups. Many Nationalist groups were also identified as Kiho-p'a, Honamp'a, Sopukp'a, and other geographical groupings'. See also Sung-Chul Yang (1981:61): 'In human terms, the Koreans were sharply divided into complicated yet familiar clusters, ranging from the traditional stalwarts to the modern reformists, from undaunted patriots to unscrupulous quislings, from radicals to moderates, and from ideologues to pragmatists. The Korean Independence movement was, in short, a composite of both politico-military daring and human drama. It had a common enemy, Japan, as its unflagging rallying point but severely lacked internal cohesion and uniform direction'.

3   On the Communist–nationalist overlap see Scalapino and Lee (1972:61) and Chong-sik Lee (1965a:ix).

4   For information on Pak's pre-1945 activities see van Ree (1989:20–3) and Sung-Chul Yang (1981:168).

5   A couple of examples of regional differentiation: tenancy rates tended to be higher near urban centres and ports in the southern provinces than in the north, intensifying pressure for land reform in those regions (Graegert 1994:141), while the concentration of industry on the northeast coast, especially in the Hamhung–Hungnam area made those centres 'one of the very few points of sustained urban Communist activity inside northern Korea before 1945' (Scalapino and Lee 1972:319).

6   The first such congress was held 28–30 August 1946, fully a year after liberation, and was called in order to ratify the union of the North Korean Communist Party and the New People's Party to form the Korean Workers' Party.

7   For the texts of extortion notes from this period, including one issued in the name of Ch'oe Hyon, later a high-ranking KWP cadre, see Dae-Sook Suh (1970:449–51).

8   Kim's autobiography contains various references to the guerillas' poor standard of education. See, for example, Kim Il Sung (1996:6).

9   See Dae-Sook Suh (1988:340): 'The huge paintings depicting him as an ever-victorious general, well-equipped with binoculars and pistol and smartly dressed with leather boots and all, hardly match the haggard look in tattered partisan clothes, lugging an old Japanese rifle, in the original photographs'. In a similar vein, Yu Song-ch'ol, a former senior Soviet–Korean cadre, recalled how when he first met Kim Il Sung in 1942 Kim was physically weak and emaciated, which 'may very well be a result of the extremely poor environment he lived in when he was involved in the anti-Japanese partisan activities throughout Manchuria (Seiler 1994:111).

10 van Ree (1989:25–6) finds evidence of direct contacts between the Manchurian guerillas and the Soviets in the mid-1930s, and maintains that the Soviets ordered the guerillas to desist in order to avoid provoking the Japanese into broader military action against the Soviet Far East. Dae-Sook Suh (1967:277ff) finds no evidence that the Soviets knew much about Kim prior to his entry into the Soviet Union, although partisans used to cross frequently into the Soviet Union after 1936–37 for resupply. Cumings (1981:37), however, cites a reference to Kim in a Soviet journal article of the late 1930s as evidence that the Soviets were aware of Kim's activities. Seiler (1994:25) cites the testimony of a former senior KWP cadre to the effect that relevant Soviet authorities became aware of Kim's activities when his mentor, Wei Zhengmin, attended the Seventh Comintern Congress in 1935 and briefed Soviet officials on guerilla activities in Manchuria.

11 Koreans began to migrate to Russia in the 1860s. By 1917 they numbered approximately 60 000, including some 20 000 who had become Russian subjects. Numbers continued to grow in the 1920s and significant numbers—7884 in 1926 alone—were granted Soviet citizenship on the explicit grounds of the services they had rendered to the Soviet cause in the Far East. For accounts of the Korean community in Russia and the Soviet Union prior to 1945 see Chong-sik Lee and Ki-wan Oh (1968), Ginsbergs (1975) and Weathersby (1990). For Soviet policy, including personnel policy in Eastern Europe in the immediate postwar period see Brus (1977), Skilling (1977), and McCauley ed. (1977).

12 Ginsbergs (1976:5) describes the policy of 'cadre export' as one where 'Soviet citizens with particular "national" attributes were systematically planted within the inner circles of the governing elites of countries gravitating in the Soviet orbit'. Also see Dae-Sook Suh (1988:108): 'Many key posts in the party, military, government, news media, and cadre training schools were occupied by the Soviet–Koreans; their challenge was not [to be] taken lightly. Ho Ka-i, perhaps the most influential Soviet–Korean, was the first secretary of the party, Kim Sung-hwa, another Soviet–Korean, headed the central party school where all new party cadres were trained. The editors of the party organs, newspapers and journals, were also Soviet–Koreans, and they controlled the information net-

works in the North. Even at Kim Il Sung University, many professors came from the Soviet Union'. According to Hak-Soon Paik (1993:791) this guidance extended to the basic laws and the constitution of the DPRK, which were written in Russian and then translated into Korean. For further details see Weathersby (1990:196) and the US State Department study *North Korea: A Case Study in the Techniques of Takeover* (1961:101). Also see the brief biographies in Chong-sik Lee and Ki-wan Oh (1968) which help us to grasp the scale of Soviet control of DPRK party and government until well into the 1950s. Perhaps the most egregious example is probably that of Pang Hak-se, a former NKVD officer in the Uzbekistan party *apparat* who, as Minister of Home Affairs (1951–60) remained in control of all domestic security matters in the DPRK throughout the 1950s. Halliday and Cumings (1988) maintain that North Korea may be likened to Yugoslavia in the degree of independence it exercised during 1945–50. For a rebuttal see van Ree (1989:174).

13 In a similar vein, Dae-Sook Suh (1970:476–7) notes of the many surviving policy documents of Korean leftist groups from the immediate post-1945 era: 'These documents are generally repetitious in nature and they contain statements expressing exuberance accompanied by strong hatred toward the defeated Japanese. Surprisingly, no major statement of the party is available which discusses the general direction or policies of the party immediately after the liberation even when the operation of the Communist party was legal'.

14 On the effect of the Moscow conference on Korean Communist support see Soon-Sung Cho (1967:92–113), Scalapino and Lee (1972:273ff), and Cumings (1981:224).

15 On Soviet behaviour see, for example, Weathersby (1990:190–2).

16 For an account of the Comintern purges see Starkov (1994). On the purging of foreign party leaders within the Comintern during the Terror also see Conquest (1973) and Volkogonov (1995).

17 Kim is frequently described as having 'charisma', but the aura he acquired came later after years of intensive cult of personality politics. On the other hand, O Yong-jin's account of Kim's first public appearance in Pyongyang on 14 October 1945 is detailed and persuasive (as befits a man who was later to become a prominent playwright in the South) in its depiction of an ordinary young man having little impact on the crowd with his 'monotonous, plain, and duck-like voice'. See Scalapino and Lee (1972:324–5). Yu Song-ch'ol, a senior KPA cadre at this time, likewise saw little personal magnetism in Kim. See Seiler (1994:111, 124–5).

18 At this stage a word of clarification about Party titles is in order. Soon after liberation the KCP divided into northern and southern bureaus and then into northern and southern parties, though under a united leadership. The exact date of the establishment of the North Korean Communist Party (NKCP) is not clear, although Scalapino and Lee (1972:355) note Kim Il Sung's use of the term 'North Korean Community Party organization' at the Third Executive Committee meeting of the Bureau during 17–18 December 1945. The NKCP and SKCP became the North Korean Workers' Party (NKWP) and the South Korean Workers' Party (SKWP) after merger with the Yan'an group's New People's Party in August 1946. The SKWP effectively ceased to exist after its leadership went North in 1949, but the NKWP retained the fiction of a separate SKWP until after the outbreak of the Korean War.

19 See Scalapino and Lee (1972:406). On Mu's actual role in the lead-up to and early stages of the Korean War see Myung-Lim Park (1995:266). Mu had been one of the members of the Yan'an group with close CCP ties and had served as Peng Dehuai's Chief of Staff (Sung-Chul Yang 1981:165). Peng was, of course, now the commander of the Chinese People's Volunteers in Korea.

20 On the Party membership policies of the Korean War years see Scalapino and Lee (1972:456–7) and Koon-Woo Nam (1974:86ff).

21 See Scalapino and Lee (1972:427) for examples of the praise generated for Kim in the official media to mark his fortieth birthday in April 1952. Stalinist polities seem to have viewed milestone birthdays as suitable occasions to intensify personality cults. Gill (1980:167) has observed how 'the cult of Stalin burst on to the public scene in the second half of December 1929, with the week beginning 18 December witnessing the saturation of the mass media by messages of greeting to Stalin from all corners of the country, by articles about Stalin, and by pictures of the general Secretary. The precipitating factor in this enormous outpouring of praise was Stalin's fiftieth birthday on 21 December'. As we shall see later, Kim Jong Il's fortieth birthday in 1982, and his fiftieth birthday in 1992 likewise marked a significant boost in the younger Kim's authority and personality cult.

22 See Chong-sik Lee (1965b) and Okonogi (1994) for an account of this policy debate and an assessment of its scale and consequences. In particular, Lee notes that in the first decade after 1953, 75 per cent of all foreign aid went on the means of production and only 25 per cent on agriculture and consumer goods. In order to finance its heavy industrialisation the DPRK enforced a compulsory savings rate of 25 per cent of national income—'even higher than those enforced in the Soviet Union and Communist China in comparable periods of their history. It is easy to perceive that the North Korean leaders demanded the utmost sacrifice and perseverance from the population' (Chong-sik Lee 1965b:122).

23 On the influence of Soviet policies on the DPRK in the immediate aftermath of Stalin's death see Okonogi (1994:177ff).

24 On the significance of the December 1955 speech 'On Eliminating Dogmatism and Formalism and Establishing Juche in Ideological Work' see Okonogi (1994:196ff) and Scalapino and Lee (1972:500).

25 See Chapter 2 for details.

26 For sociological analysis of the 914 delegates to the Third KWP Congress see Scalapino and Lee (1972:505ff). In age, education and occupation, nearly 60 per cent were 40-years old or younger and had limited formal education. Eight per cent were college graduates. Veterans whose experience extended into the pre-1945 period represented a mere 8 per cent of the total.

27 From an examination of the contents of the KWP's theoretical organ Kulloja, Chong-sik Lee (1965b:123) argues that Juche first began to develop as a consistent ideology about 1957. Dae-Sook Suh (1988:147) notes how within two to three years after the 1956 Congress 'many historical studies blending grossly exaggerated accounts of [Kim's] partisan exploits with traditional Korean history began to appear', while Scalapino and Lee (1972:565) similarly remark on the major DPRK rewriting of the history of the Communist movement that occurred in the late 1950s.

CHAPTER 2—THE POLITICAL INSTITUTIONS OF THE DPRK

1   For details of KWP mass organisations see Scalapino and Lee (1972:490ff) and Chin-wee Chung (1983:81ff).

2   Bylaw 21. See Dae-Sook Suh (1981:534) for translation.

3   For the few facts that are known about these two Party conferences see Scalapino and Lee (1972:718–19). On the Second Party Conference also see Dae-Sook Suh (1988:220).

4   The Sixth KWP Congress in October 1980 elected 248 full and 103 alternate Central Committee members. Alternative members are also often referred to in the literature as candidate members.

5   See Scalapino and Lee (1972:727) and Dae-Sook Suh (1981:277) for informed guesses as to what actually transpires at these meetings.

6   For discussion of KWP plenums in the period 1946–70 see Scalapino and Lee (1972:720–6). For a list of all known KWP plenums to 1980 see Dae-Sook Suh (1981:273–308).

7   For analysis of re-election patterns from the Second to the Fifth KWP Congress see Dae-Sook Suh (1976:163). Chong-sik Lee (1982:443) reports that 175 out of 248 full members of the Sixth KWP Congress, or 70.6 per cent, were new appointments, marginally more than the 68.0 per cent of the Fifth KWP Congress Central Committee. Also see Scalapino and Lee (1972:749), whose analysis of the Fifth KWP Congress Central Committee suggests that considerable calculation goes into assigning individuals a place in the Central Committee hierarchy. Again the correlation with Stalinist practice as described by Daniels (1989:102) is striking.

8   See Dae-Sook Suh (1976:168): 'The role of the Candidate Central Committee members is not clear. Contrary to practice elsewhere relatively few candidate members are promoted to full membership, and fewer still are re-elected to candidate status. The tenure is not long and their characteristic patterns are similar to those of the full members. It does not seem to be a step up towards higher office'.

9   For the sake of clarity, in this work we shall use the term 'Politburo' to describe this committee.

10 See Fainsod (1962:154, 262–3).

11 For a description of the establishment of these institutions and their early history see Fainsod (1962:154ff) and Schapiro (1971:319ff).

12 The membership of the Secretariat in October 1990 was as follows: Kim Il Sung, Kim Jong Il, Kim Chung-nin, Pak Nam-gi, So Kwan-hui, Hwang Chang-yop, Kim Yun-hyok, Kim Hwan, Kim Ch'ang-ju, Kim Tal-hyon, Chang Ch'ol, Yun Ki-bok, and Kim Yong-sun. For a list of Party Secretaries present at the forty-fifth anniversary of the founding of the KWP on October 1990 see *PT* 13 October 1990.

13 It is not always possible to pinpoint the date of cadres' departures from the Secretariat since the DPRK media does not give this information. Such departures are revealed by checking the names of Party Secretaries listed in the hierarchy in media coverage of significant Party meetings and ceremonies.

14 The English text of the 1972 constitution is contained in Dae-Sook Suh (1981:499), who gives bibliographical information on both the 1948 and 1972

documents. Major articles dealing with the 1972 constitution include Chong-sik Lee (1976), and Chin-Wee Chung (1983).

15 For further discussion see Chin-Wee Chung (1983:24).

16 Chong-sik Lee (1976:209): 'There is no doubt that the CPC is a super-power agency in which all executive, legislative and judicial powers are rolled into one'.

17 On this point see Chin-Wee Chung (1983:29, 40–1).

18 On the role of the president under the 1972 constitution see Chong-sik Lee (1976:195–6) and Chin-Wee Chung (1983.31–6).

19 Of the seventeen members, eight were either full or alternate Politburo members, and nine were non-members of the Politburo. They were as follows (Politburo members' names in italics): *Kim Il Sung, Pak Song-ch'ol, Yi Chong-ok, Han Song-yong, Kang Song-san, So Yun-sok, Cho Se-ung, Hong Si-hak,* Ch'oe Mun-son, Kim Hak-bong, Kang Hyon-su, Pak Sung-il, Yi Pong-il, Im Hyong-gu, Yom Ki-sun, Kim Ki-son, and Ch'i Ch'ang-ik (CPC Secretary) (*PT* 26 May 1990).

20 Chin-Wee Chung has calculated a re-election rate for SPA members of 35–40 per cent (Chin-Wee Chung 1983:26ff).

21 Useful sources on the operations of the SPA include Dae-Sook Suh (1981:360–443), Chin-Wee Chung (1983:29), and Chong-sik Lee (1976:197).

22 See Scalapino and Lee (1972:56): 'The Leader and the Party remain conceptually unintegrated, despite the elaborate institutional structure that has been created around them . . . Today, Kim Il Sung *is* the Party—and the Party is currently the state in every meaningful sense.'; C.I. Eugene Kim and Byung-Chul Koh (1983:142): 'North Korea is Kim Il Sung: the two are not only inseparable but form a symbolic unity . . .'; Byung-Joon Ahn (1988:138): 'Kim Il Sung himself represents the very incarnation of the party, for he is the ultimate source of power, ideology, policy, and leadership'.

23 In the following section I have drawn on material that first appeared in Buzo (1995).

24 This brief description cannot, of course, do full justice to a multifaceted and dynamic phenomenon. For a more detailed description of the core features of Stalinism in particular see Tucker (1977) and Gill (1990:1–20).

25 Cumings (1982–83), however, does offer some comparisons.

26 The trenchant language with which the DPRK daily assails its adversaries ('puppet fascist bandit clique' etc.) often attracts attention, but Volkogonov (1995:120) describes how in Stalin's case 'The polemics with his ideological opponents wrought a transformation in Stalin. He learned to use rhetoric and added a personal and offensive dimension to his customary trenchancy, calling people such names as "chatterer", "slanderer", "muddlehead", "ignoramus"'.

27 Stalin's 1935 pronouncement that '. . . we must understand that of all the capital values which the world possesses the most precious and the most decisive in its influence is man himself, and the cadre' represents a core Kimist position. See de Jonge (1986:327).

28 See, for example, Clark (1977:192): 'Even though there had been a hierarchy in previous Marxist–Leninist models for Soviet society, that is, in Lenin's doctrine of the vanguard, this hierarchy was not to be a permanent feature, and the ultimate kinship model was fraternal. But from the mid-thirties on, different systemic goals emerged. While it was true that in future most citizens would relate to each other as brothers, they would also look up to a father (or fathers)

... The new anthropology provided for a higher order man than had been envisaged before . . . One is struck by the wealth of kinship metaphors . . .'. This newly established environment of kinship metaphors was firmly in place by the mid-1930s and, of course, Kim entered into contact with the Soviet Union shortly afterwards.

29 Kim's obliteration of all streams of pre-1945 anti-Japanese resistance other than his own has a parallel in a similar process in the Soviet Union by which reference to practically all Bolshevik heroes other than Stalin ceased and the centrality of Stalin's role in the October Revolution was stressed (Ulam 1974:390). Byung-Chul Koh (1978b:143), among others, notes that Kim Il Sung had a respectable revolutionary record which he traduced by hagiography.

30 Gill (1980:170) notes: 'As a consequence of the claimed infallibility of Stalin's words, the population was continually exhorted to pay the closest attention to his instructions and to be guided in all their activities by them. The people were portrayed as accepting without question what Stalin said, not because of any objectively established criteria of truth and falsehood, but simply because Stalin had said it; if Stalin said something, by definition it must be so'. The parallels with the operation of the Kimist cult are striking.

31 Although Lenin's writings contain scattered references to the need for centralisation, his era was characterised chiefly by the New Economic Plan of 1921, which recognised the need for state and private sectors to coexist under prevailing circumstances. The vision of a centrally planned economy derives partly from the Marxian vision of a unified economy that could impose itself over the vagaries of the capitalist system, but its implementation derives from a series of measures taken by Stalin in the period 1928–30 with the objective of destroying the economic power of all groups outside the direct control of the CPSU and redirecting resources into heavy industry.

32 Collectivisation first became CPSU policy under Stalin's advocacy at the Fifteenth CPSU Party Congress in 1927.

33 In the DPRK the pharaonic excesses of the Pyongyang skyline go further than what might ordinarily be expected in a country attempting a rapid transformation to industrialisation. Moreover, as Tucker (1963: 93) has pointed out in the context of postwar Stalinism, 'transformism' was not just a particular form of ambitious economic planning, but had a strong philosophical basis in the pseudo-scientific doctrines of Michurin and Lysenko.

34 de Jonge (1986:262) notes Stalin's tendency to be dismissive of the whole field of mathematical economics on the ground that it was 'idealist' and not Marxist. In a similar vein Ulam (1974:444) records a toast to science proposed by Stalin in 1938: 'To the flourishing of science, of that science whose exponents, though they understand and exploit the strength and meaning of scientific tradition, refuse to be slaves of those traditions. To the science which has the courage to break with old traditions, norms, directions if they have outlived their usefulness, if they have become a brake on progress'. In Kim Il Sung's case this trait took various forms, chiefly the levelling of the accusation of 'empiricism' against his opponents, a charge characteristically brought against technicians and economic planners seeking to apply rational calculations to industrial output. See, for example, Scalapino and Lee (1972:510).

35 See Ulam (1974:638) for Stalin's practice.

36 Unlike Hitler, who left vast areas of governance to others, and Mao, who

concentrated on setting ideological parameters, Kim was highly interventionist in a style typified by his on-the-spot guidance tours. Stalin rarely left the Kremlin, but his eye for detail and selective intervention in routine matters of state are well documented. Relevant sources for this include Ulam (1974:264) and Deutscher (1966:362). Deutscher in particular relates how during World War Two foreign statesmen and generals were impressed by Stalin's extraordinary grasp of the technical details of the Soviet war effort. The following reminiscence by Averell Harriman describing Stalin in wartime also illustrates this point: 'He had an enormous ability to absorb detail and to act on detail . . . He had a masterly knowledge of the sort of equipment that was important for him. He knew the calibre of the guns he wanted, the weight of the tanks his roads and bridges would take, and the details of the type of metal he needed to build aircraft' (Urban 1981:27). Kim Il Sung's penchant for detail emerges not only from his extensive on-the-spot guidance tours but also from his interviews with foreign dignitaries and journalists. It is also worth recalling that former US President Jimmy Carter, himself a nuclear engineer by training, was reportedly impressed with Kim's grasp of technical detail in their June 1994 discussions.

37 See, for example, van Ree (1989), Weathersby (1990), Goncharov et al (1993), Hak-Soon Paik (1993, 1995), and Myung-Lim Paik (1995).

38 See Tucker (1977:78). A succinct summary of these features, including the overt adoption of Ivan the Terrible and Peter the Great as historical antecedents of the Stalinism order, may also be found in Lewin (1977:124).

39 Palais in particular sees royal authority as constrained by a number of factors, including the external legitimisation of Korean dynastic rule by the Chinese imperial court, lack of royal control over the bureaucracy, lack of control over the civil and military examination system which functioned as the bureaucracy's instrument of recruitment, the operation of institutions such as the Censorate, the Royal Secretariat and the Royal Lectures, the monarch's inability to exercise decisive control over land ownership and use, and the normative restraints of Neo-Confucian thought which abhorred excessive concentration of royal power (Palais 1975:10–16, Palais 1976:4).

40 This role is described in detail by anthropologists such as Han (1949:70) and Osgood (1951:48–50).

41 On remonstration see Haboush (1988). Haboush (1996) also contains examples of remonstration, including an especially poignant example in 1756, when four high-ranking ministers took King Yongjo to task for his overbearing attitude toward his mentally unbalanced son, Crown Prince Sado (Haboush 1996:80).

42 See Schapiro (1971:469) for a chronicle of the early stages of the Stalin cult.

43 See Clark (1977: 180–98) for a detailed account of how this process took hold in the Soviet Union in the 1930s.

44 On the public acclamation given to Stalin see the descriptions given in by Gill (1990:293).

45 The father-and-son system has been referred to extensively in the literature since the public emergence of Kim Jong Il in 1980, but of necessity it lacks primary source material. The description above accords with the system described to this author by various DPRK cadres and foreign diplomats in Pyongyang during May–October 1975.

46 From this author's observation in 1975, cadres and bureaucrats received a Korean-language, daily bulletin of news drawn from international wire services

covering a broad range of international events. Coverage of ROK political, economic and social affairs was especially detailed and was drawn directly from the ROK media without apparent modification. This bulletin contained no reference to restricted distribution channels and was apparently widely, though not publicly, available. It was available to foreign embassies and was keenly read by locally engaged staff members. Conversations with Foreign Ministry officials would occasionally reveal knowledge gleaned from this source, but this knowledge often formed the basis of somewhat dogmatic interpretations, especially of social conditions in the ROK, that left little room for further discussion.

47 See Dae-Sook Suh (1981:523ff) for an English translation of an unofficial Korean version of the bylaws as updated at the Fifth KWP Congress in November 1970.
48 See Chapter 6.
49 Also see Chapter 6.

CHAPTER 3—THE EMERGING TYRANNY, 1958–70

1 Kim used the term 'equal emphasis' to describe this policy (Scalapino and Lee 1972:594). For the sake of clarity we shall also use this term in referring to the policy framework which emerged at this time.
2 Kim first elaborated on the 'strategy of the triple revolutions' at the Eighth Plenum of the Fourth KWP Central Committee in February 1964. For the open sections of Kim's speech see Kim Il Sung (1984), vol. 18, pp. 213–31. For analysis see Byung-Chul Koh (1984a:123ff).
3 DPRK sources quoted by Byung-Chul Koh (1984a:133).
4 In his speech to the All-Nation Agricultural Cooperatives Conference on 5 January 1959, Kim asserted: 'As Marxism–Leninism teaches us and the experience of the Soviet Union demonstrates, the farm problem can be ultimately solved only through the [transformation of] individual farm management to socialistic cooperativization' (Chong-sik Lee 1962:12).
5 For example, Alexander Joungwon Kim (1975:313–14) quotes Kim in the late 1960s as saying '. . . it is in the countryside where the survivals and leftovers of the old society are found more than anywhere else, and it is again in the countryside where the material and technical foundations of socialism are weakest'.
6 On the sub-team system see Hy-Sang Lee (1994:190).
7 On the Chollima Movement see Alexander Joungwon Kim (1965:260–1), Joseph Chung (1974:96–7), Ho-Min Yang (1988), and Jae-Jean Suh (1994:21–2).
8 On the origins and development of the Chongsanri Method see Scalapino and Lee (1972:562–3) and Ki-Hyuk Pak (1983:224).
9 Article 12: 'The State, in all its work, thoroughly implements the great Chongsanri spirit and Chongsanri method that assist the work of the lower echelon by the upper echelon, respect the public opinion, and arouse self-conscious enthusiasm of the masses by giving priority to political work and work with the people'. Translation from Dae-Sook Suh (1981:503).
10 Kim's official biographer Baik Bong (1969, vol. 3, p. 225) uses the same term for the Fourth KWP Congress as the Soviet leadership used for the Seventeenth

CPSU Congress in February 1934, which confirmed the personal dictatorship of Stalin, who convened only two more congresses in the remaining nineteen years of his life. Likewise Kim convened only two more congresses in the remaining thirty-four years of his life.

11 Koon-Woo Nam (1974:121–2) offers the following affiliations for the 85 full Central Committee members:

Prewar Manchurian guerilla	57
Post-1945 cadres	13
Prewar domestic Communists	8
Yan'an	3
Soviet–Korean	1
Unknown background	3
Total	85

For a more detailed analysis of the Fourth KWP Congress Central Committee see Scalapino and Lee (1972:732–52).

12 Light (1988:26) defines peaceful coexistence as 'competition between socialist and capitalist states stopping short of military confrontation'. In terms of the history of Soviet foreign policy, in the 1920s it entailed business-like relations with the capitalist world which would enable the Soviet economy to be rebuilt. After Lenin's death it was adopted as a policy by Stalin and was an essential element in his doctrine of Socialism in One Country. It then gradually became a long-term strategy, despite 'an unambiguous tenet of Marxism–Leninism that there is every objective reason for conflict between capitalism and socialism' (Light 1988:40). Light (1988:41–2) further notes that under Mao Zedong, the Chinese rejected the long-term perspective and argued that although peaceful coexistence might be in the security interests of the international working class, it could hardly be in its revolutionary interests if it served to delay the revolution. As we shall see, this is the position that Pyongyang has consistently adopted.

13 On the DPRK reaction to the outcome of the Cuban missile crisis, see Dae-Sook Suh (1988:213) and Scalapino and Lee (1972:594).

14 For coverage of a 28 October 1963 Rodong Shinmun editorial which criticises the Soviet Union for its opposition to DPRK economic policy ('In the past some comrades neither understood nor supported our party's policies on socialist construction'.) and argues against the Comecon concept of division of labour on the grounds that it would eliminate the economic independence of nations, see Chong-sik Lee (1965b:133) and Zagoria (1983:356). Also see Dae-Sook Suh (1988:179–88) for details of other DPRK public criticism of the Soviet Union at this time.

15 The official version of Kim's concluding speech at the Fifth Plenum makes no direct mention of military matters. However, the extended attention he pays to shortcomings in economic planning and execution—and his attribution of these shortcomings to failures in the full implementation of the Chollima Movement, the Chongsanri Method and the Taean Work System foreshadows the return to intensive mobilisation methods. See Kim Il Sung (1984), vol. 16, pp. 464–75. For commentary on the decisions of the Fifth Plenum see Chong-sik Lee (1964:663) and Dae-Sook Suh (1988:213–20).

16 The reader may wonder how this policy might be applied at the kindergarten

level. By the mid-1970s foreign visitors to showpiece kindergartens in Pyongyang could observe preschool children, aged three to six, receiving detailed instruction in the guerilla tactics applied by Kim Il Sung at the battle of Bochonbo in 1937 by means of a giant model of the surrounding terrain. Rows of coloured lights marked lines of attack and retreat and flint sparks indicated the location of actual skirmishes. The school musical performance consisted of military songs sung while marching in step while the playground featured pedal tanks instead of pedal cars, revolving artillery positions instead of carousels, and miniature fighter airplanes in swings. Moreover, at after-school hobby centres called Children's Palaces, visitors could observe primary school-age students receiving instruction in basic marksmanship using air rifles on miniature targets labelled 'US imperialist', 'Japanese militarist', and 'Park Chung-hee'. For a perceptive account of one visitor's encounter with the DPRK education system in 1981 see Sung-Chul Yang (1983).

17 Dae-Sook Suh (1988:219–20) charts the rise in military expenditures as a proportion of the total state budget as follows: 1961—2.6 per cent, 1964—5.8 per cent, 1966—10 per cent, 1967—30.4 per cent. Similarly Joseph Chung (1972:94) calculates that defence expenditure rose from an average of 4.3 per cent for the period 1956–66 to 31.2 per cent for the period 1967–70. On comparison with the Soviet military-industrial complex, Trigubenko (1991:106) maintains that in the 1980s the military economy in the DPRK accounted for 30 per cent of aggregate social product compared with 8 per cent in the USSR at its height. In terms of value the products of the military-industrial complex exceeded output of the civilian sectors, and the rate of growth in the military industrial complex had risen every year since 1966.

18 On 2 August 1964 the USS *Maddox* exchanged fire with a number of North Vietnamese torpedo boats in the Gulf of Tonkin. In the wake of this incident the US Senate passed the Gulf of Tonkin Resolution, which gave President Johnson sufficient authority to begin a major build-up of US military forces in Vietnam.

19 For the context of these remarks see Kim's speech 'The Present Situation and the Tasks of Our People', delivered to the Second KWP Conference on 5 October 1966 in Kim Il Sung (1984), vol. 20, pp. 318–97.

20 The direct language of these treaties reflected a strong commitment in Beijing and Moscow to the defence of the DPRK. They consisted of six concise articles, and were more precise in obligation to 'immediately render military and other assistance' than the 1953 US–ROK Defence Treaty (Boulychev 1994:85).

21 For a comparison of rates of investment in the heavy and light industry sectors see Joseph Chung (1974:73). Relevant percentage figures throughout this period are as follows:

	1956	1960	1961	1962	1963	1964	1965	1970
Heavy industry	93.3	80.6	69.7	63.7	68.2	73.8	87.3	80.7
Light industry	6.7	19.4	30.3	36.3	32.8	26.2	12.7	19.3

22 In his 1965 New Year speech Kim Il Sung acknowledged the slowdown: 'It is true that the economic development of our country has been delayed somewhat compared with what was expected, because we had to direct great strength to

further increase the defence capacity in the last two or three years to meet the changing turn of events' (quoted in Joseph Chung 1974:93).

23 On the calculation of these rates in conditions of statistical blackout see Scalapino and Lee (1972:125–60). As Soviet aid resumed after rapprochement with Moscow in 1965 following Khrushchev's ouster, and as the economy absorbed the initial strain on resources, production returned to higher rates of growth.

24 For the terms of this confrontation see Scalapino and Lee (1972:611): 'Confronted with the sharp setbacks of 1966 in the economic field, they presumably argued that both men and machinery were being driven too hard; that greater attention should be paid to providing a truly modern scientific basis so that the quality of production could be improved, with less focus upon sheer quantity; and that priorities should be readjusted, with some possibility of reducing the mushrooming military expenditures and stretching out the military preparedness program'. Also see Scalapino and Lee (1972:1258–60).

25 If ever there was a period where Kim Il Sung achieved a level of terror and paranoia that approached that of Stalin it was during this period. Something of the atmosphere into which the country descended at this time may be gained from the account of Ali Lameda, a Venezuelan Communist working for the Department of Foreign Publications under the Ministry of Foreign Affairs at the time. Lameda was arrested along with a French colleague in September 1967 and imprisoned without trial for twelve months, released, rearrested and found guilty of attempting to sabotage, spy and introduce infiltrators. Comparison of Lameda's account with accounts of Soviet practice during the Great Terror in Conquest (1973) and elsewhere reveal close similarities, not only in the functioning of the DPRK and the Stalin era judicial system but also in the technique of blaming foreign 'saboteurs' for political and economic reversals. See Amnesty International (1979).

26 They included Kim Ch'ang-bong, Ho Pong-hak, Ch'oe Kwang, Ch'oe Hyon, and O Chin-u. Kim and Ho were purged the following year, Ch'oe Kwang was also purged but rehabilitated in the 1970s, and Ch'oe Hyon and O remained at the very pinnacle of the military establishment until their end of their careers. By contrast, while Kim lived, the economic cadres never again approached their pre-1967 level of Politburo representation. We should also note that during 1968 the DPRK media increasingly began to focus attention on the 'revolutionary family' of Kim Il Sung, highlighting the achievements of selected members of his family, including his parents. See Chong-sik Lee (1982:441), who also quotes Rin-Sup Shinn as having been told that the process began in 1966.

27 For example, in a March 1967 speech titled 'On Improving Party Work and Implementing The Decisions of the Party Conference' he described the background to the current crisis as follows: 'Establishing the Party's monolithic ideological system is the most fundamental problem arising in Party building . . . So far we have endeavoured for many years to establish this system within the Party. Up to 1956 I took care mainly of administrative work in the Cabinet. I therefore had no time to give consideration to inner-Party work. Taking advantage of this, factional elements within the Party came to the fore and secretly came together to cause mischief with the aim of destroying our Party's monolithic ideological system . . . I therefore took personal charge of Party work in 1956 and have been guiding it ever since. For more than ten years since then I have

striven to establish a monolithic ideological system in the Party and put the Party work as a whole to rights' (Kim Il Sung 1984, vol. 21, pp. 116–17).

28 For details see Koh (1984a:133). Significant DMZ incidents increased eleven-fold from 1966 to 1967 (1965—59; 1966—50; 1967—566), and declined from 1969 (1968—629; 1969—111; 1970—113; 1971—47; 1972—none). At the same time, during 1967 the characteristic form of infiltration across the DMZ underwent a qualitative change from individuals or two-man teams on surveillance missions to larger, well-armed groups evidently seeking to establish bases for guerilla warfare, as the DPRK had done in the period immediately prior to the Korean War.

29 For further information on these incidents see Byung-Chul Koh (1969) and Zagoria and Zagoria (1981).

30 We do not know the extent of DPRK–North Vietnam military ties during this period, but we have already noted the influence of North Vietnamese strategy on DPRK thinking. In this light, the timing of the Blue House attack one week before the Tet offensive in South Vietnam, which began on 31 January 1968, may not have been a coincidence but a planned diversion.

31 See Scalapino and Lee (1972:969–73) for details. They cite what purport to be notes taken at the meeting where Kim Il Sung made his allegations against the three, the most credible of which consisted of 'cliquism' and failure to carry out proper political and technical training in the armed forces.

32 Compared with an average of $170.2 million p.a. in the period 1962–66, two-way trade with the USSR increased rapidly after 1966: 1967—$218.3 million; 1968—$293.1 million; 1969—$328.2 million; See Joseph Chung (1974:110). For details of Soviet military assistance to the DPRK 1965–68 see Zagoria (1983:358).

33 For the Soviet perspective on this era see Boulychev (1994:90): 'The post-1965 Kosygin visit thaw never managed to restore relations to their former closeness. Soviet ideology, internal and external policy was viewed with suspicion in Pyongyang and the Soviet people in North Korea were virtually isolated'.

34 After signing the 1961 mutual defence treaty China and the DPRK settled a long-standing territorial dispute in 1963, with the Chinese negotiators under instructions from Zhou Enlai to accommodate DPRK demands as far as possible in order to retain DPRK goodwill in the ongoing Sino–Soviet rivalry (Chae-Jin Lee 1996:99). It was this settlement, and especially the agreement to share sovereignty over Ch'onji, the crater-lake in Paekdu-san, that appears to have temporarily unravelled in the late 1960s. Also see Hunter (1983:198).

35 For example, Scalapino and Lee (1972:559): 'By a process of weaving and feinting, first to one side, then to the other, Kim and his Party had established a certain independence and neutrality'; Sung-Chul Yang (1994:183): 'Kim's consummate balancing act throughout the years of the slowly changing Sino–Soviet rivalry has, in fact, been one of his political trademarks'; Sung-Joo Han (1983:162): 'For nearly two decades North Korea has been able to exploit the Sino–Soviet conflict to its advantage'; Joseph M. Ha (1983:226): 'North Korea, fearful of becoming overly dependent upon the Soviet Union for economic or military assistance, has played a skillful game of manoeuvring between the USSR and China'.

CHAPTER 4—SETBACKS TO SOCIALISM, 1970–80

1   See Simmons (1971:108–9), Byung-Chul Koh (1971:22–36), and Scalapino and Lee (1972:653–68) for coverage of the Fifth KWP Congress.

2   Kim Yong-ju, who was ranked 41 in the Fourth KWP Congress Central Committee, was the first but by no means the last member of Kim's extended family to gain high rank. In the 1970s and 1980s he was joined by other family members and relatives by blood and by marriage, including, of course, Kim Jong Il. While there has been some suggestion that Kim Il Sung wished his younger brother to succeed him (e.g. Chong-sik Lee 1982:442) this is doubtful. Kim Il Sung would not have accomplished much by the succession of someone only nine years younger. Moreover, by the time that Kim Yong-ju appeared in the Politburo rankings, plans for the succession of his nephew were already well advanced. Before his recall to the Politburo in 1993, Kim Yong-ju had spent only the period 1966–75 in high office. These were precisely the early years of the Kim Jong Il ascendancy, and it seems probable that his prominence at this time was in support of his nephew.

3   Most commentators accept that Kim Jong Il was born in the Siberian village of Vyatsuk. His official biography describes his birthplace as 'a secret camp of anti-Japanese guerillas on Mt Paekdu' (Tak, Kim and Pak 1985:9). Apparently his birth did not go unnoticed: 'At that time, a number of impressive stories about the birth of Comrade Kim Jong Il began to circulate, instant legends among the public. Some of the myths were: the Sobaeksu Valley, where the birthplace of Comrade Kim Jong Il is situated, was mistified [sic] as a holy place for a saint from the heavens; a new general star rose in the sky over Mt Paektu, predicting the birth of a new general; and a swift horse appeared on Mt Paektu and a young general trained military arts and cultivated his strength, riding the horse' (See 'Secret Camp on Mt. Paektu', DPRK no. 478, February 1996). Kim Jong Il was the eldest of three children born to Kim Il Sung and Kim Chong-suk. A younger brother died as a child and a younger sister is presumed to be still alive. After Kim Chong-suk's death in 1949, Kim Il Sung remarried and had four children by his second wife, Kim Song-ae (Dae-Sook Suh 1988:282, 395). Apart from Kim Jong Il, none of Kim Il Sung's children has played a prominent political role.

4   Tak, Kim and Pak (1985:108–27). His biographers seem entirely straight-faced in listing major early activities as fighting nepotism and upholding 'the prestige of the leader' in the face of revisionism. For a more objective account of this phase of Kim's career see Clippinger (1981:290).

5   As a matter of comparative interest, by all accounts the Soviet leader was a cold and indifferent parent who made little or no effort to bring on his two sons Yakov and Vasili. As a consequence, they cut somewhat tragic figures in their adult lives. See, for example, Volkogonov (1995).

6   Author's personal observations at the time.

7   Cited by Dong-Bok Lee (1981b:415), who also noted that this reference disappeared from the 1973 edition.

8   As usual, the DPRK portrays this movement as beginning from below, when in December 1975 the Komdok Mine in the industrial domain and the Chongsan Cooperative Farm in the agricultural domain 'raised first the torch of this

movement and called upon the whole country to launch this movement' (*PT* 9 January 1982). See Clippinger (1981:294–8) for further details.

9   See Clippinger (1981:292) for a table listing the frequency of the use of the term 'Party Centre' in *Kulloja* from 1973–80. The significance of this table is, of course, that it reflects the extent to which coded reference was being made to the activities of Kim Jong Il during this period. Clippinger's table lists 378 references in 1976, falling to 163 in 1977, all of which occurred in the period January–March, then falling to just four references in 1978.

10   Kim Chung-nin was reinstated in 1980, and Yang in 1993.

11   For more details on these purchases see Zagoria & Kim (1976:37).

12   These observations are chiefly the outcome of conversations between the author and trade and business representatives from a number of European countries in Pyongyang in 1975. Many had come to the DPRK to oversee the installation of machinery or carry out construction work, and anecdotes of machinery abuse, lack of basic tradesman's skills, lack of basic infrastructure, and shoddy construction work on a scale which surprised experienced international traders and construction workers figured prominently in their conversation—as it continues to do in the case of their counterparts in the 1990s. Two examples that stick in the author's mind are the British technicians overseeing construction at a petrochemical works who found it difficult to dissuade local workers from stress welding on gas balloons and laying electrical cables in bare soil; and the Swiss engineer who, assuming that his firm's precision watch manufacturing plant would be installed in a dust-free environment, arrived to find he could detect daylight through the brick walls of the factory building.

13   In 1977 debts accumulated in the early 1970s were consolidated into a loan agreement with a consortium of European banks with an aggregate principal debt of approximately US$700 million. The loan arrangements were rescheduled in March 1980 and May 1984. The DPRK did not repay any of the principal and ceased interest repayments in 1984. For details of Japanese efforts to recover money owed by the DPRK to Japanese companies see Hong-Nack Kim (1983:322–3).

14   For example, minor changes aimed at stimulating consumer goods production took place with the inception of the local budget system in 1973. See Namkoong and Yoo (1994:130) and Hy-Sang Lee (1994:195ff).

15   Byung-Chul Koh (1984a) and others stress the force of domestic political considerations in Park Chung-hee's turn toward autocracy in the early 1970s. Kyung-won Kim (1977), on the other hand, argues against this linkage. While Park would of course have had domestic considerations strongly on his mind, we should not lose sight of the broader security context for ROK domestic policies. The detailed account by Clifford (1994:78) of the 26 March 1970 ROK–US discussions, for example, leaves little doubt of the traumatic effect of US policy shifts on the ROK leadership at the time.

16   *PT* 14 August 1971, quoted by Byung-Chul Koh (1984a:87).

17   Jong-Hwan Song (1984:627) lists the key Chinese attributes as:

  • a propensity to modulate between fighting and negotiating, depending which tactic is appropriate at the time;
  • tenacity in the definition of wider interests. In Mao's words: 'A comprehension of the whole makes it easier to handle the part . . . because the part belongs to the whole';

- flexibility within the scope of this whole; and
- negotiating in a group.

18 Jong-Hwan Song (1984: 648ff) also lists the following specific DPRK negotiation tactics:

- pre-emptive agenda setting: hijacking the agenda by making public the subjects of forthcoming negotiations; minor counterproposing on dates and venues;
- controlling the pace of negotiation: speedy at first for pressure through propaganda, then dilatory to build up pressure of expectation on the adversary;
- image projection: using the talks as a platform for speeches aimed at an international audience and at its presumed constituency in the South;
- obfuscatory multiple proposals in multiple forums;
- extortionary demands: demands that have no hope of succeeding, but which might draw forth a concession in return for their withdrawal;
- the Sibylline Books tactic: ultimatum tactics that persuade the opponent to accept terms before they grow more unfavourable; and
- controlling the atmosphere of the talks through sudden replacement of delegates, alternation between open and closed sessions, calculated rudeness, control of the media, and working in groups.

19 Text in Hakjoon Kim (1992:587–8).
20 For details of Kim's abduction see Clifford (1994:85–6).
21 See Young C. Kim (1976:90): 'My conversations with North Koreans [in Pyongyang in August 1975] led me to believe that: 1) North Korean leaders feel that the international situation is developing in their favour. The international isolation of South Korea is becoming more pronounced while the international standing of North Korea is improving; 2) There is a tremendous degree of genuine confidence and arrogance North Koreans exude in this regard; [and] 3) There is a North Korean perception, consistent with their ideology, that revolutionary forces in South Korea are gaining strength, political instability is growing ever more acute, and that South Korea is in the process of disintegration'. This author received similar presentations from senior DPRK officials in Pyongyang at precisely the same time as Kim.
22 For details see Niksch (1981) and Young-ho Lee (1981). For an extended discussion of the factors influencing DPRK strategy during the 1970s, see Sung-Joo Han (1983).
23 In 1989 the DPRK released detailed population statistics to UN representatives for the first time. These statistics revealed that the armed forces had been excluded from the census from the early 1970s on. Calculations based on the otherwise unaccountable fall in the gender ratio from 95.1 to 86.9 in the period 1970–75, down to 84.2 in 1987 provided a basis for the estimates of armed forces manpower given above. Eberstadt (1995:22) concludes that these statistics 'raise some questions which must still go unanswered and point to discrepancies as yet unresolved. Nevertheless, they seem inadvertently to confirm the proposition that a steady and enormous increase in the country's military population took place between the mid-1970s and the late 1980s'.
24 Dealing with the ROK was a very peripheral issue to the Soviets at this stage, and it faded from the agenda as domestic political repression in the ROK grew in 1974, raising questions about the longer term stability of the Park regime.

For further details on Soviet–ROK contacts during this period see Boulychev (1994:93).

25 A common anecdote in Pyongyang diplomatic circles in 1975 related how Kim had been unaware of the full extent of the Soviet withholding until leading military cadre O Chin-u visited Egypt and Syria in late 1973. He reported to Kim Il Sung that the Soviet equipment supplied to those countries was far more advanced and sophisticated than any being supplied to the DPRK. Kim immediately asked the Soviets for comparable equipment and the Soviet refusal led to a major diplomatic row in which the Soviets declined to discuss the matter with Kim's envoys and in retaliation Kim refused to see the outgoing Soviet Ambassador in late 1974.

26 On 18 August 1976 Korean People's Army (KPA) guards in the Panmunjom Joint Security Area (JSA) attacked a group of South Korean civilian labourers and their ROK and US military escort while the labourers were trimming a poplar tree that was obscuring the view of a UN observation post. Two American officers were killed with axes seized from the working party, and other injuries were inflicted. The assault appeared to be premeditated and there was some question both as to what level of KPA command had ordered it and whether or not it signalled the start of a wider confrontation. As a result, the US put its forces in Korea on alert, the carrier *Midway* moved toward the east coast of Korea, and on 21 August the tree was felled by the United Nations Command in a show of force. At a Military Armistice Commission meeting on 21 August the KPA side conveyed an unprecedented message from Kim Il Sung expressing regret over the incident. On 6 September the two sides agreed to redivide the JSA to minimise instances of direct contact. On the Soviet reaction see Zagoria and Zagoria (1981).

27 For further details see Hunter (1983:201–2).

28 See Zagoria (1983:360) and Hunter (1983:204) for details of the DPRK's unfavourable reaction to the Sino–Japanese treaty and the US–China normalisation.

29 Although from the 1960s on, his full laudatory title was 'Comrade Kim Il Sung, the great leader of the 40 million Korean people, peerless patriot, national hero, ever-victorious, iron-willed commander, one of the outstanding leaders of the international Communist movement and working-class movement, and general secretary of the Central Committee of our Party' (e.g. Scalapino and Lee 1972:654), Kim clearly lacked international credentials. Beginning in the early 1970s, therefore, the DPRK took to placing large advertisements in leading Western newspapers such as *The London Times* and *The Washington Post* featuring extended extracts from Kim Il Sung's major speeches (though the practice soon ceased as it became clear that it was making Kim into a figure of fun). DPRK missions abroad also made the dissemination of Kim Il Sung's writings and the establishment of 'Juche study groups' a priority in their work. The DPRK media in turn gave high prominence to this largely self-generated evidence of Kim's prestige abroad, and an unsophisticated, isolated population may well have come to believe that Kim Il Sung had become a major international statesman—as perhaps did an unsophisticated, isolated leader who allowed such practices to continue.

30 The First Committee effectively negated this achievement, however, by also passing a conflicting pro-ROK resolution. On the Korean Question at UNGA 30 see Byung-Chul Koh (1976).

31 For accounts of the DPRK's participation in the Colombo Summit, see Byung-Chul Koh (1977:65) and Dae-Sook Suh (1988:265).

CHAPTER 5—THE CONFIRMATION OF KIM JONG IL, 1980–83

1 For background see, among others, Oh and Hassig (1994).
2 Based on the ages given in Dong-Bok Lee (1981a).
3 For the English text of Kim Il Sung's report to the Sixth KWP Congress see *PT* 11 October 1980.
4 For an account of Kim's struggles with bureaucratism see, for example, Chong-sik Lee (1982:435ff).
5 See *PT* 15 October 1980 for full details of the membership of these bodies.
6 *PT* 15 February 1982. For discussion see Induk Kang (1982:92).
7 They are Han Sok-yong, who became a Politburo member in 1990, and Hong Song-nam who was briefly a member from 1987–89.
8 The information in this paragraph comes from a variety of sources, including the author's interviews with specialists in DPRK politics and published compilations of material assembled from ROK sources, such as in *FBIS, Biographical Information on DPRK Figures*, FBIS-EAS-95-015-S, 24 January 1995.
9 *FBIS, Biographical Information on DPRK Figures*, FBIS-EAS-95-015-S, 24 January 1995, p. 3.
10 On 20 October 1980, for example, Hyon Chun-guk, Vice Chairman of the KWP International Department, was reported as telling visiting Japanese newsmen that the younger Kim was 'the sole confirmed heir' of Kim Il Sung. See *FBIS* 21 October 1980, North Korea D1.
11 See, for example, *PT* 21 August 1982.
12 *PT* 21 August 1982. See Induk Kang (1982:91–8) and Byung-Chul Koh (1986:21–6) for further discussion of *On the Juche Idea*.
13 Unless otherwise stated, these calculations are based on figures given in Koo (1992).
14 The Party seemed keenly aware that poor performance in the nonferrous metals sector was seriously affecting the balance of trade and depriving it of hard currency. The Sixth Party Plenum, held in the industrial city of Hamhung, during 29–31 August 1982, was given over almost entirely to ways and means of increasing nonferrous metal production and machine industry output. In its own words, if the Second Seven-Year Plan target of 1.5 million tonnes annual production were to be met, 'it would be possible to strengthen economic cooperation and exchange with many countries of the world, further develop foreign trade and successfully solve many problems arising in attaining the high targets of socialist economic construction' (*PT* 4 September 1982). For this reason, in the early 1980s the DPRK had also approached Western European firms with joint venture mining proposals, but without success (Kawai 1983:18; the *Asia Yearbook* 1982:180).
15 For details of these negotiations see Dong-Bok Lee (1981b:37–8).
16 The relevant passage read: 'We must do away with the colonial fascist rule of the US imperialists and their stooges in south Korea . . . In order to achieve

266

the independent, peaceful reunification it is imperative to eliminate military fascist rule and democratize society in south Korea. As long as democracy is stamped out and harsh military fascist rule is maintained in south Korea as today, there can be no national rapprochement and solidarity nor can the country be reunified by peaceful means' (*PT* 11 October 1980).

17 See Hongkoo Lee (1983:16) for a discussion of divergent interpretations of Kim's 1980 reformulation of the Confederal Republic proposal. At this point it is worth noting that DPRK talks proposals typically consist of public statements, often purposefully couched in vague, obfuscatory language. They are rarely clarified or qualified by DPRK officials, almost all of whom are restricted to robotic repetition of policy statements and, of course, are not made subject to any subsequent clarification or explanation process through interaction with the media. It is, therefore, hardly surprising that differing interpretations of DPRK positions abound and that DPRK intentions require assessment across a range of issues and over an extended period of time.

18 See Dong-Bok Lee (1981b). The DPRK, likewise, rejected subsequent ROK proposals such as a Consultative Conference for National Reunification made in January 1982 (*KWA* 1982, vol. 6, no. 2, pp. 195–7), and discussion of twenty pilot projects for inter-Korean cooperation proposed in February 1982 (*KWA* 1982, vol. 6, no. 2, pp. 198–200).

19 For a detailed coverage of the Burmese government's action see 'The verdict is guilty', *FEER*, 17 November 1983.

20 For details of these two visits see Byung-Chul Koh (1985b:265).

21 The number of Chinese delegations visiting the DPRK rose from 38 in 1982 to 62 in 1983. Visits at the Vice-Ministerial level or above rose from 10 to 16. The corresponding figures for DPRK delegations to China were 34 (9 Vice-Ministerial or above) in 1982 and 54 (18) in 1983 (Chong-Wook Chung 1986:54).

22 In private, however, Chinese leaders were telling foreign leaders at the time that they found the Kims difficult to deal with and that China's influence on the DPRK was less than many outsiders imagined (DFAT Cable from Tokyo to Canberra, 22 November 1984: CRS A9737; 91/004008–1).

23 On this passage of China–DPRK diplomacy see Zagoria (1983:367).

24 On the Soviet view of developments in the Northeast Asian region at the time, particularly as they affected relations with the DPRK, see Zhebin (1995).

25 For details see Byung-joon Ahn (1986:16).

26 Zhebin (1995:728). The delegation was led by CPSU Politburo alternate member Pyotr Demichev. Zhebin does not mention if the level of representation was decided on in the aftermath of the KAL incident.

27 Not only did the DPRK warmly praise Andropov's achievements, but Suck-ho Lee (1986:21) notes that the DPRK declared two days of mourning and devoted a *Rodong Shinmun* editorial to Andropov. Neither obsequy was tendered on the death of Brezhnev. Also see *PT* 14 February 1984.

28 Zhebin (1995:728) maintains that final approval for Kim's May 1984 visit to the Soviet Union was only given after the Director-General of TASS visited Pyongyang and reported on his discussions with Kim Il Sung. One must assume that in this interview Kim's warning of the threat of revived Japanese militarism and his indirect criticism of China for developing ties with Japan while Japan remained a staunch supporter of US military policy in the region were vivid

and persuasive enough to convince the Soviets that real scope existed for a major development of the bilateral relationship.

CHAPTER 6—SIGNS OF REFORM, 1984–86?

1   At that time Byung-Chul Koh (1985a:241) surmised: 'One cannot . . . rule out the possibility, albeit remote, that the Rangoon incident may have been the product not of a well-coordinated policy decision but of a strategically-placed hard-line faction of Pyongyang's power elite', and others have speculated in a similar vein. However, from this author's subsequent conversation with a Chinese diplomat close to the events in Rangoon, the Chinese were convinced from the behaviour of the DPRK Ambassador in Rangoon that he had knowledge of the bombing operation at least some weeks before it happened. While little is known of the internal communication networks of the DPRK government, it seems far-fetched to believe that the Ambassador could know of the operation without Ho Tam also knowing. Ho's subsequent promotion also strongly suggests that both Kim Il Sung and Ho had full knowledge of the Rangoon operation and that Kim endorsed Ho's role in it.

2   For details of the government personnel changes made at this time see *PT* 1 February 1984.

3   The following comments on changes in the months following December 1983 are representative: 'Drastic changes in government positions took place, perhaps in reaction to economic failures at home and diplomatic setbacks abroad' (Kihl 1985:67); 'It is evident from the pattern of new assignments that there has been a generational change among DPRK political leaders in favour of Kim Jong Il. Supporters of Kim Jong Il from the Party are rapidly replacing the old revolutionaries and aging technocrats in important positions' (Dae-Sook Suh 1986:14); 'At present, another transition appears to be taking place as Kim Jong Il, heir to his father's position, rises. The replacement of the veteran Ho Tam as Foreign Minister by Kim Yong-nam, who appears to be a key element in the new team, is but one indication of the passing of the old guard' (Scalapino 1986:x); 'Kim Chong Il is said to have strengthened the function of the 10-member Secretariat, recruiting relatively young technocrats who are generally Kim Chong Il's alumni . . . we may tentatively conclude that North Korea's announcement of her economic policy advocating cooperation with foreign "capitalist" countries should be interpreted as a departure from past policies. In other words, North Korea is slowly, within limits, beginning to open her door to the outside world, and is prepared to introduce "pragmatism" in her economy, science and technology' (Hakjoon Kim 1984:18, 24–5); 'A generational shift in the political power structure was begun after the 6th Party Congress in 1980 when people of the revolution's second generation started to be recruited in large numbers . . . In particular, almost all newly appointed Alternate Politburo members were economic experts who introduced Party policy directions in the economy, science and technology' (Hyun-Joon Chon 1994:59); 'We have seen a replacement of young technocrat elites who are particularly close to Kim Jong Il between the 6th party congress in October 1980 and change of the key members of the

Administration Council in July 1985' (Jae-Kyu Park 1987:8). The extensiveness and persistence of this literature can also be illustrated by some of the titles of articles reviewing annual developments in North Korea published in the journal *Asian Survey* during the period: 'North Korea in 1983: Transforming "The Hermit Kingdom?"'; 'North Korea in 1984: "The Hermit Kingdom" Turns Outward'; 'North Korea in 1985: A New Era After Forty Years'.

4   When promoted to full Politburo membership status at the Sixth KWP Congress in 1980, Paek was a 63-year-old three-star General and Vice Defence Minister, while Chon was a 64-year-old four-star General and chief bodyguard to Kim Il Sung.

5   For the text of the Joint Venture Law see *PT* 15 September 1984.

6   On the DPRK's light industry policy during this period also see Hy-Sang Lee (1994:199).

7   From this author's conversations with a foreign company active in trading with the DPRK during this period, the major features of this streamlining were the delegation of authority to conduct foreign trade in certain commodities to select ministries and the facilitation of transactions with non-socialist countries by administratively separating barter trade from normal commercial transactions. Other signs of minor adjustment during this period include renewed emphasis on independent accounting within economic units, various forms of decentralisation at the operational level by permitting horizontal contacts between industrial complexes and economic ministries (Merrill 1991:150), allowing local factories to fix prices for locally made goods, the creation of 'proto-chaebols' comprising a core major industry with direct links to a cluster of feeder industries, and a number of measures aimed at encouraging industries toward more rational economic behaviour, including applying market mechanisms to the supply and demand for raw materials, the right of industries to retain a portion of their profits and also to apply greater differentiation in wages and conditions (Namkoong and Yoo 1994:130).

8   EIU 4/1981:22. Also note Kawai (1983:18), who reports a DPRK proposal to West Germany on the possible collaborative development of nonferrous metal resources in the country and a Japanese feasibility study on a joint coal mining venture, neither of which proceeded past the stage of preliminary negotiation. For details of the UNDP program, which amounted to $18.4 million during 1983–86 see EIU 2/1983:22.

9   Koh (1984:46) also makes the point that there was little new in this emphasis of the importance of foreign trade for the DPRK, and cites various supportive statements on the subject by Kim Il Sung during the 1970s. Also see Joseph Chung (1987:123) who quotes a Kim Il Sung speech of 4 March 1975: 'But from now on we must actively trade with emerging independent countries and capitalist nations. Under the circumstances when the economy is developing rapidly and new economic branches are being created, we cannot satisfactorily meet all our needs if we depend only on socialist markets'.

10   We should also note in passing that former Soviet specialists on the DPRK economy reject the notion that the DPRK was pursuing a path of economic reform during this period. Mikheev (1991:446) notes: 'Attempts to open the door a little way, granting more rights and freedom to some selected companies have nothing to do with real reform. The only purpose of those attempts is to satisfy the supreme leadership's demands within the bounds of the court

economy', while Trigubenko (1991:108) states: 'There are no grounds whatsoever to call them reforms, because the communist regime is not being reformed, just as the socialist model of development is not reforming either'.

There is often a wide gap between announced policy and implementation measures, and it is therefore interesting to note on an anecdotal level that at least one regular Australian business traveler to the DPRK over this period with whom this author spoke regularly at the time, noted as evidence of active government interest in facilitating the conduct of foreign trade the provision of more skilled interpreter services and more internationally oriented entertainment in Pyongyang hotels in the form of a disco with foreign hostesses. These changes lasted from early 1984 to about mid-1985 before they petered out. Business in the DPRK at the end of 1985 was, in this businessman's assessment, being conducted in an atmosphere and by methods essentially indistinguishable from those that had prevailed before 1984.

11 Zhebin (1995:728): 'That trip and another made by Kim Il Sung in 1986 seemed to improve relations to a level unprecedented during the previous thirty years. The Politburo of the DPRK's ruling Korean Worker's Party (KWP) adopted a special resolution on promoting friendly relations with the USSR. Bilateral agreements and understandings seemed at the time to lay down a rock-solid base for development of bilateral ties'.

12 For details of Soviet weaponry supplied to the DPRK during this period see Pfaltzgraff (1986).

13 For the report by the Central Statistical Bureau see PT 20 February 1984. See Joseph Chung (1987:109ff) for a detailed assessment of the Second Seven-Year Plan.

14 See Trigubenko (1991:119) for comment on the quality of DPRK manufactures.

15 On 28 December 1984 Kim gave an interview to the Yugoslavian journal Review of International Affairs of Yugoslavia (text in PT 20 February 1985) and on 9 June 1985 gave an interview to the Japanese journal Sekai (text in PT 17 July 1985).

16 For example, The Korea Herald, 14 January 1984, 'D.C. discussions on Korea "encouraging": US official', where the anonymous briefing official describes the DPRK statement as not a breakthrough, but 'a new statement of position'. Nevertheless, there is ample evidence that both the US and the ROK looked at the proposal very carefully. The US in particular, convinced of Chinese good intentions, sought to extend the tripartite formula to include the Chinese and, despite Washington's preliminary assessment that the proposal 'looked, in large part, to be propaganda', were also particularly concerned not to be dismissive of a proposal that had been actively brokered by Beijing (AA Cable from Washington to Canberra, 20 January 1984: CRS A1838; 3126/1/1).

17 For the text of ROK Premier Chin Iee-chong's 10 March response to Kang's letter see KWA 1984, vol. 8, no. 1, pp. 190–3.

18 This formula was far from new. This author participated in a lengthy discussion between then Foreign Minister Ho Tam and then Australian Ambassador to the DPRK Stephen FitzGerald in September 1975. In endeavouring to tease out some of the possibilities of the DPRK's long-established double bipartite talks policy of negotiating a peace treaty with the US and then a political settlement with the ROK, I retain a clear memory of suggesting to our ambassador that he ask if these two processes could in fact occur as consecutive agenda items at the same set of talks. Ho's reply, to the extent that he understood the question, was

couched in general terms, but he did not dismiss the notion—nor should he have, since it was a logical telescoping of the double bipartite strategy.

19 In fact, in the wake of Kim Il Sung's visit, Soviet Deputy Foreign Minister Kapitsa stated that the Soviet Union did not endorse the tripartite formula and did not find the prospect of direct DPRK–US negotiations to be realistic (AA Cable from Moscow to Canberra, 10 July 1984: CRS A1838; 3126/1/1).

20 For details see 'The 3 + 1/2 formula', FEER, 31 May 1984, p. 40. See also an account in Newsweek 14 May 1984, p. 9 suggesting that then US Ambassador to China Arthur Hummel had been aggressive in pushing the plan before the US finally approached the Chinese on the matter formally through Secretary of State George Schultz in late 1983.

21 Byung-joon Ahn (1984:44) states that Pyongyang initially passed its tripartite proposal to the Chinese on 8 October and that Beijing conveyed it to Washington on 12 October 1983. The Rangoon bombing took place on 9 October. Also see 'The shadow of the bomb', FEER, 26 January 1984, p. 14, for details of these exchanges.

22 For the text of the South's acceptance see KWA 1984, vol. 8, no. 4, pp. 967–8. Significant as the breakthrough was, the act of giving was far from a gracious one, with the DPRK imposing a number of conditions on delivery that were contrary to the International Red Cross rule of respecting the wishes of the recipient country, and at one stage walked out of the delivery negotiations. For the atmospherics surrounding the DPRK offer, see Korea Newsreview, 22 September 1984. For the official announcement of the DPRK's offer, see PT 12 September 1984.

23 According to a senior ROK official connected with these negotiations whom the author interviewed, the predominant assessment in Seoul was that the flood relief proposal was originally a propaganda ploy. The ROK had already advised the International Red Cross on 3 September that it did not require assistance. It was caught by surprise when the DPRK made its proposal, but after some deliberation accepted it. The DPRK in turn gave evidence of having been caught by surprise. It vacillated, and then calculated that its best interest was served by proceeding with the offer. Perhaps it sensed the hesitation in Seoul and calculated that that further negotiation might exploit dissension in Seoul ruling circles.

24 For details of the ROK proposal see KH 14 October 1984. The DPRK account of the 15 November meeting concentrates on the contrast between the DPRK preference for a single, all-embracing agenda item titled 'On North–South Cooperation and Exchange in the Economic Field' and the ROK preference to separate the complementary trade ('exchange' in DPRK parlance) aspect from the cooperation aspect in a two-point agenda (PT 21 November 1984).

25 The US had expected Pyongyang to respond in this manner, but maintained that calling off the exercise 'would have been to make a military requirement hostage to political events' and this was not acceptable even in the European theatre. They offered scant comfort to Pyongyang with their observation that the scope of the 1985 exercise would be slightly smaller than previous years (AA Cable from Seoul to Canberra, 9 January 1985: CRS A1838; 3126/1/1).

26 For the full text of the proposal, delivered by Ho Tam at the SPA session in his capacity as Chairman of the Committee for the Peaceful Reunification of the Fatherland, see PT 13 April 1985.

27 The display was replayed on television in Seoul and described by one observer as follows: 'It was in fact a pseudo military pageant with 50 000 goose-stepping youths all shouting their support for North Korea and Kim Il Sung. The event was watched by a further 100 000 people with flash cards depicting revolutionary scenes and slogans. Not only did the display go well beyond the bounds of propriety, but it had all the hallmarks of careful planning and orchestration. The only surprise must be that the ROK delegation endured the display for half an hour before walking out'. (AA cable from Seoul to Canberra, 29 August 1985: CRS A1838; 3126/1/2). For documents relating to the ninth full-dress talks see KWA 1985, vol. 9, no. 3, pp. 585–95.

28 Sadly, the chief revelation from these exchanges was the extent to which the two societies and cultures had diverged, while 'the obvious backwardness of the North Korean family members and evidence of their thorough-going indoctrination has dumbfounded many in the South' (AA Cable from Seoul to Canberra, 25 September 1985: CRS A1838; 3126/1/2). This was especially noticeable with the art troupes. As one observer in Seoul noted: 'For those here who had in past years braved the risks of reading or listening to the north's literature . . . there was a tendency to believe the north's claim that it alone had truly preserved the cultural traditions and arts of the past. In one night's entertainment by the north's folk art troupe this particular balloon was pricked: the thigh-slapping, dervish-like whirling that years of Soviet cossack advice had superimposed on the stately peasant drum dance of Korean tradition was not well received. The absence of traditional music instruments and repeated resort to the march-like rhythms of socialist realism too had this effect. One contact, active in the student protest movement, expressed astonishment and disappointment at what he had seen' (AA Australian Embassy Memorandum from Seoul to Canberra, 24 September 1985: CRS A1838; 3126/1/2). Issuing out of a somewhat different critical tradition, Radio Pyongyang's domestic service also expressed disappointment at the performance of the South's art troupe: 'The dance entitled 'Kkotpora' featured the traditional Korean hat and costume. The frenzy of naked bodies prevailing on the stages and in the films in the southern half strikes us dumb. This results from the direct import of the Yankee-style culture of the US imperialist aggressors. What we should not overlook here, apart from the crime of the US imperialists who are the aggressors, is the anti-national crime of the South Korean flunkeyist traitors who are accepting such culture gratefully. They opened the gates of the South so that the Yankee pig, covered with dirt, can rush in and run wildly about at will in the beautiful and noble flower garden of our national culture' (Transcript in AA cable from FBIS Seoul to Canberra, 5 October 1985, CRS A1838; 3126/1/2).

29 AA Cable from Seoul to Canberra, 5 December 1985: CRS A1838; 3126/1/2. For the chief delegates' speeches see KWA 1984, vol. 9, no. 4, pp. 888–91.

30 'You sell workers to countries like West Germany and Brazil because there are so many unemployed in south Korea. Do not do that but send them to us. The northern half of the Republic is rich in underground resources. Let us exploit them jointly, you contributing the manpower and we providing the equipment' (PT 17 July 1985).

31 'The fishing grounds off our East Sea abound in fish because the cold and warm currents meet there. In winter many cold-water fish shoal there and in summer

a large number of warm-water fish gather there. Let the south Korean fishermen catch fish in our fishing grounds' (*PT* 17 July 1985).

32   'You cannot solve the fundamental [agricultural] problem by carrying out this type of New Community Movement which is confined merely to replacing the thatched roofs. If you are to make the south Korean peasants prosperous you must undertake irrigation projects so that they will farm well. We have rich experience in irrigation. Therefore we can go to south Korea and help you in undertaking irrigation projects' (*PT* 17 July 1985). Kim proceeded to relate how the South Korean representatives departed expressing enthusiasm for these schemes, but nothing positive came of it: 'After that we waited for a positive answer from the south Korean side. However, there was no reply after one month or even after two months. I think that it is probable that they went to ask the Americans their opinion. A reply came from the south Korean side only after a lapse of some three or four months. They suggested that we should not do any of the things which we had proposed, but instead put forward the idea of building a hotel at Mt Kumgang and running a joint tourist enterprise providing *kisaeng* girls for pleasure. We did not reply to them because their proposal was so disgusting and despicable' (*PT* 17 July 1985).

33   The North had in mind a committee with co-chairmen of vice-premier level, deputy chairmen of ministerial rank and seven members of ministerial or vice-ministerial level. For details of the North's proposal see *PT* 21 May 1985. For the ROK's revisions to the 20 June agreements, proposed at the Fourth Inter-Korean Economic Meeting, held at Panmunjom on 18 September 1985 see *KWA* 1985, vol. 9, no. 4, pp. 873–80.

34   This was known as the Kumgang Dam. The ROK concern was based on intelligence assessments, later reassessed as faulty, that the DPRK could inundate the Han River valley including much of Seoul were it to deliberately blow up the dam, presumably in conjunction with other military activity. In what was to become one of the major financial scandals of the Chun Administration, US$70 million was raised to construct a containing dam downstream, known as the Peace Dam, and the money was then used for political purposes. The project was finally shelved by the Roh Tae-woo Administration in 1988 and publicly discredited by the Kim Young Sam Administration in 1993. See Clifford (1994:213–14).

35   For example, see 'Militant brotherhood—Kim tilts to Moscow', *FEER*, 20 June 1985, which quotes a speech by DPRK Vice President Pak Song-ch'ol in which he said: 'We are grateful to the Soviet comrades for the sincere help they gave us, shedding blood and sweat in a time of need. We respect the Soviet people as our liberator, helper and ally'. DPRK generosity of spirit had its limits, however, for, as the article noted, this portion of the speech was omitted from domestic media reports. On Soviet irritation at DPRK 'ingratitude' see Zhebin (1995:733). Also see Roy Kim (1987:391ff) for an analysis of the different emphases employed by DPRK and Soviet leaders on the occasion of the fortieth anniversary of the liberation of Korea in August 1985.

36   Zhebin (1995:733) notes that while the DPRK media carried the word '*per-estroika*' it never commented on its substance: 'Especially taboo were any references to democratization, condemnation of Stalin's personality cult, and rehabilitation of the victims of Stalinism. Pyongyang feared that such

information would draw parallels with the purges that had taken place in the DPRK in the 1950s and 1960s'.

37 Practically the only visible sign of substantial Soviet diplomatic gain out of all this was the distance Kim Il Sung now placed between himself and the anti-Heng Samrin government forces in Cambodia. As Prince Norodom Sihanouk himself complained at the time, the DPRK media ceased to mention his regular visits to the DPRK, where Kim had provided him with a villa. See *FEER*, 9 April 1987, p. 11.

38 For further details on these contacts see Chae-Jin Lee (1996:109–10).

CHAPTER 7—THE DPRK AND THE COLLAPSE OF THE SOVIET BLOC, 1987–91

39 See *PT* 3 January 1987 for the official communique of the Twelfth Plenum.

40 One ROK source attributed it to a personality clash with O Chin-u (FBIS-EAS–95–015-S, 24 January 1995, p. 24). More authoritatively, a Soviet source interviewed by this author maintained that O had expressed displeasure at the large-scale redeployment of troops onto civil construction projects on the grounds that it was disrupting military preparedness. This practice was already widespread in the DPRK. Troops had played a major role in the construction of the huge Nampo Lock Gate project, and when Kim Jong Il, accompanied by O Chin-u and O Kuk-yol among others, gave on-the-spot guidance at Nampo on 11 April 1984, he 'highly appreciated the success registered by the soldier-builders in their endeavours' (*PT* 18 April 1984). On 5 September 1986 the KCNA announced that 150 000 KPA soldiers had been mobilised 'for the purpose of peace-related construction' (Komaki 1987:13). In opening the first stage of the Sunchon Vynalon Complex in October 1989 Kim Il Sung highlighted the role of 'the soldiers of our People's Army and other builders of the Complex' (*PT* 14 October 1989). O's fall from grace was not total, and six years later he was listed No. 45 in the Party hierarchy for Kim Il Sung's Funeral Committee.

41 'Younger' is, of course, a strictly relative description here. If we assume that the earliest officer candidates in 1945 were about 20 years of age, then at the time of O's dismissal the postwar generation comprised all military officers under the age of 60.

42 On this incident see *VP* vol. XVIII, no. 5, pp. 28–9.

43 Also see FBIS-EAS–95–015-S, 24 January 1995, p. 3.

44 From this author's discussions at the time, Japanese analysts attributed Yi's departure to his misgivings over the scale of resources, estimated at about $4 billion, allocated to the 13th World Festival of Youth and Students, held in Pyongyang in July 1989. This explanation is consistent with the known facts. Yi's fall from grace was not complete. Not only was the face-saving attribution of Yi's departure to health problems unprecedented, but he later returned to high office. In 1992 he became Secretary of the North Hamgyong Province Party Committee, and was ranked No. 73 in Kim Il Sung's Funeral Committee in July 1994.

45 See *PT* 19 March 1988 for a summary of the theory. For subsequent passing references in the Kims' speeches and writings see *PT* 9 December 1989 and *PT*

26 May 1990. For analysis see Byung-Chul Koh (1991:3–4) and Jae-Jean Suh (1994:29–32).

46 See Chapter 8.

47 For the text of Prime Minister Yi Kun-mo's speech to the SPA announcing the plan see PT 25 April 1987. For sector-by-sector analysis see Komaki (1987:14–15) and Uehara (1987:20).

48 The new Plan envisaged an annual growth rate for the plan period of 7.9 per cent, which represented a scaling back from previous plans, such as the 9.6 per cent annual growth targets in the Second Seven-Year Plan (1978–84). In major production and construction sectors, the new plan postponed the completion date for eight of the ten Long Term Economic Goals for the 1980s from 1990 to 1993. The two exceptions were cement and marine production, both relatively low-technology industries.

49 For reasons outlined by Trigubenko (1991:123) and Moiseyev (1991:76). Trigubenko describes the contents of a long-range energy plan developed by the DPRK in 1987–88 which called for the doubling of aggregate installed capacity of the power industry to 14.5 million kW and a trebling of annual output from 32 billion kWh to 100 billion kWh between 1990 and 2000. She notes that the proposed installed capacity was incapable of achieving the desired output, that no provision was made for losses in the network, which were estimated at least 25 per cent of the total output, and that the planners made no provision for the financing of the construction of the eighteen new power generating facilities required.

50 Ten years later, as the DPRK encountered serious food shortages and its past agricultural performance came under closer scrutiny, the consensus was that it had rarely, if ever, exceeded 6 million tonnes production per annum. The most notable form of exaggerating output was the sample harvesting method, whereby estimates of production for a whole region were based on samples drawn from high-yield fields. See Hy-Sang Lee (1994:193).

51 Kim Jong Il's views on this subject and on the course of world history since 1945 emerge with exceptional clarity in his 1987 treatise Let us march forward dynamically along the road of socialism and communism under the unfurled banner of the anti-imperialist struggle (PT 1 October 1988). For discussion see p. 197.

52 The statistics in the table show a balance of trade in favour of the Soviet Union, but the Soviet export figures are inflated by inclusion of items such as oil, coking coal, industrial equipment and textiles provided largely on credit to the DPRK for processing and re-export to the Soviet Union (Zhebin 1995:735). Zhebin also criticises what he terms 'the DPRK's selfish approach to, and its interest in gaining unilateral benefits and advantages from its relations with the Soviet Union', and cites falsification of statistics and repeated non-delivery of contracted goods as standard DPRK practices during this period. He further notes: 'As a result of these trade practices, the Soviets, in order to balance the trade and [to] purchase in the world market the products that were not supplied by the DPRK, were constrained to reduce exports to North Korea and sell part of the goods meant for Pyongyang to third countries'. Under these circumstances, it is doubtful that the Soviets derived much benefit from their trade with the DPRK during this period.

53 For the text of the Administration Council decision establishing the zone see PT 1 January 1992. The zone covered 621 square kilometres, and was supported

by the declaration of Rajin, Sunbong and Chongjin ports as free trade ports. In the zone 'foreigners are allowed to establish and run various forms of business including co-production, joint venture and foreign-funded business and engage in service business of various forms' with their capital and income protected under DPRK law.

54 In a survey of 116 foreign investment projects initiated in the period 1984–93, Young Namkoong (1995b:468) found that they totalled US$150 million and that the foreign partner was from the pro-North section of the Korean community in Japan in 90 per cent of the cases. By sector they comprised light industry (35 per cent); retail stores including shops and restaurants (30 per cent); agriculture (11 per cent); metal and machinery (8 per cent) and mining (7 per cent). Namkoong contrasts this with the $7.46 billion in foreign investment attracted by Vietnam in the period 1986–94.

55 A UNDP-sponsored meeting in Pyongyang in October 1991 established a management committee to conduct a feasibility study of the plans submitted by China, Russia and the DPRK, with the aim of advancing a master plan acceptable to all parties by June 1993. For further information see Soo-Jin Kim (1993), Marton, McGill and Paterson (1995), and Si-Joong Kim (1996).

56 Kwang-Yong Kim (1994:98) quotes a survey of firms interested in doing business with the North conducted in 1991 by the Korea Trade Promotion Corporation (KOTRA) which revealed the following major sources of motivation:

- in order to secure a bridgehead for future advancement: 41.5 per cent;
- interest in cheap labour: 31.5 per cent; and
- interest in exploiting natural resources: 24.4 per cent.

57 For details see 'Order on the Border', FEER 20 March 1986.

58 Because of the illegal nature of most of the transactions involved, there is little literature on this subject. According to one estimate, by the mid-1990s the trade had grown to involve up to 100 000 people, some of whom traded in major commodities including lumber, automobiles and artifacts. Estimates of its annual value vary from $30 million to $300 million, compared with a reported $550 million in official DPRK–China trade in 1995. See 'Barter on the Border', FEER 10 October 1996.

59 For further details see Hy-Sang Lee (1994:199–202).

60 For a detailed, sector by sector comparison of ROK and DPRK economic capability as of 1992, see Young Namkoong (1995a).

61 For the texts of the DPRK proposal and the ROK response see KWA 1987, vol. 11, no. 2, pp. 351–7.

62 See KWA 1987, vol. 11, no. 2, pp. 362–3.

63 The woman, Kim Hyon-hui, recounted how she and an accomplice, assuming false identities as Japanese nationals, had planted the bomb while en route from Baghdad to Abu Dhabi where they had disembarked. The pair aroused suspicions while waiting for a connecting flight out of Abu Dhabi and were arrested. The woman's companion died after swallowing a suicide pill but she herself was arrested, interrogated and handed over to the ROK authorities. Eventually, she admitted she was the daughter of a DPRK diplomat who had been recruited for special operations by the KWP in 1980. For official ROK documents relating to the incident, including Kim Hyon-hui's statement, see KWA 1988, vol. 12, no. 1, pp. 181–4. For reports on the incident see 'The Pyongyang factor' and 'Seeking forgiveness', FEER 28 January 1988, and KH 22 January and 9 February 1988.

64   For the text of this declaration see *KWA* 1988, vol. 12, no. 3, pp. 627–30.

65   For detailed analysis see Byung-Chul Koh (1989a) and Sang-Woo Rhee (1991).

66   On the DPRK's 1980 DCRK proposal see, for example, Young C. Kim (1981), Chong-sik Lee (1986) and Sung-Chul Yang (1994b).

67   For a detailed account of the 1988 interparliamentary negotiations see Dong-Bok Lee (1988:785–808).

68   For details see *KWA* 1989, vol. 13, no. 1, pp. 191–3, 207–10, and 215–19.

69   For the North's position on the various talks proposals at the time, expressed in characteristic robust language, see *PT* 21 October 1989 on the officials' and Red Cross talks; *PT* 28 October 1989 on the sports talks; and *PT* 4 November 1989 on the joint parliamentary talks.

70   For the official minutes of their discussion see *KWA* 1989, vol. 13, no. 3, pp. 583–5.

71   See Yonhap Press Agency report in FBIS DR/EAS, 4 August 1989, p. 32.

72   With this decision, sports once again disappeared from the talks agenda. The atmosphere surrounding the 1989–90 sports talks was never very promising. Amid mutual accusations of delaying tactics and unreasonable demands, matters finally came to a head on 7 February 1990 when the North presented the South with what it termed 'a three-point demand of principle'. This called upon the South to: 1) reaffirm jointly with the North that it would participate as a united team or not at all; 2) 'admit that it has delayed the formation of a single team by coming out with problems which have nothing to do with the talks'; and 3) revoke remarks concerning the sending of a separate team (*PT* 24 March 1990). With the South's rejection of these demands, the talks effectively ceased.

73   For official ROK statements on the discovery see *KWA* 1990, vol. 14, no. 1, pp. 190–1.

74   These references concentrated on the withdrawal of US forces from Korea and the implementation of a 'free travel and a full-scale open-door policy between the north and south'. The principal impediment to cross-DMZ exchanges was, Kim blandly asserted, a series of anti-tank obstacles on the southern side of the DMZ. As Dae-Sook Suh (1990:613) noted at the time: 'What Kim wants from the South is the withdrawal of US troops, tearing down of the tank barrier, free travel for the South Korean dissidents to the North, and an opportunity for the North to strengthen the dissident groups in the South and form a united front with them'.

75   For speeches and news conference transcripts see *KWA* 1990, vol. 14, no. 4, pp. 568–77.

76   For analysis of the prime ministerial talks see Dae-Sook Suh (1990:617–20).

77   The relevant portion of Kim's address read: 'We deem it necessary to settle the humanitarian question of visit and exchange, but cannot compromise with the attempt to delay the settlement of the question of peace, the military question, which is more pressing. Home-town visits or economic exchange, to be effective, require before anything else that the daggers hidden in the bosom should be thrown away and that the fear of invasion from the south or "invasion from the north" should be dispelled. Evading the settlement of the military question and insisting only on exchange in the situation of our country where there is a real danger of war, is in fact tantamount to wishing no peace, no normal visit or no exchange itself' (*PT* 1 January 1991).

78   See *KWA* 1991, vol. 15, no. 4, pp. 757–71.

79 Boulychev (1994:97) maintains that the decision to expand contacts with the ROK was made by the CPSU CC in October 1986, a few days before Kim Il Sung arrived in Moscow on a state visit.

80 AA Memorandum from Tokyo to Canberra, 2 July 1987: CRS A1838; 3107/40/91. Kim was accompanied by Vice President Yi Chong-ok, Foreign Minister Kim Yong-nam and Chairman of the Democratic Front for the Unification of the Fatherland Ho Tam (PT 30 May 1987).

81 On negotiations between the two Koreas and the IOC during this period see Dong-Bok Lee (1988:782–5).

82 In the lead-up to the Olympics the DPRK continued its efforts to persuade friendly states not to participate and produced a steady stream of strident propaganda against the Olympics. Typical of these efforts was the release in May 1987 of what the DPRK called a 'white paper to condemn the US imperialists and the Chon Du-hwan puppet clique who have turned south Korea into an AIDS-infested area'. Issued in the name of the Secretariat of the Committee for the Peaceful Reunification of the Fatherland, a united front organisation, and obviously inspired by growing international concern at the spread of the disease, the paper stated, inter alia, 'The only disease strictly of US origin, AIDS called "American pest" has spread all over the world with rapidity in recent several years [sic]. It poses a big social problem for south Korea, an outright colony of the USA' (PT 30 May 1987).

83 For details see KWA 1987, vol. 11, no. 1, pp. 172–4.

84 The key reference to the ROK read: 'I think that, in the context of a general amelioration of the situation on the Korean Peninsula, opportunities can also be opened up for varying economic ties with South Korea' (KWA 1988, vol. 12, no. 3, pp. 652–7).

85 According to Hua (1991:31), who was a foreign affairs adviser to Deng Xiaoping at the time, in the autumn of 1988 Deng approved a policy that set three preconditions for establishing diplomatic relations with Seoul: a corresponding move by the Soviet Union, the suspension of the annual Team Spirit exercises, and the withdrawal of US nuclear weapons from the Korean peninsula. Deng saw the latter two as concessions to Pyongyang in order to make DPRK acceptance of the Chinese move easier.

86 Boulychev (1994:103–4) gives a vivid account of the state of Soviet–DPRK relations at this stage: 'When Soviet foreign minister E. Shevardnadze arrived in Pyongyang at the beginning of September 1990, and tried to explain why the USSR cannot avoid diplomatic normalization with South Korea, he received very harsh treatment and a well-prepared answer with a whole set of menaces [sic]. They included recognizing the Soviet republics [at that time still a part of (the) Soviet Union] as independent states, setting up relations with Japan and joining Japan's positions on the "Northern territories". Pyongyang also pointed out that the setting up of relations with the "enemy" would "take away any meaning" from [the] alliance treaty and, therefore, would force the DPRK to "produce different kinds of weapons". This was the most ominous threat of all [because] it was the first time that Pyongyang's hitherto top secret nuclear program was brought into the open. Bringing up the subject of nuclear weapons precisely showed the degree of animosity and irritation or even hysteria which the Soviet intentions in regard to the ROK stirred up in Pyongyang.' The reference to relations with Japan is significant because, as we shall see, within

a month the DPRK and Japanese political leaders signed a joint declaration on the normalisation of relations.

87 See, for example, *PT* 6 October 1990, '"Diplomatic relations" bargained for dollars', which described Soviet–ROK negotiations as 'characterized by hypocrisy and betrayal urged by double dealing'. On the ROK agreement to extend $2.3 billion in economic assistance to the Soviet Union, Pyongyang alleged: 'south Korea is not in a position to issue such a colossal sum of money. It is highly probable that it will come from the special fund of the US imperialists for disorganizing socialism'. On the other hand, Boulychev argues that the DPRK had good reason to feel aggrieved. Soviet policy on Korean issues in the *perestroika*-era was confused and confusing. The more conservative Soviet Ministry for Foreign Affairs dealt with Pyongyang while Gorbachev's staff forced the pace on recognising the ROK. The result was that many significant steps were taken without consultation or advance warning to Pyongyang (Boulychev 1994:100ff).

88 The DPRK paid a price for this. As Zhebin (1995:737) notes: 'After August 1991 and until the dissolution of the USSR that December, North Korea actually ceased to exist in Soviet foreign policy thinking'. As a postscript, also note that when Kim Jong Il received his first foreign visitor in December 1995, eighteen months after the death of his father, it was none other than former Soviet Defence Minister Dmitri Yazov, who led the abortive coup.

89 AA Cable from Beijing to Canberra, 17 October 1991: CRS A1838; 3107/40/91.

90 For a perceptive description of the DPRK attitude to the US, see Zweig (1989:77–8).

91 For the text of the US announcement see *KWA* 1988, vol. 12, no. 4, pp. 856–9.

92 On the earlier history of US–DPRK relations see Scalapino (1983) and Byung-Chul Koh (1984a). For further details on the US–DPRK dialogue after 1988 see Sung-Joo Han (1991), Chae-Jin Lee (1994), and Eberstadt (1995).

93 These initiatives meant that ROK opposition to the notion of expanded Japan–DPRK contacts was no longer a major factor, and by the middle of 1988 the ROK was encouraging such contact. The scope and significance of this change in ROK policy was considerable and is worth noting. Japanese officials confessed that in discussions with ROK officials they had been 'taken aback by the boldness of the ROK's unilateral and unsolicited gesture of support [for Japan–DPRK contacts]' AA Cable from Tokyo to Canberra, 12 July 1988: CRS A1838; 3125/11/87.

94 For a detailed account of DPRK–Japan relations from 1960–77 see Jung-Hyun Shin (1981). On relations in the 1980s see Jung-Hyun Shin (1986) and Hong-Nack Kim (1983, 1994a, 1994b).

95 For the text of this agreement, see *PT* 29 September 1990. On 10 October 1990, *The Japan Times* published an 'inside account' of the events leading up to the signing of the joint declaration. According to this account there were 'sharp disagreements' between the Japanese and DPRK parties until the final moments before the signing. In this account Kanemaru Shin emerges as having insisted on acceptance of the postwar compensation concept in order to resolve disagreements among the Japanese delegation. At this, 'Officials of the North Korean Workers' Party reportedly were delighted at the Japanese concession. They described the outcome of the talks as nearly 100 per cent in their favor'. See

'Japan–N. Korea talks controversial until the end', *The Japan Times*, 10 October 1990.

96 See Hong-Nack Kim (1994a:677). The DPRK agent who had confessed to planting the bomb on KAL Flight 858 also stated that as part of her training to assume a Japanese identity she had received intensive language training from a Japanese woman whom she identified from Japanese missing persons photographs. The DPRK refused to discuss the issue, maintaining that it was both fabricated and irrelevant to the talks. As a DPRK spokesman put it at a subsequent news briefing: 'The Japanese side brought forward such a question at the talks discussing the normalization of diplomatic relations on the hypothetical assumption that it is highly probable that an unidentified imaginary Japanese woman who is said to be related with a bogus criminal of a drama enacted by the United States and the south Korean military fascist clique is in the DPRK . . . This is an intolerable insult and challenge to us and an act to break up the talks' (*PT* 25 May 1991).

97 For a detailed account of the normalisation talks see Bridges (1993:143–62).

98 For a more detailed account of the ROK's campaign for separate UN membership see Samuel S. Kim (1994:34–40).

99 On the background to the DPRK's nuclear program see Mack (1991) and Oh and Hassig (1994). For negotiations during the period 1989–92 in particular see Mazarr (1992).

100 For example, the size of the reactor itself was unnecessarily large for research purposes, while satellite photographs also revealed the existence of what appeared to be a reprocessing plant. For details see Mack (1993:3).

101 On the eve of the launching of Desert Storm, Kim Il Sung described the conflict as follows: 'Taking advantage of the destruction of the balance of forces in international relations, the imperialists are acting more outrageously, launching piratic armed aggression against the sovereign countries without hesitation and creating the danger of devastating war by paving the road to a new, larger-scale aggression on the plea of opposing aggression' (*PT* 1 January 1991).

102 For Roh's assurances made on 18 December 1991 see *KWA* 1992, vol. 16, no. 1, pp. 123–5.

103 Some focus attention on the DPRK's nuclear program as the development of a 'nuclear card', to be exchanged for diplomatic and economic benefits (Chung-In Moon 1993, Byung-Chul Koh 1994) while others see the nuclear option not as a bargaining tool per se, but as a counterweight to growing ROK conventional military superiority (Mack 1991, Byung-Joon Ahn 1993).

104 On the DPRK's armament industry with particular reference to the development of biochemical weapons see Young-Tai Jeung (1995:40–51).

105 For the text of this treatise, entitled *Let us march forward dynamically along the road of socialism and communism under the unfurled banner of the anti-imperialist struggle*, see *PT* 1 October 1988.

106 Boulychev (1994:97) relates how Kim Il Sung, after meeting Gorbachev in October 1986, is rumoured to have remarked privately that he found Gorbachev 'a revisionist worse than Khrushchev'.

107 For discussion see Byung-Chul Koh (1994:210).

108 This bizarre perspective merits elaboration: 'U.S. President Bush cheered the removal of the Berlin Wall, but he does not even mention the existence of the concrete barrier that divides the north and the south of Korea. The South

Korean authorities have camouflaged the concrete barrier and refuse to allow the public to see it. This reveals their intention to keep Korea divided. However, the existence of the concrete barrier on the southern side of the Military Demarcation Line can not be concealed. Last year, on the initiative of the International Liaison Committee for the Reunification and Peace of Korea, an international investigation commission to confirm the existence of the concrete wall composed of prominent figures from many countries came to our country, took photographs of the wall and showed them to the world' (*PT* 8 June 1991).

109 AA Cable from Beijing to Canberra, 13 November 1991: CRS A1838; 3107/40/91.

CHAPTER 8—A MATTER OF SURVIVAL, THE 1990s

1   Kang's reformist credentials rested largely on the coincidence of his earlier time in office and Party interest in Chinese-style economic policies, though his pragmatic outlook also impressed former Soviet economists (Trigubenko 1991:131). On the other hand, one should exercise caution in assessing Kang's pragmatic credentials. Shinn (1988:413–14), for example, points out that Kang first rose to prominence in the late 1960s in the wake of the major purges of 1967–68 that expunged the last traces of economic rationalism from the Party.

2   See, for example, the article titled 'Supreme Leader of the Party, State and Army', *Democratic People's Republic of Korea*, no. 474, pp. 6–9, October 1995.

3   *Democratic People's Republic of Korea*, no. 476, p. 9, December 1995.

4   *Democratic People's Republic of Korea*, no. 477, p. 7, December 1995.

5   *Democratic People's Republic of Korea*, no. 474, p. 7, October 1995.

6   ibid.

7   *Democratic People's Republic of Korea*, no. 474, p. 8, October 1995.

8   ibid.

9   By the late 1980s, the DPRK owed approximately $2.3 billion to a large consortium of Western banks on loans contracted in 1974 and 1977. As we have previously noted, no principal repayments had ever been made and, after a rescheduling agreement in 1984, interest repayments ceased in the same year. In August 1987 the banks declared the DPRK to be in formal default. One major syndicate, led by Morgan Grenfell, lobbied other banks in support of a joint proposal to the DPRK to settle the issue on the basis of a 70 per cent write-off of the loans but was unsuccessful. In 1990 a committee acting on behalf of the banks instituted legal action in a number of jurisdictions. In 1992 the banks obtained an award by the International Chamber of Commerce requiring immediate payment of the debt. The award was enforceable in over seventy countries and, theoretically at least, opened the way for the sequestering of DPRK goods and property (AA Note for File, 22 January 1992; CRS A1838; 3125/10/1). At the time of writing, a stand-off still prevails: the DPRK has made no move to re-establish its bona fides with the banks, while the banks have displayed no interest in pursuing the matter further than the ICC judgment.

10 The major committees were the North–South Military Joint Committee, and the Joint North–South Cooperation and Exchange Committee. The two sides

also agreed to establish liaison offices at Panmunjom. For details on these agreements see *PT* 16 May 1992. At the eighth prime ministerial level talks, held in Pyongyang 15–17 September, the two sides then established a North–South Joint Reconciliation Committee and reached a series of supplementary agreements on military, economic and cultural negotiations (*PT* 26 September 1992). For the official joint statement by the delegations at the conclusion of the May talks see *KWA* 1992, vol. 16, no. 2, pp. 367–74. For the September talks communique see *KWA* 1992, vol. 16, no. 3, p. 585.

11 On the implications for the ROK of abolishing or substantially amending the National Security Law see Young-Ju Koh (1995).

12 For the text of this statement see *KWA* 1992, vol. 16, no. 2, pp. 378–80.

13 For a detailed report on the DPRK's stance on signing a nuclear safeguards agreement see the text of Minister of Nuclear Energy Industry Ch'oe Hak-gun's speech at the SPA session in *PT* 11 April 1992.

14 For documents from this meeting see *KWA* 1992, vol. 16, no. 2, pp. 376–8.

15 For its part, Pyongyang made the program subject to the release of an aging former DPRK agent, Yi In-mo, from imprisonment in the ROK. For Pyongyang's explanation of the failure of the visits program see *PT* 29 August 1992. For criticism of the South's position at the eighth prime ministerial level talks, see *PT* 19 September 1992. The Yi In-mo affair was resolved in March 1993 when he was allowed to 'visit' the North.

16 For the Joint Communique of this meeting see *KWA* 1992, vol. 16, no. 3, p. 585.

17 For the official ROK Government statement on the uncovering of a 62-man DPRK spy ring on 6 October and a statement of the ROK–US position on the DPRK's nuclear policy see *KWA* 1992, vol. 16, no. 4, pp. 757–64.

18 This statement was widely quoted in the international media at the time. For its context see *The Korea Times* 21 March 1993.

19 As an insight into DPRK thinking, *The Wall Street Journal* 8 June 1994 related how at the Kim-Kanter talks, the DPRK had suggested a joint DPRK–US front against the real threat to both parties in the region—namely, Japan. As the *Journal* related, 'Mr Kanter was startled by the proposal . . .'

20 For details of the China–ROK negotiations see Chae-Jin Lee (1996:122–8).

21 On Russian policy toward the Koreas during this period see Bazhanov and Bazhanov (1994), Davidov (1994), Blank (1995), and Seung-Ho Joo (1996).

22 For a discussion of Russia's position on the DPRK nuclear issue see Seung-Ho Joo (1996:43–7).

23 For the DPRK Ministry of Foreign Affairs statement on the signing of the safeguards accord see *PT* 8 February 1992.

24 *KWA* 1993, vol. 17, no. 1, p. 176.

25 For the text of the DPRK announcement on the NPT withdrawal and a DPRK Ministry of Foreign Affairs memorandum on the inspections issue see *PT* 20 March 1993.

26 For text see *KWA* 1993, vol. 17, no. 4, p. 776.

27 For the 21 March 1994 statement of IAEA Secretary General Hans Blix see *KWA* 1994, vol. 18, no. 1, p. 154.

28 For analysis of the Geneva Framework Agreement see Cotton (1995).

29 For a summary of the evidence for a bona fide nuclear weapons program see Mack (1993:350–4).

30 However, it is almost certainly thinking along the lines described by Bracken

(1995:55): 'North Korea in recent years has linked its survival to that of its neighbors through a dangerous but nonetheless carefully designed military structure that makes its survival press sharply on that of its neighbors. The fragility of its internal position—food shortages, economic deprivation, and the lack of legitimate succession—becomes a perverse strength when linked to nuclear weapons and an army capable of destroying some significant part of the South, even if it is ultimately defeated. *North Korea's national security policy consists of linking internal and external pressures, so that outsiders had better not pressure North Korea where it may implode, or they may cause it to explode*' [italics in original].

31 For details of the DPRK actions see *Vantage Point*, vol. XVIII, no. 8, pp. 4–6.

BIBLIOGRAPHY

Information on the DPRK usually comes from one of three sources: the official DPRK media; reports of foreign residents, visitors and defectors; and outside documentation reportage, interpretation and analysis. Each has advantages and disadvantages, and while the totality of information on the DPRK falls a long way short of that available for other countries and political systems, more is available than is generally supposed—especially when used judiciously.

The DPRK official media attracts a good deal of suspicion, if not outright derision, for obvious reasons, but it would be a mistake to dismiss it out of hand. It is a statement of record, by which information that the regime judges to be important is made public. However opaque and at times mendacious this record may be, it is an official, continuing record of the regime's priorities, of its ideological concerns, and of key personnel changes. Sustained exposure to the DPRK media is an essential requirement for the would-be analyst, both in itself and as an essential check on the reportage of the DPRK's adversaries. Interviews with DPRK officials can also be revealing, not so much because of the unexpected inside information that might emerge, but because of the 'reality check' they can provide. For example, years after it had become an established thesis among external observers that the DPRK had embarked upon a process of economic reform in 1984–85, DPRK officials at home and abroad were still routinely denying this to visitors. Thus, although DPRK media analysis reveals little by itself, it remains an indispensable point of departure and a vital reference tool. My extensive reading of the Korean language DPRK media over the years provided the background for this work, though for practical reasons the DPRK's official English language media are the source of my citations in most cases.

Reports of foreign residents, visitors, and defector debriefings still play a relatively minor role in analytical work. There are almost no foreign residents, other than representatives of foreign governments. These representatives move in highly circumscribed circles and are almost always effectively screened off from the DPRK government and political process. The same applies in the case of visitors, the value of whose reports tends to lie in anecdote rather than analysis. Defectors' accounts are an increasingly important source of first-hand information. They are not always neutral or objective, but they often provide a wealth of detailed information that is otherwise hard to obtain. One only has to consider the contribution played by such reports in assembling a detailed picture of life in the former Soviet Union to appreciate the importance of this source of information.

Interpretation and analysis of the DPRK by outsiders has features in common with literature purporting to analyse closed societies everywhere, as well as a few special characteristics. The main generic feature is the variable quality of the literature, but while discerning readers can often assess this in accordance with their needs, it also produces the phenomenon of the 'balanced' view, whereby analysis reflects an aggregate of different views without much concern for the merits of these views in their disaggregated state. Moreover, where the secondary literature is based almost entirely on short analyses of specific topics, the nature of the overall pattern becomes difficult to discern. It still seems incredible, for example, that after some fifty years of passing reference, there has been virtually no serious analysis of the ideological debt Kim Il Sung owed to Stalinism.

Sectoral imbalances are also present in the secondary literature. Even a cursory survey of this literature reveals a tendency to concentrate on topics relating to international relations, foreign policy and the reunification question, while works that deal with DPRK domestic politics and economy, or else link domestic and international developments in a sustained, cogent manner are few and far between. This phenomenon is almost certainly market-driven; interest in the international ramifications of the Korean question attracts a far greater audience than do the seemingly esoteric practices of the DPRK leadership. Nevertheless, it imposes an important limitation on the degree to which we may safely rely on this source of information. It is common, for example, to sit through entire conferences on the Korean question without hearing discussion of topics as vital as the composition of the DPRK Politburo or the ideological foundations for state policy.

There are also specific difficulties of interpretation. In the academic sphere, the vast bulk of interpretation and analysis is carried out by a relatively small coterie of people who are strongly reliant on two localities—Seoul and Washington—as centres for information and discussion. Inevitably, this can produce deference to orthodox opinion and a tendency to reflect prevailing theories uncritically. In Seoul, obviously, there are also deeper, historical influences at work which arise more directly out of the Korean conflict. While these are often trivialised into the Communist/anti-Communist polarity, there are more pervasive intellectual influences at work than can be discussed here. Public opinion, the local media, and a number of government-sponsored agencies all influence the debate, and often reflect widespread Korean hopes and expectations that may not easily be distinguished from wishful thinking. Each of the above sources has its limitations, but broad reading and judicious use of materials can help overcome the bias of over-reliance on any single type of material.

CITED WORKS

Ahn, Byeonggil 1995, 'Domestic Uncertainty and Coordination between North and South Korea', in *Rationality and Politics in the Korean Peninsula*, eds HeeMin Kim and Woosang Kim, International Society for Korean Studies, Osaka University of Economics and Law/Michigan State University International Studies and Programs, Seoul, pp. 119–42.

Ahn, Byung-joon 1984, 'North Korea's Proposal for a Tripartite Conference and Changes in Four Power Relations in East Asia', *Korea and World Affairs*, vol. 8, no. 1, pp. 17–47.

——1986, 'North Korea and the United States in Global and Regional Perspective', in *North Korea in a Regional and Global Context*, eds Robert A. Scalapino and Hongkoo Lee, Institute of East Asian Studies, University of California, Berkeley, pp. 284–300.

——1987, 'North Korean Foreign Policy: An Overview', in *The Foreign Relations of North Korea: New Perspectives*, eds Jae-Kyu Park, Byung-Chul Koh and Tae-Hwan Kwak, Westview Press and Kyungnam University Press, Seoul, pp. 15–38.

——1988, 'Changing Roles of the Party in Asian Communist Societies', in *Asian Communism Continuity and Transition*, eds Robert A. Scalapino and Dalchoong Kim, Institute of East Asian Studies, University of California, Berkeley, pp. 137–50.

——1993, 'Arms Control and Confidence-building on the Korean Peninsula', in *Asian Flashpoint: Security and the Korean Peninsula*, ed Andrew Mack, Allen & Unwin, Sydney, & Australian National University, Canberra, pp. 97–112.

Amnesty International 1979, *Ali Lameda: A Personal Account of the Experience of a Prisoner of Conscience in the Democratic People's Republic of Korea*, AI Index: ASA 24/02/79. Amnesty International Secretariat, 1979.

Asia Yearbook, Far Eastern Economic Review, Hong Kong.

Australian Archives. See under Department of Foreign Affairs and Trade (DFAT).

Baik, Bong 1969, *Kim Il Sung: Biography*. 3 volumes, Miraisha, Tokyo.

Bazhanov, Eugene and Bazhanov, Natasha 1994, 'The Evolution of Russian–Korean Relations', *Asian Survey*, vol. XXXIV, no. 9, pp. 789–98.

Blank, Stephen 1995, 'Russian Policy and the Changing Korea Question', *Asian Survey*, vol. XXXV, no. 8, pp. 711–25.

Boulychev, Georgi D. 1994, 'Moscow and North Korea: the 1961 Treaty and After', in *Russia in the Far East and Pacific Region*, eds Il-Yung Chung and Eunsook Chung, The Sejong Institute, Seoul , pp. 81–118.

Bracken, Paul 1993, 'Nuclear Weapons and State Survival in North Korea', *Survival*, vol. 35, no. 3, pp. 137–53.

——1995, 'Risks and Promises in the Two Koreas', *Orbis*, vol. 39, no. 1, pp. 55–64.

Brandt, Vincent S.R. 1983, 'North Korea: Anthropological Speculation', *Korea and World Affairs*, vol. 7, no. 4, pp. 617–28.

Bridges, Brian 1993, *Japan and Korea in the 1990s: From Antagonism to Adjustment*, Edward Elgar, Aldershot.

Brus, Wlodzimierz 1977, 'Stalinism and the "People's Democracies"', in *Stalinism: Essays in Historical Interpretation*, ed Robert C. Tucker, W.W. Norton & Company Inc, New York, pp. 239–58.

——1995, 'Pathways to the Present: Stalinism and Traditionalism in the DPRK', *Korean Observer*, vol. XXVI, no. 3, pp. 345–77.

Chirot, Daniel 1994, *Modern Tyrants: The Power and Prevalence of Evil in Our Age*, The Free Press, New York.

Cho, Soon-Sung 1967, *Korea in World Politics 1940–50: An Evaluation of American Responsibility*, University of California Press, Berkeley.

——1968, 'Korea', *Asian Survey*, vol. VIII, no. 1, pp. 39–41.

Chon, Hyun-Joon, 'Structure of the Power Elite of North Korea,' *The Korean Journal of National Unification*, Special Edition, 1994.

Chun, In-Young (Chon In-yong) 1990, *Pukhan ui chongch'i* (The Politics of North Korea), Ulyu munhwa-sa, Seoul.

Chung, Chin-wee 1983, 'The Evolution of a Constitutional Structure in North Korea', in *North Korea Today: Strategic and Domestic Issues*, eds Robert A. Scalapino and Jun-Yop Kim, Institute of East Asian Studies, University of California, Berkeley, pp. 19–42.

Chung, Chong-Wook 1983, 'Mass Organizations and Campaigns in North Korea', in *North Korea Today: Strategic and Domestic Issues*, eds Robert A. Scalapino and Jun-Yop Kim, Institute of East Asian Studies, University of California, Berkeley, pp. 81–113.

——1986, 'China's Role in Two-Korea Relations in the 1980s', *Journal of Northeast Asian Studies*, vol. V, no. 3, pp. 52–66.

——1988, 'Political Institutions in Asian Communist Societies: China and North Korea', in *Asian Communism Continuity and Transition*, eds Robert A. Scalapino and Dalchoong Kim, Institute of East Asian Studies, University of California, Berkeley, pp. 100–12.

Chung, Joseph S. 1971, 'The Six Year Plan (1971–76) of North Korea: Targets, Problems and Prospects', *Journal of Korean Affairs*, vol. I, no. 2, pp. 15–27.

——1972, 'North Korea's "Seven-Year Plan" (1961–70): Economic Performance and Reforms', *Asian Survey*, vol. XII, no. 6, pp. 527–45.

——1974, *The North Korean Economy: Structure and Development*, Hoover Institution Press, Stanford, 1974.

——1983, 'Economic Planning in North Korea', in *North Korea Today: Strategic and Domestic Issues*, eds Robert A. Scalapino and Jun-Yop Kim, Institute of East Asian Studies, University of California, Berkeley, pp. 164–96.

——1986, 'Foreign Trade of North Korea: Performance, Policy, and Prospects', in *North Korea in a Regional and Global Context*, eds Robert A. Scalapino and Hongkoo Lee, Institute of East Asian Studies, University of California, Berkeley, pp. 78–114.

——1987, 'North Korea's Economic Development and Capabilities', in *The Foreign Relations of North Korea: New Perspectives*, eds Jae-Kyu Park, Byung-Chul Koh and Tae-Hwan Kwak, Westview Press and Kyungnam University Press, Seoul, pp. 107–38.

Clark, Katerina 1977, 'Utopian Anthropology as a Context for Stalinist Literature', in *Stalinism: Essays in Historical Interpretation*, ed Robert C. Tucker, W.W. Norton & Company Inc, New York, pp. 180–98.

Clifford, Mark 1994, *Troubled Tiger: Businessmen, Bureaucrats, and Generals in South Korea*, M.E. Sharpe, Armonk, N.Y.

Clippinger, Morgan E, 1981, 'Kim Jong Il in the North Korean Mass Media: a Study of Semi-Esoteric Communication', *Asian Survey*, vol. XXI, no. 3, pp. 289–309.

Commonwealth Record Series. See under Department of Foreign Affairs and Trade (DFAT).

Conquest, Robert 1973, *The Great Terror*, Collier, New York.

Cumings, Bruce 1981, *The Origins of the Korean War: Liberation and the Emergence of Separate Regimes 1945–47*, Princeton University Press, Princeton, New Jersey.

——1982–83, 'Corporatism in North Korea', *Journal of Korean Studies*, vol. 4, pp. 241–68.

——1993, 'The Corporate State in North Korea', in *State and Society in Contemporary Korea*, ed Hagen Koo, Cornell University Press, Ithaca, pp. 197–230.

Daniels, Robert V. 1989, 'Political Processes and Generational Change', in *Political Leadership in the Soviet Union*, ed Archie Brown, MacMillan Press, Basingstoke, pp. 96–126.

Davidov, Oleg V. 1994, 'Russia's Position towards North Korea's Development as a Nuclear Power', in *Russia in the Far East and Pacific Region*, eds Il-Yung Chung and Eunsook Chung, The Sejong Institute, Seoul, pp. 357–88.

de Jonge, Alex 1986, *Stalin and the Shaping of the Soviet Union*, Collins, Glasgow.

Democratic People's Republic of Korea, 1958, Foreign Languages Publishing House, Pyongyang.

Democratic People's Republic of Korea (periodical), Pyongyang.

Department of Foreign Affairs and Trade (DFAT) Commonwealth Record series A9737, Correspondence files, annual single series 1990–; Commonwealth Record series A1838, Correspondence files, multiple number series, 1948–89, recorded by the Department of Foreign Affairs from 1970–87 and thereafter by DFAT. All files consulted were made available to the author under the Special Access provisions of s. 56 of the *Archives Act, 1983* (Cwlth).

Deutscher, Isaac 1966, *Stalin: A Political Biography*, rev. Pelican edn, Penguin, Harmondsworth.

Eberstadt, Nicholas 1995, *Korea Approaches Reunification*, M.E. Sharpe, Armonk, N.Y.

Eckert, Carter J. 1991, *Offspring of Empire: The Koch'ang Kims and the Colonial Origins of Korean Capitalism, 1876–1945*, University of Washington Press, Seattle.

Eckert, Carter J., Lee, Ki-baik, Lew, Young-Ick, Robinson, Michael and Wagner, Edward 1990, *Korea Old and New: A History*, Ilchogak Publishers, Seoul.

Economist Intelligence Unit, Country Profile: North Korea, 1995–96. The Economist Publications Limited, London.

Economist Intelligence Unit, Country Report: China, North Korea, The Economist Publications Limited, London.

Economist Intelligence Unit, Quarterly Economic Review of China and North Korea, The Economist Publications Limited, London.

Eisenstadt, S.N. 1966, *Modernization: Protest and Change*, Prentice-Hall, Inc, Englewood Cliffs, N.J.

——1973, 'Post-Traditional Societies and the Continuity and Reconstruction of Tradition', *Daedalus*, vol. 102, no. 1, pp. 1–28.

Fainsod, Merle 1962, *How Russia is Ruled*, Harvard University Press, Cambridge, Mass.

Far Eastern Economic Review, Hong Kong.

Foreign Broadcast Information Service, FBIS-EAS-95. Springfield, Virginia.

Foster-Carter, Aidan 1993, 'The Gradualist Pipe Dream: Prospects and Pathways for Korean Reunification', in *Asian Flashpoint: Security and the Korean Peninsula*, ed Andrew Mack, Allen & Unwin, Sydney, & Australian National University, Canberra, pp. 159–75.

Gill, Graeme 1990, *The Origins of the Stalinist Political System*, Cambridge University Press, Cambridge.

Ginsbergs, George 1975, 'The Citizenship Status of Koreans in Pre-Revolutionary Russia and the Early Years of the Soviet Regime', *Journal of Korean Affairs*, vol. V, no. 2, pp. 1–19.

——1976, 'The Citizenship Status of Koreans in the USSR: Post-World War II Developments', *Journal of Korean Affairs*, vol. VI, no. 1, pp. 1–18.

Goncharov, Sergei N, Lewis, John W, and Xue, Litai 1993, *Uncertain Partners: Stalin, Mao, and the Korean War*, Stanford University Press, Stanford.

Graegert, Edwin H. 1994, *Landownership Under Colonial Rule: Korea's Japanese Experience, 1900–35*, University of Hawaii Press, Honolulu.

Ha, Joseph M. 1983, 'The Impact of the Sino–Soviet Conflict on the Korean Peninsula', in *The Two Koreas in World Politics*, eds Tae-Hwan Kwak, Wayne Patterson and Edward A. Olsen, The Institute for Far Eastern Studies, Kyungnam University, Seoul, pp. 211–30.

Haboush, JaHyun Kim 1985, 'The Education of the Yi Crown Prince: A Study in Confucian Pedagogy', in *The Rise of Neo-Confucianism in Korea*, eds Wm Theodore de Bary and JaHyun Kim Haboush, Columbia University Press, New York.

——1988, *A Heritage of Kings: One Man's Monarchy in the Confucian World*, Columbia University Press, New York.

——trans. 1996, *The Memoirs of Lady Hyegyong: The Autobiographical Writings of a Crown Princess of Eighteenth-Century Korea*. University of California Press, Berkeley.

Haggard, M.T. 1965, 'North Korea's International Position', *Asian Survey*, vol. V, no. 8, pp. 375–89.

Halliday, Jon and Cumings, Bruce 1988, *Korea: the Unknown War*, Viking Press, London.

Han, Sung-Joo 1991, 'The Korean Triangle: The United States and the Two Koreas', in *North Korea in Transition*, eds Chong-sik Lee and Se-Hee Yoo, Institute of East Asian Studies, University of California, Berkeley, pp. 43–53.

Henderson, Gregory 1987, 'The Politics of Korea', in *Two Koreas—One Future?*, eds John Sullivan and Roberta Foss, University Press of America, Lanham, pp. 123–66.

Hua, Di 1991, 'Recent Developments in China's Domestic and Foreign Affairs: The Political and Strategic Implications for Northeast Asia', Strategic and Defence Studies Centre, Australian National University, Canberra.

Huh, Moon-Young and Jeung, Young-Tai 1994, 'External Policies and Relations', in *Prospects for Change in North Korea*, eds Tae-Hwan Ok and Hong-Yung Lee, Institute of East Asian Studies, University of California, Berkeley.

Hunter, Helen-Louise 1983, 'North Korea and the Myth of Equidistance', in *The Two Koreas in World Politics*, eds Tae-Hwan Kwak, Wayne Patterson and Edward A. Olsen, The Institute for Far Eastern Studies, Kyungnam University, Seoul, pp. 195–210.

Hwang, Eui-Gak 1993, *The Korean Economies: A Comparison of North and South*, Clarendon Press, Oxford.

Jeong, Kap-Young 1992, 'The North Korean Economy: Structure, Performance and International Comparison', in *Korea and World Affairs*, vol. 16. no. 1, pp. 22–39.

Jeung, Young-Tai 1995, 'North Korea's Armament Industry, and the Buildup of the Biochemical Warfare Capability', *East Asian Review*, vol. VII, no. 2, pp. 40–51.

Johnson, Chalmers 1982, *MITI and the Japanese Miracle: The Growth of Industrial Policy 1925–1975*, Stanford University Press, Stanford, California.

Joo, Seung-Ho 1996, 'Russian Policy on Korean Unification in the Post-Cold War Era', *Pacific Affairs*, vol. 69, no. 1, pp. 32–48.

Kang, Induk 1982, 'Kim Jong Il's Guidance Activities as Mirrored in the Recent Korean Press', in *Journal of Northeast Asian Affairs*, vol. I, no. 4, pp. 91–9.

Kawai, Hiroko 1983, 'Trade of the Democratic People's Republic of Korea in 1982', *China Newsletter*, no. 44, pp. 18–20.

Kelley, Donald R. 1987, *Soviet Politics from Brezhnev to Gorbachev*, Praeger, New York.

Keum, Hieyeon 1997, 'Beijing Between Seoul and Pyongyang: Chinese Foreign Policies towards the Korean Peninsula', *The Economics of Korean Reunification*, vol. 2, no. 1, pp. 86–111.

Kihl Young-Whan 1985, 'North Korea in 1984: The Hermit Kingdom Turns Outward!', *Asian Survey*, vol. XXV, no. 1, pp. 65–79.

Kim, Alexander Joungwon 1965, 'The "Peak of Socialism" in North Korea: The Five and Seven-Year Plans', *Asian Survey*, vol. V, no. 5, pp. 255–69.

——1975, *Divided Korea: The Politics of Development 1945–72*, East Asian Research Center, Harvard University, Harvard University Press, Cambridge, Mass.

Kim, C.I. Eugene, and Koh, Byung-Chul. (eds) 1983, *Journey to North Korea: Personal Perceptions*, Institute of East Asian Studies, University of California, Berkeley.

Kim, Hakjoon 1984, 'Current Major Trends in North Korea's Domestic Politics', *Journal of Northeast Asian Studies*, vol. III, no. 3, pp. 16–29.

——1992, *Unification Policies of South and North Korea 1945–91: A Comparative Study*, Seoul National University Press, Seoul.

Kim, Hong-Nack 1983, 'Japan's Policy Toward the Korean Peninsula Since 1965', in *The Two Koreas in World Politics*, eds Tae-Hwan Kwak, Wayne Patterson and Edward A. Olsen, The Institute for Far Eastern Studies, Kyungnam University, Seoul, pp. 305–30.

——1984, 'Japan's Two Koreas Policy and Its Implications for Korean Unification', in *Korean Reunification: New Perspectives and Approaches*, eds Tae-Hwan Kwak, Chonghan Kim and Hong-Nack Kim, The Institute for Far Eastern Studies, Kyungnam University, Seoul, pp. 197–224.

——1994a, 'Japan's North Korea Policy in the Post-Cold War Era', *Korea and World Affairs*, vol. 18, no. 4, pp. 669–94.

——1994b, 'Japan and North Korea: Normalization Talks between Pyongyang and Tokyo', in *Korea and·the World: Beyond the Cold War*, ed Young-Whan Kihl, Westview Press, Boulder, pp. 111–32.

Kim, Il Sung 1984, *Works Vols 1–39*, The Foreign Languages Publishing House, Pyongyang.

——1993, *Reminiscences With the Century 3*, The Foreign Languages Publishing House, Pyongyang.

——1994a, *Reminiscences With the Century 4*, The Foreign Languages Publishing House, Pyongyang.

——1994b, *Reminiscences With the Century 1*, The Foreign Languages Publishing House, Pyongyang.

——1994c, *Reminiscences With the Century 2*, The Foreign Languages Publishing House, Pyongyang.

——1994d, *Reminiscences With the Century 5*, The Foreign Languages Publishing House, Pyongyang.

——1995, *Reminiscences With the Century 6*, The Foreign Languages Publishing House, Pyongyang.

——1996, *Reminiscences With the Century 7*, The Foreign Languages Publishing House, Pyongyang.

Kim, Ilpyong J. 1988, 'China and the Two Koreas in the Post-Seoul Olympics Era', *Korea Observer*, vol. XIX, no. 3, pp. 267–83.

——1994, 'The Soviet Union/Russia and Korea: Dynamics of 'New Thinking', in *Korea and the World: Beyond the Cold War*, ed Young-Whan Kihl, Westview Press, Boulder, pp. 83–96.

Kim, Jong Il 1982. *On the Juche Idea*, The Foreign Languages Publishing House, Pyongyang.

——1992–93, *Kim Jong Il: Selected Works, Vols I and II*, The Foreign Languages Publishing House, Pyongyang.

Kim, Kihwan 1983, 'Korea's Economy: Reforms, Prospects and Implications for the Balance of Power on the Peninsula', *Korea and World Affairs*, vol. 7, no. 3, pp. 353–61.

Kim, Kwang-Yong 1994, 'Inter-Korean Economic Cooperation—Current Status and Future Prospects', *East Asian Review*, vol. VI, no. 3, pp. 91–110.

Kim, Kyung-won 1977, 'South Korea: The Politics of Detente', in *The Future of the Korean Peninsula*, eds Young C. Kim and Abraham M. Halpern, Praeger Publishers, New York.

Kim, Roy U.T. 1968, 'Sino–North Korean Relations', *Asian Survey*, vol. VIII, no. 8, pp. 708–22.

——1987, 'Gorbachev's Asian Policy and Its Implications for Peace and Unification of Korea', *Korea Observer*, vol. XVIII, no. 4, pp. 380–408.

Kim, Samuel S. 1991, 'North Korea and the Non-Communist World: The Quest for National Identity', in *North Korea in Transition*, eds Chong-sik Lee and Se-Hee Yoo, Institute of East Asian Studies, University of California, Berkeley, pp. 17–42.

——1994, 'The Two Koreas and World Order', in *Korea and the World: Beyond the Cold War*, ed Young-Whan Kihl, Westview Press, Boulder, pp. 29–68.

Kim, Young C. 1976, 'The Democratic People's Republic of Korea in 1975', *Asian Survey*, vol. XVI, no. 1, pp. 82–94.

——1981, 'North Korea in 1980: the Son Also Rises', *Asian Survey*, vol. XXI, no. 1, pp. 112–24.

Koh, Byung-Chul 1969, 'The Pueblo Incident in Perspective', *Asian Survey*, vol. IX, no. 4, pp. 264–80.

——1971, 'Anatomy of a Revolution: Some Implications of the Fifth KWP Congress', *Journal of Korea Studies*, vol. I, no. 3, pp. 22–36.

——1976, 'The Battle Without Victors: The Korean Question in the UN General Assembly', *Journal of Korean Affairs*, vol. V, no. 4, pp. 43–63.

——1977, 'North Korea 1976: Under Stress', *Asian Survey*, vol. XVII, no. 1, pp. 61–70.

——1978a, 'The Impact of the Chinese Model on North Korea', *Asian Survey*, vol. XVIII, no. 6, pp. 626–43.

——1978b, 'Political Leadership in North Korea: Toward a Conceptual Understanding of Kim Il Sung's Leadership Behaviour', *Korean Studies*, vol. 2, pp. 139–57.

——1978c, 'North Korea in 1977: Year of "Readjustment"', *Asian Survey*, vol. XVIII, no. 1, pp. 36–44.

——1983, 'The Cult of Personality and the Succession Issue', in *Journey to North Korea: Personal Perceptions*, eds C.I. Eugene Kim and Byung-Chul Koh, Institute of East Asian Studies, University of California, Berkeley, pp. 25–41.

——1984a, *The Foreign Policy Systems of North and South Korea*, University of California Press, Berkeley.

——1984b, 'Political Succession in North Korea', *Korean & World Affairs*, vol. 8, no. 3, pp. 557–76.

——1985a, 'North–South Korean Relations in the Year 2000', in *Korea in the Year*

2000: Prospects for Development and Change, ed Sung-Joo Han, Asiatic Research Center, Korea University, Seoul, pp. 229–66.

——1985b. 'China and the Korean Peninsula', *Korea and World Affairs*, vol. 9, no. 2, pp. 254–79.

——1986, 'Ideology and North Korean Foreign Policy', in *North Korea in a Regional and Global Context*, eds Robert A. Scalapino and Hongkoo Lee, Institute of East Asian Studies, University of California, Berkeley, pp. 20–36.

——1989a, 'Seoul's New Unification Formula: An Assessment', *Korea and World Affairs*, vol. 13, no. 4, pp. 656–71.

——1989b, 'North Korea in 1988: The Fortieth Anniversary', *Asian Survey*, vol. XXIX, no. 1, pp. 39–45.

——1991, 'Political Change in North Korea', in *North Korea in Transition*, eds Chong-sik Lee and Se-Hee Yoo, Institute of East Asian Studies, University of California, Berkeley, pp. 1–15.

——1993, 'The Politics of Succession in North Korea: Consolidation or Disintegration?', *The Journal of East Asian Affairs*, vol. VII, no. 3, pp. 58–79.

——1994, 'Ideology and Pragmatism in North Korean Foreign Policy', in *Korean Studies: New Pacific Currents*, ed Dae-Sook Suh, Center for Korean Studies, University of Hawaii, Honolulu, pp. 207–26.

Koh, Young-Ju 1995, 'Prerequisites for Abolishing South Korea's National Security Law—With Regard to North Korea's Criminal Law Provisions', *East Asian Review*, vol. VII, no. 2, pp. 83–103.

Komaki, Teruo 1987, 'Economic Trends in North Korea and the Third Seven-Year Plan', *China Newsletter*, no. 70, pp. 12–15.

——1992, 'North Korea Inches Toward Economic Liberalization', *Japan Review of International Affairs*, Summer 1992, pp. 155–74.

Koo, Bon-Hak 1992, *Political Economy of Self-Reliance: Juche and Economic Development in North Korea 1961–90*, Research Centre for Peace and Reunification of Korea, Seoul.

The Korea Herald, Seoul, ROK.

Korea Newsreview, Seoul, ROK.

The Korea Times, Seoul, ROK.

Korea and World Affairs, Seoul, ROK.

Kwak, Tae-Hwan 1986, *In Search of Peace and Unification on the Korean Peninsula*, Seoul Computer Press, Seoul.

Lee, Chae-Jin 1988, 'China's Pragmatic Policy Orientation and Its Implications for Korean Unification', *Korea Observer*, vol. XIX, no. 1, pp. 1–28.

——1994, 'The United States and Korea: Dynamics of Changing Relations', in *Korea and the World: Beyond the Cold War*, ed Young-Whan Kihl, Westview Press, Boulder, pp. 69–82.

——1996, *China and Korea: Dynamic Relations*, The Hoover Press, Stanford, California.

Lee, Chinkook 1990, 'An Analysis of North Korea's Economic Development with Special Reference to Agriculture', *Journal of Northeast Asian Studies*, vol. IX, no. 3, pp. 23–33.

Lee, Chong-sik 1962, 'The "Socialist Revolution" in the North Korean Countryside', *Asian Survey*, vol. II, no. 8, pp. 1–22.

——1964, 'Korea: In Search of Stability', *Asian Survey*, vol. 4, no. 1, pp. 656–65.

——1965a, *The Politics of Korean Nationalism*, University of California Press, Berkeley.

——1965b, 'Stalinism in the East', in *The Communist Revolution in Asia: Tactics, Goals and Achievements*, ed Robert A. Scalapino, University of California, Berkeley, pp. 114–39.

——1976, 'The 1972 Constitution and Top Communist Leaders', in *Political Leadership in Korea*, eds Dae-Sook Suh and Chae-Jin Lee, University of Washington Press, Seattle, pp. 192–222.

——1982, 'Evolution of the Korean Workers' Party and the Rise of Kim Chong-il', *Asian Survey*, vol. XXII, no. 5, pp. 434–48.

——1983, 'The Evolution of the Korean Workers' Party and the Rise of Kim Chong-il', in *North Korea Today: Strategic and Domestic Issues*, eds Robert A. Scalapino and Jun-Yop Kim, Institute of East Asian Studies, University of California, Berkeley, pp. 65–80.

——1986, 'The Evolution of North–South Korean Relations', in *North Korea in a Regional and Global Context*, eds Robert A. Scalapino and Hongkoo Lee, Institute of East Asian Studies, University of California, Berkeley, pp. 115–32.

Lee, Chong-sik and Oh, Ki-wan 1968, 'The Russian Faction in North Korea', *Asian Survey*, vol. VIII, no. 4, pp. 270–88.

Lee, Dong-Bok 1981a, 'North Korea after Sixth KWP Congress', *Korea and World Affairs*, vol. 5, no. 3, pp. 415–40.

——1981b, 'Present and Future of Inter-Korean Relations: The January 12 Proposal and the Sixth Congress of the KWP', *Korea and World Affairs*, vol. 5, no. 1, pp. 36–52.

——1988, 'North–South Korean Parliamentary Talks: Positions of Two Sides and Prospects', *Korea and World Affairs*, vol. 12, no. 4, pp. 782–808.

Lee, Hongkoo 1983, 'North Korea: One South Korean Perspective', in *North Korea Today: Strategic and Domestic Issues*, eds Robert A. Scalapino and Jun-Yop Kim, Institute of East Asian Studies, University of California, Berkeley, pp. 10–18.

Lee, Hy-Sang 1994, 'Economic Factors in Korean Reunification', in *Korea and the World: Beyond the Cold War*, ed Young-Whan Kihl, Westview Press, Boulder, pp. 189–216.

Lee, Manwoo 1994, 'Domestic Politics and Unification: Seoul's Perspective', in *Korea and the World: Beyond the Cold War*, ed Young-Whan Kihl, Westview Press, Boulder, pp. 167–88.

Lee, Suck-Ho 1986, 'Evolution and Prospects of Soviet–North Korean Relations in the 1980s', *Journal of Northeast Asian Studies*, vol. V, no. 2, pp. 19–34.

——1989, *Party-Military Relations in North Korea: A Comparative Analysis*, Research Center for Peace and Reunification of Korea, Seoul.

Lee, Young-Ho 1981, 'Military Balance and Peace in the Korean Peninsula', *Asian Survey*, vol. XXI, no. 8, pp. 852–64.

Levin, Norman D. 1993, 'US Interests in Korean Security in the Post-Cold War World', in *Asian Flashpoint: Security and the Korean Peninsula*, ed Andrew Mack, Allen & Unwin, Sydney, & Australian National University, Canberra, pp. 21–8.

Lewin, Moshe 1977, 'The Social Background of Stalinism', in *Stalinism: Essays in Historical Interpretation*, ed Robert C. Tucker, W.W. Norton & Company Inc, New York, pp. 111–36.

Light, Margot 1988, *The Soviet Theory of International Relations*, Wheatsheaf Books, Brighton, Sussex.

McCauley, Martin (ed.) 1977, *Communist Power in Europe 1944–1949*, The Macmillan Press Ltd, London.

Mack, Andrew 1991, 'North Korea and the Bomb', *Foreign Policy*, no. 83, pp. 87–104.

——1993, 'Security and the Korean Peninsula in the 1990s', in *Asian Flashpoint: Security and the Korean Peninsula*, ed Andrew Mack, Allen & Unwin, Sydney, & Australian National University, Canberra, pp. 1–20.

Marton, Andrew, McGee, Terry and Paterson, Donald G. 1995, 'Northeast Asian Economic Cooperation and the Tumen River Area Development Project', *Pacific Affairs*, vol. 68, no. 1, pp. 8–33.

Mazarr, Michael J. 1992, 'North Korea's Nuclear Program: The World Responds, 1989–92', *Korea and World Affairs*, vol. 16, no. 2, pp. 294–318.

Merrill, John 1991, 'North Korea's Halting Efforts at Economic Reform', in *North Korea in Transition*, eds Chong-sik Lee and Se-Hee Yoo, Institute of East Asian Studies, University of California, Berkeley, pp. 139–53.

——1993, 'North Korea in 1992', *Asian Survey*, vol. XXXIII, no. 1, pp. 43–53.

——1994, 'North Korea in 1993: In the Eye of the Storm', *Asian Survey*, vol. XXXIV, no. 1, pp. 10–18.

Mikheev, Vasily V. 1991, 'New Soviet Approaches to North Korea', *Korea and World Affairs*, vol. 15, no. 3, pp. 442–56.

Moiseyev, Valentin I. 1991, 'USSR–North Korea Economic Cooperation', in *Pukhan kyongje ui hyonhwang gwa chonmang* [Current Situation and Outlook for the North Korean Economy], Korea Development Institute, Seoul, pp. 69–93.

Moon, Chung-In 1993, 'The Political Economy of Security on the Korean Peninsula in the Regional Context', in *Asian Flashpoint: Security and the Korean Peninsula*, ed Andrew Mack, Allen & Unwin, Sydney, & Australian National University, Canberra, pp. 113–36.

Nam, Koon-Woo 1974, *The North Korean Communist Leadership, 1945–65: A Study of Factionalism and Political Consolidation*, The University of Alabama Press, Alabama.

Namkoong, Young 1995a, 'A Comparative Study on North and South Korean Economic Capability', *The Journal of East Asian Affairs*, vol. IX, no. 1, pp. 1–43.

——1995b, 'An Analysis of North Korea's Policy to Attract Foreign Capital: Management and Achievement', *Korea and World Affairs*, vol. 19, no. 3, pp. 459–81.

——1996, 'Trends and Prospects of the North Korean Economy', *Korea and World Affairs*, vol. 20, no. 2, pp. 219–35.

Namkoong, Young and Yoo, Ho-Yeol 1994, 'North Korea's Economic System', in *Prospects for Change in North Korea*, eds Tae Hwan Ok and Hong Yung Lee, Institute of East Asian Studies, University of California, Berkeley.

Nelson, Daniel N. (ed) 1992, *Romania After Tyranny*, Westview Press, Boulder.

Niksch, Larry A. 1981, 'US Troop Withdrawal from South Korea: Past Shortcomings and Future Prospects', *Asian Survey*, vol. XXI, no. 3, pp. 325–41.

Nisbet, Robert 1976, *The Social Philosophers*, Paladin, St Albans.

Oh, Kongdan 1990, 'North Korea in 1989: Touched by Winds of Change?', *Asian Survey*, vol. XXX, no. 1, pp. 74–80.

Oh, Kongdan and Hassig, Ralph C. 1994, 'North Korea's Nuclear Program', in *Korea and the World: Beyond the Cold War*, ed Young-Whan Kihl, Westview Press, Boulder , pp. 233–52.

Oh, Yong-Suk 1992, 'Chinese and Soviet Reforms and Korea's Northward Policy: An Economic Perspective', in *The Changing Socialist Systems and the Korean Peninsula in the Post-Cold War Era*, ed Chong-Wook Chung, Seoul Press, Seoul, pp. 163–96.

Okonogi, Masao 1994, 'North Korean Communism: In Search of Its Prototype', in

Korean Studies: New Pacific Currents, ed Dae-Sook Suh, Center for Korean Studies, University of Hawaii Press, Honolulu 1994, pp. 177–206.

Paige, Glenn D. 1964, 'North Korea and the Emulation of Russian and Chinese Behaviour', in *Communist Strategies in Asia: A Comparative Analysis of Governments and Parties*, ed A. Doak Barnett, Praeger, New York, pp. 228–61.

——1967, 'Korea', *Asian Survey*, vol. VII, no. 1, pp. 25–9.

Paik, Hak-Soon 1993, North Korean State Formation 1945–50, PhD thesis, University of Pennsylvania.

——1995, 'The Soviet Union's Objectives and Policies in North Korea, 1945–50', *Korea and World Affairs*, vol. 19, no. 2, pp. 269–93.

Pak, Ki-Hyuk 1983, 'Agricultural Policy and Development in North Korea', in *North Korea Today: Strategic and Domestic Issues*, eds Robert A. Scalapino and Jun-Yop Kim, Institute of East Asian Studies, University of California, Berkeley, pp. 214–29.

Palais, James B. 1975, *Politics and Policy in Traditional Korea*, Harvard University Press, Cambridge, Mass.

——1976, 'Political Leadership in the Yi Dynasty', in *Political Leadership in Korea*, eds Dae-Sook Suh and Chae-Jin Lee, University of Washington Press, Seattle, pp. 3–40.

Palthiel, Jeremy T. 1983, 'The Cult of Personality: Some Comparative Reflections on Political Culture in Leninist Regimes', in *Studies in Comparative Communism*, vol. XVI, nos. 1–2, pp. 49–64.

Park, Jae-Kyu 1983, 'North Korea's Policy Toward the Third World: The Military Dimension', in *The Two Koreas in World Politics*, eds Tae-Hwan Kwak, Wayne Patterson and Edward A. Olsen, The Institute for Far Eastern Studies, Kyungnam University, Seoul, pp. 87–103.

Park, Kwon-sang 1982, 'North Korea under Kim Jong Il', in *Journal of North East Asian Studies*, vol. I, no. 2, pp. 57–77.

Park, Myung-Lim 1995, 'North Korea's Inner Leadership and the Decision to Launch the Korean War', *Korea and World Affairs*, vol. 19, no. 2, pp. 240–68.

Pfaltzgraff, Robert L. Jr. 1986, 'Soviet Strategy and North Korea', *Korea and World Affairs*, vol. 10, no. 2. pp. 324–45.

Powell, David E. 1992, '*Perestroika* in the (Former) USSR: Psychological, Political, and Economic Dimensions', in *Studies in Comparative Communism*, vol. XXV, no. 2, pp. 193–207.

Pyongyang Times, Pyongyang, DPRK.

Ree, Erik van 1989, *Socialism in One Zone: Stalin's Policy in Korea 1945–1947*, Berg Publishers Limited, Oxford UK.

Rhee, Sang-Woo 1986, '*Chuch'e* Ideology as North Korea's Foreign Policy Guide', in *North Korea in a Regional and Global Context*, eds Robert A. Scalapino and Hongkoo Lee, Institute of East Asian Studies, University of California, Berkeley, pp. 37–54.

——1991, 'From National Unification to State Unification: A Realistic Design for One Korea', in *North Korea in Transition*, eds Chong-sik Lee and Se-Hee Yoo, Institute of East Asian Studies, University of California, Berkeley, pp. 129–37.

Rigby, T.H. 1977, 'Stalinism and the Mono-Organizational Society', in *Stalinism: Essays in Historical Interpretation*, ed Robert C. Tucker, W.W. Norton & Company Inc, New York, pp. 53–76.

Robinson, Michael Edson 1988, *Cultural Nationalism in Colonial Korea, 1920–25*, University of Washington Press, Seattle.

Roeder, Phillip G. 1993, *Red Sunset: the Failure of Soviet Politics*, Princeton University Press, Princeton, New Jersey.

Scalapino, Robert A. (ed) 1965, *The Communist Revolution in Asia: Tactics, Goals and Achievements*, University of California, Berkeley.

——1983, 'North Korean Relations with Japan and the United States', in *North Korea Today: Strategic and Domestic Issues*, eds Robert A. Scalapino and Jun-Yop Kim, Institute of East Asian Studies, University of California, Berkeley, pp. 331–50.

——1986, 'Polemics and Realities: U.S.–North Korean Relations', in *North Korea in a Regional and Global Context*, eds Robert A. Scalapino and Hongkoo Lee, Institute of East Asian Studies, University of California, Berkeley, pp. 301–26.

Scalapino, Robert A. and Kim, Dalchoong (eds) 1988, *Asian Communism Continuity and Transition*, Institute of East Asian Studies, University of California, Berkeley.

Scalapino, Robert A. and Lee, Chong-sik 1972, *Communism in Korea Part 1: The Movement*, University of California Press, Berkeley.

——1972, *Communism in Korea Part 2: The Society*, University of California Press, Berkeley.

Schapiro, Leonard 1971, *The Communist Party of the Soviet Union*, 2nd edn, Vintage Books, New York.

Segal, Gerald 1990, *The Soviet Union and the Pacific*, The Royal Institute of International Affairs, Unwin Hyman, London.

Seiler, Sydney A. 1994, *Kim Il-song 1941–48: The Creation of a Legend, The Building of a Regime*, University Press of America, Lanham, Maryland.

Shin, Jung-Hyun 1981, *Japanese–North Korean Relations: Lineage Politics in the Regional System of East Asia*, Kyunghee University Press, Seoul.

——1986, 'North Korea's Relations with Japan: the Possibilities for Bilateral Reconciliation', in *North Korea in a Regional and Global Context*, eds Robert A. Scalapino and Hongkoo Lee, Institute of East Asian Studies, University of California, Berkeley, pp. 240–62.

Shinn, Rin-Sup 1988, 'Political Trends in North Korea and Their Implications for Inter-Korean Relations,' *Korea Observer*, vol. XIX, no. 4, pp. 397–423.

——1990, '"Democratic Confederal Republic of Koryo"—Motives, Contexts, and Implications', *Korea and World Affairs*, vol. 14, no. 4, pp. 626–48.

Shirk, Susan 1993, *The Political Logic of Economic Reform in China*, University of California Press, Berkeley.

Simmons, Robert 1971, 'North Korea: Silver Anniversary', *Asian Survey*, vol. XI, no. 1, pp. 104–10.

Sin, Sam-Soon 1991, 'The Repressions of Kim Il-sung: a Historical Memoir', *Korea and World Affairs*, vol. 15, no. 2, pp. 279–301.

Skilling, H. Gordon 1977, 'Stalinism and Czechoslovak Political Culture', in *Stalinism: Essays in Historical Interpretation*, ed Robert C. Tucker, W.W. Norton & Company Inc, New York, pp. 257–80.

Song, Jong-Hwan 1984, 'How the North Korean Communists Negotiate: A Case Study of the South–North Korean Dialogue of the Early 1970s', *Korea and World Affairs*, vol. 8, no. 3, pp. 610–64.

Starkov, Boris A. 1994, 'The Trial that Was Not Held', *Europe-Asia Studies*, vol. 46, no. 8, pp. 1297–315.

Suh, Dae-Sook 1967, *The Korean Communist Movement 1918–48*, Princeton University Press, Princeton, New Jersey.

——1970, *Documents of Korean Communism 1918–48*, Princeton University Press, Princeton, New Jersey.

——1973, 'The Korean Revolutionary Movement: A Brief Evaluation of Ideology and Leadership', in *Korea Under Japanese Colonial Rule: Studies of the Policy and Techniques of Japanese Colonialism*, ed Andrew C. Nahm, The Centre for Korean Studies, Institute of International and Area Studies, Western Michigan University, pp. 185–92.

——1976, 'Communist Party Leadership', in *Political Leadership in Korea*, eds Dae-Sook Suh and Chae-Jin Lee, University of Washington Press, Seattle, pp. 159–91.

——1981, *Korean Communism 1945–80: A Reference Guide to the Political System*, The University of Hawaii Press, Honolulu.

——1983, 'Kim Il-song: His Personality and Politics', in *North Korea Today: Strategic and Domestic Issues*, eds Robert A. Scalapino and Jun-Yop Kim, Institute of East Asian Studies, University of California, Berkeley, pp. 43–64.

——1986, 'The Organization and Administration of North Korean Foreign Policy', in *North Korea in a Regional and Global Context*, eds Robert A. Scalapino and Hongkoo Lee, Institute of East Asian Studies, University of California, Berkeley, pp. 1–19.

——1988, *Kim Il Sung: The North Korean Leader*, Columbia University Press, New York, 1988.

——1990, 'Changes in North Korea and Inter-Korean Relations', *Korea and World Affairs*, vol. 14, no. 4, pp. 610–25.

Suh, Dae-Sook and Lee, Chae-Jin 1976, *Political Leadership in Korea*, University of Washington Press, Seattle.

Suh, Jae-Jean 1994, 'North Korea's Social System', in *Prospects for Change in North Korea*, eds Tae Hwan Ok and Hong Yung Lee, Institute of East Asian Studies, University of California, Berkeley.

Tak, J., Kim, G I., and Pak, H. J. 1985, *Great Leader Kim Jong Il* (2 vols), Sorinsha Publishers, Tokyo.

Trigubenko, Marina 1991, 'Industry of the DPRK: Specific Features of the Industrial Policy, Sectoral Structure and Prospects', in *Pukhan kyongje ui hyonhwang gwa chonmang* [Current Situation and Outlook for the North Korean Economy], Korea Development Institute, Seoul, pp. 101–35.

Tucker, Robert C. 1963, *The Soviet Political Mind: Studies in Stalinism and Post-Stalin Change*, Praeger, New York.

——1977, 'Stalinism as Revolution from Above', in *Stalinism: Essays in Historical Interpretation*, ed Robert C. Tucker, W.W. Norton & Company Inc, New York, pp. 77–110.

Uehara, Takashi 1987, 'North Korea's External Trade in 1986', *China Newsletter*, no. 70, pp. 16–21.

Ulam, Adam B. 1974, *Stalin: The Man and His Era*, Allen Lane, London.

Urban, George 1981, 'Was Stalin Really a "Great Man"?: A Conversation with Averell Harriman', *Encounter*, vol. LVII, no. 5, pp. 20–38.

US Department of State 1961, *North Korea: A Case Study in the Techniques of Takeover*, Department of State Publication 7118, Far Eastern Series 103, Washington.

Vantage Point, Seoul, ROK.

Volkogonov, Dmitri 1995, *Stalin: Triumph and Tragedy*, Weidenfeld and Nicolson, London.

Wall Street Journal, New York, New York.

Weathersby, Kathryn 1990, Soviet Policy toward Korea: 1944–46, PhD thesis, Indiana University.

Weber, Max 1964, *The Theory of Social and Economic Organization*, ed Talcott Parsons, The Free Press, New York.

Yang, Ho-Min 1988, 'Mao Zedong's Ideological Influence on Pyongyang and Hanoi: Some Historical Roots Reconsidered', in *Asian Communism Continuity and Transition*, eds Robert A. Scalapino and Dalchoong Kim, Institute of East Asian Studies, University of California, Berkeley, pp. 37–75.

Yang, Sung-Chul 1981, *Korea and two Regimes: Kim Il Sung and Park Chung Hee*, Schenckman Publishing Company Inc, Cambridge, Mass.

——1983, 'Socialist Education in North Korea', in *Journey to North Korea: Personal Perceptions*, eds C.I. Eugene Kim and Byung-Chul Koh, Institute of East Asian Studies, University of California, Berkeley, pp. 63–83.

——1990, 'A Leftist Antithesis against the Rightist Thesis on Post-Liberation Korean Politics and a Need for Its Synthesis', *Korea and World Affairs*, vol. 14, no. 2, pp. 371–87.

——1994a, *The North and South Korean Political Systems: A Comparative Analysis*, Westview Press, Boulder, & Seoul Press, Seoul.

——1994b, 'The Lessons of Divided Germany for Divided Korea', in *Korea and the World: Beyond the Cold War*, ed Young-Whan Kihl, Westview Press, Boulder, pp. 261–78.

Zagoria, Donald S. 1983, 'North Korea: Between Moscow and Beijing', in *North Korea Today: Strategic and Domestic Issues*, eds Robert A. Scalapino and Jun-Yop Kim, Institute of East Asian Studies, University of California, Berkeley, pp. 351–71.

——1986a, 'Soviet Policy toward North Korea', in *North Korea in a Regional and Global Context*, eds Robert A. Scalapino and Hongkoo Lee, Institute of East Asian Studies, University of California, Berkeley, pp. 177–89.

——1986b, 'The Soviet Union's Military-Political Strategy in the Far East', *Korea and World Affairs*, vol. 10, no. 2, pp. 346–69.

Zagoria, Donald S. and Kim, Young Kun 1976, 'North Korea and the Major Powers', in *The Two Koreas in East Asian Affairs*, ed William J. Barnds, New York University Press, New York, pp. 19–59.

Zagoria, Donald S. and Zagoria, Janet D. 1981, 'Crisis on the Korean Peninsula', in *The Diplomacy of Power: Soviet Armed Forces as a Political Instrument*, ed Stephen Kaplan et al, The Brookings Institute, Washington, pp. 357–411.

Zhebin, Alexander 1995, 'Russia and North Korea: An Emerging, Uneasy Partnership', *Asian Survey*, vol. XXXV, no. 8, pp. 727–39.

Zweig, David 1989, 'A Sinologist's Observations on North Korea', *Journal of Northeast Asian Studies*, vol. VII, no. 3, pp. 62–82.

OTHER WORKS CONSULTED

Ahn, Byung-joon 1982, 'Unification of Korea: Reality and Policy', *Journal of Northeast Asian Studies*, vol. I, no. 1, pp. 71–88.

——1985, 'The Soviet Union and the Korean Peninsula', *Asian Affairs*, vol. 11, no. 4, pp. 1–20.

Ahn, Suck-Kyo 1988, 'A Comparative Study of the Socialist Economic Systems of China and North Korea', in *Asian Communism Continuity and Transition*, eds Robert A. Scalapino and Dalchoong Kim, Institute of East Asian Studies, University of California, Berkeley, pp. 268–82.

An, Tai-Sung 1983, *North Korea in Transition*, Greenwood Press, Westport Conn.

Baek, Jong-Chun 1984, 'Probe for an Alternative Strategy of Conflict Resolution in the Korean Peninsula', in *Korean Reunification: New Perspectives and Approaches*, eds Tae-Hwan Kwak, Chonghan Kim and Hong-Nack Kim, The Institute for Far Eastern Studies, Kyungnam University, Seoul, pp. 425–66.

——1987, 'North Korea's Military Capabilities', in *The Foreign Relations of North Korea: New Perspectives*, eds Jae-Kyu Park, Byung-Chul Koh and Tae-Hwan Kwak, Westview Press, Boulder, & Kyungnam University Press, Seoul, pp. 81–106.

Baek, Jong-Chun and Rhee, Seong-Han 1992, 'Inter-Korean Relations in a New Era: A Breakdown?', in *The Changing Socialist Systems and the Korean Peninsula in the Post-Cold War Era*, ed Chong-Wook Chung, Seoul Press, Seoul, pp. 211–32.

Barnds, William J. (ed) 1976, *The Two Koreas in East Asian Affairs*, New York University Press, New York.

——1976, 'Old Issues in a New Context', in *The Two Koreas in East Asian Affairs*, ed William J. Barnds, New York University Press, New York, pp. 19–59.

Bracken, Paul 1993, 'The North Korean Nuclear Program as a Problem of State Survival', in *Asian Flashpoint: Security and the Korean Peninsula*, ed Andrew Mack, Allen & Unwin, Sydney, & Australian National University, Canberra, pp. 85–96.

Brandt, Vincent S.R. 1971, *A Korean Village between Farm and Sea*, Harvard University Press, Cambridge, Mass.

——1979, 'Sociological Aspects of Political Participation in Rural Korea', *The Journal of Korean Studies*, vol. 1, pp. 206–23.

Buzo, Adrian 1981, 'North Korea—Yesterday and Today', *Transactions of the Royal Asiatic Society Korea Branch*, vol. 56, pp. 1–26.

——1995, 'The DPRK and Late De-Stalinisation', *Korean Journal of National Reunification*, vol. 4, pp. 151–71.

Cha, Young-Koo 1986, 'North Korea's Strategic Relations: Pyongyang's Security Cooperation with Beijing and Moscow', in *North Korea in a Regional and Global Context*, eds Robert A. Scalapino and Hongkoo Lee, Institute of East Asian Studies, University of California, Berkeley, pp. 371–86.

Cho, Soon-Sung 1969, 'North and South Korea: Stepped-up Aggression and the Search for New Security', *Asian Survey*, vol. IX, no. 1, pp. 29–39.

——1985, 'South–North Korean Relations in the Year 2000', in *Korea in the Year 2000: Prospects for Development and Change*, ed Sung-Joo Han, Asiatic Research Center, Korea University, Seoul, pp. 213–28.

Choi, Chang-Yoon 1983, 'Interests and Policies of the Soviet Union and China

Toward the Korean Peninsula As Viewed from the Sino–Soviet Conflict', in *The Two Koreas in World Politics*, eds Tae-Hwan Kwak, Wayne Patterson and Edward A. Olsen, The Institute for Far Eastern Studies, Kyungnam University, Seoul, pp. 231–54.

Choi, Chong-Ki 1984, 'The Role of the United Nations and the Korean Question', in *Korean Reunification: New Perspectives and Approaches*, eds Tae-Hwan Kwak, Chonghan Kim and Hong-Nack Kim, The Institute for Far Eastern Studies, Kyungnam University, Seoul, pp. 269–94.

Chufrin, Gennady 1993, 'Russian Interests in Korean Security in the Post-Cold War World', in *Asian Flashpoint: Security and the Korean Peninsula*, ed Andrew Mack, Allen & Unwin, Sydney, & Australian National University, Canberra, pp. 29–36.

Chun, Hae-jong 1968, 'Sino–Korean Tributary Relations during the Ch'ing Period', in *The Chinese World Order*, ed John K. Fairbank, Harvard University Press, Cambridge, Mass.

Chun, In-Young 1992, 'North Korea's Change and Inter-Korean Relations', in *The Changing Socialist Systems and the Korean Peninsula in the Post-Cold War Era*, ed Chong-Wook Chung, Seoul Press, Seoul, pp. 233–44.

Chung, Chin O. 1978, *Pyongyang between Peking and Moscow: North Korea's Involvement in the Sino–Soviet Dispute 1958–75*, The University of Alabama Press, Alabama.

Chung, Chin-Wee 1986, 'North Korea's Relations with China', in *North Korea in a Regional and Global Context*, eds Robert A. Scalapino and Hongkoo Lee, Institute of East Asian Studies, University of California, Berkeley, pp. 226–39.

Chung, Chong-Wook (ed) 1992, *The Changing Socialist Systems and the Korean Peninsula in the Post-Cold War Era*, Seoul Press, Seoul.

Cohen, Stephen F. 1977, 'Bolshevism and Stalinism', in *Stalinism: Essays in Historical Interpretation*, ed Robert C. Tucker, W.W. Norton & Company Inc, New York, pp. 3–29.

Confino, M. 1987, 'Traditions, Old and New: Aspects of Protest and Dissent in Modern Russia', in *Patterns of Modernity, Volume II: Beyond the West*, ed S.N. Eisenstadt, Frances Pinter, London, pp. 12–36.

Cotton, James 1987, 'The Prospects for the North Korean Political Succession', *Korea and World Affairs*, vol. 11, no. 4, pp. 745–68.

Cotton, James 1989, 'North–South Korean relations: another false start?', *The World Today*, vol. 45, no. 6, pp. 104–8.

——1991, 'Conflict and Accommodation in the Two Koreas', in *The End of the Cold War in Northeast Asia*, eds Stuart Harris and James Cotton, Longman Cheshire, Boulder.

——1992, 'Civil Society in the Political Transition of North Korea', *Korea and World Affairs*, vol. 16, no. 2, pp. 319–37.

——1993, 'The Two Koreas and Rapprochement: Foundations for Progress?', in *Asian Flashpoint: Security and the Korean Peninsula*, ed Andrew Mack, Allen & Unwin, Sydney, & Australian National University, Canberra, pp. 137–46.

——1995, 'The North Korea/United States Nuclear Accord: Background and Consequences', *Korea Observer*, vol. XXVI, no. 3, pp. 321–44.

Cotton, James and Neary, Ian 1989, *The Korean War in History*, Manchester University Press, Manchester.

Cumings, Bruce 1987, 'The Division of Korea', in *Two Koreas—One Future?* eds John Sullivan and Roberta Foss, University Press of America, Lanham.

De Bary, Wm Theodore and Haboush, JaHyun Kim eds 1985, *The Rise of Neo-Confucianism in Korea*. Columbia University Press, New York.

Dernberger, Robert F. 1988, 'The Economies of China, North Korea, and Vietnam: A Comparative Study', in *Asian Communism Continuity and Transition*, eds Robert A. Scalapino and Dalchoong Kim, Institute of East Asian Studies, University of California, Berkeley, pp. 241–67.

Deuchler, Martina, 1980, 'Neo-Confucianism: The Impulse for Social Action in Early Yi Korea', *Journal of Korean Studies*, vol. 2, pp. 71–111.

Dittmer, Lowell 1988, 'Marxist Ideology in China and North Korea', in *Asian Communism Continuity and Transition*, eds Robert A. Scalapino and Dalchoong Kim, Institute of East Asian Studies, University of California, Berkeley, pp. 13–36.

Eisenstadt, S.N. 1966, *Modernization: Protest and Change*, Prentice-Hall, Englewood Cliffs, New Jersey.

——ed. 1987, *Patterns of Modernity, Volume II: Beyond the West*, Frances Pinter, London.

Erlich, Alexander 1977, 'Stalinism and Marxian Growth Models', in *Stalinism: Essays in Historical Interpretation*, ed Robert C. Tucker, W.W. Norton & Company Inc, New York, pp. 137–54.

Garrett, Banning and Glaser, Bonnie 1995, 'Looking Across the Yalu: Chinese Assessments of North Korea', *Asian Survey*, vol. XXXV, no. 6, pp. 529–45.

Gill, Graeme 1980, 'The Soviet Leader Cult: Reflections on the Structure of Leadership in the Soviet Union', *British Journal of Political Science*, vol. 10, no. 2, pp. 167–86.

Ha, Yong-chool 1988, 'Party-Military Relations in North Korea: A Comparative Perspective', in *Asian Communism Continuity and Transition*, eds Robert A. Scalapino and Dalchoong Kim, Institute of East Asian Studies, University of California, Berkeley, pp. 218–40.

Han, Chungnim C, 1949 'Social Organization of Upper Han Hamlet in Korea', PhD thesis, University of Michigan 1949, reprinted in *Transactions of the Royal Asiatic Society Korea Branch*, vol. 62, pp. 1–142.

Han, Sung-Joo 1983, 'North Korea's Security Policy and Military Strategy', in *North Korea Today: Strategic and Domestic Issues*, eds Robert A. Scalapino and Jun-Yop Kim, Institute of East Asian Studies, University of California, Berkeley, pp. 144–63.

——1987, 'Peaceful Reunification Policy: An Appraisal', *Korea and World Affairs*, vol. 11, no. 1, pp. 80–93.

——1976, 'Korea: Militarist or Unification Policies?', in *The Two Koreas in East Asian Affairs*, ed William J. Barnds, New York University Press, New York, pp. 123–66.

Henderson, Gregory 1968, *Korea: The Politics of the Vortex*, Harvard University Press, Cambridge, Mass.

——1989, 'Korea, 1950', in *The Korean War in History*, eds James Cotton, and Ian Neary, Manchester University Press, Manchester, pp. 175–82.

Huh, Moon-Young, Chung, Kyu-Sup, and Chon, Hyun-Joon 1994, 'The Advent of Kim Jong Il Regime in North Korea and Prospects for Its Policy Direction', in *The Research Institute for National Unification, Series No. 1 Policy Studies Report*, the Research Institute for National Unification, Seoul.

Hwang, Byung-Moo 1988, 'North Korea's Insurgency in Historical and Comparative Perspective', in *Asian Communism Continuity and Transition*, eds Robert A. Scalapino and Dalchoong Kim, Institute of East Asian Studies, University of California, Berkeley, pp. 283–309.

Hwang, In-Kwan 1984, 'A Question for Korean Reunification via Permanent Neutrality', in *Korean Reunification: New Perspectives and Approaches*, eds Tae-Hwan Kwak, Chonghan Kim and Hong-Nack Kim, The Institute for Far Eastern Studies, Kyungnam University, Seoul, pp. 377–404.

——1994, 'Korean Unification in a Comparative Perspective', in *Korea and the World: Beyond the Cold War*, ed Young-Whan Kihl, Westview Press, Boulder, pp. 279–300.

Huntington, Samuel P. 1966, 'The Political Modernization of Traditional Monarchies', *Daedalus*, vol. 95, no. 3, pp. 763–88.

Jencks, Harlan W. 1988, 'The Party, the Gun, and the Great Leader: Civil-Military Relations in North Korea', in *Asian Communism Continuity and Transition*, eds Robert A. Scalapino and Dalchoong Kim, Institute of East Asian Studies, University of California, Berkeley, pp. 187–217.

Johnson, Chalmers (ed) 1973, *Ideology and Politics in Contemporary China*, University of Washington Press, Seattle.

Kang, David C. 1995, 'Rethinking North Korea.' *Asian Survey*, vol. XXXV, no. 3, pp. 253–67.

Kawai, Hiroko 1984, 'Trade of the Democratic People's Republic of Korea in 1983', *China Newsletter*, no. 50, pp. 20–4.

——1985, 'North Korea's Foreign Trade in 1984', *China Newsletter*, no. 57, pp. 12–16.

Kawashima, Fujiya 1980, 'The Local Gentry Association in Mid-Yi Dynasty Korea: A Preliminary Study of the Ch'angnyong Hyangan, 1600–1838', *Journal of Korean Studies*, vol. 2, pp. 113–37.

Keum, Hieyeon and Campbell, Joel R. 1994, 'The Price of Change: Policy Reform and Leadership Transitions in post 1978 Chinese Politics with Comparison to Gorbachev's Soviet Union', in *The Journal of East Asian Affairs*, vol. VII, no. 1, pp. 90–134.

Kihl, Young-Whan 1983, 'The Issue of Korean Unification', in *Journey to North Korea: Personal Perceptions*, eds C.I. Eugene Kim and Byung-Chul Koh, Institute of East Asian Studies, University of California, Berkeley, pp. 99–117.

——1984, *Politics and Policies in Divided Korea: Regimes in Contest*. Westview Press, Boulder.

——1984, 'South Korea's Unification Policy in the 1980s: An Assessment', in *Korean Reunification: New Perspectives and Approaches*, eds Tae-Hwan Kwak, Chonghan Kim and Hong-Nack Kim, The Institute for Far Eastern Studies, Kyungnam University, Seoul, pp. 23–48.

——1984, *Politics and Policies in Divided Korea: Regimes in Contest*, Westview Press, Boulder.

——(ed) 1994, *Korea and the World: Beyond the Cold War*, Westview Press, Boulder.

——1994, 'The Politics of Inter-Korean Relations: Coexistence or Reunification?', in *Korea and the World: Beyond the Cold War*, ed Young-Whan Kihl, Westview Press, Boulder, pp. 133–52.

Kim, C.I. Eugene 1982, 'North Korea Today', *Korea and World Affairs*, vol. 6, no. 4, pp. 509–26.

——1983, 'Introduction: A Long Journey', in *Journey to North Korea: Personal*

Perceptions, eds C.I. Eugene Kim and Byung-Chul Koh, Institute of East Asian Studies, University of California, Berkeley, pp. 1–24.

——1984, 'An Evaluation of Korean Reunification Formulas', in *Korean Reunification: New Perspectives and Approaches*, eds Tae-Hwan Kwak, Chonghan Kim and Hong-Nack Kim, The Institute for Far Eastern Studies, Kyungnam University, Seoul, pp. 307–24.

——1985, 'The Two Koreas—Leadership, System Characteristics and Domestic and Foreign Policy Performances', *Korea and World Affairs*, vol. 9, no. 1, pp. 116–27.

——1986, 'In the Shadow of *chuch'e*: North Korea's Relations with Japan', in *North Korea in a Regional and Global Context*, eds Robert A. Scalapino and Hongkoo Lee, Institute of East Asian Studies, University of California, Berkeley, pp. 263–83.

Kim, Dalchoong 1984, 'Two Koreas and Four Major Powers: Mutually Balanced Contact for Peace and Reunification', in *Korean Reunification: New Perspectives and Approaches*, eds Tae-Hwan Kwak, Chonghan Kim and Hong-Nack Kim, The Institute for Far Eastern Studies, Kyungnam University, Seoul, pp. 251–68.

Kim, Deok 1986, 'The Evolution of North–South Korean Relations: Reassessment and Prospects', in *North Korea in a Regional and Global Context*, eds Robert A. Scalapino and Hongkoo Lee, Institute of East Asian Studies, University of California, Berkeley, pp. 133–51.

Kim, Dong-Sung 1994, 'China's Policy Toward North Korea and Cooperation Between South Korea and China', *The Korean Journal of International Studies*, vol. XXV, no. 1, pp. 29–46.

Kim, Hakjoon 1983, 'Prospects for Korean Unification in the Changing East Asian International Politics', in *The Two Koreas in World Politics*, eds Tae-Hwan Kwak, Wayne Patterson and Edward A. Olsen, The Institute for Far Eastern Studies, Kyungnam University, Seoul, pp. 383–400.

——1984, 'The Tripartite Conference Proposal for Korean Settlement: Its Origin, Evolution and Prospects', in *Korean Reunification: New Perspectives and Approaches*, eds Tae-Hwan Kwak, Chonghan Kim and Hong-Nack Kim, The Institute for Far Eastern Studies, Kyungnam University, Seoul, pp. 103–22.

——1988, 'The Dual Character of the Korean Division: Implications for a Korean Settlement', in *Asian Communism Continuity and Transition*, eds Robert A. Scalapino and Dalchoong Kim, Institute of East Asian Studies, University of California, Berkeley, pp. 329–42.

——1995, 'On the Nature of the North Korean State', *Korea and World Affairs*, vol. 9, no. 4, pp. 686–704.

Kim, Ilpyong J. 1984, 'The People's Republic of China and Korean Reunification', in *Korean Reunification: New Perspectives and Approaches*, eds Tae-Hwan Kwak, Chonghan Kim and Hong-Nack Kim, The Institute for Far Eastern Studies, Kyungnam University, Seoul, pp. 171–90.

——1995, 'The Sino–Soviet Alliance and the Korean War: The Decision Making of Stalin, Mao and Kim Il Sung', *Korea and World Affairs*, vol. 19, no. 2, pp. 337–48.

Kim, Kook-Chin 1988, 'A Comparative Study of the Politics of Leadership Succession in China, Vietnam, and North Korea', in *Asian Communism Continuity and Transition*, eds Robert A. Scalapino and Dalchoong Kim, Institute of East Asian Studies, University of California, Berkeley, pp. 170–86.

——1992, 'De-bipolarization and Prospects for Peace in Northeast Asia', in *The*

Changing Socialist Systems and the Korean Peninsula in the Post-Cold War Era, ed Chong-Wook Chung, Seoul Press, Seoul, pp. 61–78.

Kim, Kwang-ok 1984, 'Some Aspects of Korean Political Behaviour: Traditional and Modern Context', *Korean Social Science Journal*, vol. 11, pp. 100–16.

Kim, Samuel S. 1983, 'Pyongyang, The Third World, and Global Politics', in *The Two Koreas in World Politics*, eds Tae-Hwan Kwak, Wayne Patterson and Edward A. Olsen, The Institute for Far Eastern Studies, Kyungnam University, Seoul, pp. 59–86.

——1991, 'North Korea and the Non-Communist World: The Quest for National Identity', in *North Korea in Transition*, eds Chong-sik Lee and Se-Hee Yoo, Institute of East Asian Studies, University of California, Berkeley, pp. 17–42.

Kim, Si-Joong 1996, 'The Tumen River Area Development Program: The Present Status and Future Prospects', *The Economics of Korean Reunification*, vol. 1, no. 1, pp. 105–19.

Kim, Soo-Jin 1993, 'Tumen River Area Development Project and Inter-Korean Economic Cooperation', *East Asian Review*, vol. V, no. 2, pp. 65–86.

Kim, Sung-Chull 1992, 'Juche Idea: Base of Regime Legitimation of North Korea in the Age of Decaying Socialism', *The Korean Journal of National Reunification*, vol. 1, pp. 151–74.

Kim, Sungwoo 1993, 'Recent Economic Policies of North Korea', *Asian Survey*, vol. XXXIII, no. 9, pp. 864–78.

Kim, Youn-Soo (ed) 1979, *The Economy of the Korean Democratic People's Republic 1945–77*. German Korea-Studies Group, Kiel.

——1987, 'The Foreign Trade of North Korea with European CMEA Countries', *Korea and World Affairs*, vol. 11, no. 4, pp. 785–803.

Kim Youn-Suk 1994, 'Economic Integration: Toward Korean Reunification', *The Journal of East Asian Affairs*, vol. VII, no. 1, pp. 1–17.

Kim, Young C. 1975, 'North Korea in 1974', *Asian Survey*, vol. XV, no. 1, pp. 43–52.

——1980, 'North Korea in 1979: National Unification and Economic Development', *Asian Survey*, vol. XX, no. 1, pp. 53–62.

——1983, 'The Political Role of the Military in North Korea', in *North Korea Today: Strategic and Domestic Issues*, eds Robert A. Scalapino and Jun-Yop Kim, Institute of East Asian Studies, University of California, Berkeley, pp. 133–43.

——1994, 'Prospects for Korean Reunification: An Assessment', in *Korea and the World: Beyond the Cold War*, ed Young-Whan Kihl, Westview Press, Boulder, pp. 253–60.

Kim, Yu-Nam 1986, 'Changing Relations between Moscow and Pyongyang: Odd Man Out', in *North Korea in a Regional and Global Context*, eds Robert A. Scalapino and Hongkoo Lee, Institute of East Asian Studies, University of California, Berkeley, pp. 152–76.

Kim, Yung-Myung 1992, 'Democratization and Changing Conditions for Reunification in Korea', in *The Changing Socialist Systems and the Korean Peninsula in the Post-Cold War Era*, ed Chong-Wook Chung, Seoul Press, Seoul, pp. 197–210.

Kiyosaki, Wayne S. 1976, *North Korea's Foreign Relations: The Politics of Accommodation, 1945–75*. Praeger, New York.

Koh, Byung-Chul 1973, 'North Korea: A Breakthrough in the Question for Unity', *Asian Survey*, vol. XIII, no. 1, pp. 83–93.

——1983, 'Unification Policy and North–South Relations', in *North Korea Today: Strategic and Domestic Issues*, eds Robert A. Scalapino and Jun-Yop Kim, Institute of East Asian Studies, University of California, Berkeley, pp. 264–308.

——1983, 'Reunification Strategies of China and North Korea', *Korea and World Affairs*, vol. 7, no. 3, pp. 395–408.

——1984, 'The Korean Impasse: The View from Pyongyang', in *Korean Reunification: New Perspectives and Approaches*, eds Tae-Hwan Kwak, Chonghan Kim and Hong-Nack Kim, The Institute for Far Eastern Studies, Kyungnam University, Seoul, pp. 49–68.

——1987, 'North Korea's Foreign Policymaking Process', in *The Foreign Relations of North Korea: New Perspectives*, eds Jae-Kyu Park, Byung-Chul Koh and Tae-Hwan Kwak, Westview Press, Boulder, & Kyungnam University Press, Seoul, pp. 39–58.

——1988, 'North Korea in 1987', *Asian Survey*, vol. XXVIII, no. 1, pp. 62–70.

——1988, 'North Korea in 1987: Launching a New Seven-Year Plan', *Asian Survey*, vol. XXVIII, no. 1, pp. 62–70.

——1988, 'Political Institutionalization in Asian Communist Societies: China, North Korea and Vietnam', in *Asian Communism Continuity and Transition*, eds Robert A. Scalapino and Dalchoong Kim, Institute of East Asian Studies, University of California, Berkeley, pp. 75–99.

——1994, 'A Comparison of Unification Policies', in *Korea and the World: Beyond the Cold War*, ed Young-Whan Kihl, Westview Press, Boulder, pp. 153–66.

Kolakowski, Leszek 1977, 'Marxist Roots of Stalinism', in *Stalinism: Essays in Historical Interpretation*, ed Robert C. Tucker, W.W. Norton & Company Inc, New York, pp. 283–98.

Koo, Youngnok 1983, 'A Framework for Transactions Between the Two Koreas', in *The Two Koreas in World Politics*, eds Tae-Hwan Kwak, Wayne Patterson and Edward A. Olsen, The Institute for Far Eastern Studies, Kyungnam University, Seoul, pp. 173–94.

Ku, Dae-Yeol 1985, *Korea Under Colonialism*, Royal Asiatic Society Korea Branch, Seoul.

Kwak, Tae-Hwan 1983, 'Problems of Korean Political Integration: A Micro-level Analysis', in *The Two Koreas in World Politics*, eds Tae-Hwan Kwak, Wayne Patterson and Edward A. Olsen, The Institute for Far Eastern Studies, Kyungnam University, Seoul, pp. 141–72.

——1994, 'The United Nations and Reunification', in *Korea and the World: Beyond the Cold War*, ed Young-Whan Kihl, Westview Press, Boulder, pp. 301–12.

Kwak, Tae-Hwan, Kim, Chonghan, and Kim, Hong-Nack (eds) 1984, *Korean Reunification: New Perspectives and Approaches*, The Institute for Far Eastern Studies, Kyungnam University, Seoul, 1984.

Kwak, Tae-Hwan and Patterson, Wayne 1983, 'U.S. Political-Security Policy Toward the Korean Peninsula', in *The Two Koreas in World Politics*, eds Tae-Hwan Kwak, Wayne Patterson and Edward A. Olsen, The Institute for Far Eastern Studies, Kyungnam University, Seoul, pp. 331–52.

Kwak, Tae-Hwan, Patterson, Wayne and Olsen, Edward A. (eds) 1983, *The Two Koreas in World Politics*, The Institute for Far Eastern Studies, Kyungnam University, Seoul.

Lane, David and Ross, Cameron 1994, 'Limitations of Party Control: The Government Bureaucracy in the USSR', *Communist and Post-Communist Studies*, vol. 27, no. 1, pp. 19–38.

Lee, Chae-Jin 1983, 'Economic Aspects of Life in North Korea', in *Journey to North Korea: Personal Perceptions*, eds C.I. Eugene Kim and Byung-Chul Koh, Institute of East Asian Studies, University of California, Berkeley, pp. 42–62.

——1986, 'China's Policy toward North Korea: Changing Relations in the 1980s', in *North Korea in a Regional and Global Context*, eds Robert A. Scalapino and Hongkoo Lee, Institute of East Asian Studies, University of California, Berkeley, pp. 190–225.

Lee, Changsoo 1983, 'Social Policy and Development in North Korea', in *North Korea Today: Strategic and Domestic Issues*, eds Robert A. Scalapino and Jun-Yop Kim, Institute of East Asian Studies, University of California, Berkeley, pp. 114–32.

Lee, Chong-sik 1967, 'Kim Il Song of North Korea', *Asian Survey*, vol. VII, no. 6, pp. 374–82.

——1991, 'Coexistence, Revolution, and the Dialogue for Unification', in *North Korea in Transition*, eds Chong-sik Lee and Se-Hee Yoo, Institute of East Asian Studies, University of California, Berkeley, pp. 73–81.

Lee, Chong-sik and Yoo, Se-Hee eds 1991, *North Korea in Transition*, Institute of East Asian Studies, University of California, Berkeley.

Lee, Hong-Yung 1988, 'Changing Roles of the Communist Parties in China, North Korea, and Vietnam: A Historical Perspective', in *Asian Communism Continuity and Transition*, eds Robert A. Scalapino and Dalchoong Kim, Institute of East Asian Studies, University of California, Berkeley, pp. 113–36.

——1990, 'Future Dynamics in Sino–Korea Relations', *Journal of Northeast Asian Studies*, vol. IX, no. 3, pp. 34–49.

——1994, 'China and the Two Koreas: New Emerging Triangle', in *Korea and the World: Beyond the Cold War*, ed Young-Whan Kihl, Westview Press, Boulder, pp. 97–110.

Lee, Kang-sok 1981, 'Sources of Kim Il-Sung's [sic] Juche Ideology with Reference to Maoist Thought', *Vantage Point*, vol. IV, no. 11, pp. 1–11.

Lee, Manwoo 1983, 'How North Korea Sees Itself', in *Journey to North Korea: Personal Perceptions*, eds C.I. Eugene Kim and Byung-Chul Koh, Institute of East Asian Studies, University of California, Berkeley, pp. 118–41.

——1984, 'Korean Reconciliation: Combining Two Track Diplomacy', in *Korean Reunification: New Perspectives and Approaches*, eds Tae-Hwan Kwak, Chonghan Kim and Hong-Nack Kim, The Institute for Far Eastern Studies, Kyungnam University, Seoul, pp. 343–58.

Levin, Moshe 1974, *Political Undercurrents in Soviet Economic Debates: From Bukharin to the Modern Reformers*, Princeton, University Press, Princeton, New Jersey.

Levin, Norman 1986, 'North Korea's Strategic Relations', in *North Korea in a Regional and Global Context*, eds Robert A. Scalapino and Hongkoo Lee, Institute of East Asian Studies, University of California, Berkeley, pp. 387–405.

Lho, Kyongsoo 1993, 'Writing the Final Chapter: Inter-Korean Rivalry in the 1990s', in *Asian Flashpoint: Security and the Korean Peninsula*, ed Andrew Mack, Allen & Unwin, Sydney, & Australian National University, Canberra, pp. 147–58.

Li, Mirok 1956, *The Yalu Flows*, The Michigan State University Press, East Lansing.

Mack, Andrew (ed) 1993, *Asian Flashpoint: Security and the Korean Peninsula*, Allen & Unwin, Sydney, & Australian National University, Canberra.

Markovic, Mihailo 1977, 'Stalinism and Marxism', in *Stalinism: Essays in Historical Interpretation*, ed Robert C. Tucker, W.W. Norton & Company Inc, New York, pp. 299–319.

Mills, Charles W. 1994, 'The Moral Epistemology of Stalinism', *Politics and Society*, vol. 22, no. 1, pp. 31–58.

Murrell, Peter 1991, 'Symposium on Economic Transition in the Soviet Union and Eastern Europe', *Journal of Economic Perspectives*, vol. 5, no. 4, pp. 3–9.

Niksch, Larry A. 1986, 'The Military Balance on the Korean Peninsula', *Korea and World Affairs*, vol. 10, no. 2, pp. 253–77.

——1988, 'Guerilla Communism in Asia', in *Asian Communism Continuity and Transition*, eds Robert A. Scalapino and Dalchoong Kim, Institute of East Asian Studies, University of California, Berkeley, pp. 310–28.

Ofer, Gur 1987, 'Economic Aspects of the Modernization of Russia and China', in *Patterns of Modernity, Volume II: Beyond the West*, ed S.N. Eisenstadt, Frances Pinter, London.

Oh, Kwan-Chi 1991, '*Chuch'e* versus Economic Interdependence: The Impact of Socialist Economic Reforms on North Korea', in *North Korea in Transition*, eds Chong-sik Lee and Se-Hee Yoo, Institute of East Asian Studies, University of California, Berkeley, pp. 101–13.

Ok, Tae-Hwan and Lee, Hong-Yung eds 1994, *Prospects for Change in North Korea*, Institute of East Asian Studies, University of California, Berkeley.

Olsen, Edward A. 1984, 'Modifying the United States' Korea Policy: Offering Pyongyang an Economic Carrot', in *Korean Reunification: New Perspectives and Approaches*, eds Tae-Hwan Kwak, Chonghan Kim and Hong-Nack Kim, The Institute for Far Eastern Studies, Kyungnam University, Seoul, pp. 153–70.

Osgood, Cornelius 1951, *The Koreans and Their Culture*, The Ronald Press Company, New York.

Palais, James B. 1975, *Politics and Policy in Traditional Korea*. Harvard University Press, Cambridge, Mass.

——1979, 'Political Participation in Traditional Korea, 1876–1910', *Journal of Korean Studies*, vol. 1, no. 1, pp. 73–121.

Park, Andus 1992, 'Gorbachev and the Role of Personality in History', *Studies in Comparative Communism*, vol. XXV, no. 1, pp. 47–56.

Park, Han-Shik 1983, 'Policy Orientations of the People's Republic of China and the Korean Peninsula', in *The Two Koreas in World Politics*, eds Tae-Hwan Kwak, Wayne Patterson and Edward A. Olsen, The Institute for Far Eastern Studies, Kyungnam University, Seoul, pp. 279–304.

——1983, '*Chuch'e*: The North Korean Ideology', in *Journey to North Korea: Personal Perceptions*, eds C.I. Eugene Kim and Byung-Chul Koh, Institute of East Asian Studies, University of California, Berkeley, pp. 84–98.

——1984, 'Two Ideologies in One Culture: The Prospect for National Integration in Korea', in *Korean Reunification: New Perspectives and Approaches*, eds Tae-Hwan Kwak, Chonghan Kim and Hong-Nack Kim, The Institute for Far Eastern Studies, Kyungnam University, Seoul, pp. 123–52.

——1987, 'Nationalism in Korea: An Assessment of the Self-Reliance Doctrine', *Korean and World Affairs*, vol. 11, no. 3, pp. 500–10.

——1994, 'Ideological Synthesis for a United Korea', in *Korea and the World: Beyond the Cold War*, ed Young-Whan Kihl, Westview Press, Boulder, pp. 313–28.

Park, Jae-Kyu 1984, 'North Korea's Democratic Confederal Republic of Koryo: A Critique', in *Korean Reunification: New Perspectives and Approaches*, eds Tae-Hwan Kwak, Chonghan Kim and Hong-Nack Kim, The Institute for Far Eastern Studies, Kyungnam University, Seoul, pp. 69–84.

——1987, 'Introduction: A Basic Framework for Understanding North Korea's Foreign Policy', in *The Foreign Relations of North Korea: New Perspectives*, eds

Jae-Kyu Park, Byung-Chul Koh and Tae-Hwan Kwak, Westview Press, Boulder, & Kyungnam University Press, Seoul, pp. 3–14.

Park, Ki-hyuk and Gamble, Sidney D. 1975, *The Changing Korean Village*, The Royal Asiatic Society Korea Branch, Seoul.

Park, Soon-Won 1994, 'Korean Factory Workers During World War II: The Case of the Onoda Cement Sungho-ri Factory', *Korea Journal*, vol. 34, no. 3, pp. 20–36.

Park, Tong-Whan 1994, 'Improving Military Security Relations', in *Korea and the World: Beyond the Cold War*, ed Young-Whan Kihl, Westview Press, Boulder, pp. 217–32.

Peterson, Mark 1979, 'Hyangban and Merchant in Kaesong', *Korea Journal*, vol. 19, no. 10, pp. 4–18.

Poznanski, Kazimierz 1993, 'An Interpretation of Communist Decay: The Role of Evolutionary Mechanisms', *Communist and Post-Communist Studies*, vol. 26, no. 1, pp. 3–24.

Pratt, Keith 1980, 'Politics and Culture Within the Sinic Zone', *Korea Journal*, vol. 20, no. 6, pp. 15–29.

Pye, Lucian W. 1988, 'Leadership in the Three Confucian–Leninist Cultures', in *Asian Communism Continuity and Transition*, eds Robert A. Scalapino and Dalchoong Kim, Institute of East Asian Studies, University of California, Berkeley, pp. 151–69.

Redfield, Robert 1956, *Peasant Society and Culture: An Anthropological Approach to Civilization*, The University of Chicago Press, Chicago.

Rhee, Sang-Woo 1983, 'North Korean Ideology, Social Change, and Policy toward the South', in *North Korea Today: Strategic and Domestic Issues*, eds Robert A. Scalapino and Jun-Yop Kim, Institute of East Asian Studies, University of California, Berkeley, pp. 230–63.

——1983, *Security and Unification of Korea*, Sogang University Press, Seoul.

Rhee, T.C. 1983, 'The World and America's Korea Policy', in *The Two Koreas in World Politics*, eds Tae-Hwan Kwak, Wayne Patterson and Edward A. Olsen, The Institute for Far Eastern Studies, Kyungnam University, Seoul, pp. 353–82.

——1984, 'Four Great Powers and Korea's Unification: What Can and Cannot Happen', in *Korean Reunification: New Perspectives and Approaches*, eds Tae-Hwan Kwak, Chonghan Kim and Hong-Nack Kim, The Institute for Far Eastern Studies, Kyungnam University, Seoul, pp. 225–50.

Roy, Denny 1994, 'The Myth of North Korean "Irrationality"', *The Korean Journal of International Studies*, vol. XXV, no. 2, pp. 129–45.

Ru'an Ye 1993, 'Historic Transformation of the Korean Peninsula and China's Concerns', in *Asian Flashpoint: Security and the Korean Peninsula*, ed Andrew Mack, Allen & Unwin, Sydney, & Australian National University, Canberra, pp. 37–44.

Scalapino, Robert A. 1963, 'Korea', *Asian Survey*, vol. III, no. 1, pp. 37–9.

——1976, 'The Two Koreas—Dialogue or Conflict?', in *The Two Koreas in East Asian Affairs*, ed William J. Barnds, New York University Press, New York, pp. 60–122.

——1988, 'The Prospects for Peace on the Korean Peninsula', *Journal of Korean and World Affairs*, vol. 12, no. 2, pp. 270–80.

——1988, 'Ideology, Populism, and Statecraft: The Mix in Asian Communist Foreign Policies', in *Asian Communism Continuity and Transition*, eds Robert A. Scalapino and Dalchoong Kim, Institute of East Asian Studies, University of California, Berkeley, pp. 343–64.

Scalapino, Robert A. and Kim, Jun-yop (eds) 1983, *North Korea Today: Strategic and*

Domestic Issues, Institute of East Asian Studies, University of California, Berkeley.

Scalapino, Robert A. and Lee, Hongkoo (eds) 1986, *North Korea in a Regional and Global Context*, Institute of East Asian Studies, University of California, Berkeley.

Scheibe, Siegfried 1991, *Kino-e son Pukhan ui kyongje-sahui: silsang-gwa chonmang* [The North Korean Economy and Society at the Crossroads: Current Situation and Prospects], Research Institute for National Unification, Seoul.

Sharlet, Robert 1977, 'Stalinism and Soviet Legal Culture', in *Stalinism: Essays in Historical Interpretation*, ed Robert C. Tucker, W.W. Norton & Company Inc, New York, pp. 155–79.

Shaw, Martin 1991, *Post-Military Society: Militarism, Demilitarization and War at the End of the Twentieth Century*, Polity Press, Cambridge, UK.

Shinn, Rin-Sup 1982, 'North Korea in 1981: First Year for De Facto Successor Kim Jong Il', *Asian Survey*, vol. XXII, no. 1, pp. 99–105.

——1983, 'North Korea in 1982: Continuing Revolution under Kim Jong Il', *Asian Survey*, vol. XXIII, no. 1, pp. 102–9.

Simmons, Robert 1972, 'North Korea: Year of the Thaw', *Asian Survey*, vol. XII, no. 1, pp. 25–31.

Solomon, Richard H. 1973, 'From Commitment to Cant: The Evolving Functions of Ideology in the Revolutionary Process', in *Ideology and Politics in Contemporary China*, ed Chalmers Johnson, University of Washington Press, Seattle, pp. 47–77.

Somerville, John 1976–77, 'Stability in Eighteenth Century Ulsan', *Korean Studies Forum*, no. 1, pp. 1–19.

Starr, John Bryan 1973, *Ideology and Culture: An Introduction to the Dialectic of Contemporary Chinese Politics*, Harper & Row, New York.

Suh, Dae-Sook 1979, 'North Korea 1978: The Beginning of the Final Push', *Asian Survey*, vol. XIX, no. 1, pp. 51–7.

——1986, 'North Korea in 1985: A New Era After Forty Years', *Asian Survey*, vol. XXVI, no. 1, pp. 78–85.

——1987, 'North Korea in 1986: Strengthening the Soviet Connection', *Asian Survey*, vol. XXVII, no. 1, pp. 56–63.

Suh, Jae-Jean 1994, 'Ideology', in *Prospects for Change in North Korea*, eds Tae-Hwan Ok and Hong-Yung Lee, Institute of East Asian Studies, University of California, Berkeley.

Suh, Sang-Chul 1983, 'North Korean Industrial Policy and Trade', in *North Korea Today: Strategic and Domestic Issues*, eds Robert A. Scalapino and Jun-Yop Kim, Institute of East Asian Studies, University of California, Berkeley, pp. 197–213.

Sullivan, John and Foss, Roberta (eds) 1987, *Two Koreas—One Future?*, University Press of America, Lanham, Maryland.

Trigubenko, Marina 1994, 'The Role of the USSR in Liberating and Partitioning Korea', in *Russia in the Far East and Pacific Region*, eds Il-Yung Chung and Eunsook Chung, The Sejong Institute, Seoul, pp. 21–58.

Tucker, Robert C. 1973, 'Culture, Political Culture, and Communist Society', *Political Science Quarterly*, vol. 88, no. 2, pp. 173–90.

——(ed) 1977, *Stalinism: Essays in Historical Interpretation*, W.W. Norton & Company Inc, New York.

Uehara, Takashi 1986, 'The North Korean Economy', *China Newsletter*, no. 65, pp. 19–20.

Urban, G.R. 1989, *Can the Soviet System Survive Reform?*, Frances Pinter, London.

White, Gordon and Bowles, Paul 1994, 'The Political Economy of Financial Reform in China', *The Journal of Communist Studies and Transition Politics*, vol. 10, no. 1, pp. 80–103.

White, Stephen 1979, *Political Culture and Soviet Politics*, Macmillan, London.

Yang, Sung-Chul 1984, 'Twain: Is One Korea Possible?', in *Korean Reunification: New Perspectives and Approaches*, eds Tae-Hwan Kwak, Chonghan Kim and Hong-Nack Kim, The Institute for Far Eastern Studies, Kyungnam University, Seoul, pp. 325–42.

Yim, Yong-Soon 1983, 'The Dynamics of North Korean Military Doctrine', in *The Two Koreas in World Politics*, eds Tae-Hwan Kwak, Wayne Patterson and Edward A. Olsen, The Institute for Far Eastern Studies, Kyungnam University, Seoul, pp. 103–28.

——1984, 'Issues and Problems of Korean Reunification', in *Korean Reunification: New Perspectives and Approaches*, eds Tae-Hwan Kwak, Chonghan Kim and Hong-Nack Kim, The Institute for Far Eastern Studies, Kyungnam University, Seoul, pp. 85–102.

Zagoria, Donald S. 1984, 'The USSR and the Issue of Korean Reunification', in *Korean Reunification: New Perspectives and Approaches*, eds Tae-Hwan Kwak, Chonghan Kim and Hong-Nack Kim, The Institute for Far Eastern Studies, Kyungnam University, Seoul, pp. 191–96.

——1991, 'North Korea and the Socialist World', in *North Korea in Transition*, eds Chong-sik Lee and Se-Hee Yoo, Institute of East Asian Studies, University of California, Berkeley, pp. 93–9.

Zhang, Baohui 1993, 'Institutional Aspects of Reforms and the Democratization of Communist Regimes', *Communist and Post-Communist Studies*, vol. 26, no. 2, pp. 165–81.

INDEX

world view, 1–2, 110–11, 237–8; effect on organisation of Party and society, 70–1; former guerillas in the oligarchy, 13, 18; guerillas in Manchuria, 8; in ideology, 110–11, 197, 204, 242; Kim Jong Il's identification with, 53–4, 106, 111–12, 119, 212; versus communism, 16
Gulf War, 195, 230

Ha Ang-ch'on, 72
Haboush, JaHyun Kim, 47
Han Ik-su, 11, 33
Han Sok-yong, 167
The historical lesson in building socialism . . . (Kim), 206
Ho Chong-suk, 135, 137
Ho Ka-i, 21, 22, 32
Ho Pong-hak, 74
Ho Tam, 132–3, 134, 136, 153, 181
Hong Si-hak, 36
Hong Song-nam, 135, 136, 165, 212
Hong Song-yong, 133, 135, 136, 165–6
Hoxha, Enver, 49
Hu Yaobang, 126, 138, 157–8
Hungary, 187
Hwang Chang-yop, 33, 36, 84
Hwang Jang-yop, 212
Hyon Chung-guk, 186
Hyon Mu-gwang, 135, 137
Hyundai, 180, 181–2

ideology: as a barrier to international dialogue, 190–1; as a barrier to reform, 138; contradictions in Kim Jong Il's ideology, 207–8; debate ceases after 1958 conference, 58; degeneration of, 242; effect on economic policy, 88–9, 103, 120, 123, 129, 139, 144–6, 169–70, 174, 216–17, 240–1, 243; effect

on reunification negotiations, 154–5; in foreign policy, 76, 81; Juche, 2, 23–4, 26, 37, 42, 105, 117–18, 141, 168–9, 213; Kim Jong Il reaffirms Kimist ideology, 108, 209–10; Leninist Party organisation, 233–6; militarism in, 57–9, 61, 69–71, 78, 241–2; monolithic ideology, 59, 108, 114; predatory view of international economic relations, 141, 145; rationalisation of hereditary succession, 87–8; rhetoric to rationalise setbacks, 164; Rural Theses, 170, 210; Stalinism in, 42–3; subservience of expertise to, 115, 120; traditionalism in, 46, 47–8, 237; use of to screen external developments, 161–2; *see also* Chollima Movement; Chongsanri Method; Taean Work System; Three Revolution Team Movement
Im Ch'un-ch'u, 134
Imjin War, 47
industrialisation, 24, 27, 42, 44, 57, 59, 61, 71–2, 84–5, 238
intelligentsia, 29, 84
International Atomic Energy Agency, 165, 194–5, 196, 205, 219, 225–9
International Monetary Fund, 215
International Olympic Committee, 155, 159, 186
Ivan the Terrible, 45

Japan: annexes Korea, 3–5; as perceived by DPRK ideology, 190; dialogue with DPRK, 191–3, 200–1, 210, 223–4; dispute over Kurile Islands, 126–7, 224; emerges as a major power, 82–3; in Manchuria, 3; loans to DPRK, 122; offers